# Beginning R

An Introduction to Statistical Programming

**Larry Pace**

Apress·

ISBN-13 (pbk): 978-1-4302-4554-4

ISBN-13 (electronic): 978-1-4302-4555-1

President and Publisher: Paul Manning
Lead Editor: Jonathan Gennick
Technical Reviewer: Myron Hylnka
Editorial Board: Steve Anglin, Ewan Buckingham, Gary Cornell, Louise Corrigan, Morgan Ertel, Jonathan Gennick, Jonathan Hassell, Robert Hutchinson, Michelle Lowman, James Markham, Matthew Moodie, Jeff Olson, Jeffrey Pepper, Douglas Pundick, Ben Renow-Clarke, Dominic Shakeshaft, Gwenan Spearing, Matt Wade, Tom Welsh
Coordinating Editor: Kevin Shea
Copy Editor: Jill Steinberg
Compositor: SPi Global
Indexer: SPi Global
Artist: SPi Global
Cover Designer: Anna Ishchenko

Distributed to the book trade worldwide by Springer Science+Business Media New York, 233 Spring Street, 6th Floor, New York, NY 10013. Phone 1-800-SPRINGER, fax (201) 348-4505, e-mail orders-ny@springer-sbm.com, or visit www.springeronline.com.

For information on translations, please e-mail rights@apress.com, or visit www.apress.com.

Apress and friends of ED books may be purchased in bulk for academic, corporate, or promotional use. eBook versions and licenses are also available for most titles. For more information, reference our Special Bulk Sales-eBook Licensing web page at www.apress.com/bulk-sales.

Any source code or other supplementary materials referenced by the author in this text is available to readers at www.apress.com. For detailed information about how to locate your book's source code, go to www.apress.com/source-code.

*To my wife Shirley Pace, who has taught me the true meaning of love and loyalty.*

—Larry Pace

# Contents at a Glance

# Contents

# About the Author

**Larry Pace** is a statistics author, educator, and consultant. He lives in the upstate area of South Carolina in the town of Anderson. He earned his Ph.D. from the University of Georgia in psychometrics (applied statistics) with a content major in industrial-organizational psychology. He has written more than 100 publications including books, articles, chapters, and book and test reviews. In addition to a 35-year academic career, Larry has worked in private industry as a personnel psychologist and organization effectiveness manager for Xerox Corporation, and as an organization development consultant for a private consulting firm. He has programmed in a variety of languages and scripting languages including FORTRAN-IV, BASIC, APL, C++, JavaScript, Visual Basic, PHP, and ASP. Larry has won numerous awards for teaching, research, and service. He is currently a Graduate Research Professor at Keiser University, where he teaches doctoral courses in statistics and research. He also teaches adjunct classes for Clemson University. When he is not reading and writing about statistics, helping others with their statistical analyses, teaching, and doing research, he likes to build spreadsheet models for various statistical analyses, tend a small vegetable garden, play his guitar, and cook on the grill. He is married to Shirley Pace, and the Paces have four grown children and two grandsons. The Paces are volunteers with Meals on Wheels and avid pet lovers with six cats and one dog, all rescued.

# About the Technical Reviewer

**Dr. Myron Hlynka** is a professor in the Department of Mathematics and Statistics at the University of Windsor in Windsor, Ontario, Canada. He received his Ph.D. in Statistics from Penn State University in 1985. His research specialties are queueing theory and applied probability, and he maintains a well-known queueing theory web page at web2.uwindsor.ca/math/hlynka/queue.html.

# Acknowledgments

No published book is ever the work of a single individual, even when only one author is listed. This book came to fruition very quickly, thanks to an excellent team and great teamwork. Jonathan Gennick of Apress approached me in the spring of 2012 with the idea of a book on beginning R. Realizing that the current R books miss the mark in significant ways, and that a book on R to help novices and intermediate programmers alike was much needed, we quickly came to an agreement. With Jonathan's expert guidance, the book went from concept to completion in only eight months. Jonathan assembled a team of professionals, and the synergy was amazing. I wish all my writing projects were as easy and fun as this one was, and as fast, too! I was privileged to have the expert technical review of Dr. Myron Hlynka of the University of Windsor, Canada. Myron caught more than a few gaffes, and made excellent suggestions for improvement in the text, almost all of which were followed. He also provided outstanding detailed reviews of the R code, making sure it worked as advertised, as well as many great ideas for improving the code and expanding the examples. The book is both better and more accurate because of Myron's eagle eye and his statistical and programming expertise. Jill Steinberg did the copyediting, and her suggestions and corrections made the book more readable, easier to understand, and more consistent. Kevin Shea, my contributing editor, kept the entire project on track, and kept me focused on both the needed details and the big picture at the same time. Thanks, Kevin! Mark Powers also pitched in from time to time, and kept the project moving along. I am grateful to the Apress production team for their excellent work in producing the final copy and the graphics for this book. I hope you enjoy reading it as much as I enjoyed writing it!

—Larry Pace

# Introduction

This is a beginning to intermediate book on the statistical language and computing environment called R. As you will learn, R is freely available and open source. Thousands of contributed packages are available from members of the R community. In this book, you learn how to get R, install it, use it as a command-line interpreted language, program in it, write custom functions, use it for the most common descriptive and inferential statistics, and write an R package. You also learn some "newer" statistical techniques including bootstrapping and simulation, as well as how to use R graphical user interfaces (GUIs) including RStudio and RCommander.

## Who This Book Is For

This book is for working professionals who need to learn R to perform statistical analyses. Additionally, statistics students and professors will find this book helpful as a textbook, a supplement for a statistical computing class, or a reference for various statistical analyses. Both statisticians who want to learn R and R programmers who need a refresher on statistics will benefit from the clear examples, the hands-on nature of the book, and the conversational style in which the book is written.

## How This Book Is Structured

This book is structured in 20 chapters, each of which covers the use of R for a particular purpose. In the first three chapters, you learn how to get and install R and R packages, how to program in R, and how to write custom functions. The standard descriptive statistics and graphics are covered in Chapters 4 to 7. Chapters 8 to 14 cover the customary hypothesis tests concerning means, correlation and regression, and multiple regression. Chapter 14 introduces logistic regression. Chapter 15 covers chi-square tests. Following the standard nonparametric procedures in Chapter 16, Chapters 17 and 18 introduce simulation and the "new" statistics including bootstrapping and permutation tests. The final two chapters cover making an R package and using the RCommander package as a point-and-click statistics interface.

## Conventions

In this book, we use TheSansMonoConNormal font to show R code both inline and as code segments. The R code is typically shown as you would see it in the R Console or the R Editor. All hyperlinks shown in this book were active at the time of printing. Hyperlinks are shown in the following fashion:

http://www.apress.com

When you use the mouse to select from the menus in R or an R GUI, the instructions will appear as shown below. For example, you may be directed to install a package by using the Packages menu in the RGui. The instructions will state simply to select Packages ➤ Install packages... (the ellipsis points mean that an additional dialog box or window will open when you click Install packages). In the current example, you will see a list of mirror sites from which you can download and install R packages.

## Downloading the code

The R code and documentation for the examples shown in this book and most of the datasets used in the book are available on the Apress web site, `www.apress.com`. You can find a link on the book's information page under the Source Code/Downloads tab. This tab is located below the Related Titles section of the page.

## Contacting the Author

I love hearing from my readers, especially fellow statistics professors. Should you have any questions or comments, an idea for improvement, or something you think I should cover in a future book—or you spot a mistake you think I should know about—you can contact me at `larry@twopaces.com`.

# CHAPTER 1

■ ■ ■

# Getting R and Getting Started

R is a flexible and powerful open-source implementation of the language S (for *statistics*) developed by John Chambers and others at Bell Labs. R has eclipsed S and the commercially available S-Plus program for many reasons. R is free, and has a variety (nearly 4,000 at last count) of contributed packages, most of which are also free. R works on Macs, PCs, and Linux systems. In this book, you will see screens of R 2.15.1 running in a Windows 7 environment, but you will be able to use everything you learn with other systems, too. Although R is initially harder to learn and use than a spreadsheet or a dedicated statistics package, you will find R is a very effective statistics tool in its own right, and is well worth the effort to learn.

Here are five compelling reasons to learn and use R.

- R is open source and completely free. It is the *de facto* standard and preferred program of many professional statisticians and researchers in a variety of fields. R community members regularly contribute packages to increase R's functionality.

- R is as good as (often better than) commercially available statistical packages like SPSS, SAS, and Minitab.

- R has extensive statistical and graphing capabilities. R provides hundreds of built-in statistical functions as well as its own built-in programming language.

- R is used in teaching and performing computational statistics. It is the language of choice for many academics who teach computational statistics.

- Getting help from the R user community is easy. There are readily available online tutorials, data sets, and discussion forums about R.

R combines aspects of functional and object-oriented programming. One of the hallmarks of R is implicit looping, which yields compact, simple code and frequently leads to faster execution. R is more than a computing language. It is a software system. It is a command-line interpreted statistical computing environment, with its own built-in scripting language. Most users imply both the language and the computing environment when they say they are "using R." You can use R in *interactive* mode, which we will consider in this introductory text, and in *batch* mode, which can automate production jobs. We will not discuss the batch mode in this book. Because we are using an interpreted language rather than a compiled one, finding and fixing your mistakes is typically much easier in R than in many other languages.

## Getting and Using R

The best way to learn R is to use it. The developmental process recommended by John Chambers and the R community, and a good one to follow, is *user* to *programmer* to *contributor*. You will begin that developmental process in this book, but becoming a proficient programmer or ultimately a serious contributor is a journey that may take years.

1

If you do not already have R running on your system, download the precompiled binary files for your operating system from the Comprehensive R Archive Network (CRAN) web site, or preferably, from a mirror site close to you. Here is the CRAN web site:

http://cran.r-project.org/

Download the binary files and follow the installation instructions, accepting all defaults. Launch R by clicking on the R icon. For other systems, open a terminal window and type "R" on the command line. When you launch R, you will get a screen that looks something like the following. You will see the label *R Console*, and this window will be in the *RGui* (graphical user interface). Examine Figure 1-1 to see the R Console.

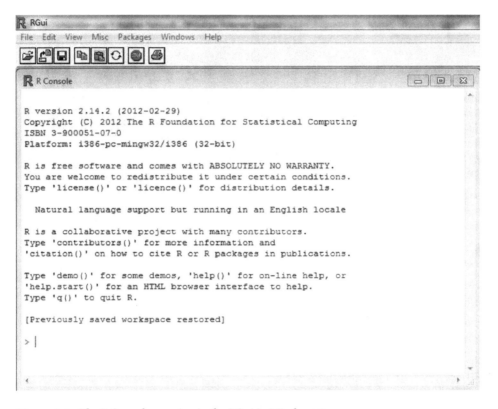

***Figure 1-1.*** *The R Console running in the RGui in Windows 7*

Although the R greeting is helpful and informative for beginners, it also takes up a lot of screen space. You can clear the console by pressing < Ctrl > + L or by selecting Edit ➤ Clear console. R's icon bar can be used to open a script, load a workspace, save the current workspace image, copy, paste, copy and paste together, halt the program (useful for scripts producing unwanted or unexpected results), and print. You can also gain access to these features using the menu bar.

---

■ **Tip**   You can customize your R Profile file so that you can avoid the opening greeting altogether. See the R documentation for more information.

---

Many casual users begin typing expressions (*one-liners*, if you will) in the R console after the R prompt (>). This is fine for short commands, but quickly becomes inefficient for longer lines of code and scripts. To open the R Editor, simply select File > New script. This opens a separate window into which you can type commands (see Figure 1-2). You can then execute one or more lines by selecting the code you want to use, and then pressing < Ctrl > + R to run the code in the R Console. If you find yourself writing the same lines of code repeatedly, it is a good idea to save the script so that you can open it and run the lines you need without having to type the code again. You can also create custom functions in R. We will discuss the R interface, data structures, and R programming before we discuss creating custom functions.

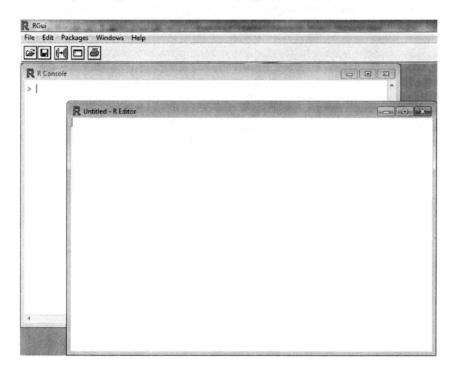

**Figure 1-2.** *The R Editor*

# A First R Session

Now that you know about the R Console and R Editor, you will see their contents from this point forward simply shown in this font. Let us start with the use of R as a calculator, typing commands directly into the R Console. Launch R and type the following code, pressing < Enter > after each command. Technically, everything the user types is an *expression*.

```
> 2 ^ 2
[1] 4
> 2 * 2
[1] 4
> 2 / 2
[1] 1
> 2 + 2
[1] 4
> 2 - 2
[1] 0
> q()
```

Like many other programs, R uses ^ for exponentiation, * for multiplication, / for division, + for addition, and - for subtraction. R labels each output value with a number in square brackets. As far as R is concerned, there is no such thing as a *scalar quantity*; to R, an individual number is a one-element vector. The [1] is simply the index of the first element of the vector. To make things easier to understand, we will sometimes call a number like 2 a *scalar*, even though R considers it a vector.

The power of R is not in basic mathematical calculations (though it does them flawlessly), but in the ability to assign values to objects and use functions to manipulate or analyze those objects. R allows three different assignment operators, but we will use only the traditional <- for assignment.

You can use the equal sign = to assign a value to an object, but this does not always work and is easy to confuse with the test for equality, which is ==. You can also use a right-pointing assignment operator ->, but that is not something we will do in this book. When you assign an object in R, there is no need to declare or type it. Just assign and start using it. We can use x as the label for a single value, a vector, a matrix, a list, or a data frame.

We will discuss each data type in more detail, but for now, just open a new script window and type, and then execute the following code. We will assign several different objects to x, and check the *mode* (storage class) of each object. We create a single-element vector, a numeric vector, a matrix (which is actually a kind of vector to R), a character vector, a logical vector, and a list. The three main types or modes of data in R are *numeric*, *character*, and *logical*. Vectors must be *homogeneous* (use the same data type), but lists, matrices, and data frames can all be *heterogeneous*. I do not recommend the use of heterogeneous matrices, but lists and data frames are commonly composed of different data types. Here is our code and the results of its execution. Note that the code in the R Editor does not have the prompt > in front of each line.

```
x <- 2
x
x ^ x
x ^ 2
mode(x)
x <- c(1:10)
x
x ^ x
mode(x)
dim(x) <- c(2,5)
x
mode(x)
x <- c("Hello","world","!")
x
mode(x)
x <- c(TRUE, TRUE, FALSE, FALSE, TRUE, FALSE, TRUE)
x
mode(x)
x <- list("R","12345",FALSE)
x
mode(x)
```

Now, see what happens when we execute the code:

```
> x <- 2
> x
[1] 2
> x ^ x
[1] 4
> x ^ 2
[1] 4
> mode(x)
[1] "numeric"
```

Note the "sequence operator" will produce the same result as c(1:10). You could produce a vector with the numbers 1 through 10 by using seq(1:10). R provides the user the flexibility to do the same thing in many different ways. Consider the following examples:

```
> seq(1:10)
 [1]  1  2  3  4  5  6  7  8  9 10
> x <- c(1:10)
> x
 [1]  1  2  3  4  5  6  7  8  9 10
> x ^ x
 [1]           1           4          27         256        3125       46656
 [7]      823543    16777216   387420489 10000000000
> mode(x)
[1] "numeric"
> dim(x) <- c(2,5)
> x
     [,1] [,2] [,3] [,4] [,5]
[1,]    1    3    5    7    9
[2,]    2    4    6    8   10
> mode(x)
[1] "numeric"
```

Here is the obligatory "Hello World" code that is almost universally included in programming books and classes:

```
> x <- c("Hello","world","!")
> x
[1] "Hello" "world" "!"
> mode(x)
[1] "character"
> x <- c(TRUE, TRUE, FALSE, FALSE, TRUE, FALSE, TRUE)
> x
[1]  TRUE  TRUE FALSE FALSE  TRUE FALSE  TRUE
> mode(x)
[1] "logical"
> x <- list("R","12345",FALSE)
> x
[[1]]
[1] "R"

[[2]]
[1] "12345"

[[3]]
[1] FALSE

> mode(x)
[1] "list"
```

List indexing is quite different from vector and matrix indexing, as you can see from the output above. We will address that in more detail later. For now, let us discuss moving around in R.

# Moving Around in R

R saves all the commands you type during an R session, even if you have cleared the console. To see the previous lines(s) of code, use the up arrow on the keyboard. To scroll down in the lines of code, use the down arrow. The left and right arrows move the cursor in the current line, and this allows you to edit and fix code if you made a mistake. As you have learned, you can clear the console when you want a clear working area, but you will still be able to retrieve the entire command history. When you are finished with a session, you may want to save the workspace image if you did something new and useful, or discard it if you were just experimenting or created something worse than what you started with! When you exit R, using the q() function, or in Windows, File > Exit, the R system will save the entire command history in your current (working) directory as a text file with the extension *.Rhistory.

You can access the R history using a text editor like Notepad. Examining the history is like viewing a recording of the entire session from the perspective of the R Console. This can help you refresh your memory, and you can also copy and paste sections of the history into the R Editor or R Console to speed up your computations.

As you have already seen, the R Editor gives you more control over what you are typing than the R Console does, and for anything other than one-liners, you will find yourself using the R Editor more than the R Console.

In addition to saving the command history, R saves the functions, loaded packages, and objects you create during an R session. The benefit of saving your workspace and scripts is that you will not have to type the information again when you access this workspace image.When you exit R, you will see a prompt asking if you want to save your workspace image (see Figure 1-3).

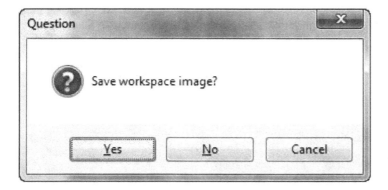

**Figure 1-3.** *When you exit R, you will receive this prompt*

Depending on what you did during that session, you may or may not want to do that. If you do, R will save the workspace in the *.RData format. Just as you can save scripts, output, and data with other statistics packages, you can save multiple workspace images in R. Then you can load and use the one you want. Simply find the desired workspace image, which will be an *.RData file, and click on it to launch R. The workspace image will contain all the data, functions, and loaded packages you used when you saved the workspace.

When you are in an R session, you may lose track of where you are in the computer's file system. To find out your working directory, use the getwd()command. You can also change the working directory by using the setwd(dir) command. If you need help with a given function, you can simply type help(function), or use the ?function shortcut. Either of these will open the R documentation, which is always a good place to start when you have questions.

To see a listing of the objects in your workspace, you can use the ls() function. To get more detail, use ls.str(). For example, here is the list of the objects in my current R workspace:

```
> ls()
 [1] "A"            "acctdata"     "address"     "B"          "b1"
 [6] "balance"      "c"            "CareerSat"   "chisquare"  "colnames"
[11] "confint"      "correctquant" "dataset"     "Dev"        "grades"
[16] "Group"        "hingedata"    "hours"       "i"          "Min_Wage"
```

```
[21] "n"            "names"        "newlist"       "P"            "pie_data"
[26] "quizzes"      "r"            "sorted"        "stats"        "stdev"
[31] "TAge"         "test1"        "test2"         "test3"        "testmeans"
[36] "tests"        "truequant"    "Tscore"        "Tscores"      "V"
[41] "x"            "y"            "z1"            "zAge"         "zscores"
[46] "ztest1"
```

Let us create a couple of objects and then see that they are added to the workspace (and will be saved when/if you save the workspace image).

```
> Example1 <- seq(2:50)
> Example2 <- log(Example1)
> Example2
 [1] 0.0000000 0.6931472 1.0986123 1.3862944 1.6094379 1.7917595 1.9459101
 [8] 2.0794415 2.1972246 2.3025851 2.3978953 2.4849066 2.5649494 2.6390573
[15] 2.7080502 2.7725887 2.8332133 2.8903718 2.9444390 2.9957323 3.0445224
[22] 3.0910425 3.1354942 3.1780538 3.2188758 3.2580965 3.2958369 3.3322045
[29] 3.3672958 3.4011974 3.4339872 3.4657359 3.4965076 3.5263605 3.5553481
[36] 3.5835189 3.6109179 3.6375862 3.6635616 3.6888795 3.7135721 3.7376696
[43] 3.7612001 3.7841896 3.8066625 3.8286414 3.8501476 3.8712010 3.8918203
>
```

Now, see that ls() will show these two vectors as part of our workspace. (This is a different workspace image from the one shown earlier.) As this is a large workspace, I will show only the first screen (see Figure 1-4).

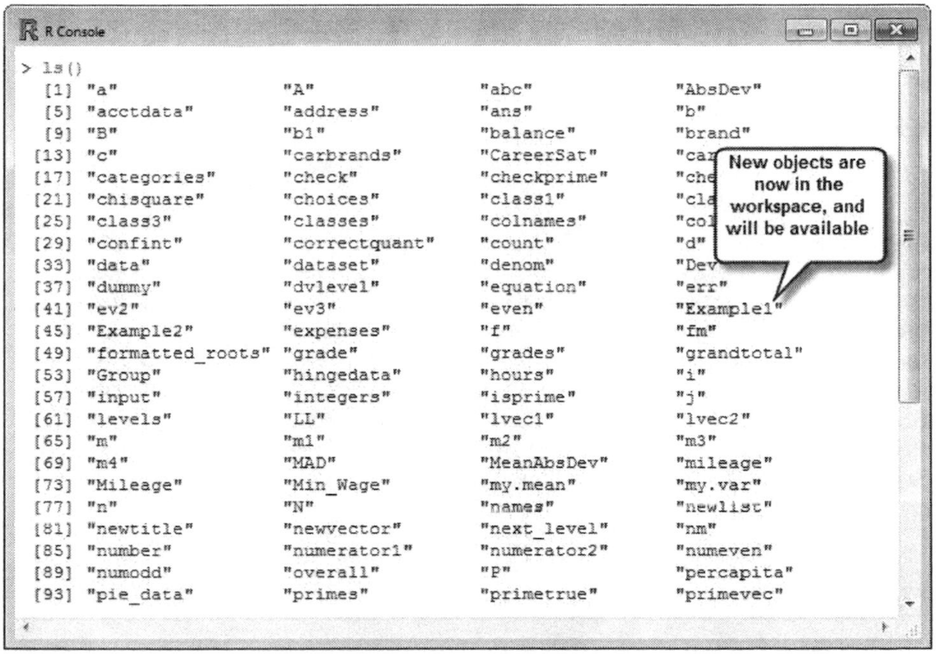

*Figure 1-4. Newly-created objects are automatically stored in the workspace*

Now, see what happens when we invoke the ls.str() function for a "verbose" description of the objects in the workspace. Both our examples are included. The ls.str() function gives an alphabetical listing of all the objects currently saved in the workspace. We will look at the descriptions of only the two examples we just created.

```
> ls.str()

ls.str()
Example1 :  int [1:49] 1 2 3 4 5 6 7 8 9 10 ...
Example2 :  num [1:49] 0 0.693 1.099 1.386 1.609 ...
```

# Working with Data in R

As the creator of the S language, John Chambers, says, in most serious modern applications, real data usually comes from a process external to our analysis. Although we can enter small amounts of data directly in R, ultimately we will need to import larger data sets from applications such as spreadsheets, text files, or databases. Let us discuss and illustrate the various R data types in more detail, and see how to work with them most effectively.

## Vectors

The most common data structure in R is the *vector*. As we have discussed, vectors must be *homogeneous*—that is, the type of data in a given vector must all be the same. Vectors can be numeric, logical, or character. If you try to mix data types, you will find that R forces (*coerces*, if you will) the data into one mode.

## Creating a Vector

See what happens when you try to create a vector as follows. R obliges, but the mode is character, not numeric.

```
> x <- c(1, 2, 3, 4, "Pi")
> x
[1] "1"  "2"  "3"  "4"  "Pi"
> mode(x)
[1] "character"
```

Let us back up and learn how to create numeric vectors. When we need to mix data types, we need lists or data frames. Character vectors need all character elements, and numeric vectors need all numeric elements. We will work with both character and numeric vectors in this book, but let us work with numeric ones here. R has a *recycling* property that is sometimes quite useful, but which also sometimes produces unexpected or unwanted results. Let's go back to our sequence operator and make a numeric vector with the sequence 1 to 10. We assign vectors using the c (for *combine*) function. Though some books call this *concatenation*, there is a different cat() function for concatenating output. We will discuss the cat() function in the next chapter. Let us now understand how R deals with vectors that have different numbers of elements. For example, see what happens when we add a vector to a different single-element vector. Because we are adding a "scalar" (really a single-element vector), R's recycling property makes it easy to "vectorize" the addition of one value to each element of the other vector.

```
> x <- c(1:10)
> x
 [1]  1  2  3  4  5  6  7  8  9 10
> length(x)
[1] 10
> y <- 10
> length(y)
[1] 1
> x+y
 [1] 11 12 13 14 15 16 17 18 19 20
```

Many R books and tutorials refer to the last command above as *scalar addition*, and that much is true. But what really matters here is that the command and its output are technically an implementation of R's *recycling* rule we discussed above. When one vector is shorter than the other, the shorter vector is recycled when you apply mathematical operations to the two vectors.

## Performing Vector Arithmetic

R is very comfortable with adding two vectors, but notice what sometimes happens when they are of different lengths, and one is not a single-element vector. Look at the output from the following examples to see what happens when you add two vectors. In some cases, it works great, but in others, you get warned that the longer object is not a multiple of the length of the shorter object!

```
> y <- c(0, 1)
> y
[1] 0 1
> x+y
 [1]  1  3  3  5  5  7  7  9  9 11
> y <- c(1,3,5)
> x+y
 [1]  2  5  8  5  8 11  8 11 14 11
Warning message:
In x+y : longer object length is not a multiple of shorter object length
```

What is happening in the code above is that the shorter vector is being recycled as the operation continues. In the first example, zero is added to each odd number, while 1 is added to each even number. R recycles the elements in the shorter vector, as it needs, to make the operation work. Sometimes R's recycling feature is useful, but often it is not. If the vectors are *mismatched* (that is, if the length of the longer vector is not an exact multiple of the shorter vector's length), R will give you a warning, but will still recycle the shorter vector until there are enough elements to complete the operation.

Before we discuss vector arithmetic in more detail, let us look at a few more computations using our example vector x:

```
> 2+3 * x        #Note the order of operations
 [1]  5  8 11 14 17 20 23 26 29 32
> (2+3) * x      #See the difference
 [1]  5 10 15 20 25 30 35 40 45 50
> sqrt(x)        #Square roots
 [1] 1.000000 1.414214 1.732051 2.000000 2.236068 2.449490 2.645751 2.828427
 [9] 3.000000 3.162278
> x %% 4         #This is the integer divide (modulo) operation
 [1] 1 2 3 0 1 2 3 0 1 2
> y <- 3+2i      #R does complex numbers
> Re(y)          #The real part of the complex number
[1] 3
> Im(y)          #The imaginary part of the complex number
[1] 2
> x * y
 [1]  3+ 2i  6+ 4i  9+ 6i 12+ 8i 15+10i 18+12i 21+14i 24+16i 27+18i 30+20i
```

Now that you understand working with numeric vectors, we are ready to explore additional vector arithmetic. First, create a vector:

```
> x <- c(1:10)        #Create a vector
```

Note that the c() function is not really needed here, as my technical reviewer pointed out! You can simply use:

```
> x <- 1:10
```

And get the same result. Following are some other possibilities, along with the results for x, y, and z.

```
> y <- seq(10)        #Create a sequence
> z <- rep(1,10)      #Create a repetitive pattern
> x
 [1]  1  2  3  4  5  6  7  8  9 10
> y
 [1]  1  2  3  4  5  6  7  8  9 10
> z
 [1] 1 1 1 1 1 1 1 1 1 1
```

As mentioned previously, R often allows users to avoid explicit looping by the use of *vectorized* operations. Looping *implicitly* through a vector is many times faster than looping explicitly, and makes the resulting R code more compact. As you will learn in the following chapter, you can loop explicitly when you need to, but should try to avoid this if possible. Vectorized operations on a single vector include many built-in functions, making R powerful and efficient. It is possible to apply many functions to data frames as well, though not all functions "do" data frames, as you will see. We can work around this by using other features and functions of R.

Although it takes some getting used to, R's treatment of vectors is logical. As we discussed earlier, a vector must have a single mode. You can check the mode of an object using the mode() function or using the typeof() function. As you have seen already in the output, R, unlike some other languages, begins its indexing with 1, not 0.

## Adding Elements to a Vector

When you add elements, you are reassigning the vector. For example, see what happens when we append the numbers 11:15 to our x vector:

```
> x <- c([1:10])
> x
 [1]  1  2  3  4  5  6  7  8  9 10
```

Now, let us reassign x by adding the numbers 11 through 15 to it. We are taking x and then appending (concatenating, in computer jargon) the sequence 11, 12, 13, 14, 15 to the 10-element vector to produce a 15-element vector we now have stored as x.

```
> x <- c(x, 11:15)
> x
 [1]  1  2  3  4  5  6  7  8  9 10 11 12 13 14 15
```

As you already know, we can use the sequence operator to create a vector. We can obtain the length of the vector with the length() function, the sum with the sum() function, and various statistics with other built-in functions to be discussed and illustrated later. To make our example a little more interesting, let us imagine a discrete probability distribution. We have a vector of the values of the variable and another vector of their probabilities. Here is a very interesting distribution known as Benford's Distribution, which is based on Benford's Law. The distribution gives the probability of first digits in numbers occurring in many (but not all) kinds of data. Some data, such as financial data, are well described by Benford's Law, making it useful for the investigation of fraud. We will return to this example later when we have the background to dig deeper, but for now, just examine the distribution itself. We will call the first digit V. Table 1-1 lists the first digits and their probabilities.

***Table 1-1.*** *Benford's Distribution*

| V | Probability |
|---|---|
| 1 | 0.301 |
| 2 | 0.176 |
| 3 | 0.125 |
| 4 | 0.097 |
| 5 | 0.079 |
| 6 | 0.067 |
| 7 | 0.058 |
| 8 | 0.051 |
| 9 | 0.046 |

If you have taken statistics classes, you may recall the mean of a discrete probability distribution is found as:

$$\mu = \sum (xp(x))$$

In the following code, notice how easy it is to multiply the two vectors and add the products in R. As experienced users quickly learn, there are often many ways to accomplish the same result in R (and other languages). In this book, I will typically show you a simple, direct way or the way that helps you learn R most effectively. In the following example, we will create a vector of the Benford Distribution probabilities, and then a vector of the initial digits. We will use P for probability and V for the first digit, to maintain consistency with Table 1-1.

```
> P
[1] 0.301 0.176 0.125 0.097 0.079 0.067 0.058 0.051 0.046
> V
[1] 1 2 3 4 5 6 7 8 9
> sum(V * P)
[1] 3.441
```

It is similarly easy to find the variance of a discrete probability distribution. Here is the formula:

$$\sigma^2 = \sum p(x)(x-\mu)^2$$

We subtract the mean from each value, square the deviation, multiply the squared deviation by the probability, and sum these products. The square root of the variance is the standard deviation. We will calculate a vector of squared deviations, then multiply that vector by the vector of probabilities, and sum the products. This will produce the variance and the standard deviation. Examine the following code:

```
> Dev <- (V - mean(V))^2
> Dev
[1] 16  9  4  1  0  1  4  9 16
> sum(Dev * P)
[1] 8.491
> stdev <- sqrt(sum(Dev * P))
> stdev
[1] 2.913932
```

# Matrices

To R, a *matrix* is also a vector, but a vector is *not* a one-column or one-row matrix. Although it is possible to create heterogeneous matrices, we will work only with numeric matrices in this book. For mixed data types, lists and data frames are much more suitable.

## Creating a Matrix

Let's create a matrix with 2 rows and 5 columns. We will use our standard 10-item vector to begin with, but will come up with some more engaging examples shortly. The following example takes the values from our 10-item vector and uses them to create a 2x5 matrix:

```
> x <- c(1:10)
> x <- matrix(x, 2, 5)
> x
     [,1] [,2] [,3] [,4] [,5]
[1,]    1    3    5    7    9
[2,]    2    4    6    8   10
```

R fills in the data column-by-column rather than by rows. The matrix is still a vector, but it has the dimensions you assigned to it. Just as with vectors, you have to reassign a matrix to add rows and columns. You can use arrays with three or more dimensions, but we will stick with vectors, two-dimensional matrices, lists, and data frames in this beginning book.

You can initialize a matrix, and assign a default value, such as zero or NA to each cell. Examine the following examples. Notice how the first parameter is replicated across all cells.

```
> matrix(0, 5, 2)
     [,1] [,2]
[1,]    0    0
[2,]    0    0
[3,]    0    0
[4,]    0    0
[5,]    0    0
> matrix(NA, 5, 2)
     [,1] [,2]
[1,]   NA   NA
[2,]   NA   NA
[3,]   NA   NA
[4,]   NA   NA
[5,]   NA   NA
```

R has a *matrix* class, and matrices have the attribute of *dimensionality*. As far as the length is concerned, a matrix is a type of vector, but as mentioned above, a vector is not a type of matrix. A little strangely, a matrix is also a kind of list as well. You'll note in the following example that we have x, which is numeric, has a length of 10, is of class "integer," and has dimensionality. Yet, somewhat surprisingly to beginning users of R, the matrix is also a list instead of a combination of numeric vectors. Although it is possible to combine data types in a matrix because the matrix is also a list, I advise against that and suggest that you use character vectors and lists as well as data frames to deal with mixed-mode data.

```
> length(x)
[1] 10
> mode(x)
[1] "numeric"
```

```
> typeof(x)
[1] "integer"
> class(x)
[1] "matrix"
> attributes(x)
$dim
[1] 2 5
> y <- c(1:10)
> length(y)
[1] 10
> mode(y)
[1] "numeric"
> typeof(y)
[1] "integer"
> class(y)
[1] "integer"
> attributes(y)
NULL
```

## Referring to Matrix Rows and Columns

As with vectors, we refer to the elements of a matrix by using their indices. It is possible to give rows and columns their own namesas a way to make your data and output easier for others to understand. We can refer to a row or column, rather than to a single cell, simply by using a comma for the index. Both indices and names work for referring to elements of the matrix. In the following code, we will create a character vector with the names of our columns. Not too creatively, we will use A, B, C, D, and E to correspond to spreadsheet programs like Excel and OpenOffice Calc.

```
> colnames(x) <- c("A","B","C","D","E")
> x
     A B C D  E
[1,] 1 3 5 7  9
[2,] 2 4 6 8 10
> x[1,"C"]
C
5
> x[1,2]
B
3
> x[, 1]
[1] 1 2
> x[1, ]
A B C D E
1 3 5 7 9
> x[2,"E"]
 E
10
>
```

Although we have the flexibility of naming columns and rows in R, unless we are working with matrices, we will usually find that for data analysis, data frames give us all the advantages of vectors, lists, and matrices. We will discuss this in more detail later in the chapter.

# Matrix Manipulation

Let us create a more interesting matrix and see how we can perform standard matrix operations on it, including transposition, inversion, and multiplication. Continuing with our example of Benford's Law, we will add some context (the data are hypothetical, though they are based on a published study and is patterned after the real data. The data in Table 1-2 represent the leading digits in the checks written by an insurance refund officer. When a financial audit was conducted, the company asked the auditor to investigate potential fraud. The expected distribution would be the occurrences of the leading digits if the data followed Benford's Law, while the actual counts are those from a sample of checks written by the refund officer.[1]

***Table 1-2.*** *Actual and Expected Values*

| Leading Digit | Actual | Expected |
|:---:|:---:|:---:|
| 1 | 132 | 86.7 |
| 2 | 50 | 50.7 |
| 3 | 32 | 36 |
| 4 | 20 | 27.9 |
| 5 | 19 | 22.8 |
| 6 | 11 | 19.3 |
| 7 | 10 | 16.7 |
| 8 | 9 | 14.7 |
| 9 | 5 | 13.2 |

We can perform a chi-square test of goodness of fit to determine whether the data are likely to have been fabricated. Fraudulence would be indicated by a significant departure of the actual from the expected values. We will do the hypothesis test later, but for now, let us see how we can calculate the value of the test statistic. We create the matrix with three columns and nine rows, and name our columns as we did previously.

A common practice in R programming is to use the spacing flexibility of R to help visualize the dimensionality of the data. See the following example, in which I intentionally spaced the data to make it appear to be a matrix. This makes the code easier to inspect and makes more obvious what we are doing. Here is the code from the R Editor. When you execute the code, you will get the result that appears after the script.

```
acctdata <- c(1,   132,  86.7,
              2,    50,  50.7,
              3,    32,  36.0,
              4,    20,  27.9,
              5,    19,  22.8,
              6,    11,  19.3,
              7,    10,  16.7,
              8,     9,  14.7,
              9,     5,  13.2)
```

---

[1]For more information, see Durtschi, C., Hillison, W., & Pacini, C. (2004). "The effective use of Benford's law to assist in detecting fraud in accounting data." *Journal of Forensic Accounting, 5,* 17–34.

Note that the following "ugly" code produces exactly the same result:

```
acctdata <- c(1,132,86.7,
2,50,50.7,
3,32,36.0,
4,20,27.9,
5,19,22.8,
6,11,19.3,
7,10,16.7,
8,9,14.7,
9,5,13.2)
```

You'll note that we have created a vector, whether we use the pretty code or the ugly code:

```
> acctdata <- c(1,132,86.7,
+ 2,50,50.7,
+ 3,32,36.0,
+ 4,20,27.9,
+ 5,19,22.8,
+ 6,11,19.3,
+ 7,10,16.7,
+ 8,9,14.7,
+ 9,5,13.2)
> acctdata
 [1]   1.0 132.0  86.7   2.0  50.0  50.7   3.0  32.0  36.0   4.0  20.0  27.9
[13]   5.0  19.0  22.8   6.0  11.0  19.3   7.0  10.0  16.7   8.0   9.0  14.7
[25]   9.0   5.0  13.2
```

Now, we will make our vector into a matrix by using the matrix() function. We will apply the colnames() function to create a character vector containing the column labels, just as we did earlier with A, B, C, D, and E.

```
acctdata<-matrix(acctdata,9,3, byrow=TRUE)
colnames(acctdata) <- c("digit","actual","expected")
> acctdata
      digit actual expected
[1,]      1    132     86.7
[2,]      2     50     50.7
[3,]      3     32     36.0
[4,]      4     20     27.9
[5,]      5     19     22.8
[6,]      6     11     19.3
[7,]      7     10     16.7
[8,]      8      9     14.7
[9,]      9      5     13.2
```

As mentioned earlier, the use of spacing to mimic the appearance of a matrix is common and useful in R code. The byrow=TRUE setting made it possible to fill the data in row by row, instead of the default column by column. Now, let us calculate our test statistic.

___

▓ **Note**  We will discuss the example in greater depth later, and you will learn how to examine the significance of the test statistic using the chi-square distribution.

___

Here is the formula for the test statistic. Note that $O$ stands for "observed" or "actual," and $E$ stands for "expected."

$$\chi^2 = \frac{\sum (O - E)^2}{E}$$

Following are the calculations. (We really would not do the analysis this way because the test is built into R, but it makes a good example.) At this point, we have accomplished nothing more than we could have done with two vectors, and we made the calculations slightly more complicated than they need to be, but this helps you see how R works.

```
> chisquare <- sum((acctdata[,2]-acctdata[,3])^2/acctdata[,3])
> chisquare
[1] 40.55482
```

The power of R's matrix operations occurs with matrix transposition, multiplication, and inversion. Two matrices with the same shape (that is, the same numbers of rows and columns) can be added and subtracted. You can also multiply and divide matrices by scalars, and multiply two matrices together to produce a new matrix. If we call the two matrices **A** and **B**, then **A** must have the same number of columns as the number of rows in **B** in order to find the matrix product **AB**. The matrix resulting from multiplying **A** and **B**, which we will call **C**, will have the same number of rows as **A**, and the same number of columns as **B**.

To keep the examples simple, let us use small matrices. We will create two matrices, and then do some basic operations including matrix addition and subtraction, component-by-component multiplication, and transposition. Here is the code:

```
> A <- matrix(c( 6,  1,
+                0, -3,
+               -1,  2),3, 2, byrow=TRUE)
> B <- matrix(c( 4,  2,
+                0,  1,
+               -5, -1),3, 2, byrow=TRUE)
>A (with output)
>B (with output)
> A+B
     [,1] [,2]
[1,]   10    3
[2,]    0   -2
[3,]   -6    1
> A - B
     [,1] [,2]
[1,]    2   -1
[2,]    0   -4
[3,]    4    3
> A * B # this is component-by-component multiplication, not matrix multiplication
     [,1] [,2]
[1,]   24    2
[2,]    0   -3
[3,]    5   -2
> t(A)
     [,1] [,2] [,3]
[1,]    6    0   -1
[2,]    1   -3    2
```

Matrix inversion is possible only with square matrices (they have the same numbers of rows and columns). We can define matrix inversion as follows. If **A** is a square matrix and **B** is another square matrix of the same size having the property that **BA** = **I** (where **I** is the *identity* matrix), then we say that **B** is the inverse of **A**. When a matrix inverse exists, we will denote it as $A^{-1}$. Let us define a square matrix **A** and invert it using R. We check that both $A^{-1}A$ and $AA^{-1}$ produce **I**, the identity matrix. Here is the code:

```
> A <- matrix(c( 4, 0, 5,
+               0, 1,-6,
+               3, 0, 4),3,3,byrow=TRUE)
> B <- solve(A)  # This finds the inverse of A.
> A %*% B #Matrix multiplication
     [,1] [,2] [,3]
[1,]    1    0    0
[2,]    0    1    0
[3,]    0    0    1
> B %*% A
     [,1] [,2] [,3]
[1,]    1    0    0
[2,]    0    1    0
[3,]    0    0    1
```

Earlier, you learned that a vector is not a one-row or one-column matrix. But you may be interested to know you can have a one-row or one-column matrix if you need that. When you want a vector, just use indexing, as shown in the preceding example. When you need a one-row or one-column matrix, just add the drop = FALSE argument. This is sometimes necessary because certain operations that work with matrices will not work with vectors. First, let us look at a matrix—in this case a $3 \times 3$ matrix. When we specify drop = FALSE, we can then create a one-row or a one-column matrix! Here is an example:

```
> A
     [,1] [,2] [,3]
[1,]    4    0    5
[2,]    0    1   -6
[3,]    3    0    4
> A[,1]
[1] 4 0 3
> A[1,]
[1] 4 0 5
> A[1,,drop=FALSE]
     [,1] [,2] [,3]
[1,]    4    0    5
> A[,1,drop=FALSE]
     [,1]
[1,]    4
[2,]    0
[3,]    3
```

# Lists

We will not work directly with lists much in this book, but you will learn something about them. A list can be very useful, as it can consist of multiple data types. Creating a list is straightforward. Remember, lists can mix data types, as we discussed earlier, and the indexing of lists is not like that of vectors and matrices.

For example, see the list created from the combination of my name, address, city, state, and zip code.

```
> address <- list("Larry Pace","102 San Mateo Dr.","Anderson","SC",29625)
> address
[[1]]
[1] "Larry Pace"

[[2]]
[1] "102 San Mateo Dr."

[[3]]
[1] "Anderson"

[[4]]
[1] "SC"

[[5]]
[1] 29625
```

See that address[1] is a list, not an element, and that address[[1]] is an element, not a list. We will use *data frames* almost exclusively from this point forward, as they are the preferred form of data for most statistical analyses. We can create data frames in R or import tables from other sources and read the data in by rows or columns. Data frames are in many ways the most flexible and useful data structure in R.

---

▪ **Note**   Although you will rarely use lists per se, you must understand how they work, because the data structure of choice for statistics in R is the data frame, which is itself a kind of list.

---

## Data Frames

A *data frame* in R combines features of vectors, matrices, and lists. Like vectors, data frames must have the same kind of data in each column. Like matrices, data frames have both rows and columns. And like lists, data frames allow the user to have a combination of numeric, character, and logical data. You can think of a data frame in the same way you would think of a data set in a statistics program or a worksheet in Excel or some other spreadsheet program.

We can build data frames from column data or from row data. We can also use the R Data Editor to build small data frames. However, most of the time, we will be importing data from other applications by reading the data into R as a data frame. As with vectors and matrices, many R functions "do" data frames, making it possible to summarize data quickly and easily. Because a data frame is a kind of list (see the next chapter for more detail), we must use the lapply() function to apply functions that do not "do" data frames to multiple columns in the data frame. For example, as you will see later in this chapter, the colMeans function works fine with numeric data in data frames, but the median function does not. You will learn in the following chapter how to use lapply() to apply the median function to multiple columns.

## Creating a Data Frame from Vectors

Say we have a small data set as follows. We have the names of 10 students and their scores on a statistics pretest. We have stored each of these in vectors, and we would like to combine them into a data frame. We will make the data in two columns, each of which will have the name of the vector we defined.

The following code shows the creation of two vectors, one of which is character (the persons' names), and the other of which is numeric (the test scores). We can then combine these two vectors into a data frame.

```
> people<-c("Kim","Bob","Ted","Sue","Liz","Amanada","Tricia","Johnathan","Luis","Isabel")
> scores<-c(17,19,24,25,16,15,23,24,29,17)
```

```
> people
 [1] "Kim"       "Bob"       "Ted"       "Sue"       "Liz"       "Amanada"
 [7] "Tricia"    "Jonathan"  "Luis"      "Isabel"
> scores
 [1] 17 19 24 25 16 15 23 24 29 17
```

Here is the code to create a data frame from the two vectors.

```
> quiz_scores <- data.frame(people, scores)
> quiz_scores
      people scores
1        Kim     17
2        Bob     19
3        Ted     24
4        Sue     25
5        Liz     16
6    Amanada     15
7     Tricia     23
8   Johathan     24
9       Luis     29
10    Isabel     17
```

We can remove any unwanted objects in the workspace by using the rm() function. Because we now have a data frame, we no longer need the separate vectors from which the data frame was created. Let us remove the vectors and see that they are "still there," but not accessible to us. The data frame clearly shows that they are still there, including their labels.

```
> rm(people,scores)
> people
Error: object 'people' not found
> scores
Error: object 'scores' not found
> quiz_scores
      people scores
1        Kim     17
2        Bob     19
3        Ted     24
4        Sue     25
5        Liz     16
6    Amanada     15
7     Tricia     23
8   Johathan     24
9       Luis     29
10    Isabel     17
```

As with matrices, we can obtain individual columns by using the column index in square brackets. We can also employ the data frame name followed by a $ sign and the column name. Finally, we can apply the attach() command to gain immediate access to our columns as vectors if we need them. See the examples following.

```
> quiz_scores[2]
   scores
1      17
2      19
3      24
```

```
4        25
5        16
6        15
7        23
8        24
9        29
10       17
> quiz_scores$scores
 [1] 17 19 24 25 16 15 23 24 29 17
> attach(quiz_scores)
> scores
 [1] 17 19 24 25 16 15 23 24 29 17
```

In more sophisticated manipulations, we can combine the contents of two data frames either in a column-wise fashionusing the cbind procedure or row-wise (stacking) using the rbind procedure. In our basic treatment of data frames, we will stick with simple data structures, examining a single data frame at a time.

## Creating a Data Frame Using the R Data Editor

When you have a very small amount of data and would like to enter the data in a spreadsheet-like table, you can invoke the R Data Editor. For example, we have the federal minimum wage for the years 1997 to 2006 in constant 1996 dollars. We will include the years and the wages, so we have 20 elements to enter. For such a small amount of data, it is easier to use the R Editor than to create and combine vectors, or to use a spreadsheet or text editor and then import the data. To create the data frame in R, we must name and type our two columns, and then edit the data frame as follows. When we close the Data Editor, the data frame is added to the workspace.

```
> Min_Wage <- data.frame(Year = numeric(), Value = numeric())
> Min_Wage <- edit(Min_Wage)
```

The first command in this example initializes the data frame and tells R the frame is empty. The second command invokes the edit() function to open the editor, reassigning the data frame. When we close the editor, the data frame is updated. To close the editor, simply click on the X in the upper-right corner of the window. Figure 1-5 shows the editor open, with the minimum wage data having just been entered.

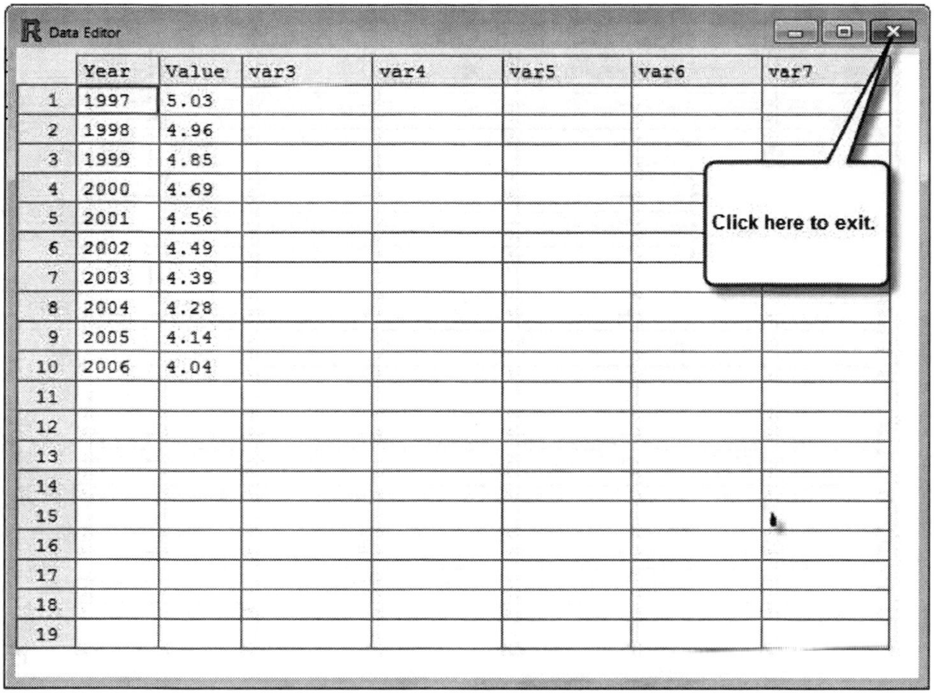

*Figure 1-5. The R Data Editor*

Our data frame is now available for use. We can use the approaches described above to access the individual columns (which are variables in the *statistical*, though not the *programming*, sense). Remember we can use the $ feature, the index number, or simply attach the data frame to have immediate access to the individual vectors. We see in the R Console the result of the input in the R Data Editor, which is:

```
> Min_Wage
   Year Value
1  1997  5.03
2  1998  4.96
3  1999  4.85
4  2000  4.69
5  2001  4.56
6  2002  4.49
7  2003  4.39
8  2004  4.28
9  2005  4.14
10 2006  4.04
```

## Reading a Table into a Data Frame

We will begin with a simple example of reading a comma-separated value (CSV) file into an R data frame. This will illustrate the technique used with many more sophisticated data types such as SPSS files or database files. Many online databases, such as those provided by the Bureau of Labor Statistics and the U.S. Census, allow users to export data as text files or as worksheets.

21

Say we are interested in the per capita income of the various states over the last few years. We find the information in Table 1-3, which we will paste into an Excel worksheet, and then save as a CSV file (only the first lines of data are shown). These data were retrieved from the following web site:

http://www.infoplease.com/ipa/A0104652.html

The averages for 2004, 2007, and 2008 are indeed absent from the table.

***Table 1-3.*** *Per Capita Income by State (Including District of Columbia)*

| State | Yr_2000 | Yr_2001 | Yr_2002 | Yr_2003 | Yr_2005 | Yr_2006 | Yr_2009 | Yr_2010 |
|---|---|---|---|---|---|---|---|---|
| Alabama | 23,521 | 24,477 | 25,128 | 26,338 | 29,136 | 30,894 | 33,096 | 33,945 |
| Alaska | 29,642 | 31,027 | 32,151 | 33,568 | 35,612 | 38,138 | 42,603 | 44,174 |
| Arizona | 24,988 | 25,878 | 26,183 | 26,838 | 30,267 | 31,936 | 32,935 | 34,999 |
| Arkansas | 21,995 | 22,750 | 23,512 | 24,289 | 26,874 | 28,473 | 31,946 | 33,150 |
| California | 32,149 | 32,655 | 32,996 | 33,749 | 37,036 | 39,626 | 42,325 | 43,104 |
| Colorado | 32,434 | 33,455 | 33,276 | 34,283 | 37,946 | 39,491 | 41,344 | 42,802 |

It is easy to copy the data table from the web page and paste it into an open Excel worksheet. Remove the extra commas from the table using Excel's search and replace function. Now you can save the file as a CSV file and read it into R. Say we have saved the CSV data file in our working directory. Following is the R code for reading the table from that CSV file into a data frame. You will use a similar approach with other types of data files.

```
> percapita <- read.csv("Percapita.csv", header = TRUE)
> head(percapita)
       State Yr_2000 Yr_2001 Yr_2002 Yr_2003 Yr_2005 Yr_2006 Yr_2009 Yr_2010
1    Alabama   23521   24477   25128   26338   29136   30894   33096   33945
2     Alaska   29642   31027   32151   33568   35612   38138   42603   44174
3    Arizona   24988   25878   26183   26838   30267   31936   32935   34999
4   Arkansas   21995   22750   23512   24289   26874   28473   31946   33150
5 California   32149   32655   32996   33749   37036   39626   42325   43104
6   Colorado   32434   33455   33276   34283   37946   39491   41344   42802
> class(percapita)
[1] "data.frame"
```

R assumes the class of the table is a data frame, so we did not have to initialize the data frame. This is a very common way to read large data sets into R. Use the head() function to display the first few lines of a data frame.

We can use the colMeans() function with numeric data in vectors or data frames, and easily find the yearly averages. The use of the mean() function for this purpose has been deprecated in the latest versions of R.

```
colMeans(percapita[2:9])
   YR2000    YR2001    YR2002    YR2003    YR2005    YR2006    YR2009    YR2010
27972.74  29019.10  29672.52  30512.02  33441.68  35328.66  38216.32  39396.50
```

We can also get a summary for each variable by using the summary() function. R provides a frequency count for the character variable (state names) and lists the first several cases.

```
> summary(percapita[2:9])
    Yr_2000          Yr_2001          Yr_2002          Yr_2003          Yr_2005          Yr_2006
 Min.   :20900   Min.   :21653   Min.   :22372   Min.   :23448   Min.   :24820   Min.   :27028
 1st Qu.:24848   1st Qu.:25838   1st Qu.:26539   1st Qu.:27537   1st Qu.:30410   1st Qu.:32063
 Median :27660   Median :28699   Median :29405   Median :29944   Median :32836   Median :34405
 Mean   :28186   Mean   :29245   Mean   :29917   Mean   :30862   Mean   :33864   Mean   :35768
 3rd Qu.:31066   3rd Qu.:32071   3rd Qu.:32728   3rd Qu.:33450   3rd Qu.:36466   3rd Qu.:38927
 Max.   :40702   Max.   :42377   Max.   :42706   Max.   :48342   Max.   :54985   Max.   :57746
    Yr_2009          Yr_2010
 Min.   :30103   Min.   :31186
 1st Qu.:34015   1st Qu.:35312
 Median :36935   Median :38446
 Mean   :38761   Mean   :40017
 3rd Qu.:41652   3rd Qu.:42974
 Max.   :66000   Max.   :71044
```

## Dealing With Missing Data in R

R is capable of dealing with missing data, but its rules are strict. Missing data are indicated by NA. Note the following vector, in which we have inserted a missing value. The mean() function returns NA, indicating that the missing value does not allow the calculation to occur.

```
> x <- c(1,2,3,4,5,6,NA,8,9,10)
> x
 [1]  1  2  3  4  5  6 NA  8  9 10
> mean(x)
[1] NA
```

By setting na.rm = TRUE, we can tell R to "remove" (*ignore*, really) the missing value and use the remaining values for the calculation. For example:

```
> mean(x, na.rm = TRUE)
[1] 5.333333
```

However, the value NA is still in the vector, as the following example shows:

```
> x
 [1]  1  2  3  4  5  6 NA  8  9 10
```

## Conclusion

In this chapter you learned what R is, how it works, where to get it, and how to use R. You also learned a bit about R's functions and its handling of various types of data. With this background out of the way, you are now ready to learn how to program in R.

# CHAPTER 2

■ ■ ■

# Programming in R

R allows you to save and reuse code, as we discussed in Chapter 1. When explicit looping is necessary, it is possible, as you will learn in this chapter. We will discuss the basics of programming in general, and the specifics of programming in R, including program flow, looping, and the use of logic. In Chapter 3, you will learn how to create your own useful R functions to keep from typing the same code repetitively. When you create functions, they are saved in your workspace image, and are available to you whenever you need them. As mentioned earlier, R programming is *functional* in the sense that each function call should perform a well-defined computation relying on the arguments passed to the function (or to default values for arguments). Everything in R is an object, including a function, and in this sense, R is an *object-oriented* programming language.

## What is Programming?

Programming is the process of writing, saving, and executing instructions that tell a computer what to do and how to do it. The set of instructions is a *program*. Every program needs a purpose, input, and output. We can think of any program, no matter how simple or complicated, as having the following steps: *starting, operations*, and *stopping*. Programs also often include branching and looping, as you will see. Becoming a good programmer usually is a developmental process. Languages like BASIC were (and still are) often used to teach the essentials of programming. If you have never written a program, you might find R initially confusing, but if you can follow the directions in this book and replicate the screens and output you see here, you will be developing both skills in R and in using R for data analysis.

Some languages like BASIC or FORTRAN are general-purpose programming languages, while others, like R, are specialized for a specific purpose such as data analysis and statistics. There is no one "best" programming language, as every language can (theoretically) be used to accomplish the same (or at least similar) results as any other one. R's strengths are apparent to those who already know statistics and want to learn to use R for data analysis.

Many casual users of R are not particularly interested in R programming. They use the base version of R and many R packages including graphical user interfaces like R Commander to accomplish quite sophisticated analyses, graphics, and output, all without programming in R. Serious users of R eventually realize they can make their lives easier by writing functions to make repetitive calculations easier and more efficient. If you learned to program in other languages, you will find those languages do not work the same way R does. R is both a functional language and an object-oriented language, as we have discussed.

Programming is both an art and a science. You can learn how to program in the same way you learn any other skill. You will progress from *unconscious incompetence* (you don't know what you don't know) to *conscious incompetence* (you know what you don't know) to *conscious competence* (you have to think about what you are doing, almost as though you are having a conversation with yourself) to *unconscious competence* (you are very good at programming, and you know how to do many things intuitively without having to ask yourself what to do next). Programmers who are unconsciously competent are skillful, while consciously competent programmers are more mechanistic in their approach, though they can still write effective programs. The unconsciously competent programmer is often much faster and often much more creative than the consciously competent one.

There is a system concept called *equifinality*, which teaches us that a given end can be reached by a variety of potential means. This is nowhere more apparent than in computer programming and the use of computer software. There are often many ways to accomplish the same purpose in R, some of which are brute force and inelegant, and others of which are simple, some of which are just matters of personal style and preference, and a few of which are elegant, clever, or even brilliant.

Every good programmer knows at least one language, and really good programmers often know many languages. Learning a new computer language is very much like learning to speak and write a new language. Every language has its rules of grammar, spelling, pronunciation, syntax, describing action, and dealing with the past, present, and future. When you learn your native language, you are immersed in it by living with and learning to converse with those who speak the language. I suggest that the immersion approach also works with programming. Some people really do have a knack for it, while for others, it is an acquired skill (and an acquired taste). Just as with a spoken language, the only way really to learn it is to practice it, especially with fluent speakers, the only way to learn programming is to do it. Reading a book about programming teaches you about programming. But writing programs and fixing your mistakes along the way teaches you to program. You will eventually stop making some mistakes and start making new ones, but in programming, we learn from our experience, and, if we are smart, from others' experiences too.

Consider the risks of not learning to program in R (or some language). If you do not know how to program, you may find that the functions written by others do not perform exactly the same computations you want. You must then either pay someone who knows how to program to write the program for you, or you will have to learn enough R and R programming to do it yourself. If you learn to program, you will save yourself both time and money in the end, and will find that the modest investments involved with using a free language with many free resources will quickly produce returns. One book on beginning programming describes the problem of the "golden handcuffs," in which you pay someone else to write a program (or do a data analysis) for you, and then you become dependent on that person to fix the program, extend the program, or do a different analysis, and every time you ask for these changes or additions, you pay that person again. This is not unethical, immoral, or illegal, as long as the person is qualified and produces the correct program, analysis, or report, but you are at his or her mercy nonetheless. First, you do not know how the program works, and you cannot modify it. Second, if that person did something incorrect, you have no way of knowing unless you hire an additional person to check the first person's work. Expensive! Third, you cannot necessarily even see the source code, because it may be the intellectual property of the person who created it, and may be copyrighted. The bottom line is the other person gets the *gold*, and you get the *handcuffs*. This book and others like it are like a key to open the handcuffs and get you programming on your own.

Some people simply program because it is enjoyable to them, while others never intend to become serious or professional-level programmers, but have a problem they can't quite solve using the tools they currently have. Others learn to program out of self-defense. To quote the editorialist Ambrose Bierce, "Plan or be planned for."

# Getting Ready to Program

According to computer scientist and educator Jeremy Penzer, programming in any language should follow best practice. Penzer's (2006) guidelines are well worth reading and heeding. Remember a program is nothing more or less than a set of instructions for a computer to follow. The advantage of programming is that when we write a program and save it, we do not have to retype the instructions every time we need to execute them. Programs do not have to be complex to be useful. You are essentially "programming" every time you develop a worksheet model, a document template, a keyboard macro, or a computer program. Penzer recommends the following (paraphrased):

- **Problem specification**. This is the starting point for any program. Just as you would develop an objective and make an outline if you had to write a paper or report, rather than simply start writing, you should specify the problem as clearly as possible.

Particularly important is determining what inputs your program needs and what outputs it should produce. It is also important to consider the problem and its solution from the perspective of those who will use the program and those who will benefit from the solution.

- **Code planning**. Contrary to what may be your notion of where to start, it is best not to start writing code, but rather to sketch out a rough version of the program with a pen and paper (or on a computer screen). If you know how to make a flow chart, that is a great idea, too (see below for a simple example). Plan the code by making a nontechnical *program prototype*. Mock up the desired format of the output.

- **Identify constants**. If you plan to use a constant or a variable, it is good to give that value an identifier at the beginning of the program. The advantage is obvious. If you assign a value to an argument or a constant, you can change that value once, and update all instances throughout the program.

- **Program documentation**. Good programs are self-documenting. Lay out the code logically and clearly. Use spacing and indentation to make the code readable, and use comments to describe the complicated parts of your program. This helps you and others. When you comment the more complicated parts of your code, you will not have to remember weeks later what was very simple and obvious to you at the time, and you can sometimes spend hours deciphering your own "once-obvious" code. This is the voice of experience speaking here.

- **Solve runtime problems**. Although books on programming are usually linear and straightforward, programming in real life is not like that at all. You may break your problem down into several steps, and work on them at different times. You will almost always find that your code does not produce the expected or desired results when you first execute it. You may or may not get much feedback about what went wrong. In this book, we will not write large programs, so we will not need any sophisticated debugging skills or tools. If your code is not working properly and you cannot figure out why, you can often "comment out" sections of the code by using the # symbol in front of each line in a section of your code and seeing if you can isolate the troublesome parts.

- **Verify your program**. As we are not developing large or sophisticated programs or functions, we are usually satisfied simply when we use some test cases for which we know the correct answers. More advanced forms of program verification are not needed in this case.

# The Requirements for Learning to Program

To learn to program, you need a combination of three things. You need *motivation*. This is sometimes internal and sometimes external. You have to either want to learn to program or need to learn to program. You also need a bit of *curiosity* about what you might be able to do better or differently if you can learn to program. Programmers by nature are curious. They want to tinker with their programs just as an automobile hobbyist would tinker with an engine. They want to make their code as effective as it can be, and good programmers like to experiment, learn new things, and see what the language they are learning can do easily, with difficulty, or simply cannot do. Finally, you need to have some *creativity*. A creative programmer uses his or her imagination to visualize the way a program should work, and to anticipate issues before they happen.

Many people see those who program computers as nerds or geeks. They imagine them with pocket pen protectors, and as boring. The reality is that people who program computers are interesting, and sometimes fascinating, people who help others solve important (or at least *meaningful*) problems. In the broadest sense of what constitutes a *computer*, there are many more "computers" in the world than there are people. And every one of those computers had to have someone to write its operating system, its programming language(s), and its computational procedures. You can program a timer, a garage-door opener, and your digital video recorder. People program everything from calculators to bar-code and laser scanners to cell phones to tablets to PCs and supercomputers. People who program this wide array of devices are constantly in demand, often make good salaries and rates, and generally have more fun at work than many other people have at play.

Programming in R is very much like programming in any other language and programming in general. When you can create and then validate a useful R program, you will have a great (and well deserved) sense of personal satisfaction. You will also find that others are often quite appreciative of your efforts.

# Flow Control

Programming requires controlling the flow from one part of the program to another. Flow control occurs through the use of loops, conditional statements and branching, and stopping conditions that cause the program to stop executing one thing and execute something else or quit entirely. All programming languages have these capabilities, and each language implements the capabilities differently. However, the more computer programming languages you are exposed to, and especially the more languages you learn, the more you see this at an abstract level before you think or of the mechanics of achieving the actual control of the flow of your program. Thus, we will discuss this topic conceptually first, and then illustrate it with very specific examples. The aspects of flow control we will discuss are looping, conditional statements, and branching. As I mentioned, these are common in all computer languages.

## Looping

Computers are much better than humans atperforming routine and repetitive operations or tasks. When we need to perform an operation that is repeated, we can use looping. The computer repeats the execution of the loop's instructions a specified number of times or until a specified stopping condition is met. At that point, the computer moves (passes program control) to the next set of instructions. Symbolically, if we wanted to perform operations A, B (five times), and C, we could write the instructions either this way:

```
A
B
B
B
B
B
C
```

Or we could write them this more compact way:

```
A
Loop (B five times)
C
```

That is essentially what looping does. R provides three types of explicit loops. You can use one type of looping to accomplish the same purpose as either or both of the other types.

## Conditional Statements and Branching

Conditional statements allow us to execute a *branch* of code when a certain condition is satisfied. They also may include an *else* branch to be executed if the condition is not satisfied. They might include an `if`, an `if then else`, or an `ifelse` option.

Say we want to execute C if A is true, but to execute B if A is false. Symbolically, we would represent this as follows:

```
if (A is TRUE) do C
else do B
```

What we have just done is to create a *branch* in our program. We must provide a way to evaluate the results of the condition, and then decide what to do based on the evaluation. Let us create a flow chart to show how our prototype program might be visualized (see Figure 2-1). The diamond represents the decision, and because there are two possible answers, creates a branch.

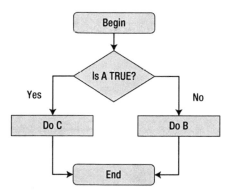

***Figure 2-1.*** *A flow chart of our prototype program*

In the flow chart, the arrows represent the *flow* of *program control*. We say the control *passes* to the object identified by the next shape the arrow points to, rectangles for tasks or operations, diamonds for decisions, and rounded rectangles for starting and stopping. If you have never developed a flow chart before, this is a good habit to get into, and you do not have to use a computer program to do that unless you want to.

# Essentials of R Programming

Now that we have defined programming and we are getting ready to program in a general way, let us see how R specifically implements these concepts. This will help us prepare for writing our own R functions in Chapter 3, which builds on Chapters 1 and 2.

Although this is not a highly technical book on software development in R, even beginning programmers need to understand how R works, its various operators and classes, and the R environment(s). We will discuss them in rather nontechnical terms. Interested readers can consult the R documentation, tutorials, and more advanced texts, but this discussion will give you the background you need to begin writing effective programs and functions.

# R Operators

You have already seen the arithmetic and some of the comparison operators in R. There are also operators for logic. You saw earlier that when you try to use more than one type of data in a vector, R will coerce the data to one type. Let us examine a more complete list of the operators available in R.

## Arithmetic Operators

We use arithmetic operators for numerical arithmetic, but it is important to realize that due to the structure of R, arithmetic operators are also functions in their own right. R accepts numeric and complex data types, and coerces any arguments that are not of these types into numeric or character. As a reminder, the arithmetic operators are shown in Table 2-1:

*Table 2-1.* *Arithmetic Operators in R*

| Operator | Description | Code Example | Result/Comment |
|---|---|---|---|
| + | Addition | 2 + 2 | 4 |
| – | Subtraction | 2 – 2 | 0 |
| * | Multiplication | 2 * 2 | 4 |
| / | Division | 2 / 2 | 1 |
| ^ or ** | Exponentiation | 2 ^ 2 or 2 ** 2 | 4 |
| %% | Modulus | 2 %% 2 | 0 |
| %/% | Integer (truncated) Division | 3 %/% 2 | 1 # R truncates the remainder |

## Comparison Operators

R provides the expected comparison operators. These are useful in flow control to check the truth or falsehood of a condition. The comparison operators evaluate to TRUE or FALSE. As I mentioned previously, you can also use T and F, but we will not do that in this book for pedagogical reasons. See Table 2-2 for the R comparison operators.

**Table 2-2.** *R Comparison Operators*

| Operator | Description | Code Example | Result/Comment |
|---|---|---|---|
| > | Greater than | 3 > 2 | TRUE |
| | | 2 > 3 | FALSE |
| < | Less than | 2 < 3 | TRUE |
| | | 3 < 2 | FALSE |
| >= | Greater than or equal to | 2 >= 2 | TRUE |
| | | 2 >= 3 | FALSE |
| <= | Less than or equal to | 2 <= 2 | TRUE |
| | | 3 <= 2 | FALSE |
| == | Equal to | 2 == 2 | TRUE |
| | | 2 == 3 | FALSE |
| != | Not equal to | 2 != 3 | TRUE |
| | | 2 != 2 | FALSE |

## Logical Operators

The logical operations "and," "or," and "not" evaluate to TRUE, FALSE, or NA. R provides both vectorized and unvectorized versions of the "and" and "or" operators. See Table 2-3 for the logical operators available in R. As with the comparison operators, logical operators are useful in program control.

**Table 2-3.** *Logical Operators in R*

| Operator | Description | Code Example | Result/Comment |
|---|---|---|---|
| & | Logical And | `> x <- 0:2`<br>`> y <- 2:0`<br>`> (x < 1) & (y > 1)`<br>`[1]  TRUE FALSE FALSE` | This is the vectorized version. It compares two vectors element-wise and returns a vector of TRUE and/or FALSE. |
| && | Logical And | `> x <- 0:2`<br>`> y <- 2:0`<br>`> (x < 1) && (y > 1)`<br>`[1] TRUE` | This is the unvectorized version. It compares only the first value in each vector, left to right, and returns only the first logical result. |
| \| | Logical Or | `> (x < 1) | (y > 1)`<br>`[1]  TRUE FALSE FALSE` | This is the vectorized version. It compares two vectors element-wise and returns a vector of TRUE and/or FALSE. |

*(continued)*

**Table 2-3.** (*continued*)

| Operator | Description | Code Example | Result/Comment |
|---|---|---|---|
| ‖ | Logical Or | `> (x < 1) \|\| (y > 1)`<br>`[1] TRUE` | This is the unvectorized version. It compares two vectors and returns only the first logical result. |
| ! | Logical Not | `> !y == x`<br>`[1]  TRUE FALSE  TRUE` | Logical negation. Returns either a single logical value or a vector of TRUE and/or FALSE. |

# Input and Output in R

Before we discuss R programming in more detail, let us explore some of the ways we can handle input and output in R, and what options we have for formatting R output and customizing our workspace. Note that R defaults to seven digits for numerical data, but you can change that with the options() function.

```
> getOption("digits")
[1] 7
> pi
[1] 3.141593
> options(digits = 4)
> pi
[1] 3.142
```

Although you can set standard options at the beginning of a session, R does not save or restore them when you exit and restart R. To see a list of all the options available to you, type ?options. For most casual users, the defaults in the R base package are acceptable, but more advanced users can increase the width of the printed output, select various output devices, and change many other options.

You can type data into the R Console, the R Data Editor, and the R Editor. You also learned how to import data in R. Occasionally, you may want to prompt the user for input from the computer keyboard. To accomplish that, you can use the readline() function. For example:

```
> size <- readline("How many digits do you want to display? ")
How many digits do you want to display? 5
> pi
[1] 3.142
> options(digits = size)
> pi
[1] 3.1416
```

This approach is only one of several different ways to get keyboard input from the user, but it is a simple place to start. The readline() function treats input as character mode. This code would obviously be more useful if we could make sure we are passing a value to R that is within the limits the base package specifies (which are up to 22 digits), and also make sure we enter a positive integer. For example, the American Psychological Association's *Publication Manual* requires probabilities to be reported to two or three decimal places, and statistics such as correlations, *z* scores, and test statistics reported for hypothesis tests (regression coefficients, *t* tests, *F* tests, and chi-square values, for example) to be reported to two decimal places of accuracy. We will return to this example later, after we discuss other aspects of R programming.

You can read data, as you learned, using the read.table() function. You can also use the scan() function. A call to read.table expects to read a rectangular table of data, and returns a data.frame object. You can also use scan() instead of c to build a vector, and you can leave out the commas when you do. For example, to enter the numbers 1, 2, 3, 4, and 5, you could simply type:

```
> x <- scan()
1: 1 2 3 4 5
6:
Read 5 items
> x
[1] 1 2 3 4 5
```

You may find this approach easier for entering data, but you could just as easily accomplish the same result with

```
x <- seq(1:5)
    or
x <- c(1,2,3,4,5)
```

Just as you can *read* data, you can also *write* data. You know that simply giving the name of an object causes its value to be written to the R Console. You can use the print() function when you need to do so, and other functions reverse the process and write results analogous to read.table and scan(). These two functions are write.table(), which obviously corresponds to read.table() and cat(), which you saw in the last chapter. The general assumption is that the file arguments are typically delimited text files, but R is capable of handling other data types as well, as you have seen with CSV files.

Here is a list of the standard classes, data types, and examples to show how these objects are displayed by R (see Table 2-4).

***Table 2-4.*** *Object Types in R*

| Class(es) | Object Type(s) | Examples |
|-----------|----------------|----------|
| logical | logical | TRUE, FALSE |
| numeric | double | 1, 0.33, 1e4 |
| integer | integer | as.integer(1) |
| character | character | "Hello world" |
| list | list | list(a=1, b="data") |
| complex | complex | 3+.5i |
| raw | raw | as.raw(c(1,2,3)) |
| expression | expression | expression(x, 1) |
| function | closure | function(x) x+1 |
|  | builtin | `mean` |
|  | special | `if` |
| call | language | quote(x+1) |
| "{", etc. (many) | S4 | New("track") |
| name | symbol | quote(x) |
| environment | environment | .GlobalEnv |

# Understanding the R Environment

As you have seen repeatedly, the central computation in R is a function call. The call is defined by the function object and the objects supplied as arguments. The result returned by the function in almost all cases is also an object. As you have also seen, R provides different classes. In R, once an object is defined, any future reference to that object will return the same value, unless we intentionally (or sometimes unintentionally, in the beginning) assign a new value to the object. Sometimes our assignments are technically replacements, as in a statement such as

```
x <- x+1
```

The R environment consists of a collection of objects, each of which has its own associated name and a reference to another environment (sometimes called the *parent*, and returned by the function parent.env()). The *global* environment is associated with the current R session. Expressions you evaluate in the session are also evaluated in the global environment. Depending on the packages you have loaded, there will be a "chain" of environments (not a list, really), with each successive environment *enclosed* by its parent environment. You can see the names of the environments and their "hierarchy" by using the search() function. For example, here is the result of the search() function for my current R workspace:

```
> search()
[1] ".GlobalEnv"        "package:stats"    "package:graphics"
[4] "package:grDevices" "package:utils"    "package:datasets"
[7] "package:methods"   "Autoloads"        "package:base"
```

When you install a package, and both the global environment (that is, your workspace or current R session), and the installed package, have a function with the same name, R will "mask" the function and use the function in the highest-level environment. R also uses the search path to locate R data sets. Sometimes, two different packages or two directories on your computer will have functions with the same name that are not really the same function. This can create headaches if you wind up using the wrong one. The moral is to be careful and know your environment(s).

Remember that to R each function and object has a name. Functions are objects, and we give each one a unique name. Here is a simple example to calculate the coefficient of variation for a data set. We pass a vector to the function, and then divide the standard deviation of x by the mean of x to calculate the coefficient of variation (CV).

```
> CV <- function(x) sd(x)/mean(x)
> x
[1] 0 1 2
> CV(x)
[1] 1
```

See that the general syntax for creating a function in R is:

```
function (formal arguments) body
```

Whenever you create a function, it gets a reference to the environment in which you created it. This reference is a built-in property of that function. When you are evaluating expressions in the command level of an R session, you are working in the global environment. When you load packages with a *namespace*, that namespace environment replaces the global environment. You can even create new environments, as well as manipulate them, but we do not cover that subject in this book.

You have already seen that R provides many built-in functions, and that using them is as simple as calling the function and supplying the necessary arguments (some authors call these *parameters*, but we will use *argument* because of the statistical meaning of *parameter*). You should take the time to get comfortable writing and using scripts and determining which functions are most useful before you plunge into creating your own functions. As you know, with R, the essential working of the language is the evaluation of a call to a function. If you cannot find a function, you can write your own, either as an *anonymous* (unnamed) function, or as a named function. Any functions you create and name will be stored in your workspace, and will be available to you if you save and reload the workspace.

To gain access to a function in the standard (core) R version, you simply type its name in an expression. To access a function in a downloaded package, you must first *load* the package. You can use the `library` function or the `require` function to load the desired package. You can also load a package from the RGui using `Packages > Load package`. To see a list of installed packages in your workspace, use the `library()` function with no arguments. Here is a partial list of the packages currently in the R workspace for this book (Figure 2-2). Note that the SoDA package has a spelling error (*exampels* rather than *examples*).

```
R R packages available                                          _ □ ✕

Packages in library 'C:/Users/Larry Pace/Documents/R/win-library/2.14':

boot                    Bootstrap Functions (originally by Angelo Canty
                        for S)
car                     Companion to Applied Regression
gmp                     Multiple Precision Arithmetic
Rcmdr                   R Commander
SoDA                    Functions and Exampels for "Software for Data
                        Analysis"

Packages in library 'C:/Program Files/R/R-2.14.2/library':

base                    The R Base Package
boot                    Bootstrap Functions (originally by Angelo Canty
                        for S)
class                   Functions for Classification
cluster                 Cluster Analysis Extended Rousseeuw et al.
codetools               Code Analysis Tools for R
compiler                The R Compiler Package
datasets                The R Datasets Package
foreign                 Read Data Stored by Minitab, S, SAS, SPSS,
                        Stata, Systat, dBase, ...
graphics                The R Graphics Package
grDevices               The R Graphics Devices and Support for Colours
                        and Fonts
```

***Figure 2-2.*** *A partial list of the packages in an R workspace*

# Implementation of Program Flow in R

Loops are implemented in some fashion in almost all programming languages, but R gives us more alternatives than most other languages to avoid explicit looping, as you learned in the previous chapter. There are three basic approaches to looping in R, which are the `for` loop, the `while` loop, and the `repeat` loop.

## For Loops

We will typically use `for` loops in this book. We can use a `break` or `next` statement to stop the execution of the loop if necessary. The `for` loop will iterate a specified number of times.

> ■ **Note**   Remember that although loops work, and although you sometimes need explicit loops, you can often avoid looping by using vectorized operations, as we discussed earlier and will illustrate throughout this book.

Let us start with a very simple example. We want to multiply 1 through 5 by 10 and show the results in the R Console. Here is a very simple example. The value of n becomes 1, then 2, then 3, then 4, then 5. We multiply each value in turn by 10 and report the rather uninteresting results.

```
> i <- c(1:5)
> for (n in i) print(n * 10)
[1] 10
[1] 20
[1] 30
[1] 40
[1] 50
```

See that the syntax of the for loop is:

```
for(names in values) expression
```

The for loop iterates through the names (number of) components of values (a list, matrix, or vector) one at a time, and names takes on the value of each successive element of values as the loop proceeds to its completion. Because we used a one-liner for our statement, we did not need to enclose the expression in curly braces.

Although the loop works, it is also unnecessary, as you can accomplish the same purpose without a loop. Remember the arithmetic operators in R are *vectorized*, which means when you apply them to a vector, they will be applied to each successive element implicitly, and you do not have to tell R to do that. It simply does. For example, to print the value of *i* multiplied by 10, simply use the built-in print function.

```
> i <- 1:5
> print(i * 10)
[1] 10 20 30 40 50
```

The for loop can also be used with lists and vectors. For example, consider the following character vector and looping through it:

```
> carbrands <- c("Honda","Toyota","Ford","GM","BMW","Fiat")
> for(brand in carbrands) {
+ print(brand)
+ }
[1] "Honda"
[1] "Toyota"
[1] "Ford"
[1] "GM"
[1] "BMW"
[1] "Fiat"
```

Programmers who learned other languages often use explicit loops in R at the beginning, because they are unfamiliar with R's vectorized operations. As you will see, the apply family of functions provides many opportunities to loop implicitly, not just with a vector, but also with a matrix or even an entire data set. Sometimes, it is not possible to avoid explicit looping, and when that is the case, the for loop is usually the best bet.

# While and Repeat Loops

The while and repeat loops are used less commonly than for loops. To use these loops effectively, we must often supply a checking condition that makes it possible to stop execution, or to halt the loop with a break or a next statement. Because while and repeat loops require extra steps, most R programmers stick with for loops when looping is unavoidable.

## The While Loop

The while loop is potentially more useful than the repeat loop, but everything you can do with while could also be accomplished with for with fewer steps. In the following while loop, loop from 0 to 9, and add 2 to each even number. Thus, our loop adds 2 to 0 for the first element of "even," 2 to 2 for the second element, and so on. The result is that we get the first five even numbers.

```
> even <- 0
> while(even < 10) {
+ even <- even+2
+ print(even)
+ }
[1] 2
[1] 4
[1] 6
[1] 8
[1] 10
```

## The Repeat Loop

In the following repeat loop, we start with $i = 1$, print the value of $i$, and then add 1 to $i$. As long as $i$ is less than 5, the loop continues. When $i$ exceeds 5, the loop halts (see the *break* statement). Our rather useless loop prints the numbers 1 through 5 one at a time.

```
> i <- 1
> repeat {
+ print(i)
+ i <- i+1
+ if(i > 5)
+ {break}
+ }
[1] 1
[1] 2
[1] 3
[1] 4
[1] 5
```

A repeat loop has the following syntax:

repeat *statement*

Be careful with repeat loops, and perhaps avoid them altogether. The statement must include a test that determines when to break the execution of the loop, and you can only stop a repeat loop with a break statement.

It is very easy to create an infinite loop. If that does happen, you can press <Esc> or click on the stop-sign icon in the RGui to regain control of the wayward loop. Either approach works. Remember: Anything you can accomplish with one type of loop can be accomplished by the other two looping types, and for that reason, in this book, we will stick with for loops.

## Avoiding Explicit Loops: The Apply Function Family

The *apply* family of functions (including apply, sapply, lapply, and tapply) makes it possible to avoid explicit loops in many cases, thus making R code both simpler and more efficient. For example, the apply() function applies the specified function to the desired elements of a data frame, matrix, list, or vector. It does so without the need for an explicit loop. Technically, apply is for matrices, so it will attempt to coerce a data frame into matrix form when you use it.

You saw an example in Chapter 1 (page 20), in which we used the colMeans() function to get the means of all the numeric columns in a data frame. There are some functions, such as median, that do not "do" data frames, but you can use apply family functions to deal with this issue. Let us return to the per capita income data frame from Chapter 1. We will find the median for the first year's data, but see what happens when we try to find the median for multiple columns. You can, however, use the lapply function to get the median per capita income for each year in the data frame. Remember from the previous chapter that a data frame is a type of list, not a matrix, and the result of its application is a list as well.

In the following code, see that the median function is not vectorized, and that because the data frame is really a list, we cannot apply the median function directly to the data frame:

```
> median(percapita[2:9])
Error in median.default(percapita[2:9]) : need numeric data
```

The lapply() function allows us to find the median for each column in the data frame:

```
> lapply(percapita[2:9], median)
$YR2000
[1] 27645

$YR2001
[1] 28611

$YR2002
[1] 29273

$YR2003
[1] 29939.5

$YR2005
[1] 32657

$YR2006
[1] 34096.5

$YR2009
[1] 36878.5

$YR2010
[1] 38439
```

Although the lapply() function works here, the output is not particularly pleasant to view. The apply() function can be used to produce a nicer-looking and more compact result. The apply function is general in that it works with arrays, matrices, and data frames. It requires at least three arguments, and an optional one. The second argument is 1 for rows, 2 for columns. The third argument is the *function* you are *applying*. In a programming sense, the apply family of functions are *wrappers* that provide implicit looping, which is far faster than explicit looping, especially with large data sets. We are again working with the per capita income data, but by using the apply() function, 2 for columns, and median for the function to be applied, we produce a two-row tabular structure with the median for each year beneath the label for the year. For example:

```
> apply(percapita[2:9], 2, median)
 YR2000  YR2001  YR2002  YR2003  YR2005  YR2006  YR2009  YR2010
27645.0 28611.0 29273.0 29939.5 32657.0 34096.5 36878.5 38439.0
```

The tapply() function applies a function to arrays of variable length (what are known as a "ragged arrays"). The grouping for this function is defined by vector. Both lapply and sapply apply a function on vector or list objects. As you just saw, lapply returns a list, while sapply (*s* stands for *simplify*) returns a more easily read (and presented) *vector* or *matrix* structure. Let us examine these two functions in more detail.

Although we generally avoid lists in this book, let us create a list from the quiz scores of three different statistics classes. The three classes are of different sizes, so if we tried to make a matrix or a data frame from these data, we would have difficulty because the lengths are mismatched. However, given such a ragged array, we can use the lapply() and sapply() functions. See that the sapply() function will attempt to produce a "table-like" vector or matrix structure format, rather than a lengthier list. Here is the code to create the three vectors and combine them into a single list, which we will call classes. First, let us create our vectors and our list:

```
> class1 <- c(17,18,12,13,15,14,20,11,16,17)
> class2 <- c(18,15,16,19,20,20,19,17,14)>
> class3 <- c(17,16,15,18,11,10)
> classes <- list(class1, class2, class3)
```

Note the differences between the lapply() and the sapply() function. Like the apply() function, the sapply tries to produce a table-like output.

```
> lapply(classes, length)
[[1]]
[1] 10

[[2]]
[1] 9

[[3]]
[1] 6

> sapply(classes, length)
[1] 10  9  6
```

Similarly, we can use sapply() to apply functions like the mean and the summary() function to the list:

```
> sapply(classes, mean)
[1] 15.30000 17.55556 14.50000
> sapply(classes, summary)
        [,1]  [,2]  [,3]
```

```
Min.     11.00 14.00 10.00
1st Qu. 13.25 16.00 12.00
Median  15.50 18.00 15.50
Mean    15.30 17.56 14.50
3rd Qu. 17.00 19.00 16.75
Max.    20.00 20.00 18.00
```

As you can see, the apply family of functions is quite helpful.

# A First R Program

You now have enough information and knowledge to write a useful R program. Although there are many different ways to do this (as always—remember *equifinality*), let us apply the skills we have learned thus far to create a program to automate the calculations for a business expense report. This makes a good example from which to learn, and with which to demonstrate how R works.

Say we need to keep track of our expenses for a business trip. We have a requirement to report our trip expenses by category (we will use *columns* for categories) and by day (we will use *rows* for days). Assume we had a recent business trip and want to fill out the expense report, which happens to be a PDF form we fill out on the computer. Rather than using a spreadsheet or calculator, we can enter the information from our saved receipts into a data frame, perhaps using the R Data Editor or writing a script that queries us for the individual entries—or, if the categories are more complex, a spreadsheet or database. All we really need are the daily and category totals, which we will unfortunately still have to enter manually, but doing the math is laborious, time-consuming, and error prone. What if our data looks like that in Table 2-5?

**Table 2-5.** *Hypothetical Expense Report Data*

| Date | Airfare | CarRental | Fuel | Parking | Taxi | Lodging | Tolls | Tips | Breakfast | Lunch | Dinner | Phone | Other |
|------|---------|-----------|------|---------|------|---------|-------|------|-----------|-------|--------|-------|-------|
| 2012-01-03 | 348.75 | 80.84 | 0 | 0 | 0 | 119 | 0 | 0 | 0 | 0 | 16.55 | 0 | 0 |
| 2012-01-04 | 0 | 0 | 0 | 0 | 0 | 119 | 0 | 0 | 0 | 0 | 7.15 | 0 | 0 |
| 2012-01-05 | 0 | 0 | 4.75 | 16 | 0 | 119 | 0 | 0 | 0 | 10.07 | 0 | 0 | 0 |

The *date* format in R is a Unix-based form. R treats the dates as a *factor*, and each date as a *level*. We will discuss factors in more detail later. Assume this information is in your smartphone and you imported it to your computer as a CSV file. Let us read in the data, and then produce the totals using the apply() function. Following is our script. Although it is not fancy, it is potentially very useful, because for the next trip, all we have to do is save the program and execute it with the new data. The R Editor is useful for building and then executing the script. The code will be saved with the R history so that you can rebuild or reload it, but if you need to create a monthly expense report, you might consider writing a function and saving that function with your R workspace.

```
> coltotals <- apply(expenses[2:14], 2, sum)
> rowtotals <- apply(expenses[2:14], 1, sum)
> coltotals
  Airfare CarRental      Fuel   Parking      Taxi   Lodging     Tolls      Tips
   348.75     80.84      4.75     16.00      0.00    357.00      0.00      0.00
Breakfast     Lunch    Dinner     Phone     Other
     0.00     10.07     23.70      0.00      0.00
> rowtotals
[1] 565.14 126.15 149.82
```

# Another Example—Finding Pythagorean Triples

Math students are often asked to generate (or locate) Pythagorean triples, that is, the values of $a$, $b$, and $c$ such that $a^2 + b^2 = c^2$. There are many ways to generate these, but one popular technique is the identification of two positive integers, $s$ and $t$, and then using the following formulas:

$$a = s^2 - t^2$$

$$b = 2st$$

$$c = t^2 + s^2$$

It is very easy to find Pythagorean triples using R. We will first simply examine the necessary computations, and then we will build a program that prompts the user for the two integers, requesting the input by using the scan() function.

```
> s <- 2
> t <- 1
> a <- s^2 - t^2
> b <- 2*s*t
> c <- s^2+t^2
> a
[1] 3
> b
[1] 4
> c
[1] 5
```

This code will produce the most commonly cited Pythagorean triple, (3, 4, 5). Now, let us make our code a little more useful by prompting the user for the two integers, specifying that $t$ should be greater than $s$. Although we used readline() to read in a single value, we will use scan() here to read in the values of $s$ and $t$. The reason is simple. The readline() and readlines() functions produce character strings rather than numeric ones, and thus we would make more work for ourselves in this case, as we just need two integers. When you use scan() with no other arguments, R prompts you for entries, and numbers them sequentially, building a vector. When you press <Enter>, the scanning ends, and you regain control of the program. We will briefly introduce R functions here, which are the primary subject of Chapter 3. Use the following script to make a function:

```
#Generate Pythagorean triples
pythag <- function(x){
s <- x[1]
t <- x[2]
a <-t^2 - s^2
b <- 2 * s * t
c <- s^2 + t^2
cat("The Pythagorean triple is: ",a,b,c,"\n")
}
```

Now, we simply scan for the input. It would be better to put a little more work into making sure we are getting two positive integers and that $s < t$ is TRUE, and we will address those details in the next chapter. See that our little function and the scan() function work perfectly:

```
> input <- scan()
1: 1
```

```
2: 2
3:
Read 2 items
> input
[1] 1 2
> pythag(input)
The Pythagorean triple is:  3 4 5

> x <- scan()
1: 2
2: 3
3:
Read 2 items
> pythag(x)
The Pythagorean triple is:  5 12 13
```

# Using R to Solve Quadratic Equations

It is also easy to make a function to use the general formula for solving a quadratic equation given a, b, and c. Remember that the formula for finding the roots of a quadratic equation is as follows.

The part of the equation under the radical (the square root symbol) is called the *discriminant*. The formula will produce imaginary roots if the discriminant is less than zero, and one real "mirror" root if the discriminant equals zero. If the discriminant is positive, there will be two real roots.

$$x = \frac{-b \pm \sqrt{b^2 - 4ac}}{2a}$$

Assume we are not interested in imaginary roots, so we will compute and evaluate the discriminant. If it is nonnegative, we will find the root(s). Here is the function:

```
#Find the real root(s) of a quadratic equation
quadratic <- function(coeff) {
a <- coeff[1]
b <- coeff[2]
c <- coeff[3]
d <- b^2 - (4*a*c)
cat("The discriminant is: ",d,"\n")
if(d<0) cat("There are no real roots. ","\n")
if(d >= 0){
        root1 <- (-b+sqrt(d))/(2*a)
        root2 <- (-b-sqrt(d))/(2*a)
        cat("root1: ",root1,"\n")
        cat("root2: ",root2,"\n")
        }
}
```

Assume we are given the following quadratic equation to solve:

$$2x^2 - x - 8 = 0$$

The coefficients are $a = 2$, $b = -1$, and $c = -8$. Here is our program (function). We will first calculate the discriminant and test to see whether it is negative or nonnegative. If it is zero or positive, the function will calculate and report the root or roots of the quadratic equation.

Scan in a vector of coefficients (or use c to combine them), and then run the function on the vector.

```
> abc <- scan()
1: 2
2: -1
3: -8
4:
Read 3 items
> quadratic(abc)
The discriminant is:  65
root1:  2.265564
root2:  -1.765564
```

# Why R is Object-Oriented

Most object-oriented programming (OOP) languages like C++, Java, Lisp, Perl, or Python (to name just a few of the most popular ones) work differently from R, but R is still *object-oriented* nonetheless, as we have discussed. Let me explain further. Now that you see how you can write code in R, and how you can get data into and out of R (much more on that later), you are able to understand R's *object orientation*.

Remember that to R everything is an *object* of some sort. R classes are, to use a somewhat technical word, *polymorphic*, which just means that if you apply the same function to different objects (that is, objects of different classes), you will get different results. Like other object-oriented languages, R also allows *inheritance*. This means you can extend a given class to a more specialized class.

We talked earlier about the environments in R, including the global environment and the "local" environment. As you will see, when you create a function, all the objects created by that function are local to the function, and disappear when the function is completed. You will have to print the results or assign the objects to the global environment.

In order to understand fully R's object orientation, you need to know something about its class structures. The original S language used a class structure known as S3, while S4 classes, which were developed later, allow more extensive capabilities, including, specifically, the ability to add a *safety* feature to R, by preventing the accidental access of a class component that does not already exist.

A *class* is just a description of a thing. You can define a class using the setClass() function. An object is an instance of a class, and you can create a new object using new(). In addition to the other features of OOP mentioned above, R supports *encapsulation*, which means you can "package" separate but related data items in the same class.

## The S3 and S4 Classes

The S3 class was written by John Chambers, one of the original creators of the S language. This class was introduced in version 3 of S, and thus the obvious name. Most of the built-in classes in the base version of R are still of the S3 version. In particular, S3 classes each have a *list*, a *name*, and a *dispatch* capability. To be less technical, we can simply call these *old-style classes*.

To create an S3 class, you first form a list. The elements of the list are the member variables of the class. We then set the class attribute by using either the class() function or the attr() function. Let's say we are building a file with the names of the members of a volunteer organization. Let us build a list with the person's name, gender, age, and salary:

```
> info <- list(name = "Ray", gender = "Male", age = 52, salary = 38500)
> class(info) <- "member"
> attributes(info)
$names
[1] "name"    "gender"    "age"    "salary"

$class
[1] "member"
```

If we simply use the generic print method for our new class, we get the expected list.

```
> info
$name
[1] "Ray"

$gender
[1] "Male"

$age
[1] 52

$salary
[1] 38500

attr(,"class")
[1] "member"
```

We can write our own methods for dealing with the classes we create. For example, we may want to format our output in a more attractive way. Here is a function to do that:

```
> print.member <- function(person) {
+ cat(person$name, "\n")
+ cat("gender", person$sex, "\n")
+ cat("age", person$age, "\n")
+ cat("salary",person$salary, "\n")
+ }
```

This is a "method" of the class "member" we created. Note what happens when we now ask R to print our list:

```
> info
Ray
gender Male
age 52
salary 38500
```

By contrast, the S4 class, which is included in the commercial S-Plus and R releases since version 1.4.0, added more formality and rigor, as well as additional safety features. We will simply call these *new-style classes*. S4 classes require the explicit definition of a class using the setClass() function. As you saw above, S3 classes are created by building a list and then setting the class attribute. On the other hand, S4 classes are created by use of the new() function. Let us continue with our member list for the volunteer organization and see how we would build an S4 class. We must set the class, define it, and build a new instance of it using the new() constructor function. Here is the code:

```
> setClass("member",
+ representation(
+ name = "character",
+ sex = "character",
+ age = "numeric",
+ salary = "numeric")
+ )
[1] "member"
```

Now, we create an instance of this new class by use of the new( ) function.

```
> ray <- new("member",name = "Ray",sex = "Male",age = 52,salary = 38500)
> ray
An object of class "member"
Slot "name":
[1] "Ray"

Slot "sex":
[1] "Male"

Slot "age":
[1] 52

Slot "salary":
[1] 38500
```

In S4 functions, the member variables are known as *slots*. We reference slots by the use of the @ symbol. For example, assume Ray just had a birthday, and we want to change his age to 53. Here's how:

```
> ray@age <- 53
> ray
An object of class "member"
Slot "name":
[1] "Ray"

Slot "sex":
[1] "Male"

Slot "age":
[1] 53

Slot "salary":
[1] 38500
```

At present, S3 and S4 classes and methods are separate systems, and can be used pretty much independently of each other in R. Developers often use the old-style classes because they still work, and are less formal, making them a "quick and dirty" solution to many programming problems. Best practice, however, is to use the S4 classes for new projects.

## Generic Functions

Many of the functions in R are *generic*, which means they *encapsulate* a generic concept such as a plot, the mean, residuals, and summaries. A generic function really does no computations itself. The implementation of a generic function for a particular class of object is called a *method*. It would be very instructive for you to read the help files for the functions in the methods package, such as setClass, setGeneric, SetMethod, and Methods.

Just as everything in R is an object, every object has a class, and every class may have one or more *methods*. In many OOPs, the nature of the classes and methods is made clear in the naming conventions. For example, in C# (which is used for programming in the .NET environment), there are *objects*, *classes*, and *structs*. In that particular language, new data types are defined by use of *classes* and *struct*. Any C# application will always contain at least one class. Unlike R, C# is strongly typed, and you cannot use a variable simply by assigning it. You have to declare the specific type of the object. After defining a type for the object, you could use the following code to produce the screen output of the number of children in a person's family. Say we called the variable MyFam and declared it to be of type integer. Here is the necessary code to write the current value of this variable to the screen using C#:

```
System.Console.WriteLine("Number of children in the family: {0}": MyFam)
```

The current value of the variable is passed to the "substitution parameter," which is a zero enclosed in curly braces. Note the hierarchy implied by the "dots" in the call to the system console to write the line. Now see how much simpler this is in R:

```
> cat("Number of children in the family: ", MyFam)
```

You simply use the cat function to write the label and the value of MyFam. Remember you do not need to declare MyFam in R, but simply use an assignment operator to give it a value. R is easier to learn and use than many other OOPs, including C# (which is a play on the musical note "C Sharp," in case you did not know).

We will not spend more time discussing the S3 and S4 classes here, but remember that best practice is to use S4 classes, and I speculate (along with many others), that eventually the S4 class will supplant the S3 case as R is continuously improved, and will eventually be replaced by something even better.

# Conclusion

Every serious programmer ultimately develops his or her own personal style, and programming allows for that individuality, especially a language like R that gives the programmer so much control over what is done and how it is done. For this reason, it is good to develop the habit of being consistent. Unless you can think of a very good reason to depart from the conventions in the base version of R, you should probably follow them, at least until you reach the status of a *contributor* to the R community. It is a great idea to be consistent in your use of spacing, capitalization, indentation, object naming, commenting, and other programming aspects so that people who use your programs will know what to expect. This will make their lives, and your life, easier.

Because R is open-source, and the community of R users and developers is a very welcoming one, it is a good idea to search for an answer to a question that is perplexing you before you ask for help, though you will find many thoughtful and helpful people in the R community who are willing to guide a novice.

Now that you have seen just how easy it is to create and save a program, and have learned how to control the program flow, use logical comparisons, and loop either implicitly or explicitly, you are ready to take the plunge into writing your own R functions. This process is a natural extension of what you learned in this chapter, and you will develop the skills to write your own functions in the next chapter. As with programs, functions do not need to be complicated or elaborate to be useful. Any function that keeps you from having to do the same computations twice, that keeps you from typing the same instructions again, or that provides a result useful or necessary to additional computations, is a good function.

# CHAPTER 3

## Writing Reusable Functions

As you learned in the previous chapters, everything in R is an object. This makes R an object-oriented programming language. There are many built-in functions and thousands more contributed by the R community. Before you consider writing your own function for a particular problem, check the R documentation and discussions to see if someone else has already done the work for you. One of the best things about the R community is that new packages appear regularly, and it is quite likely someone else has already faced and solved the same programming problem. If they haven't, it is easy enough to create your own functions.

To be useful, functions do not have to be complex, elaborate, or sophisticated, though many of the built-in R functions are all of these. A function that is useful simply keeps you from having to write the same expressions repeatedly, thus saving you time and effort.

When you write functions, remember the guidelines of good programming, program control, looping, and conditional statements you learned in the previous chapters. Try to make your functions self-documenting, and try to make them as visually appealing as you can, especially if you plan to share them with others. Think about how you want the output to look, and what you intend to do with the output. Think about whether there should be default values for the function arguments. Think of the function as a program in its own right, and use best practices.

## Examining an R Function from the Base R Code

A good place to start is to examine one of the many functions provided in the base R code. You can see the code of a function simply by typing the function name with no arguments. Following is the mad function (for *median absolute deviation*). The function uses six arguments, five of which have a preassigned default value. You can supply a numeric data frame, a matrix, or a vector as the first argument, and the function calculates the median absolute value of the deviations of the values of x from the median or some other measure of center, such as the mean.

```
> mad
function (x, center = median(x), constant = 1.4826, na.rm = FALSE,
    low = FALSE, high = FALSE)
{
    if (na.rm)
        x <- x[!is.na(x)]
    n <- length(x)
    constant * if ((low || high) && n%%2 == 0) {
        if (low && high)
            stop("'low' and 'high' cannot be both TRUE")
        n2 <- n%/%2 + as.integer(high)
        sort(abs(x - center), partial = n2)[n2]
    }
    else median(abs(x - center))
}
```

Note the use of indentation to make the code easier to understand. Especially when you use loops or nested statements, this indentation clarifies how the function works and makes it easier for others to decipher. Any comments included by the author of this function in the original script are not displayed with the function. You can get help for any function in the base R package or any package you have loaded into your workspace by typing either help(function) or ?function in the R Console. Figure 3-1 shows the first part of the documentation for the mad function.

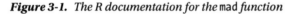

mad {stats}                                                                                    R Documentation

## Median Absolute Deviation

### Description

Compute the median absolute deviation, i.e., the (lo-/hi-) median of the absolute deviations from the median, and (by default) adjust by a factor for asymptotically normal consistency.

### Usage

```
mad(x, center = median(x), constant = 1.4826, na.rm = FALSE,
    low = FALSE, high = FALSE)
```

### Arguments

x            a numeric vector.
center       Optionally, the centre: defaults to the median.
constant     scale factor.
na.rm        if TRUE then NA values are stripped from x before computation takes place.
low          if TRUE, compute the 'lo-median', i.e., for even sample size, do not average the two middle values, but take the

**Figure 3-1.** *The R documentation for the* mad *function*

Examining the R functions is a good way to learn how they work and how you can write your own. By studying functions written by others, you can quickly grasp how to create your own function that is serviceable and quite simple to write and use.

# Creating a Function

Having taken a look at the built-in mad function, we can follow the same pattern and write a related function of our own. In this section, we'll write a function to return the *mean*, as opposed to the median, absolute derivation.

First, let us find the median absolute deviation for the Age variable from our data frame called dataset. Remember to attach the data frame if it is not already attached. Here is the code to execute:

```
> attach(dataset)
> mad(Age)
[1] 2.2239
```

Now we can create a simple function of our own to calculate the mean absolute deviation. Ours will be far less complicated than the mad function, but will show, once again, how to build a function in R. Here is the function:

```
#Function for calculating the mean absolute deviation
MeanAbsDev <- function(x)
{
        AbsDev <- abs(x - mean(x))
        MAD <- mean(AbsDev)
        cat("The mean absolute deviation is: ",MAD,"\n")
}

> MeanAbsDev(Age)
The mean absolute deviation is:  1.56
```

See how the mean absolute deviation is quite different from the median absolute deviation?

Note that you can use both upper and lower case in R function names. Some people label this mixed usage with the term "camel type" because the different cases make the words look like the humps on a camel's back. Camel type can help you and others more easily see what the function does, long after you remember writing it the first time.

The names you give your objects in R are largely a matter of personal preference, but you should avoid using names that conflict with those already in the R system. For example, using *names* as a vector name presents a slight problem because there is an object called names in R. Try to use labels that are descriptive and that help users (including yourself) understand the object's use or features.

# Calculating a Confidence Interval for a Mean

Although R has many built-in functions, somewhat surprisingly it does not have a function for a confidence interval for a mean (although, as you will learn in a later chapter, you can use the t.test function for the same purpose). Say we wanted to create a function to calculate and report a confidence interval, and we wanted to be able to make it generic so that we could pass a vector of numbers as one argument and the alpha level as our other argument. We want to provide a default alpha level of .05, which corresponds to a 95 % confidence interval, but we want the flexibility of changing the alpha level should we choose to do so. We tell R that we are creating a function by using the function keyword.

We will develop a function to calculate a confidence interval for a mean using the *t* distribution. This is the approach taken by most modern statistical packages. The reason for this is the *t* distribution was developed to deal with small samples, while the standard normal distribution works fine with larger samples. In statistics, we generally consider any sample of size $n < 30$ to be "small" and any sample of size $n \geq 30$ to be "large."

See in the following table the critical values of $z$ and $t$ for samples of various sizes using an $\alpha$ level of .05. Obviously, as the sample size increases, the differences between the $t$ and $z$ distributions become smaller and smaller. In the limit, the $t$ distribution converges to the normal distribution. By the time the sample sizes are 500 or larger, the difference is one without any real distinction. See the following critical values of $t$ for various degrees of freedom, and compare them with the critical value of $z$ for a 95 % confidence interval, or a hypothesis test with alpha = .05. Notice that with larger sample sizes, $t$ becomes virtually indistinguishable from $z$. A confidence interval based on the $t$ distribution will always be wider (often much wider) than one based on the standard normal distribution, and most modern statistical software uses the *t* distribution for confidence intervals for means, as we discussed earlier.

```
> cbind(zcrit,df,tcrit)
       zcrit   df     tcrit
 [1,]   1.96    1 12.706205
 [2,]   1.96    4  2.776445
 [3,]   1.96    9  2.262157
 [4,]   1.96   29  2.045230
 [5,]   1.96   49  2.009575
 [6,]   1.96   99  1.984217
 [7,]   1.96  199  1.971957
 [8,]   1.96  499  1.964729
 [9,]   1.96  999  1.962341
[10,]   1.96 9999  1.960201
```

Figure 3-2 shows our function for calculating a confidence interval. You see the function as it appears from within the R editor.

```
R confint - R Editor
#############################################################
#                                                           #
#   R function to calculate confidence interval for mean    #
#                   written by Larry A. Pace                #
#                                                           #
#############################################################
confint <- function(x, alpha = .05) { # x is our data vector, default alpha =.05
conflevel = (1 - alpha)*100 # confidence level
stderr <- sd(x)/sqrt(length(x))# standard error of the mean
tcrit <- qt(1-alpha/2, length(x)-1) #critical value of t
margin <- stderr * tcrit #margin of error
lower <- mean(x) - margin #calculate lower limit
upper <- mean(x) + margin #calculate upper limit
#Report results
cat(conflevel,"Percent Confidence Interval","\n")
cat("Mean:", mean(x), "Std. Error:", stderr,"\n")
cat("Lower Limit:", lower, "\n")
cat("Upper Limit:", upper, "\n")
}
```

***Figure 3-2.*** *The commented function open in the R Editor*

In the process of building the function in Figure 3-2, we made use of some of R's own built-in functions. For example, we used the cat function for formatting the output.

Open a script window and type the following. We will pass a data vector to the function and set our alpha (probability of Type I error) level at the customary default of .05. We will then calculate the standard error of the mean, determine the critical value of *t* using the qt function, and then calculate the margin of error. Subtracting the margin of error from the sample mean produces the lower confidence limit, and adding the margin of error to the sample mean produces the upper confidence limit. We will discuss confidence intervals in greater depth in Chapter 8.

```
confint <- function(x, alpha = .05) {
  conflevel = (1 - alpha)*100
  stderr <- sd(x)/sqrt(length(x))
  tcrit <- qt(1-alpha/2, length(x)-1)
  margin <- stderr * tcrit
  lower <- mean(x) - margin
  upper <- mean(x) + margin
  cat(conflevel,"Percent Confidence Interval","\n")
  cat("Mean:", mean(x), "Std. Error:", stderr,"\n")
  cat("Lower Limit:", lower, "\n")
  cat("Upper Limit:", upper, "\n")
  }
```

Now, let us try our confidence interval function on the ages in our data frame named dataset:

```
> confint(Age)
95 Percent Confidence Interval
Mean: 20.05 Std. Error: 0.4321001
LL: 19.1456
UL: 20.9544
```

When we accept the default alpha level, we will get a 95 percent confidence interval, but we can change that as we see fit by supplying the second argument. Our function is saved in the workspace image and will be available whenever we want to use (or edit) it. It is a good idea to save the script from which you built the function, and if you are planning to reuse or share the function with others, you might consider commenting the code so that you and they will understand what the function is doing. I saved the script in an R script file named confint to make it easier for me to remember and access it. Here the 90 percent and 99 percent confidence intervals for the Age variable. From a statistical perspective, see that as the confidence level increases, the width of the confidence interval does as well.

```
> confint(Age, .10)
90 Percent Confidence Interval
Mean: 20.05 Std. Error: 0.4321001
LL: 19.30284
UL: 20.79716
> confint(Age, .01)
99 Percent Confidence Interval
Mean: 20.05 Std. Error: 0.4321001
LL: 18.81379
UL: 21.28621
```

---

■ **Tip**  The use of comments makes it easier for you to remember what you were thinking when you wrote the code, and helps others understand your code, too. If you save the script, the comments will be saved, too, but when you load the function into the computer's memory, the comments, except those that you place in-line, and any indentation will be removed. This is why it is a good idea to save the script as well as the function itself.

---

As mentioned in the tip above, note how the function appears when we ask R to display it in our workspace:

```
function(x, alpha = .05) { # x is our data vector, default alpha = .05
conflevel = (1 - alpha)*100 # confidence level
stderr <- sd(x)/sqrt(length(x))# standard error of the mean
tcrit <- qt(1-alpha/2, length(x)-1) #critical value of t
margin <- stderr * tcrit #margin of error
lower <- mean(x) - margin #calculate lower limit
upper <- mean(x) + margin #calculate upper limit
#Report results
cat(conflevel,"Percent Confidence Interval","\n")
cat("Mean:", mean(x), "Std. Error:", stderr,"\n")
cat("Lower Limit:", lower, "\n")
cat("Upper Limit:", upper, "\n")
}
```

As with all the examples in this book, you may decide to take the basic idea and expand on it. It would be very easy, for example, to produce a function that uses both the *t* distribution and the standard normal distribution to produce confidence intervals, to produce confidence intervals for other statistics besides the mean (as you will learn in Chapter 8), and for many other purposes. We will explore these additional applications in the chapter on confidence intervals. For now, concentrate on how a function works, how its arguments are passed to the function, and how the results are communicated back to you. In the next sections, we will begin to unravel the mysteries of R functions, so you can write your own when you need them as well as understand how the functions others write work, what they do, and how to customize them as necessary.

# Avoiding Loops with Vectorized Operations

In the previous chapters, you learned about R's vectorized operations. You also learned about looping and the use of logic. Before we talk more about functions per se, let us revisit looping and logic. Remember that R supports iteration through vectors, but not through nonvector sets. We have to use indirect (but still convenient) means of accomplishing such looping. The `lapply()` function and the `get()` functions, for example, make this possible.

You learned a little about logic in the previous chapter. Let us expand on that knowledge. Remember: There is an `if` function we can use to perform a comparison. An `if-else` capability provides the opportunity to make our code more streamlined. Finally, there is also an `ifelse` function. Let us look at each of these in a little more detail than we did previously.

Programmers coming to R with backgrounds in different languages may use more loops than necessary at first. As an example, following is a formula from one of my math books. The famous mathematician Leonhard Euler proposed this formula for generating prime numbers. Students are asked to pick five numbers, one of them 0, two of them odd, and the other two even, and then determine if the formula reliably produces prime numbers. The students eventually figure out that the formula does work for numbers up to 40, but only a few students understand the formula does not work reliably for numbers higher than 40. This is the formula.

$$x^2 - x + 41$$

Note that if $x = 41$, the formula produces $x^2 - x + 41 = 41^2 - 41 + 41 = 41^2 = 1681$, which is clearly a composite number. Say we would like to test the numbers 0 through 50 and determine the results of the application of the formula. We could write a function with a loop, such as the following. Note that if we did not flush the console, we would get only the output for the last value of x.

CHAPTER 3 ▧ WRITING REUSABLE FUNCTIONS

```
#Function to create "prime numbers."
#Formula is x^2 - x + 41
TryIt <- function(x)
flush.console()
for (n in x) {
        result <- n^2 - n + 41
        cat("For x = ","n","Result is",result,"\n")
}
```

Now, if we let x be the vector of the numbers 1 to 50 (remember you can use the seq() function to create this vector), we can then apply this function as follows. (Only the first few rows of output are shown.)

```
For x = 0 the generated number is 41
For x = 1 the generated number is 41
For x = 2 the generated number is 43
For x = 3 the generated number is 47
For x = 4 the generated number is 53
For x = 5 the generated number is 61
For x = 6 the generated number is 71
For x = 7 the generated number is 83
For x = 8 the generated number is 97
For x = 9 the generated number is 113
For x = 10 the generated number is 131
```

Students usually pick small numbers, and conclude the formula produces prime numbers consistently, but the formula begins to break down when $x > 40$. For example, for 41 and 50, the formula produces composite numbers:

```
For x = 40 the generated number is 1601
For x = 41 the generated number is 1681
For x = 42 the generated number is 1763
For x = 43 the generated number is 1847
For x = 44 the generated number is 1933
For x = 45 the generated number is 2021
For x = 46 the generated number is 2111
For x = 47 the generated number is 2203
For x = 48 the generated number is 2297
For x = 49 the generated number is 2393
For x = 50 the generated number is 2491
```

Although the function works, R's vectorized operations make it completely unnecessary, as we can accomplish exactly the same purpose by a simple line of code. This is what new R programmers soon appreciate. Looping for its own sake is possible, but often unnecessary, and is wasteful for large datasets. Here is how to get the same result without the need for a loop:

```
> x <- 0:50
> y <- x^2 - x + 41
> y
 [1]    41   41   43   47   53   61   71   83   97  113  131  151  173  197  223
[16]   251  281  313  347  383  421  461  503  547  593  641  691  743  797  853
[31]   911  971 1033 1097 1163 1231 1301 1373 1447 1523 1601 1681 1763 1847 1933
[46]  2021 2111 2203 2297 2393 2491
```

---

■ **Tip**  Think about what you are trying to do when you are considering writing a for (or other loop). Consider whether it is possible to use R's vectorization abilities to avoid the loop altogether by making the loop implicit, and thus much faster than the explicit loop.

---

# Vectorizing If-Else Statements Using ifelse()

We have already looked at if statements and if-else statements, but we can vectorize this operation using the ifelse() function. This is really an if-then-else function, and its syntax is as follows.

```
ifelse(test, yes, no)
```

test is an object or a test that can be coerced to logical mode. yes is the vector of return values for true elements of test, and no is the vector of return values for false elements of test. As with many vectorized operations, if yes or no are too short, R will recycle their elements.

---

■ **Note**  The yes object will be evaluated if and only if at least one element of test is TRUE, and the same is true for no.

---

Missing values in test give missing values in the result, too. Following is an example modified from the R documentation. You can create sequences including 0, as you just saw, but you can also create sequences using negative numbers as well. The sqrt() function, like most others, is vectorized. Let us create a sequence from –5 to +5, and then attempt to take the square roots of the elements of the vector. R gives us a warning that we have tried to take the square roots of negative numbers. The NaN designation means "Not a Number." But we can easily avoid these warnings simply by taking the square roots of only positive numbers. The ifelse() function makes this simple.

```
> x <- -5:5
> x
 [1] -5 -4 -3 -2 -1  0  1  2  3  4  5
> sqrt(x)
 [1]      NaN      NaN      NaN      NaN      NaN 0.000000 1.000000 1.414214
 [9] 1.732051 2.000000 2.236068
Warning message:
In sqrt(x) : NaNs produced
```

Here is how we can avoid the warning using ifelse():

```
> sqrt(ifelse(x >= 0, x, NA))
 [1]       NA       NA       NA       NA       NA 0.000000 1.000000 1.414214
 [9] 1.732051 2.000000 2.236068
>
```

You cannot avoid the warning by writing the following code. Study this next example carefully to note the subtle difference between the two examples. In the first example, the ifelse() function is embedded in the sqrt function. In the second example (below), we attempt unsuccessfully to embed the sqrt function in the ifelse() function.

```
> ifelse( x >= 0, sqrt(x), NA)
 [1]      NA       NA       NA      NA       NA 0.000000 1.000000 1.414214
 [9] 1.732051 2.000000 2.236068
Warning message:
In sqrt(x) : NaNs produced
```

The vectorized operations provided by the ifelse() function are quite handy.

# Making More Powerful Functions

Thus far, we have been writing simple functions. Let us return to our math problem of generating prime numbers, and figure out how to write a function that will determine whether or not a number is prime.

Remember a prime number is evenly divisible only by 1 and the number itself. There are no other factors. There are several rules of thumb that help us determine whether a number is prime. You probably learned a few of these in school. Remember 2 is the only prime number that is even. The number 1 is not defined as a prime number, though historically it was considered by many to be prime. We know a number can be divided by 5 if the number ends in 0 or 5, and all numbers ending in 0, 2, 4, 6, and 8 are considered even. We know 3 can divide a number if the sum of its separate digits is a multiple of 3. But we eventually wind up getting stuck with large numbers, and the only reliable way to determine whether a number has factors other than itself and 1 is to use a brute-force approach.

Remember we found that 1681 is $41^2$, and is therefore composite. But you also know (because I told you) that the number 2491 is a composite number. We could simply find a list of, say, the first 100 prime numbers (such lists are all over the web), and then start dividing the target number by successively larger prime numbers until we find a factor.

Let us find a more elegant (and more easily programmable) approach to this problem. Math teachers (of whom I am one) teach the following method of determining whether a number has any factors besides itself and 1:

> *Find the square root of the number. Then divide the next higher integer by successively higher prime numbers until you find a factor.*

If we do not find a factor, the number is prime. This is a rather mechanical (and therefore programmable) process, but it is slow and time consuming. Let us speed it up substantially by creating a function. We can use the approach called "trial division." With this method, we find the square root of $x$, and then round it up to the next integer. Let us call this integer $y$. We create a vector from 2 to $y$ (remember 1 is not a prime number and is a factor of all numbers), and then divide $x$ by each number in the vector. If any of the numbers in the vector divide evenly into $x$, then $x$ is not a prime number. If none of the numbers divide evenly into $x$, then $x$ is prime.

Here is the list of the first 100 prime numbers. (You can find these lists in books and on the Internet.) I read a web table into Excel, saved the table as a CSV file, imported the data into R, and made the data frame into a vector. These are all things you should already know how to do, so I will not illustrate the steps.

```
> primes
 [1]    2    3    5    7   11   13   17   19   23   29   31   37   41   43   47   53   59   61
[19]   67   71   73   79   83   89   97  101  103  107  109  113  127  131  137  139  149  151
[37]  157  163  167  173  179  181  191  193  197  199  211  223  227  229  233  239  241  251
[55]  257  263  269  271  277  281  283  293  307  311  313  317  331  337  347  349  353  359
[73]  367  373  379  383  389  397  401  409  419  421  431  433  439  443  449  457  461  463
[91]  467  479  487  491  499  503  509  521  523  541
```

Below is the function to test primality. The stopifnot() function returns an error if $x$ is less than 2. Note the use of the any() function to determine if one or more numbers in the test vector will divide exactly (with a zero remainder) into *x*. We will examine the any, all, and which functions in more depth in the next section. Because 2 is the only even prime, the result of the modulo operation for 2 is 0, so we needed to tell the program that 2 is a prime number.

```
primality <- function(x) {
stopifnot(x >= 2)
limit <- trunc(sqrt(x) + 1)
testvec <- 2:limit
results <- x %% testvec
check <- any(results == 0)
outcome <- "Yes."
if(check == TRUE) outcome <- "No."
if(x == 2) outcome <- "Yes."
cat("Is",x,"prime?",outcome,"\n")
}
```

As a test case, let us check the primality of the numbers 2 through 10.

```
> primality(2)
Is 2 prime? Yes.
> primality(3)
Is 3 prime? Yes.
> primality(4)
Is 4 prime? No.
> primality(5)
Is 5 prime? Yes.
> primality(6)
Is 6 prime? No.
> primality(7)
Is 7 prime? Yes.
> primality(8)
Is 8 prime? No.
> primality(9)
Is 9 prime? No.
> primality(10)
Is 10 prime? No.
```

We will also test the sample numbers we used previously: 1681 and 2491.

```
> primality(1681)
Is 1681 prime? No.
> primality(2491)
Is 2491 prime? No.
```

As a final check, we will use our function to test the primality of a few of the first 100 prime numbers.

```
> primality(163)
Is 163 prime? Yes.
> primality(197)
Is 197 prime? Yes.
> primality(449)
```

```
Is 449 prime? Yes.
> primality(457)
Is 457 prime? Yes.
```

# Any, All, and Which

The any() and all() functions are quite useful. You saw the use of the any() function in the primality() function we created in the previous section. To understand how it works, consider what happens when we perform the modulus operation with the test vector.

Say we want to know not only whether a number is prime, but what the prime number is that divides exactly into the number in question if the number is not prime. Let us return to our example of 2491. We can clearly see that this is not an even number. We sum the digits $2+4+9+1=17$ and determine this number is not a multiple of 3. It cannot be a multiple of 5 because it does not end in a 5 or a 0.

When we are taught to do prime factorization, we learn ultimately that without the use of technology, we are quickly overwhelmed with the trial division approach, so we are thankful that R has come to our rescue here. So, what is the lowest prime number that divides into 2491? Let us do the integer division by going through our entire test vector and dividing x by each number in succession. Taking the square root of 2491 and then rounding up to the nearest integer, we get the number 50. Our test vector should include 2 through 50:

```
> x <- 2491
> limit <- trunc(sqrt(x)+1)
> limit
[1] 50
> testvector <- 2:50
> testvector
 [1]  2  3  4  5  6  7  8  9 10 11 12 13 14 15 16 17 18 19 20 21 22 23 24 25 26
[26] 27 28 29 30 31 32 33 34 35 36 37 38 39 40 41 42 43 44 45 46 47 48 49 50
> x %% testvector
 [1]  1  1  3  1  1  6  3  7  1  5  7  8 13  1 11  9  7  2 11 13  5  7 19 16 21
[26]  7 27 26  1 11 27 16  9  6  7 12 21 34 11 31 13 40 27 16  7  0 43 41 41
```

Because the only zero is close to the end of the vector, we can intuitively see that the number 2491 is divisible by the prime number in the fourth from the last position, and we can deduce that number is 47. Because our vector started with 2 and not 1, the prime number represented in the 46th position in our test vector is 47. Doing the division, we quickly learn that the other prime factor of 2491 is 53:

```
> 2491 / 47
[1] 53
```

But looking for zeros in our results is error prone and slow. If all we need to know is whether *any* of the numbers are zero, we can use the any() function:

```
> any(x %% testvector == 0)
[1] TRUE
```

That's an improvement, but what if we do want to know the actual position of the number in the vector, so we can identify the prime factors? We can use the which() function in that case, as in the following example:

```
> testvector
 [1]  2  3  4  5  6  7  8  9 10 11 12 13 14 15 16 17 18 19 20 21 22 23 24 25 26
[26] 27 28 29 30 31 32 33 34 35 36 37 38 39 40 41 42 43 44 45 46 47 48 49 50
```

```
> results <- x %% testvector
> results
 [1]  1  1  3  1  1  6  3  7  1  5  7  8 13  1 11  9  7  2 11 13  5  7 19 16 21
[26]  7 27 26  1 11 27 16  9  6  7 12 21 34 11 31 13 40 27 16  7  0 43 41 41
> which(results == 0)
[1] 46
```

The which() function returns the index or indexes in the vector that match our test condition. We can also turn around and use the function to determine the position in the prime vector that corresponds to the prime number 47. Here's an example:

```
> primes
 [1]    2   3   5   7  11  13  17  19  23  29  31  37  41  43  47  53  59  61
[19]   67  71  73  79  83  89  97 101 103 107 109 113 127 131 137 139 149 151
[37]  157 163 167 173 179 181 191 193 197 199 211 223 227 229 233 239 241 251
[55]  257 263 269 271 277 281 283 293 307 311 313 317 331 337 347 349 353 359
[73]  367 373 379 383 389 397 401 409 419 421 431 433 439 443 449 457 461 463
[91]  467 479 487 491 499 503 509 521 523 541
> which(primes == 47)
[1] 15
```

The all() function is similar to the any() function. These functions simply report whether any or all of their arguments are true. As a quick example, you know from the above discussion that 2 is the only even prime number. So if we look at our vector, we can ask if any of the primes are even or if all of them are odd in two different ways. We can use the which() function to identify the even prime if we like:

```
> all(primes %% 2 != 0)
[1] FALSE
> any(primes %% 2 == 0)
[1] TRUE
> which(primes %% 2 == 0)
[1] 1
```

# Making Functions More Useful

R functions are capable of calling and even modifying other functions. Doing so is powerful, but potentially risky, so you should be careful to understand the inheritance we talked about in the previous chapter and to determine what effects your functions will have on other functions.

When we examine functions in the R source code, we note that most of them make use of default values, and many of them also call other functions. For example, we wrote a function to create a two-tailed confidence interval for the mean (though you can easily get the same result by using the t.test() function, as I have said). However, what if we would like to have one-sided confidence intervals? For example, if we are doing a one-tailed hypothesis test, it makes little sense to construct a two-sided confidence interval. If we are doing a left-tailed test, the entire alpha probability should be in the left tail (from $-\infty$ to the appropriate quantile). Similarly, the right-tailed test places the entire alpha probability in the right tail of the standard normal distribution.

Thus, for a left-tailed hypothesis test, we will find a critical value of $t$ for the appropriate degrees of freedom that will place all of alpha in the left tail. Similarly, for a right-tailed test, we put all of alpha in the right tail. Let us modify our confidence interval function to take this information into account, and in the process see how one function can call, or even modify, another function. This has a cascading inheritance, so you need to be careful when using this technique, but it is quite powerful and useful.

Examining the various quantile functions in R will give you a hint. Because we are using the standard normal distribution, let us take a closer look at the R documentation for the qt() function, which provides quantiles for the *t* distribution. We will examine the *t* distribution in more detail in Chapter 9, but for now, simply type in the following code to get the documentation for the "Student" t distribution. You can use either a question mark followed by the function name or you can use help(function). Either approach will launch the help files to access the R documentation for the function you supplied.

```
> ?qt
starting httpd help server ... done
```

See the documentation for the "Student" *t* distribution in Figure 3-3.

TDist {stats}                                                                        R Documentation

## The Student t Distribution

### Description

Density, distribution function, quantile function and random generation for the t distribution with df degrees of freedom (and optional non-centrality parameter ncp).

### Usage

```
dt(x, df, ncp, log = FALSE)
pt(q, df, ncp, lower.tail = TRUE, log.p = FALSE)
qt(p, df, ncp, lower.tail = TRUE, log.p = FALSE)
rt(n, df, ncp)
```

### Arguments

| | |
|---|---|
| x, q | vector of quantiles. |
| p | vector of probabilities. |
| n | number of observations. If length(n) > 1, the length is taken to be the number required. |
| df | degrees of freedom (> 0, maybe non-integer). df = Inf is allowed. |
| ncp | non-centrality parameter *delta*; currently except for rt(), only for abs(ncp) <= 37.62. If omitted, use the central t distribution. |
| log, log.p | logical; if TRUE, probabilities p are given as log(p). |
| lower.tail | logical; if TRUE (default), probabilities are $P[X \leq x]$, otherwise, $P[X > x]$. |

***Figure 3-3.*** *Partial view of the R documentation for the t distribution functions*

See that the qt() (for quantiles) function has a default value called lower.tail, which is set to TRUE by default. Now, look at the documentation for the t.test() function. First, let's see the function itself.

```
> t.test
function (x, ...)
UseMethod("t.test")
<environment: namespace:stats>
```

That rather unassuming four-line code actually calls another function, namely UseMethod(), which does the bulk of the work. Figure 3-4 shows the documentation for the t.test() function.

## Student's t-Test

## Description

Performs one and two sample t-tests on vectors of data.

## Usage

```
t.test(x, ...)

## Default S3 method:
t.test(x, y = NULL,
      alternative = c("two.sided", "less", "greater"),
      mu = 0, paired = FALSE, var.equal = FALSE,
      conf.level = 0.95, ...)

## S3 method for class 'formula'
t.test(formula, data, subset, na.action, ...)
```

## Arguments

| | |
|---|---|
| x | a (non-empty) numeric vector of data values. |
| y | an optional (non-empty) numeric vector of data values. |
| alternative | a character string specifying the alternative hypothesis, must be one of "two.sided" (default), "greater" or "less". You can specify just the initial letter. |
| mu | a number indicating the true value of the mean (or difference in means if you are performing a two sample test). |
| paired | a logical indicating whether you want a paired t-test. |
| var.equal | a logical variable indicating whether to treat the two variances as being equal. If TRUE then the pooled variance is used to estimate the variance otherwise the Welch (or Satterthwaite) approximation to the degrees of freedom is used. |
| conf.level | confidence level of the interval. |
| formula | a formula of the form lhs ~ rhs where lhs is a numeric variable giving the data values and rhs a factor with two levels giving the corresponding groups. |
| data | an optional matrix or data frame (or similar: see model.frame) containing the variables in the formula formula. By default the variables are taken from environment(formula). |
| subset | an optional vector specifying a subset of observations to be used. |
| na.action | a function which indicates what should happen when the data contain NAs. Defaults to getOption("na.action"). |
| ... | further arguments to be passed to or from methods. |

*Figure 3-4.* *The documentation for the t.test function*

# Confidence Intervals Revisited

The t.test function provides all the options one would expect from a statistical package. We will discuss the t.test function in more depth in Chapter 9, where you will learn how to conduct all three types of *t* tests. You can do a one-sample *t* test, a paired-samples *t* test, and an independent-samples *t* test either assuming equal variances or unequal variances. You can do a two-tailed, a left-tailed, or a right-tailed test. We will explore these in more detail when we get to hypothesis testing, but for now, let us return to the point of the confidence intervals.

The average adult male between ages 20 and 74 weighed 166.3 pounds in 1960, and according to the Centers for Disease Control and Prevention (CDC), the average adult male in the same age group weighed 191 pounds in 2002. Let us assume we do not know the population standard deviation, and we want to test the hypothesis that a sample of 40 men who exercise regularly has a lower mean weight than 191 pounds. This will be a one-tailed test. Let us imagine we have a sample of 40 men who exercise at least three times weekly, and we have recorded their weights. See the following:

```
> weights
 [1] 169.1 144.2 179.3 175.8 152.6 166.8 135.0 201.5 175.2 139.0 156.3 186.6
[13] 191.1 151.3 209.4 237.1 176.7 220.6 166.1 137.4 164.2 162.4 151.8 144.1
[25] 204.6 193.8 172.9 161.9 174.8 169.8 213.3 198.0 173.3 214.5 137.1 119.5
[37] 189.1 164.7 170.1 151.0
```

Recall from our previous discussion that we used the qt function to find a critical value of *t*. Let us use our previously developed confint function to derive a 90 % confidence interval for the men's weights. Next, we will perform a one-sample *t* test with the test value of 191, and a "less than" alternative hypothesis. We will get the same confidence interval with our confint() function and the t.test() function.

```
> confint(weights, alpha = .10)
Mean: 172.55 LL: 165.5364 UL: 179.5636

> t.test(weights, mu = 191, conf.level = .90)

        One Sample t-test

data:  weights
t = -4.4322, df = 39, p-value = 7.369e-05
alternative hypothesis: true mean is not equal to 191
90 percent confidence interval:
 165.5364 179.5636
sample estimates:
mean of x
   172.55
```

Now, examine the slightly revised confint() function. I created a new function that gives us more flexibility. When we simply accept the defaults, the function will produce the same confidence intervals as the t.test() function, but when we state that we are not doing a two-tailed test, the function uses flow control to determine the appropriate boundaries and reports them to the user.

```
> confint
function(x, alpha = .05) {
conflevel = 1 - alpha/2
stderr <- sd(x)/sqrt(length(x))
tcrit <- qt(conflevel, length(x)-1)
margin <- stderr * tcrit
lower <- mean(x) - margin
upper <- mean(x) + margin
cat("Mean:", mean(x), "LL:", lower, "UL:", upper, "\n")
}
```

Our new function will make use of flow control to determine whether the user is conducting a one-tailed test or a two-tailed test. Here is a first pass at the new function (shown as it appears in the R Editor):

```
confint.1 <- function(x, alpha = .05, two.tailed = TRUE) {
  cat("Mean:",mean(x),"\n")
  df <- length(x) - 1
  stderr <- sd(x)/sqrt(length(x))
  cat("Standard error of the mean:",stderr,"\n")
  conflevel <- 1 - alpha/2
```

```
  if (two.tailed == FALSE) {
    conflevel <- 1 - alpha
    }
  tcrit <- qt(conflevel, df)
  margin <- stderr * tcrit
  LL <- mean(x) - margin
  UL <- mean(x) + margin
  if (two.tailed == FALSE) {
    cat("You are doing a one-tailed test.","\n")
    cat("If your test is left-tailed, the lower bound","\n")
    cat("is negative infinity. If your test is right-tailed","\n")
    cat("the upper bound is positive infinity.","\n")
    cat("Either add the margin",margin,"to or subtract it from","\n")
    cat("the sample mean as appropriate.","\n")
    cat("For a left-tailed test, the upper bound is",LL,"\n")
    cat("For a right-tailed test, the lower bound is",UL,"\n")
    }
  if (two.tailed == TRUE) {
    cat((1-alpha)*100,"percent confidence interval","\n")
    cat("lower bound:",LL,"\n")
    cat("upper bound:",UL,"\n")
  }
}
```

The default output of our new function is identical to that of the t.test() function, as we would hope.

```
> confint.1(weights)
Mean: 172.55
Standard error of the mean: 4.16269
lower limit: 164.1302
upper limit: 180.9698
> t.test(weights)

        One Sample t-test

data:  weights
t = 41.4516, df = 39, p-value < 2.2e-16
alternative hypothesis: true mean is not equal to 0
95 percent confidence interval:
 164.1302 180.9698
sample estimates:
mean of x
   172.55
```

However, when we specify that we are not doing a two-tailed confidence interval, the function tells us what our "confidence" interval should be.

```
> confint.1(weights, two.tailed = FALSE)
Mean: 172.55
Standard error of the mean: 4.16269
You are doing a one-tailed test.
```

```
If your test is left-tailed, the lower bound
is negative infinity. If your test is right-tailed
the upper bound is positive infinity.
Either add the margin 7.013613 to or subtract it from
the sample mean as appropriate.
For a left-tailed test, the upper bound is 165.5364 .
For a right-tailed test, the lower bound is 179.5636 .
upper bound: 165.5364
lower bound: 179.5636
```

The limits reported now are based on a 90 % confidence level and, if we were constructing a two-tailed confidence interval, would correspond to a two-tailed confidence interval with alpha = .10.

```
> t.test(weights, conf.level = .90)

        One Sample t-test

data:  weights
t = 41.4516, df = 39, p-value < 2.2e-16
alternative hypothesis: true mean is not equal to 0
90 percent confidence interval:
 165.5364 179.5636
sample estimates:
mean of x
   172.55
```

# Conclusion

In this chapter, you learned about R functions and how to write your own reusable functions. We illustrated the applicability of writing functions for solving various mathematical and statistical problems. We have discussed confidence intervals in this chapter, but will discuss them in more depth in Chapter 8. In the Chapter 4, you will learn how to use R for basic summary statistics.

■ ■ ■

# Summary Statistics

You have already seen many of the statistical functions in R, but in this chapter, you get a more complete list. You also will learn how R calculates and, more important, reports the statistical results. We cover the standard descriptive statistics from a business statistics class. If you have not taken statistics or are a little rusty, I recommend David Moore's business statistics books. Although it is a toss-up whether to cover graphs or numerical summaries first, we will start with numerical summaries. We will cover measures of central tendency and spread, and the shape of a distribution. For this chapter, and for others, we will use common examples, and the same data will be used several different times.

## Measuring Central Tendency

The three most common measures of central tendency are the mean, the median, and the mode. As you have already learned, data may have no mode, a single mode, or multiple modes. As you learned in Chapter 1, the R function mode( ) returns the *storage class* of the object supplied as the argument, not the modal value(s) of a data vector. The mean is the arithmetic average of the data, and the median is the midpoint, or the 50th percentile.

### The Mean

We define the mean for a population as follows:

1. Identify every element of the population.

2. Sum the elements.

3. Divide the sum by the number of elements to determine the mean.

The definition for the *sample mean* is identical:

1. Add up all the values.

2. Divide the total by the sample size.

3. The resulting value is the sample mean.

The mean can be properly calculated and reported only for data that are interval or ratio in nature. The R function for the mean is simply mean( ). Many other R functions also report (or return) the mean as part of their results.

From a statistical standpoint, the mean has several attractive properties:

1. The sample mean is an unbiased estimate of the population mean.

2. The mean is particularly useful because the variance, skewness, and kurtosis coefficients are based on deviations from the mean.

3. The mean is unique. Every data vector has one and only one mean.

There are several variations on the mean, and we will address a few of them briefly. The summary() function returns a six-number summary of a vector, as you have seen previously, including the mean. Recall the state per capita income from Chapter 1, and remember the use of the summary() function as well as the colMeans() function to report the means of the various years. First, recall the output from the summary() function.

```
> summary(percapita[2:9])
     Yr_2000          Yr_2001          Yr_2002          Yr_2003          Yr_2005          Yr_2006
 Min.   :20900    Min.   :21653    Min.   :22372    Min.   :23448    Min.   :24820    Min.   :27028
 1st Qu.:24848    1st Qu.:25838    1st Qu.:26539    1st Qu.:27537    1st Qu.:30410    1st Qu.:32063
 Median :27660    Median :28699    Median :29405    Median :29944    Median :32836    Median :34405
 Mean   :28186    Mean   :29245    Mean   :29917    Mean   :30862    Mean   :33864    Mean   :35768
 3rd Qu.:31066    3rd Qu.:32071    3rd Qu.:32728    3rd Qu.:33450    3rd Qu.:36466    3rd Qu.:38927
 Max.   :40702    Max.   :42377    Max.   :42706    Max.   :48342    Max.   :54985    Max.   :57746
     Yr_2009          Yr_2010
 Min.   :30103    Min.   :31186
 1st Qu.:34015    1st Qu.:35312
 Median :36935    Median :38446
 Mean   :38761    Mean   :40017
 3rd Qu.:41652    3rd Qu.:42974
 Max.   :66000    Max.   :71044
```

Now, recall the use of the colMeans() function:

```
> colMeans(percapita[2:9])
  Yr_2000   Yr_2001   Yr_2002   Yr_2003   Yr_2005   Yr_2006   Yr_2009   Yr_2010
 28185.78  29244.98  29916.59  30861.63  33864.10  35768.22  38761.10  40017.04
```

Variations on the mean are useful in certain situations. The median is a robust statistic, in that outliers or extreme values do not affect it. The mean, on the other hand, is highly affected by extremely low or high values. One obvious example is income, which is positively skewed by very wealthy individuals. The U.S. government typically reports *median* income rather than the *mean*. The R function for mean() allows us to remove (trim) up to 50% of the observations from each end of the data distribution. Examples of commonly used trimmed means are a 5% trimmed mean and a 10% trimmed mean. The median is technically the 50% trimmed mean, as trimming to 50% would remove half the observations above the middle of *x* and half the observations below the middle of *x*.

Let us use the data from the Yr_2010 in the percapita income data set discussed above. See that the 50% trimmed mean corresponds exactly to the median:

```
> mean(Yr_2010)
[1] 40027.94
> median(Yr_2010)
[1] 38859
> mean(Yr_2010, trim = .5)
[1] 38859
```

The use of the trimmed mean is an effective way to deal with outliers in the data distribution. Other variations on the mean include the geometric and harmonic mean. The interested reader should consult a statistics text for more detail on these indices.

## The Median and Other Quantiles

The median is the midpoint of a data set, and as you have seen, corresponds to the 50% trimmed mean. We can define the median as the value in the ordered data vector that is located at position:

$$(n + 1) / 2$$

R's built-in median() function locates this value, and several other R functions, such as the summary() function, provide the median as well. Remember, the median() function is not vectorized, so we need to use the apply() function to get the medians for the various years:

```
> apply(percapita[2:9], 2, median)
Yr_2000 Yr_2001 Yr_2002 Yr_2003 Yr_2005 Yr_2006 Yr_2009 Yr_2010
  27660   28699   29405   29944   32836   34405   36935   38446
```

The median is the 50th percentile, and you can use R's quantile function to locate the median as well as other quantiles (or percentiles):

```
> apply(percapita[2:9], 2, quantile)
       Yr_2000 Yr_2001 Yr_2002 Yr_2003 Yr_2005 Yr_2006 Yr_2009 Yr_2010
0%       20900   21653 22372.0 23448.0 24820.0 27028.0 30103.0 31186.0
25%      24848   25838 26538.5 27536.5 30410.0 32062.5 34014.5 35312.0
50%      27660   28699 29405.0 29944.0 32836.0 34405.0 36935.0 38446.0
75%      31066   32071 32728.0 33450.0 36465.5 38926.5 41651.5 42973.5
100%     40702   42377 42706.0 48342.0 54985.0 57746.0 66000.0 71044.0
```

Note that if we do not supply an argument for the quantile function, we get the minimum, the first quartile, the median, the third quartile, and the maximum. This is the five-number summary discussed earlier. You can find any particular percentile of interest by specifying the value as a decimal between 0 and 1. For example, let us find the 90th percentile for the Year 2010 data:

```
> quantile(Yr_2010, 0.90)
  90%
48821
```

## The Mode

We have already discussed the fact that the base version of R does not have a built-in function for identifying the modal value or values in a data set. I suggest the use of a frequency table to determine the mode or modes of a vector, if there is a mode. We can use the table() function, combined with the sort() function to identify the modal value or values of a data vector if there are any. For example, we see that two states had a per capita income of $36,421 in 2010. Because no other value was repeated, $36,421 is the mode of the data set.

```
> sort(table(Yr_2010))
Yr_2010
31186 32257 32595 32641 33150 33163 33348 33837 33865 33945 34943 34999 35307
    1     1     1     1     1     1     1     1     1     1     1     1     1
35317 35490 35597 35638 36979 36997 37095 37300 38281 38432 38446 39272 39493
    1     1     1     1     1     1     1     1     1     1     1     1     1
39557 39737 39962 40283 40596 41021 41152 42579 42802 42843 43104 43159 43564
    1     1     1     1     1     1     1     1     1     1     1     1     1
44084 44174 44762 47851 48821 49025 50781 51552 56001 71044 36421
    1     1     1     1     1     1     1     1     1     1     2
```

You may be interested in identifying the mode, and the sorted table does that, but if you want a better solution, you can download and install the prettyR package from the CRAN web site or, preferably, an R mirror site. You must download the package to your computer, and then follow the instructions to install the package. After that, you must use the require() function or the load() function to make the package active in your current workspace. To see a list of all the packages in your workspace, you can use the library() function. Here is a list of the packages in my current workspace. See that prettyR is among them (Figure 4-1).

```
Packages in library 'C:/Users/Larry Pace/Documents/R/win-library/2.15':

abind                   Combine multi-dimensional arrays
aplpack                 Another Plot PACKage: stem.leaf, bagplot,
                        faces, spin3R, and some slider functions
car                     Companion to Applied Regression
colorspace              Color Space Manipulation
e1071                   Misc Functions of the Department of Statistics
                        (e1071), TU Wien
effects                 Effect Displays for Linear, Generalized Linear,
                        Multinomial-Logit, Proportional-Odds Logit
                        Models and Mixed-Effects Models
Hmisc                   Harrell Miscellaneous
leaps                   regression subset selection
lmtest                  Testing Linear Regression Models
matrixcalc              Collection of functions for matrix differential
                        calculus
multcomp                Simultaneous Inference in General Parametric
                        Models
mvtnorm                 Multivariate Normal and t Distributions
prettyR                 Pretty descriptive stats.
Rcmdr                   R Commander
relimp                  Relative Contribution of Effects in a
                        Regression Model
rgl                     3D visualization device system (OpenGL)
```

***Figure 4-1.*** *Partial listing of the packages in an R workspace*

The prettyR package provides functions for conventionally formatted descriptive statistics, and includes a Mode() function (note the capital M) for finding the modal value or values of a data set. See the use of the Mode() function as follows for the Yr_2010 data. We will use the require() function to make sure the prettyR package is available.

```
> require(prettyR)
Loading required package: prettyR
> Mode(Yr_2010)
[1] "36421"
```

# Measuring Location via Standard Scores

In addition to the various quantiles discussed above, we can also find standard scores using R's scale() function. To review briefly, the deviation between a raw score and the mean divided by the standard deviation is a z score. We define a z score in the population as follows:

$$z = \frac{x - \mu}{\sigma}$$

In a sample, we substitute sample statistics as estimators of the population parameters.

$$z = \frac{x - \overline{x}}{s}$$

By definition, z scores have a mean of zero and a standard deviation of one. Let us find the z scores for the Yr_2010 data. If we accept the defaults, the scale() function will use the mean as the measure of center and the standard deviation as its scaling value. Only the first 10 values appear below.

```
> zYr_2010 <- scale(Yr_2010)
> zYr_2010
              [,1]
 [1,] -0.854741447
 [2,]  0.585162010
 [3,] -0.706373254
 [4,] -0.966651042
 [5,]  0.434541549
 [6,]  0.392029980
 [7,]  2.250010792
 [8,] -0.007747694
 [9,]  4.367565559
[10,] -0.104876776
```

Just to prove the point, let us calculate the mean and standard deviation of our z scores. Because the output of the scale function was a matrix, we will use apply() to calculate the standard deviation. Note the accumulation of minute amounts of rounding error in the calculation of the mean z score. Remember, the argument 2 is used to specify that the function is applied to a column of data.

```
> mean(zYr_2010)
[1] 2.638906e-16
> apply(zYr_2010, 2, sd)
[1] 1
```

# Measuring Variability

There are various measures of dispersion or spread. Among these are the variance and standard deviation, the range, the mean absolute deviation (and the median absolute deviation, as we discussed), the interquartile range (IQR), and the coefficient of variation. R provides functions for these (or provides functions which, like mad(), can be adapted for these indexes).

# Variance and Standard Deviation

In a population, the variance is defined as follows, where $N$ is the number of elements in the population.

$$\sigma_x^2 = \frac{\sum (x - \mu)^2}{N}$$

We estimate the sample variance as follows, using $n$ as the sample size.

$$s_x^2 = \frac{\sum (x - \bar{x})^2}{n - 1}$$

This is the value returned by the var() function in R. The square root of the variance is the standard deviation. Let us calculate these indices for the Year 2010 data:

```
> var(Yr_2010)
[1] 50466084
> sd(Yr_2010)
[1] 7103.948
```

As in other areas, the vectorization features of R mean that when you calculate the variance for a data frame, you will get a variance-covariance matrix rather than the variance. For example, see what happens when we calculate the variance for the per capita income data:

```
var(percapita[2:9])
          Yr_2000  Yr_2001  Yr_2002  Yr_2003  Yr_2005  Yr_2006  Yr_2009  Yr_2010
Yr_2000 20626819 21133669 20970587 21519028 24678280 25596421 26927213 27893195
Yr_2001 21133669 21792373 21691271 22360067 25643044 26726923 28386039 29466440
Yr_2002 20970587 21691271 21699502 22496055 25771187 26864249 28845630 30016171
Yr_2003 21519028 22360067 22496055 24082187 27706415 28922607 31810939 33234378
Yr_2005 24678280 25643044 25771187 27706415 32572732 33621320 36842826 38333658
Yr_2006 25596421 26726923 26864249 28922607 33621320 35903108 39291556 41123248
Yr_2009 26927213 28386039 28845630 31810939 36842826 39291556 45037045 47140509
Yr_2010 27893195 29466440 30016171 33234378 38333658 41123248 47140509 50466084
```

# Range

The range is most commonly defined as the difference between the highest value and the lowest value in a data vector. Rather than report the difference, R reports the minimum value and the maximum value. You can, of course, write a function to calculate the range if you like. See the following code. We will use the 40 weights of adult males who exercise regularly (see Chapter 3).

```
> range(weights)
[1] 119.5 237.1
> range.diff <- function(x) max(x) - min(x)
> range.diff(weights)
[1] 117.6
```

# Median and Mean Absolute Deviation

Continuing with our example of the weights, let us use the mad() function to find the median and mean absolute deviations. Remember, we can specify the measure of central tendency by supplying the argument. In this particular case, we see that the values are fairly close to each other, and that both are not very different from the standard deviation.

```
> mad(weights)
[1] 27.27984
> mad(weights, center = mean(weights))
[1] 28.54005
> sd(weights)
[1] 26.32716
```

This is a bit of a hint that the data is symmetrical in nature. Let us verify this by using the hist() function to produce a histogram (see Figure 4-2). Note the code to produce the histogram requires the data vector to be supplied as an argument.

```
> hist(weights)
```

The command line returns a prompt, >, and the R Graphics Device opens in a separate window, displaying the resulting histogram.

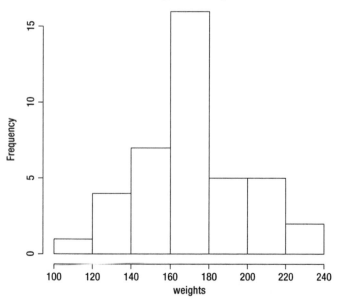

*Figure 4-2.* The histogram reveals the weights are roughly symmetrical in shape

## The Interquartile Range

The interquartile range (IQR) is the difference between the third quartile and the first quartile, and provides a view of the middle 50% of the data. The IQR is frequently displayed in a box-like shape via a box-and-whiskers plot, as you will see in the next chapter. The IQR() function provides the interquartile range.

```
> IQR(weights)
[1] 37.2
```

## The Coefficient of Variation

Occasionally, we will want to measure the size of the standard deviation of a population or sample relative to the size of the mean. For this purpose, we can use the coefficient of variation, or CV.

$$CV = \frac{standard\ deviation}{mean}$$

The CV is often used as a measure of relative risk, as it shows the amount of variability relative to the size of the average. For example, when analyzing rates of return, we might be interested in calculating the CV for different investments. R does not have a built-in function for calculating the CV, but it is simple enough to create one. We will return to this statistic later when we talk about bootstrapping in Chapter 18. For now, look at the following code:

```
> CV <- function(x) sd(x)/mean(x)
> CV
function(x) sd(x)/mean(x)
> CV(weights)
[1] 0.152577
```

The code shows that we are simply implementing the formula shown above by writing an R function to calculate the coefficient of variation.

# Covariance and Correlation

Thus far, we have been talking about one or more data vectors but have not distinguished between independent and dependent variables. Let us make that distinction, and in the process examine covariance and correlation. By convention, we will label the dependent variable $y$ and the independent variable $x$. We often call the dependent variable the criterion or the response variable, and the independent variable the predictor or explanatory variable. Say we are studying the relationship between advertising expenditures ($x$) in ten different sales regions for a fast-food restaurant, and the sales volume ($y$) for each region. Assume the sales regions were selected in such a way that each had the same sales opportunity, and we then calculated annual sales for each region. The (fabricated) data set is shown in Table 4-1.

*Table 4-1.* *Hypothetical advertising and sales figures (all figures in 1,000s)*

| Region | Advertising (x) | Sales (y) |
|--------|-----------------|-----------|
| 1 | 5.5 | 101 |
| 2 | 5.8 | 110 |
| 3 | 6.9 | 120 |
| 4 | 7.2 | 125 |
| 5 | 6.3 | 117 |
| 6 | 6.5 | 118 |
| 7 | 6.4 | 120 |
| 8 | 5.7 | 108 |
| 9 | 6.1 | 115 |
| 10 | 6.8 | 116 |

Because we are dealing with only 20 data points, we just enter the data directly into R, though you could use the R Data Editor or a spreadsheet program as well. Let us call our data frame sales. The steps for creating the vectors and creating the data frame are shown in Chapter 1 and will not be repeated here.

Let us define (theoretically) the sample covariance between *x* and *y* as follows.

$$s_{xy} = \frac{\sum (x - \bar{x})(y - \bar{y})}{n - 1}$$

Note that unlike the variance, the covariance is based on the cross products of deviation scores, and can thus be positive, zero, or negative. We can find the value of the covariance in R using the cov() function. We must supply the two variable names:.

```
> cov(Advertising, Sales)
[1] 3.5
```

The covariance is positive, which means there is a general trend for *x* and *y* to increase together, but the covariance is affected by the units of measurement of both *x* and *y*. By dividing the covariance by the products of the two standard deviations, we achieve the correlation coefficient. This value can be found directly by use of the cor() function:

```
> cor(Advertising, Sales)
[1] 0.9108064
> (cov(Advertising, Sales)/(sd(Advertising) * sd(Sales)))
[1] 0.9108064
```

As with the var() function, the cor() function will produce an intercorrelation matrix when multiple data vectors are supplied. The following example uses the per capita income data.

```
(percapita[2:9])
          Yr_2000    Yr_2001    Yr_2002    Yr_2003    Yr_2005    Yr_2006    Yr_2009
Yr_2000 1.0000000 0.9967965 0.9912189 0.9655140 0.9520761 0.9405829 0.8834670
Yr_2001 0.9967965 1.0000000 0.9974884 0.9760518 0.9624767 0.9555000 0.9060822
Yr_2002 0.9912189 0.9974884 1.0000000 0.9840871 0.9693541 0.9624625 0.9227206
Yr_2003 0.9655140 0.9760518 0.9840871 1.0000000 0.9892482 0.9836112 0.9659254
Yr_2005 0.9520761 0.9624767 0.9693541 0.9892482 1.0000000 0.9831542 0.9619243
Yr_2006 0.9405829 0.9555000 0.9624625 0.9836112 0.9831542 1.0000000 0.9771208
Yr_2009 0.8834670 0.9060822 0.9227206 0.9659254 0.9619243 0.9771208 1.0000000
Yr_2010 0.8645345 0.8885372 0.9070487 0.9533224 0.9454822 0.9660989 0.9888024
          Yr_2010
Yr_2000 0.8645345
Yr_2001 0.8885372
Yr_2002 0.9070487
Yr_2003 0.9533224
Yr_2005 0.9454822
Yr_2006 0.9660989
Yr_2009 0.9888024
Yr_2010 1.0000000
```

# Measuring Symmetry (or Lack Thereof)

We are often concerned with knowing whether our data distribution is roughly symmetrical in shape. An index commonly used for examining symmetry is the skewness coefficient, and an index for peakedness is the kurtosis coefficient. By definition, the normal distribution has zero skew and zero kurtosis.

Data may be positively skewed, negatively skewed, or unskewed. Similarly, data may be platykurtic (flat), mesokurtic (like the normal distribution), or leptokurtic (peaked). We typically look at graphical displays of the data to determine the amount or appearance of skew and kurtosis, but we can also calculate indices or coefficients to measure the degree of each. If you have studied calculus or derivational statistics, you will recognize the skewness coefficient as the third moment about the mean and the kurtosis coefficient as the fourth moment about the mean. The base version of R does not provide built-in functions for determining the amount of skew and kurtosis, but several different packages do provide them. Be careful, as not all similarly titled functions produce exactly the same result.

Here is a data frame consisting of the gasoline mileage for 1129 automobiles from the 2012 model year. The data set was compiled by the U.S. Environmental Protection Agency. Only the first few records are shown. We will look at the skewness and kurtosis estimates of the city, highway, and combined mileage estimates. We will use the skewness and kurtosis coefficients from the psych package. The function names are skew() and kurtosi(), respectively. For example:

```
> head(Mileages)
  Year          Mfr           Division    Carline Displ Cyl       Trans City Hwy Combined
1 2012 aston martin Aston Martin Lagonda Ltd  V12 Vantage   5.9  12 Manual(M6)   11  17       13
2 2012 aston martin Aston Martin Lagonda Ltd   V8 Vantage   4.7   8  Auto(AM6)   14  20       16
3 2012 aston martin Aston Martin Lagonda Ltd   V8 Vantage   4.7   8  Auto(AM7)   14  21       16
4 2012 aston martin Aston Martin Lagonda Ltd   V8 Vantage   4.7   8 Manual(M6)   13  19       15
5 2012 aston martin Aston Martin Lagonda Ltd V8 Vantage S   4.7   8  Auto(AM7)   14  21       16
6 2012         Audi                     Audi        R8   4.2   8  Auto(AM6)   13  21       16
        Trans.Desc X..Gears         Drive.Desc
1          Manual       6 2-Wheel Drive, Rear
2 Automated Manual       6 2-Wheel Drive, Rear
3 Automated Manual       7 2-Wheel Drive, Rear
```

```
4             Manual        6 2-Wheel Drive, Rear
5 Automated Manual          7 2-Wheel Drive, Rear
6 Automated Manual          6     All Wheel Drive
```

Although we can test the significance of these coefficients, in general a good rule of thumb is that the distribution is "roughly" normal or "normal enough" when the coefficients are in the range from –2 to +2. When distribution is not symmetrical, we may choose to transform the data or to use nonparametric techniques. Clearly, this data distribution is far from normally distributed, as the large skewness and kurtosis coefficients reveal. See how to install and require the package:

```
> install.packages("psych")
Installing package(s) into 'C:/Users/Larry Pace/Documents/R/win-library/2.15'
(as 'lib' is unspecified)
--- Please select a CRAN mirror for use in this session ---
trying URL 'http://lib.stat.cmu.edu/R/CRAN/bin/windows/contrib/2.15/psych_1.2.4.zip'
Content type 'application/zip' length 2441657 bytes (2.3 Mb)
opened URL
downloaded 2.3 Mb

package 'psych' successfully unpacked and MD5 sums checked

The downloaded binary packages are in
        C:\Users\Larry Pace\AppData\Local\Temp\Rtmpg7vifJ\downloaded_packages

> require(psych)
Loading required package: psych
Warning message:
package 'psych' was built under R version 2.15.1
```

Now, we can use the skew() and kurtosis() functions for our data frame.

```
> skew(City)
[1] 6.117783
> skew(Hwy)
[1] 2.98726
> skew(Combined)
[1] 4.769474
> kurtosi(City)
[1] 65.917
> kurtosi(Hwy)
[1] 23.6899
> kurtosi(Combined)
[1] 45.89908
```

To see why the data appear to be so skewed and leptokurtic, let us examine a histogram, which you can see in Figure 4-3. (We will use the city mileage only.) We will discuss graphics in more detail in the next chapter.

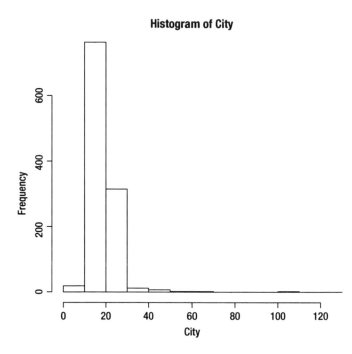

**Figure 4-3.** *Histogram of city gas mileages*

# Conclusion

In Chapter 4, you learned how to use R for the most common summary statistics. You also got a preview of the histogram as we examined the shape of data distributions. We will return to several of these examples in future chapters. For now, let us move on to summarizing data in tables and graphical form, which is the topic of Chapter 5.

# CHAPTER 5

# Creating Tables and Graphs

In the last chapter, you learned how to use R for the most common numerical descriptive statistics. In this chapter, you learn how to use R for summary tables and for various graphical representations of data. As with many of the other functions of R, you will learn that the methods R provides often produce quite different results depending on the input.

R's graphical capabilities are quite extensive, and the plots and other graphs it produces are highly customizable. After discussing frequency tables in detail, we will examine pie charts, bar charts, histograms, boxplots, line graphs, and scatter plots. Although there are many other choices, these graphics are the ones most frequently covered in basic statistics texts, and we will use many of the same examples from previous chapters for the sake of continuity.

## Frequency Distributions and Tables

You have already seen that the table() function produces a simple frequency distribution. When we have more than a few data points, we are more likely to want to produce a grouped frequency distribution. We can do this in R by establishing intervals and then determining the frequency of data values within each interval. We also sometimes are more interested in cumulative frequency distributions than in relative ones. We can produce all these in R with little difficulty.

Examine the first several records from the data set named faithful supplied with the R base package. This data set contains 272 observations of the duration of the eruption and the waiting time between the eruptions of Old Faithful, a geyser at Yellowstonc National Park. Both measurements are in minutes. Let us determine the minimum and maximum waiting times by using the range() function:

```
> head(faithful)  #head() prints the first few rows of the data set
  eruptions waiting
1     3.600      79
2     1.800      54
3     3.333      74
4     2.283      62
5     4.533      85
6     2.883      55
> waiting<-faithful[,2]
> range(waiting)
[1] 43 96
```

With 272 observations, we have too many data points for the table to be very meaningful.

```
> table(waiting)
waiting
43 45 46 47 48 49 50 51 52 53 54 55 56 57 58 59 60 62 63 64 65 66 67 68 69 70
 1  3  5  4  3  5  5  6  5  7  9  6  4  3  4  7  6  4  3  4  3  2  1  1  2  4
71 72 73 74 75 76 77 78 79 80 81 82 83 84 85 86 87 88 89 90 91 92 93 94 96
 5  1  7  6  8  9 12 15 10  8 13 12 14 10  6  6  2  6  3  6  1  1  2  1  1
```

Let us create intervals or bins and use these to get a better view of the frequency distribution. Note the creation of intervals is not an exact science, so a little trial and error may be helpful in establishing a good set of intervals. We will use the range 40 to 100, to accommodate both the lowest and highest values, and shoot for, say, 12 intervals of width 5.

Here is how to create the intervals. We will first create our sequence with our lower-class boundaries using the seq() function. Then we will use the cut() function with our breaks, specifying right = FALSE because we have left the right boundaries open. Observe the following code, and note that the grouped frequency table is more helpful than the simple frequency table.

```
> breaks <- seq(40, 100, by = 5)
> breaks
 [1]  40  45  50  55  60  65  70  75  80  85  90  95 100
> wait_time <- cut(waiting, breaks, right = FALSE)
> table(wait_time)
wait_time
 [40,45)  [45,50)  [50,55)  [55,60)  [60,65)  [65,70)  [70,75)  [75,80)
       1       20       32       24       17        9       23       54
 [80,85)  [85,90)  [90,95) [95,100)
      57       23       11        1
```

Using the cbind() function allows us to produce a columnar grouped frequency distribution, which is a more familiar presentation of the frequency distribution. For example:

```
> cbind(table(wait_time))
          [,1]
[40,45)      1
[45,50)     20
[50,55)     32
[55,60)     24
[60,65)     17
[65,70)      9
[70,75)     23
[75,80)     54
[80,85)     57
[85,90)     23
[90,95)     11
[95,100)     1
```

When we use the table() function with two variables, we get a cross tabulation. We can do that for quantitative or qualitative variables. We can also mix variable types. Here is the cross tabulation of Sex and Age from the data frame we called dataset. Recall we created this data frame in Chapter 1.

```
> attach(dataset)
> table(Sex, Age)
   Age
Sex 17 18 19 20 21 22 23
  0  2  2  2  2  2  0  0
  1  0  1  1  2  1  2  3
```

Here are the first few lines of a distribution of students' gender, grade, and GPA collected by one of my doctoral students as part of her dissertation. As mentioned previously, all the students were in grades 10, 11, and 12. Remember the head() function will produce the first few lines of a data frame, and the tail() function will report the last few lines.

```
> head(grades)
  Gender Grade  GPA
1      F     11 1.84
2      M     10 1.29
3      F     10 1.51
4      M     10 1.72
5      F     10 3.64
6      F     11 1.82
```

We will use the table() function to summarize the qualitative information (gender). See that R produces a two-way contingency table when we supply two variables to the table() function:

```
> attach(grades)
> table(Gender, Grade)
       Grade
Gender 10 11 12
     F  4 12  7
     M  3  3  3
```

# Pie Charts and Bar Charts

Pie charts and bar charts (what R calls "bar plots") are useful for graphical representation of nominal and ordinal data. For bar charts (also frequently known as bar graphs), the x axis does not represent an underlying continuum, but separate categories, and thus the bars should be separated with a gap between bars. Although the same information can be shown in a pie chart and a bar chart, the human eye is better able to judge linear distance than area, and therefore the bar chart will typically be more informative than the corresponding pie chart.

## Pie Charts

Table 5-1 shows the results of DuPont's 2010 survey of global automobile color preferences.

**Table 5-1.** *DuPont's 2010 survey of global automobile color preferences*

| Color | Percentage |
|-------|------------|
| Silver | 26 |
| Black/Black Effect | 24 |
| White/White Pearl | 16 |
| Gray | 16 |
| Red | 6 |
| Blue | 5 |
| Brown/Beige | 3 |
| Green | 2 |
| Other | 2 |

Let us simplify the color names and create a small data frame. It is easier to build such small data frames directly in R by using the Data Editor than it is to go to an application like Excel and create and export the data, which you then must read into R. We will create the data frame, defining Color as a *factor* rather than a character variable. Then we will edit the data frame in the R Data Editor.

```
> Car_Colors <- data.frame(Color = factor(), Percent = numeric())
> Car_Colors <- edit(Car_Colors)
```

Here, you type in the data, and the data frame is updated with your entries when you exit the R Editor. See the data frame below:

```
> Car_Colors
    Color Percent
1 Silver      26
2  Black      24
3  White      16
4   Gray      16
5    Red       6
6   Blue       5
7  Brown       3
8  Green       2
9  Other       2
```

Now, we can make a pie chart (and embellish it a little) as well as a bar chart from these data. Use the pie() function to create a pie chart. Note that R will default to pastel colors for the pie slices, but you can create a vector of color names and use that instead to make the graph more meaningful. For example:

```
> attach(Car_Colors)
> pie(Percent)
```

Figure 5-1 is our first pass at the pie chart. After showing the Graphics Device once, I will remove some of the white space to make the graphics more compact.

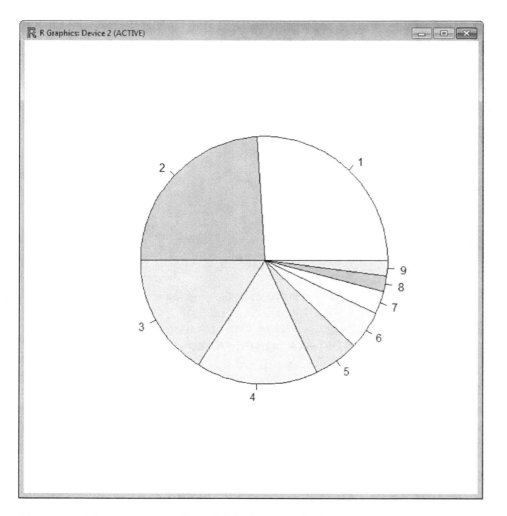

**Figure 5-1.** *A first pass at a pie chart. R defaults to pastel colors*

Now, let's create a vector of color names as well as a vector of colors for our reconfigured pie graph. We will use some RGB codes to get a better representation of the colors for silver, gray, and khaki, which I used for the "other" category. See the code below. I do not show the use of the c() function to create the character vector of colors, as you have already learned how to do this. To see a list of the colors R recognizes, you can use colors() or colours(). You can also use RBG codes if you like. A quick Internet search will reveal these codes. Here are the colors we will use for our improved chart.

```
> colors
[1] "#C0C0C0" "black"   "white"    "#696969" "red"      "blue"     "brown"
[8] "green"   "#F0E68C"
> pie(Percent, col = colors)
```

Figure 5-2 is our improved (but not complete) pie chart.

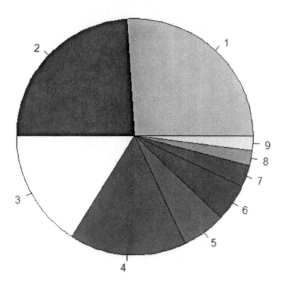

**Figure 5-2.** *Specificying color by RGB or color names helps improve the chart's appearance*

Finally, we will add a names attribute for our labels, and use the main attribute to give our pie chart a title. We combine these features for the final pie chart. Note that the result is more meaningful than our first two passes (see Figure 5-3).

```
> names(Percent)<- c("Silver","Black","White","Gray","Red","Blue","Brown",
+ "Green","Other")
> names(Percent)
[1] "Silver" "Black"  "White"  "Gray"   "Red"    "Blue"   "Brown"  "Green"
[9] "Other"
> pie(Percent, col = colors, main = "Pie Graph of Auto Color Preferences")
```

**Pie Graph of Auto Color Preferences**

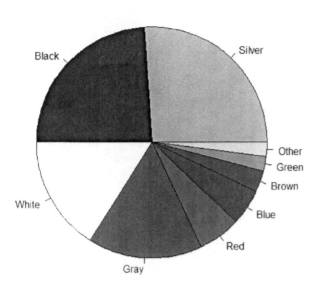

***Figure 5-3.*** *Names and a title complete the pie chart*

## Bar Charts

The same information used in the pie chart can be used in a bar chart. The generic R function to produce a bar chart is known as barplot(). As we have discussed the addition of labels and a chart title already, we will simply add those elements to our bar chart without further comment. Here is the code to produce the bar graph. Figure 5-4 shows the result.

```
barplot(Percent, col = colors, main = "Bar Chart of Auto Color Preferences")
```

**Bar Chart of Auto Color Preferences**

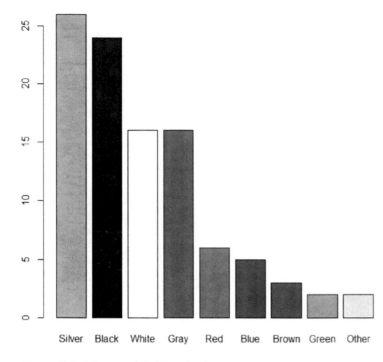

***Figure 5-4.*** *The completed bar chart*

We can also use the `table()` function with the `barplot()` function. Look at the following code, which uses the students' grade levels from a previous example. Remember that these students were all 10th, 11th, and 12th graders.

```
attach(grades)
> barplot(table(Grade), col = c("red","green","blue"), main = "Grade Level")
```

See the completed bar chart in Figure 5-5.

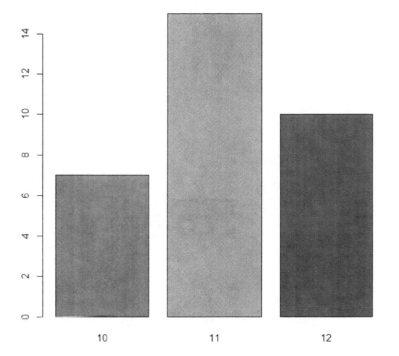

**Grade Level**

***Figure 5-5.*** *Combining the table and barplot functions*

# Boxplots

The boxplot (also called a box plot or a box-and-whiskers plot) was popularized by statistician John Tukey, and is a graphical representation of the five-number summary we discussed earlier. The function for producing a boxplot is boxplot().

Boxplots are very useful, as the examination of the relative lengths of the "whiskers" can give an idea of how skewed or unskewed the data are. The interquartile range (IQR) is the the length of the "box," and the median is represented by a line in the middle of the box. If the data distribution is relatively unskewed, the median will be close to the center of the box, and the whiskers will be roughly the same length. The whiskers extend from the center of the box to the minimum and the maximum, unless some of the data points data are considered to be outliers. When there are outliers, the whiskers extend to 3/2 of the interquartile range (IQR, and then are bounded by a "fence" or "fences." Data values between the two fences are considered "mild outliers," and data values beyond the second fence are considered "extreme outliers." Tukey's practice was to represent these outliers with small circles, and R's boxplot() function does the same thing.

Let us use the age variable from our data frame called dataset. Examine the following code and the resulting boxplot (Figure 5-6). Because the values is fabricated, the boxplot looks "very normal," but not all boxplots will be so nice in appearance. Remember we can use the main attribute to add a title to our boxplot.

```
attach(dataset)
> boxplot(Age, main = "Boxplot for Age")
```

**Boxplot for Age**

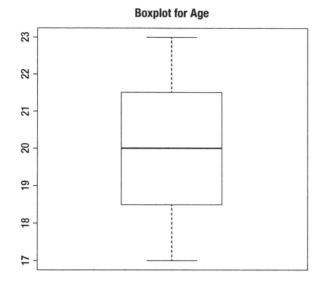

**Figure 5-6.** *Boxplot of Age variable*

As you see from examining Figure 5-6, the data (probably because I made it up) looks to be very close to normally distributed. The median is very close to the center of the box, the whiskers are of equal length, and there are no outliers. If you apply the boxplot() function to a data frame with more than one variable, R will produce very helpful side-by-side boxplots. See the example from the quiz data discussed earlier and which is repeated below for your convenience).

```
> quizzes
  test1   test2  test3
1 72.41   92.71 73.63
2 72.73   86.35 90.97
3 71.63   87.80 44.59
4 70.26  107.92 67.04
5 77.98   58.54 78.57
6 83.48   91.93 82.36
7 87.25  103.85 72.96
8 84.25  101.56 78.55
> boxplot(quizzes)
```

Take a look at the resulting boxplots in Figure 5-7, which reveals that all three quizzes are positively skewed, and that apart from the score of 58.54 on Test 2, which is identified as a mild outlier, this test (going by the median) was considerably easier than the other two.

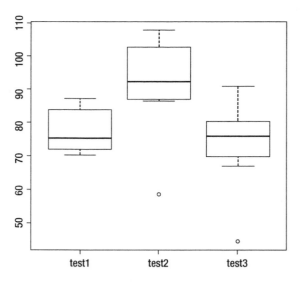

**Figure 5-7.** *R produces side-by-side boxplots for multiple variables in a data frame*

# Histograms

The R function for producing a histogram is hist(). Histograms are similar to bar charts, but because of the underlying continuum on the *x* axis, there should be no gaps between the bars. You already saw a histogram in Chapter 4 (Figure 4-1). The hist() function will produce a simple frequency histogram, but can also be used with the break attribute to produce a grouped frequency histogram. Following is the code to create a histogram of the waiting data for Old Faithful, the example we used earlier for a grouped frequency distribution.

```
attach(faithful)
> hist(waiting)
```

The grouped frequency histogram appears in Figure 5-8, and the distribution is clearly not normal, and appears to be bimodal.

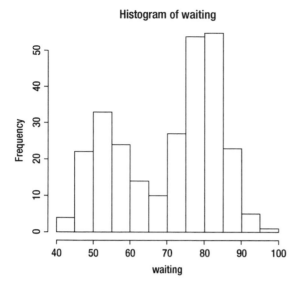

**Figure 5-8.** *R produced the histogram using the breaks we defined earlier to separate intervals*

# Line Graphs

Line graphs are produced by the generic plot() function, which has a number of uses, as you will find. Let us reexamine the minimum wage data from Chapter 1 (repeated below for your convenience). We must tell R what to plot. We can set the type option to "l" for line or to "o" for both a line and data points. (The "o" stands for "overplotting.")

```
> attach(Min_Wage)
> Min_Wage
   Year Value
1  1997  5.03
2  1998  4.96
3  1999  4.85
4  2000  4.69
5  2001  4.56
6  2002  4.46
7  2003  4.39
8  2004  4.28
9  2005  4.14
10 2006  4.04
> plot(Value, type = "o", xlab = "Year", col = "blue", main = "Minimum Wage")
```

The line graph appears in Figure 5-9. We could have used the year as the x variable, and achieved exactly the same line graph with the following code. The advantage of this approach is that the actual year labels are shown, rather than the year numbers.

```
plot(Year, Value, type = "o")
```

**Figure 5-9.** *Line graph produced by R*

# Scatterplots

The plot() function is also used to produce scatterplots (also called scatter plots and scatter diagrams). Examine the following data, which shows the weekly study hours and the grade point averages (GPAs) of 20 college students. I collected this information in one of my classes.

|    | Hours | GPA  |
|----|-------|------|
| 1  | 10    | 3.33 |
| 2  | 12    | 2.92 |
| 3  | 10    | 2.56 |
| 4  | 15    | 3.08 |
| 5  | 14    | 3.57 |
| 6  | 12    | 3.31 |
| 7  | 13    | 3.45 |
| 8  | 15    | 3.93 |
| 9  | 16    | 3.82 |
| 10 | 14    | 3.70 |
| 11 | 13    | 3.26 |
| 12 | 12    | 3.00 |
| 13 | 11    | 2.74 |
| 14 | 10    | 2.85 |
| 15 | 13    | 3.33 |
| 16 | 13    | 3.29 |
| 17 | 14    | 3.58 |
| 18 | 18    | 3.85 |
| 19 | 17    | 4.00 |
| 20 | 14    | 3.50 |

Now, we will plot sHours as our *x* variable and GPA as our *y* variable.

```
> plot(Hours, GPA)
```

See the resulting scatterplot in Figure 5-10.

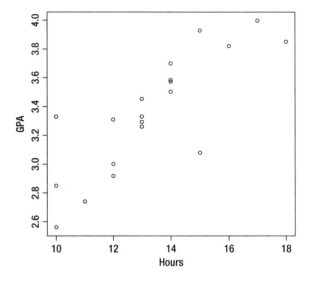

***Figure 5-10.*** *Scatterplot of study hours per week and GPA*

To add a trend line, we can use the abline attribute (think "a, b line," not *ab* line") combined with the lm() function (for linear model—more on this later). Let us add a title to our scatterplot as well. Here is the code.

```
> plot(Hours, GPA, abline(lm(GPA~Hours)), main = "Scatterplot of Hour and GPA")
```

The resulting scatterplot is shown in Figure 5-11.

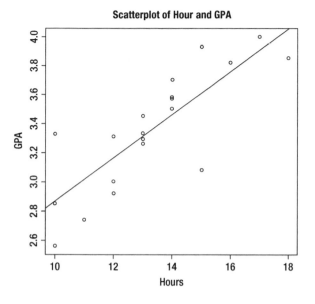

**Figure 5-11.** *Scatterplot with trend line and title added*

# Saving and Using Graphics

When you create graphics and they are displayed in the R Graphics Device, you can easily copy and save these graphics in a variety of formats including metafiles, bit maps, and postscript files. (For those importing graphics into LaTeX documents, you can save the postscript files with the extension ".eps".) You can also print graphics directly from the R Graphics Device. See the following dialog box from the Graphics Device. To access the dialog in Windows, simply right-click anywhere inside the graphic image itself (Figure 5-12).

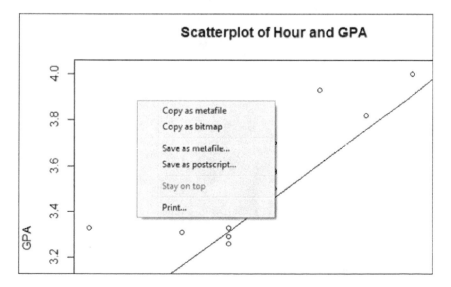

**Figure 5-12.** *Copying, saving, and printing output from the R Graphics Device*

# Conclusion

In Chapter 5, you learned how to use R for the most common tables and graphs. We will build on this knowledge in future chapters, so you can consider this an introduction. In later chapters, you will learn how to include two or more frequency polygons on the same graph, and how to use the locator() function to place text in a precise location on your graph. But for now, you have mastered the basics. In Chapter 6, we move on to discrete probability distributions.

# CHAPTER 6

■ ■ ■

# Discrete Probability Distributions

In Chapter 6, you learn how to use R for the binomial distribution and the Poisson distribution. We quickly review the characteristics of a discrete probability distribution, and then you learn the various functions in R that make it easy to work with both discrete and continuous distributions.

A discrete probability must satisfy the following conditions:

- The sum of the probabilities is 1.

- The probability of any particular outcome is between 0 and 1.

- The list of simple outcomes is exhaustive (there are no other possible outcomes) and mutually exclusive (no outcome can be in more than one category).

R's coverage of discrete probability distributions is extensive, and in the process of learning how the binomial and Poisson distribution functions work in R, you will learn how to work with other discrete probability distributions as needed. The R documentation will be of assistance as you explore additional discrete probability distributions.

## Discrete Probability Distributions

As we discussed briefly in Chapter 1, we can calculate the mean of any discrete probability distribution as:

$$\mu = \sum [xP(x)]$$

We can find the variance of a discrete probability distribution as follows:

$$\sigma^2 = \sum \left[ (x-\mu)^2 P(x) \right]$$

For many discrete probability distributions, these formulas can be simplified, as you will soon learn.

Let us use a concrete example to illustrate discrete probability distributions. Jonathan is a car salesman at the local Honda dealership. The most he has ever sold on a Saturday is five vehicles. He has kept track of the number of vehicles he sells on Saturdays, and has arrived at the distribution in Table 6-1. The mean is the sum of the third column and the variance is the sum of the fourth column in the table.

***Table 6-1.*** *An Example of a Discrete Probability Distribution*

| Number of Vehicles Sold | Probability | xP(x) | $(x - \mu)^2P(x)$ |
|---|---|---|---|
| 0 | .60 | 0.00 | 0.4753 |
| 1 | .15 | 0.15 | 0.0018 |
| 2 | .10 | 0.20 | 0.1232 |
| 3 | .08 | 0.24 | 0.3562 |
| 4 | .05 | 0.20 | 0.4836 |
| 5 | .02 | 0.10 | 0.3378 |
| Sum | 1.00 | 0.89 | 1.7779 |

Now, let us do the same calculations in R. First, we build a small data frame using the R Data Editor (see Figure 6-1).

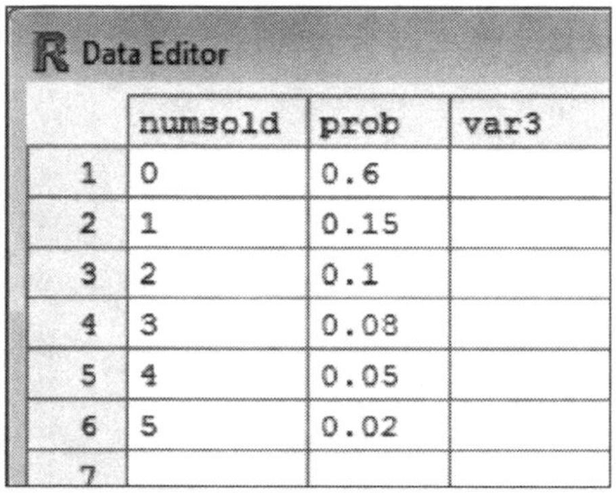

R Data Editor

| | numsold | prob | var3 |
|---|---|---|---|
| 1 | 0 | 0.6 | |
| 2 | 1 | 0.15 | |
| 3 | 2 | 0.1 | |
| 4 | 3 | 0.08 | |
| 5 | 4 | 0.05 | |
| 6 | 5 | 0.02 | |
| 7 | | | |

***Figure 6-1.*** *Probability distribution of cars sold on Saturday*

I saved the data frame with the name `saturday_sales`. Now, examine the following code to see how to calculate the mean and variance of the probability distribution using the formulas shown earlier. R produces the same results as the manual calculations given in Table 6-1.

```
> mu <- sum(numsold * prob)
> mu
[1] 0.89
> variance <- sum((numsold - mu)^2 * prob)
> variance
[1] 1.7779
```

# Bernoulli Processes

Two of the most frequently used discrete probability distributions are the binomial distribution and the Poisson distribution. We will explore each of them separately. But first, let us understand the nature of a Bernoulli process.

A very simple discrete probability distribution is one with only two possible outcomes. For example, we toss a coin and record either heads or tails. We randomly select an adult and record his or her gender. A Bernoulli process is one in which there are a series of independent trials, with the result of each being one of two outcomes. For example, we may select samples or batches of a manufactured product and decide to accept or reject the batch according to the presence or absence of defects. A person may choose an answer to a multiple-choice question, and we record a 1 for a correct answer and a 0 for an incorrect answer.

Generally, we call one of the outcomes "success," and the other "failure." In many cases, there is some logic to this (1 means "correct," and 0 means "incorrect," for example). In other cases, the distinction is purely arbitrary. We will use $p$ for the probability of success and $q = 1 - p$ for the probability of failure. We can use the notion of a Bernoulli process to develop a number of discrete probability functions.

## The Binomial Distribution: The Number of Successes as a Random Variable

If we have a series of $N$ trials taken from a Bernoulli process, the number of successes is a discrete random variable, which can take on the values 0 through $N$. Let us examine the distribution of X, the number of "successes." Any random variable X with a probability function given by

$$P(X = r) = \binom{N}{r} p^r q^{N-r}$$

where

$$\binom{N}{r} = \frac{N!}{r!(N-r)!}$$

is a binomial distribution. To make our example more specific, let us develop a binomial distribution of the number of heads in five tosses of a fair coin, in which $p$ and $q$ both equal .50. See the calculations in Table 6-2. The probabilities sum to 1, as expected. We can use the command Choose(N,r) to compute the binomial coefficient.

**Table 6-2.** *The Number of Heads in Five Tosses of a Fair Coin*

| r (number of heads) | P(r) |
| --- | --- |
| 0 | $\binom{N}{r}p^r q^{N-r} = \binom{5}{0}.5^0(.5)^5 = 1 \times 1 \times .5^5 = .03125$ |
| 1 | $\binom{N}{r}p^r q^{N-r} = \binom{5}{1}.5^1(.5)^4 = 5 \times .5 \times .5^4 = .15625$ |
| 2 | $\binom{N}{r}p^r q^{N-r} = \binom{5}{2}.5^2(.5)^3 = 10 \times .5^2 \times .5^3 = .3125$ |
| 3 | $\binom{N}{r}p^r q^{N-r} = \binom{5}{3}.5^3(.5)^2 = 10 \times .5^3 \times .5^2 = .3125$ |
| 4 | $\binom{N}{r}p^r q^{N-r} = \binom{5}{4}.5^4(.5)^1 = 5 \times .5 \times .5^4 = .15625$ |
| 5 | $\binom{N}{r}p^r q^{N-r} = \binom{5}{5}.5^5(.5)^0 = 1 \times .5^5 \times .1 = .03125$ |

R provides several functions (some of which you have already seen) for working with both discrete and continuous probability distributions. Every probability distribution covered by R includes a root name prefixed by one of the letters *p*, *q*, *d*, or *r*. The *p* is the cumulative density or mass function for the distribution. The *q* is the quantile function and can be used as a "reverse lookup," to find the value of the random variable associated with any probability. The *d* is the density (or mass) function. The *r* is the random function and will generate random samples from the probability distribution. For the binomial distribution, these functions are pbinom, qbinom, dbinom, and rbinom, respectively. Use the ?pbinom command to get more details.

In addition to the binomial distribution, R provides the negative binomial distribution, which treats the number of *failures*, rather than the number of successes, as a random variable. The negative binomial random variable represents the number of failures that occur in a series of Bernoulli trials before a specified number of successes is reached. The functions are dnbinom, pnbinom, qnbinom, and rnbinom. The R documentation contains sufficient instruction for those needing to explore or use the negative binomial distribution.

For the binomial distribution, we can calculate the distribution shown in Table 6-1 very easily by creating a vector of 0 to 6, and then finding the binomial probabilities as follows. Use the "names" attribute as before to label the rows 0 through 5, and use the cbind function to put the distribution into a column. Unsurprisingly, R produced the same values as our manual calculations.

```
> cbind(dbinom(x, size = 5, prob = .5))
      [,1]
0 0.03125
1 0.15625
2 0.31250
3 0.31250
4 0.15625
5 0.03125
```

We can use the formulas shown at the beginning of this chapter to calculate the mean and variance of the binomial distribution. However, we can simplify the computation of the mean of the binomial distribution to the following:

$$\mu = np$$

The variance can also be simplified:

$$\sigma^2 = npq$$

As another, perhaps more interesting, example, consider the use of the MicroSort technique to increase the likelihood of having a child of a particular gender. The technique involves the use of "flow cytometry" to separate sperm cells with X and Y chromosomes. Although not perfect, the sorting technique does have about a .91 probability of success for conceiving a female child and about .76 for a male child. This procedure requires "assisted reproductive techniques," such as artificial insemination, intrauterine insemination, or in vitro fertilization. Let us imagine 10 families, each with at least one female child, in which the parents have chosen to use MicroSort techniques to try to conceive a male child. What is the probability that of the 10 families, exactly 8 will have a male child? What is the probability that all 10 families will have a male child? What is the probability that 6 or fewer families will have a male child? Finally, what is the probability that at least 6 of the families will have a male child? We will use the binomial distribution and R's built-in functions to answer these questions. In the process, you will see how the binomial distribution works.

See that $p(\text{male}) = .76$, and thus that $q = p(\text{failure}) = 1 - .76 = .24$. We will treat the 10 families as "trials," and determine the probabilities.

The probability that exactly 8 families will have a male child is found using the dbinom() function:

```
> dbinom(8, size = 10, prob = .76)
[1] 0.2884986
```

The probability that all 10 families will have a male child is:

```
> dbinom(10, size = 10, prob = .76)
[1] 0.06428889
```

To find the probability of six or fewer families having a male child, we can, as we did before, sum the individual probabilities:

```
xvec <- 0:6
> sum(dbinom(xvec, 10, .76))
[1] 0.2012487
```

We can also use the pbinom() function for the cumulative binomial mass function. The pbinom() function calculates the cumulative probability from $r = 0$ to $r = 6$.

```
> pbinom(6, 10, .76)
[1] 0.2012487
```

The rbinom() function generates a random binomial distribution. Say we would like to generate 100 samples of size $N = 10$, with $p = .76$, as in our previous example. The function will return the number of successes, $r$, as the random variable. Examine the following code to see how to do this. We will save our vector of "successes" as randombinom.

```
> randombinom <- rbinom(100, 10, .76)
> randombinom
  [1]  8  9  7  7  8  7  9  7  8  8  8  7  5  4  9  8  7  9  7  7  6  8  9  9  7  9  9
 [27]  8  7  7  6  6  9 10  8  9  6  7  7  9 10  9  8  7  8  8  7  6  5 10  7  8  7
 [53]  9  7  7  9  7  8  7  8  7  9  9  9  8  4  9 10 10  8  5  6  6  8  7  8  7  6
 [79]  7  9  7  5  8  7  9  7  9  8  8  9  9  8  8  8  9  8  9  8  7  5
```

Although we will discuss confidence intervals in more detail later, note for the present that you can find the quantiles of this distribution and observe the 95% empirical confidence limits of this particular distribution. These will not be precise intervals because of the discrete nature of the binomial distribution.

```
> quantile(randombinom, .025)
2.5%
   5
> quantile(randombinom, .975)
97.5%
   10
```

These limits show us that we can be 95% confident that in a sample of 10 families, between 5 and 10 will conceive a male child using the MicroSort technique.

## The Poisson Distribution

Consider a situation where we have an *interval* (such as a day or a distance) or a region (such as an acre of land or a volume of a liquid). We might be interested in the number of "occurrences" per interval. The following conditions specify a "Poisson experiment":

1. The experiment results in outcomes that can be classified as successes or failures.

2. The average number of successes ($\mu$) that occurs in a specified region is known.

3. The probability that a success will occur is proportional to the size of the region.

4. The probability that a success will occur in an extremely small region approaches zero.

Under those conditions, we find the probability of exactly $x$ occurrences in a specified interval is

$$p(x) = \frac{e^{-\mu}\mu^x}{x!}$$

where $e$ is the base of the natural logarithms (approximately 2.71828), and $\mu$ is the mean or expected number of occurrences in a given interval.

One of the interesting properties of the Poisson distribution is that the mean and variance are equal. If we let $\lambda$ equal the number of occurrences per unit interval, and $t$ equal the length of the interval, then $\lambda t = \mu = \sigma^2$. Note that the value of $\mu$ is not required to be an integer, as it is an average or expected value.

The Poisson distribution is quite useful. For example, we might be interested in the number of vehicles going through a traffic intersection every half hour. We can model this as a Poisson process. Assume we find that the average number of vehicles per half hour is 25. Now, we can use the Poisson functions in R to find such probabilities as the probability that 20 or fewer vehicles would pass through the intersection in a given half hour period, the probability of exactly 25, or the probability that 30 or more vehicles would pass through the intersection. These functions are similar to those for the binomial distribution. Examine the following code and results. See that the ppois() function provides the cumulative probability, which you can also obtain by adding the independent densities. Here is the probability of 20 or fewer vehicles.

```
> xvec
 [1]  0  1  2  3  4  5  6  7  8  9 10 11 12 13 14 15 16 17 18 19 20
> sum(dpois(xvec, 25))
[1] 0.1854923
> ppois(20, 25)
[1] 0.1854923
```

Here is the probability of exactly 25:

```
> dpois(25, 25)
[1] 0.07952295
```

Because the number of occurrences of a Poisson random variable theoretically has no upper bound, we can use the complement rule of probability for finding the probability of 30 or more vehicles by subtracting the probability of 29 or fewer from 1.

```
> ppois(29, 25)
[1] 0.8178961
> 1-ppois(29, 25)
[1] 0.1821039
```

The Poisson distribution is also useful for business applications including the study of manufacturing defects, call center waiting times, the study of web traffic, and many other situations.

You can also search for other common discrete distributions like the geometric or the hypergeometric, (using commands ?dgeom, ?dhyper, and so on). You may also want to glance ahead to Chapter 20 to see the list of common discrete probability distributions available through R Commander.

# Relating Discrete Probability to Normal Probability

The Poisson distribution is a special type of limit of the binomial distribution, and the binomial distribution converges to the normal distribution as the number of trials increases. The Poisson distribution converges to the normal distribution as the mean increases. Although we will not develop any mathematical proofs, observe the distribution of the PMF (probability mass function) for a binomial random variable with $N = 10$ and $p = .5$. Observe how "normal"-looking this distribution appear to be even though it is discrete rather than continuous (see Figure 6-2). I added the lines to make this more obvious. Here is how to add the lines in R. The type "o" plots both points and connecting lines.

```
> x <- seq(0, 10)
> x
 [1]  0  1  2  3  4  5  6  7  8  9 10
> prob <- dbinom(x, 10, 0.5)
> plot(x, prob, type = "o", main = "Binomial Approximates Normal)
```

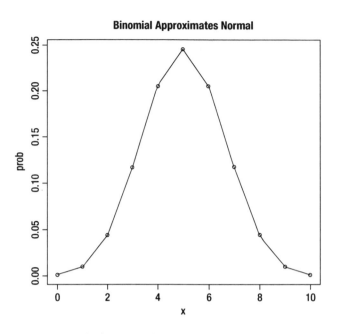

**Figure 6-2.** *The binomial distribution approaches the normal distribution*

Similarly, even though the Poisson distribution is always positively skewed, and the random variable has no specific upper limit, as the mean becomes larger, the Poisson distribution becomes more symmetrical. For example, consider the distribution of the number of sets of tires installed per day at a local Firestone dealer when the average per day is six sets of tires (data are hypothetical; see Figure 6-3). Here is the code:

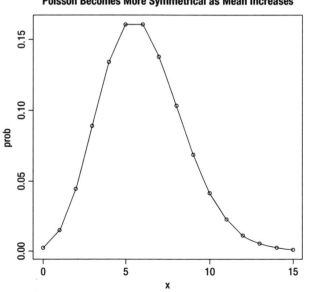

**Figure 6-3.** *The Poisson distribution becomes more symmetrical as the mean increases*

```
x <- seq(0, 15)
> prob <- dpois(x, 6)
> plot(x, prob, type = "o", main = "Poisson Becomes More Symmetrical as Mean Increases")
```

The binomial probability distribution and its associated functions and formulas are practical when the number of trials is relatively small, but become unwieldy, even for software, when the number of trials becomes very large. We can take advantage of the fact that as the number of trials increases, the binomial distribution becomes close to a normal distribution. Thus we can use the continuous normal distribution to approximate binomial probabilities in the case of large $N$. Just as with the discrete probability distributions, the normal probability distribution in R has the "lookup," (dnorm), the cumulative probability (pnorm), the "reverse lookup" (qnorm), and the random generator (rnorm) functions. We will explore these in detail in the next chapter, but for now, let's look at the normal approximation to the binomial distribution.

The current population in the United States is approximately 313.6 million, and estimates are that of these people, about 200 million have high-speed Internet access at home. Thus we can estimate the population proportion of high-speed home Internet users to be .6378. Imagine we randomly select a sample of 1500 people and we are interested in determining the probability that at least 1000 of those responding to the survey have high-speed home Internet access.

As before, we will apply the complement rule of probability and find the probability of 1000 or more by subtracting the probability of 999 or fewer from 1. R handles these calculations, but not all software packages will do so easily.

```
> 1 - pbinom(999, 1500, .6378)
[1] 0.01042895
```

We can use the standard normal curve to our advantage here and approximate the binomial probability by employing the following equalities

$$\mu = np = 1500(.6378) = 956.7$$

$$\sigma = \sqrt{npq} = \sqrt{1500(.6378)(.3622)} = 18.615$$

Now, we can simply calculate a z score as follows:

$$z = \frac{1000 - 956.7}{18.615} = \frac{43.3}{18.615} = 2.3261$$

We can determine the area to the right of $z = 2.3261$ using the complement rule and the pnorm() function.

```
> 1 - pnorm(2.3261)
[1] 0.01000661
```

Note in this case the two probabilities are very close, and differ only by a little more than .0004. Thus the normal approximation to the binomial probability was accurate in this case.

# Conclusion

In this chapter you've learned what a discrete probability distribution is and how to calculate the mean and variance of any discrete probability distribution. You also learned how to use R's built-in functions to find densities, cumulative probabilities, quantiles, and random samples from a distribution. You learned how to work with two common discrete probability distributions: the binomial and the Poisson. Finally, you learned that the normal distribution has an interesting relationship to the binomial distribution. We will study the standard normal distribution in more detail in Chapter 7.

# CHAPTER 7

# Computing Normal Probabilities

The normal distribution is the backbone of traditional statistics. We learn very early in our statistics training that the distribution of sample means, regardless of the shape of the parent distribution, approaches a normal distribution as the sample size increases. This fact permits us to use the normal distribution and distributions theoretically related to it, such as $t$, $F$, and $\chi^2$, for testing hypotheses about means and functions of means (such as the differences between two or more means, or variances, which are derived from means).

There is really nothing particularly "normal" about the normal distribution. Karl Pearson, who popularized the term, regretted doing so in his later years. Still, there is much usefulness in making inferences about means knowing that the sampling distribution of means or the differences between means follows the normal distribution with sufficient sample sizes. You saw in the last chapter that we can use the normal distribution to approximate the binomial distribution when the number of trials becomes large. In Chapter 7, you learn how to use the various functions of the normal distribution to find areas under the normal curve, to find critical values of $z$, and to create random samples from the normal distribution. You also learn more about the sampling distribution of means. Finally, you learn how to conduct a one-sample $z$ test.

Recall from Chapter 4 that you can use the scale() function to produce standard scores, and that the default center is the mean and the default scaling value is the standard deviation. Thus the scale() function by default produces $z$ scores for any set of data. The $z$ score is a "combination" statistic, providing information both about the location of the raw score relative to the mean and the number of standard deviation units the raw score is away from the mean. We can use $z$ scores both as descriptive statistics and as inferential statistics. When we know (or are willing to assume we know) the population standard deviation, we can use the standard normal distribution to make inferences about means and the differences between means. We also use the standard normal distribution to make inferences and create confidence intervals for proportions, as we have discussed previously.

The functions for the normal distribution in R are similar to those for the binomial and Poisson probability distributions you learned about in the previous chapter. The functions include pnorm, qnorm, dnorm, and rnorm.

## Characteristics of the Normal Distribution

The normal distribution is continuous, and we rarely are interested in the density function per se, but rather in finding areas under the normal curve. Technically, the lower bound of the normal distribution is $-\infty$, and the upper bound is $+\infty$. Although finding areas under a continuous distribution requires calculus, R does not "do" much calculus, though you can do simple integration and differentiation. However, using the R functions, we can avoid the difficulty of finding areas under the continuous normal curve simply by making use of a bit of basic algebra.

# Finding Normal Densities Using the dnorm Function

For any normal distribution with a nonzero standard deviation, the probability density function is

$$f(x) = \frac{1}{\sqrt{2\pi\sigma^2}} e^{-(x-\mu)^2/2\sigma^2}$$

For the *standard normal distribution* with a mean of zero and a standard deviation of 1, this simplifies to

$$f(z) = \frac{1}{\sqrt{2\pi}} e^{-z^2/2}$$

The standard normal distribution is also often called the "unit" normal distribution because it has a standard deviation of 1, a variance of 1, and as with all probability distributions, an entire area under the curve of 1. Examination of the density function shows that the distribution will be at its highest at the mean, that it will be symmetrical, and that the probabilities will taper off in the tails. This is the so-called "bell-shaped curve" students learn about in their statistics classes.

The R function for the density function is dnorm, and we can use it to draw a graph of a normal distribution. Let us compare two normal distributions, both with a mean of 20, and one with a standard deviation of 3 and the other with a standard deviation of 6. In the process, I will show you how to put both curves on the same plot, which is something we did not cover in Chapter 5. First, we will generate a vector for the *x* axis with a sequence from 0 to 40, using an increment of .5. Then, we will apply the dnorm function with a mean of 20 and standard deviations of 3 and 6, respectively. We will produce a scatter diagram of the densities as our y axis and the raw scores as our x axis. Finally, we will add the second curve to the same graph using the points function. Here is the code in R. Note that I used the type = "l" (for lines) attribute and added color to the second curve for emphasis.

```
> xaxis <- seq(0, 40, .5)
> xaxis
 [1]  0.0  0.5  1.0  1.5  2.0  2.5  3.0  3.5  4.0  4.5  5.0  5.5  6.0  6.5  7.0
[16]  7.5  8.0  8.5  9.0  9.5 10.0 10.5 11.0 11.5 12.0 12.5 13.0 13.5 14.0 14.5
[31] 15.0 15.5 16.0 16.5 17.0 17.5 18.0 18.5 19.0 19.5 20.0 20.5 21.0 21.5 22.0
[46] 22.5 23.0 23.5 24.0 24.5 25.0 25.5 26.0 26.5 27.0 27.5 28.0 28.5 29.0 29.5
[61] 30.0 30.5 31.0 31.5 32.0 32.5 33.0 33.5 34.0 34.5 35.0 35.5 36.0 36.5 37.0
[76] 37.5 38.0 38.5 39.0 39.5 40.0
> y1 <- dnorm(xaxis, 20, 6)
> y2 <- dnorm(xaxis, 20, 3)
> plot(xaxis, y2, type = "l", main = "Comparing Two Normal Distributions")
> points(xaxis, y1, type = "l", col = "red")
```

Our plot now displays both curves (see Figure 7-1).

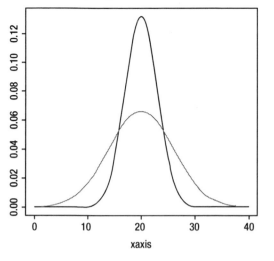

**Figure 7-1.** *Plotting two normal curves on the same graph*

## Converting a Normal Distribution to the Standard Normal Distribution

As you see, different normal distributions have different amounts of spread, based on the size of the standard deviation. It is often helpful to convert a normal distribution to the standard normal distribution and work with z scores. We can convert any normal distribution to the standard normal distribution by using the following formula:

$$z = \frac{x - \mu}{\sigma}$$

By definition the standard normal distribution has a mean of 0 and a standard deviation of 1 (see Figure 7-2).

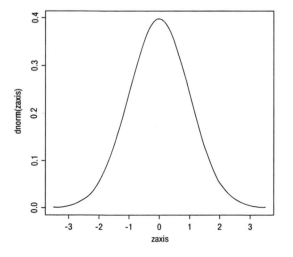

**Figure 7-2.** *The standard normal distribution*

# Finding Probabilities Using the pnorm Function

The pnorm function finds a left-tailed probability. Recall from Chapter 3 that the critical value of $z$ for a 95% confidence interval is $z = \pm 1.96$, and that the area between $-1.96$ and $+1.96$ is equal to 95% of the standard normal distribution. The pnorm function defaults to a mean of zero and a standard deviation of 1, which of course means you will be working with the standard normal distribution by default. When you need to work with a normal distribution with a different mean and standard deviation, you can supply these values as the second and third arguments to the function.

## Finding a Left-tailed Probability

Here is the R code for finding the cumulative probability under the standard normal distribution up to a $z$ score of 1.96.

```
> pnorm(1.96)
[1] 0.9750021
```

As expected, we find that the area .9750 lies to the left of $z = 1.96$. This also means that .0250 of the standard normal distribution lies to the right of $z = 1.96$.

## Finding the Area Between Two *z* Scores

We can easily find the area between any two $z$ scores by a simple subtraction strategy. For example, to find the area between $z = -1.96$ and $z = 1.96$, we can simply calculate the following:

```
> pnorm(1.96) - pnorm(-1.96)
[1] 0.9500042
```

We confirm that these two critical values separate the middle 95% of the standard normal distribution from the extreme 5%. You can use the approach shown here to find the area between any two z scores. Just remember to subtract the area to the left of the lower $z$ score from the area to the left of the higher $z$ score. Otherwise, you will wind up with a theoretically impossible negative probability.

## Finding a Right-tailed Probability

A subtraction strategy also helps us find right-tailed probabilities under the standard normal curve. For example, the area to the right of $z = 1.96$ will be very close to .025, as the previous discussion implies.

```
> 1 - pnorm(1.96)
[1] 0.0249979
```

Assume you took a standardized test with a mean of 500 and a standard deviation of 100. Your score was 720. Let's use the scale and the pnorm function to find your z score and then to find your approximate percentile on the test.

```
Scale(720, 500, 100)
        [,1]
[1,]   2.2
attr(,"scaled:center")
[1] 500
```

```
attr(,"scaled:scale")
[1] 100
> pnorm(2.2)
[1] 0.9860966
```

You did extremely well on the standardized test, and your percentile is approximately 98.6.

## Finding Critical Values Using the qnorm Function

The qnorm function finds the $z$ score associated with a given probability (quantile), and thus can be used to find critical values of $z$. The use of the pnorm and qnorm functions renders the use of tabled values of $z$ obsolete. To stay with our example, let us find the $z$ score associated with the cumulative .975 area of the normal curve (from the left tail). Of course, the answer will be very close to $z = 1.96$, as we have shown above.

```
> qnorm(.975)
[1] 1.959964
```

To find a one-tailed critical value, simply provide 1 – alpha as the argument to the qnorm function. For a left-tailed test, change the sign of the z score. We will find the one-tailed critical value of z for a test with alpha equal to .05 as follows:

```
> qnorm(1 - .05)
[1] 1.644854
```

## Using rnorm to Generate Random Samples

The rnorm function generates $n$ random samples from a normal distribution with a specified mean and standard deviation. If these arguments are omitted, they default to the standard normal distribution. Let us generate 50 random samples of a normal distribution with a mean of 100 and a standard deviation of 15.

```
> samples <- rnorm(50, 100, 15)
> samples
 [1]  78.01098 121.45292  85.49143 118.57669  79.38243 103.31105 108.12121
 [8] 108.25030  88.70047  88.80726 121.25570 104.00160  88.26656  86.81201
[15] 110.02104  90.77677  73.89115  89.95446  95.19429  96.48586  80.71891
[22] 109.79158  98.08166  77.45765  98.66197 112.28072 114.74301  89.44302
[29] 106.52937 107.67420 117.31145 107.56163 109.80694 114.41821  90.97140
[36] 104.91494 105.86462  71.82157 107.66722 122.22257  92.63734 116.42602
[43] 123.49171  79.20546 120.43231 114.48543  76.20359  97.97885  96.28731
[50]  83.78939
```

The histogram of our sample does not appear to be very "normal" (see Figure 7-3).

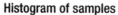

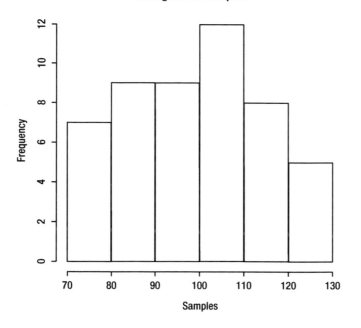

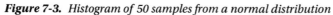

*Figure 7-3.* *Histogram of 50 samples from a normal distribution*

However, when we increase the number of samples to 1000, the histogram becomes more symmetrical and begins to look more "normal" (Figure 7-4).

```
> sample2 <- rnorm(1000, 100, 15)
> hist(sample2)
```

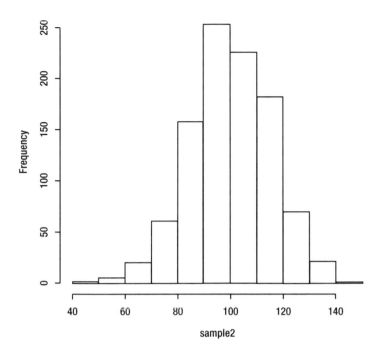

**Figure 7-4.** *Histogram of 1000 samples from a normal distribution*

# The Sampling Distribution of Means

As mentioned at the beginning of this chapter, the sampling distribution of means approaches a normal distribution as the sample size increases. This allows us to use the normal distribution to make inferences about sample means even when the parent distribution is not normal. We make use of this statistical fact when we make inferences about means or about the differences of means. Specifically, the sampling distribution of means for samples of size $n$ has a mean equal to the population mean, $\mu$, and a variance and standard deviation equal to

$$\sigma_{\bar{x}}^2 = \frac{\sigma^2}{n}$$

and

$$\sigma_{\bar{x}} = \sqrt{\frac{\sigma^2}{n}} = \frac{\sigma}{\sqrt{n}}$$

respectively. The standard deviation of the sampling distribution of means is known as the "standard error of the mean." In the absence of population parameters, we use the sample statistics as reasonable estimators, and we calculate the standard error of the mean from the sample standard deviation as follows:

$$s_{\bar{x}} = \frac{s_x}{\sqrt{n}}$$

109

# A One-sample *z* Test

By using the standard error of the mean, we can now calculate a different *z* score, in this case an inferential statistic, using the following simple formula, where $\bar{x}$ is the sample mean and $\mu$ is the known or hypothesized population mean. When we know the population standard deviation, we can use the following formula:

$$z = \frac{\bar{x} - \mu}{\sigma_{\bar{x}}}$$

or, when we do not know the population standard deviation, we can use:

$$z = \frac{\bar{x} - \mu}{s_{\bar{x}}}$$

---

■ **Note**    When you calculate the value in the last equation above, the *z* score is distributed as *t* when the sample sizes are small. We will discuss *t* tests in Chapter 9.

---

We find the *p* value using the pnorm function to determine whether to reject the null hypothesis. This simple test is not built into R, but we can easily write a function to accomplish our purpose. We will call the function ztest, and will pass three arguments, the sample mean, the population mean, and the sample standard deviation. The function will return the *z* score, and we can then use pnorm( ) to determine the *p* value.

```
ztest <- function(xbar, mu, stdev, n){
        z = (mean(xbar) - mu) / (stdev/ sqrt(n))
        return(z)
}
```

Let us return to our previous example of the weights of adult males who exercise. Remember the distribution was fairly "normal" in appearance (see Figure 7-5).

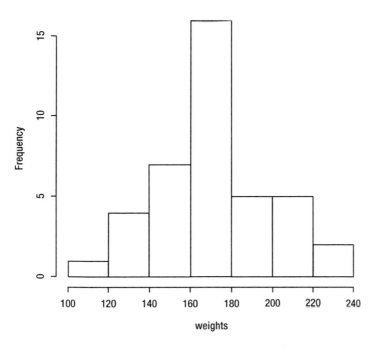

**Figure 7-5.** *Histogram of weights of 40 adult males who exercise*

Recalling that the average male adult weighs approximately 191 lbs., let us now calculate the *z* test results using the sample standard deviation as our reasonable estimate of the population standard deviation. We will make use of the *z* test function we just created.

```
> ztest(mean(weights), 191, sd(weights), length(weights))
[1] -4.43223
> pnorm(-4.43223)
[1] 4.663173e-06
```

The low *p* value indicates we can reject the null hypothesis and conclude that adult males who exercise regularly weigh significantly less than the average adult male.

# Conclusion

The normal distribution is the backbone of traditional statistics. In Chapter 7 you learned about the normal and standard normal distributions. You learned the R functions for working with the normal distribution.

You also learned about the sampling distribution of means and how to conduct a one-sample *z* test by writing a simple function. In Chapter 8, you will learn more about confidence intervals, and we will use the standard normal distribution as well as statistical distributions theoretically related to the normal distribution, such as the *t* distribution and the $\chi^2$ distribution.

■ ■ ■

# Creating Confidence Intervals

We have already discussed using the standard normal and *t* distributions for confidence intervals for means. We can construct confidence intervals for other statistics as well. Confidence intervals avoid some of the logical problems of null hypothesis testing and therefore is recommended as an alternative in many cases.

In this chapter, we review the use of R for deriving confidence intervals for means, and then examine the use of confidence intervals for other statistics, such as proportions and variances. To reiterate, a confidence interval (or interval estimate) is a range of possible values used to estimate the true value of a population parameter. We often abbreviate confidence interval as CI. We associate each confidence interval with some level of confidence, such as 90%, 95%, or 99%. The confidence level is the complement of our alpha level, so these three confidence levels correspond to alpha levels of .10, .05, and .01.

The general idea behind a confidence interval (for symmetric distributions like the normal and *t* distributions) is that we have an estimate of a parameter and we calculate a margin of error, adding the margin to the estimate to get an upper limit and subtracting the margin from the estimate to get a lower limit. Interpreting a confidence interval requires us to give a confidence estimate. Continuing with our example from Chapter 7 of the weights of 40 adult males who exercise regularly, if our confidence interval for a population mean has a lower limit of 164.13 and an upper limit of 180.97, we can say we are 95% confident that the true population mean (for men who exercise) is contained within that range. It is incorrect to say that there is a 95% chance (or .95 probability) that the true value of μ will fall between 164.13 and 180.97. It is equally incorrect to say that 95% of sample means fall between 164.97 and 180.97.

## Confidence Intervals for Means

Choosing the appropriate distribution for confidence intervals for the mean requires a bit of logic. The three candidate approaches are to use the standard normal distribution, to use the *t* distribution, or to use bootstrapping or nonparametric methods. The flow chart in Figure 8-1 will help you visualize this and determine which approach is best for a particular situation.

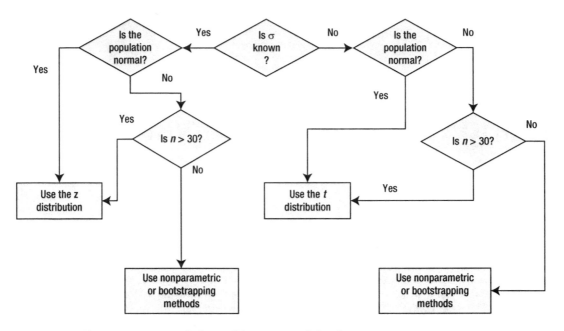

***Figure 8-1.*** *Choosing an approach for confidence intervals for the mean*

## Confidence Intervals for the Mean Using the Normal Distribution

When we know the population standard deviation and can assume the population is normally distributed, we can justify the use of the standard normal distribution for confidence intervals and hypothesis tests concerning means. We will find the critical values of z that place half our alpha level in the right tail and the other half in the left tail of the standard normal distribution.

As discussed previously, as the sample size gets larger, the differences between the standard normal distribution and the t distribution become negligible. Most statistics texts introduce z-based confidence intervals more as a pedagogical device than as a recommendation for their use in applied work.

The confidence interval for the mean when the population standard deviation is known is calculated as follows:

$$(\bar{x} - z_{\alpha/2}\sigma_{\bar{x}}) < \mu < (\bar{x} + z_{\alpha/2}\sigma_{\bar{x}})$$

We can make use of a little algebra and manipulate the formula for the margin of error in such a way that we can find the required sample size for a particular level of accuracy. Let E be the desired margin of error. Assuming we know the population standard deviation, we can solve for n, the required sample size. We make the further assumption that the sample is a simple random one. Here is our formula for determining the required sample size. Recall that the standard error of the mean, $\sigma_{\bar{x}}$, is the population standard deviation divided by the square root of the sample size. The margin of error is

$$E = z_{\alpha/2}(\sigma / \sqrt{n})$$

We can manipulate this formula algebraically to solve for n:

$$n = \left(\frac{z_{\alpha/2}\sigma}{E}\right)^2$$

As an example, let us develop a 95% confidence interval for the weights of 40 men who exercise regularly. After determining the margin of error, we will find the required sample size for a smaller margin of error. Recall the weights have a mean of 172.55, with a standard deviation of 26.3272. We will use the sample standard deviation as a reasonable estimate of the population standard deviation, and find the margin of error to be

$$E = z_{\alpha/2}(s/\sqrt{n}) = 1.96(26.3272/\sqrt{40}) = 8.1589$$

Thus, the confidence interval (reported in the format required by the *Publication Manual of the American Psychological Association*) is 95% CI [164.39, 180.71]. Assume we would like the margin of error to be no more than 5 pounds. Let us solve for the required sample size. When using this formula, always round up to the next integer. We see we will need a sample of more than 100 men to narrow the margin of error from 8.15 to 5.

$$n = \left(\frac{1.96(26.3272)}{5}\right)^2 = 107$$

Let us develop an R function for estimating the required sample size based on the above formulas. The function code is shown from the R Editor. As I have stated numerous times, a function does not have to be complex to be useful. It simply needs to automate a calculation that you might perform regularly. Note the use of the `ceiling()` function to round to the next higher integer.

```
sampsize.est <- function(E, sigma, alpha = .05){
       # E is the desired margin of error
       n <- ((qnorm(alpha/2)*sigma)/E)^2
       estsize <- ceiling(n)
       cat("for a desired margin of error of:",E,"the required sample size is:",estsize,"\n")
       }
```

Our function produces the same results as our manual calculations:

```
> sampsize.est(5, sd(weights))
for a desired margin of error of: 5 the required sample size is: 107
```

## Confidence Intervals for the Mean Using the *t* Distribution

When we do not know the population standard deviation, we use the sample standard deviation as a reasonable estimate. We use the *t* distribution instead of the normal distribution, and calculate the confidence interval as follows:

$$(\overline{x} - t_{\alpha/2}s_{\overline{x}}) < \mu < (\overline{x} + t_{\alpha/2}s_{\overline{x}})$$

In Chapter 2, we built a function for generating confidence intervals for the mean using the *t* distribution. Also, recall our previous discussion in which we found the one-sample *t* test will produce a confidence interval for the mean. We could embellish this a bit if we chose, but the application is serviceable enough as it is. Because the function for a confidence interval in the stats package is also labeled `confint()` we will change the name of our R function to `confint.mean`. Here is our updated confidence interval function:

```
confint.mean <- function(x, alpha = .05, two.tailed = TRUE) {
  cat("\t","Confidence Interval for the Mean","\n")
  cat("Mean:",mean(x),"\n")
  df <- length(x) - 1
  stderr <- sd(x)/sqrt(length(x))
```

```
  cat("Standard error of the mean:",stderr,"\n")
  conflevel <- 1 - alpha/2
  if (two.tailed == FALSE) {
    conflevel <- 1 - alpha
  }
  tcrit <- qt(conflevel, df)
  margin <- stderr * tcrit
  LL <- mean(x) - margin
  UL <- mean(x) + margin
  if (two.tailed == FALSE) {
    cat("You are doing a one-tailed test.","\n")
    cat("If your test is left-tailed, the lower bound","\n")
    cat("is negative infinity. If your test is right-tailed","\n")
    cat("the upper bound is positive infinity.","\n")
    cat("Either add the margin",margin,"to or subract it from","\n")
    cat("the sample mean as appropriate.","\n")
    cat("For a left-tailed test, the upper bound is",LL,".","\n")
    cat("For a right-tailed test, the lower bound is",UL,".","\n")
  }
  cat("upper bound:",LL,"\n")
  cat("lower bound:",UL,"\n")
}
```

Using the weights of 40 adult men who exercise, let us calculate both the t.test and the confint.mean confidence intervals for the sake of comparison. As the following R output shows, the two produce identical results.

```
> confint.mean(weights)
        Confidence Interval for the Mean
Mean: 172.55
Standard error of the mean: 4.16269
upper bound: 164.1302
lower bound: 180.9698

> t.test(weights)

        One Sample t-test

data:  weights
t = 41.4516, df = 39, p-value < 2.2e-16
alternative hypothesis: true mean is not equal to 0
95 percent confidence interval:
 164.1302 180.9698
sample estimates:
mean of x
   172.55
```

Remember that when we are doing a one-sided test, the confidence intervals are not symmetrical about the mean , but instead, the upper bound of a right-sided test is $+\infty$ and the lower bound of a left-sided test is $-\infty$. Our confidence interval function covers both possibilities by combining them when we specify two.tailed = FALSE:

```
> confint.mean(weights, two.tailed = FALSE)
        Confidence Interval for the Mean
Mean: 172.55
```

Standard error of the mean: 4.16269
You are doing a one-tailed test.
If your test is left-tailed, the lower bound
is negative infinity. If your test is right-tailed
the upper bound is positive infinity.
Either add the margin 7.013613 to or subract it from
the sample mean as appropriate.
For a left-tailed test, the upper bound is 165.5364 .
For a right-tailed test, the lower bound is 179.5636 .
upper bound: 165.5364
lower bound: 179.5636

See that the t.test function will give us the same limits with one-sided tests.

```
> t.test(weights, alternative = "less")

        One Sample t-test

data:  weights
t = 41.4516, df = 39, p-value = 1
alternative hypothesis: true mean is less than 0
95 percent confidence interval:
     -Inf 179.5636
sample estimates:
mean of x
   172.55

> t.test(weights, alternative = "greater")

        One Sample t-test

data:  weights
t = 41.4516, df = 39, p-value < 2.2e-16
alternative hypothesis: true mean is greater than 0
95 percent confidence interval:
 165.5364      Inf
sample estimates:
mean of x
   172.55
```

# Confidence Intervals for Proportions

Most people readily identify with the "margin of error" for opinion polls, and the margin of error is simply one-half the width of the confidence interval. As with the mean, we use the standard normal distribution for confidence intervals for proportions. Statistically, the reason we are using the normal distribution with proportions is that we are making use of the normal approximation to the binomial distribution, which we discussed in Chapter 6.

To construct a confidence interval for a proportion, we use the following formula:

$$(\hat{p}-E)<p<(\hat{p}+E)$$

where $E$ is the margin of error, $\hat{p}$ is the sample proportion, and $p$ is the population proportion. We calculate the margin of error as follows:

$$E = z_{\alpha/2}\sqrt{\frac{\hat{p}\hat{q}}{n}}$$

As an example, imagine that we are interested in constructing a 95% confidence interval for a population proportion. A market research company found that of 1500 respondents, 70% or .70 were in favor of allowing cell phone users to purchase any product and have it activated by the carrier of their choice (these are fictitious data). Our values are $z = 1.96$, $n = 1500$, $\hat{p} = .70$, and $\hat{q} = .30$. Here is our confidence interval:

$$E = 1.96\sqrt{\frac{(.70)(.30)}{1500}} = 1.96\sqrt{\frac{.21}{1500}} = 1.96\sqrt{\frac{.21}{1500}} = 1.96\sqrt{.00014} = .0232$$

$$(.70 - .0232) < p < (.70 + .0232)$$

$$95\%\text{CI}\,[.6768, .7232]$$

It would be easy with the R programming skills you have learned thus far to write a function to calculate a confidence interval for a proportion. Let us calculate the margin of error and the confidence limits. Our function will default to an alpha level of .05 for a 95% confidence interval, as we did with the confidence interval for the mean. Here is a sample function to calculate the confidence interval:

```
confi.prop <- function(phat, n, alpha = .05) {
        zcrit <- qnorm(1 - alpha/2)
        margin <- zcrit*sqrt((phat*(1 - phat)/n))
        upper <- phat + margin
        lower <- phat - margin
        cat("Sample proportion:",phat,"\n")
        cat(100*(1 - alpha),"confidence interval:","\n")
        cat("lower limit:",lower,"\n")
        cat("upper limit:",upper,"\n")
        }
```

As expected, our function produces the same limits as our hand calculations above.

```
> confi.prop(.70, 1500)
        Confidence Interval for a Proportion

sample proportion: 0.7
lower limit: 0.6768094
upper limit: 0.7231906
```

# Understanding the Chi-square Distribution

We will use the chi-square distribution to develop confidence intervals for the population variance. The chi-square distribution is not symmetrical like the normal and $t$ distributions, so the intervals will not be symmetrical, either. The chi-square distribution functions in R are similar to those for the normal distribution and $t$ distribution. The functions are dchisq, pchisq, qchisq, and rchisq.

The chi-square distribution is a family of distributions, each based on the parameter known as the degrees of freedom. Let us examine two chi-square distributions, one with 9 degrees of freedom and the other with 19 degrees of freedom. We will use the same device we used with the normal distribution in Chapter 7 by plotting the two distributions on the same graph. As a reminder, we will use the plot function and then the points function. Let us create an x axis from 0 to 50, and then use the dchisq function to create the two distributions. Here is the R code to produce the graph shown in Figure 8-2.

```
> xaxis <- seq(0,50)
> y1 <- dchisq(xaxis, 9)
> y2 <- dchisq(xaxis, 19)
> plot(y1, type="l", main="Chi-Square Distributions",xlab = "Chi-Square")
> points(xaxis, y2, type="l", col = "red")
```

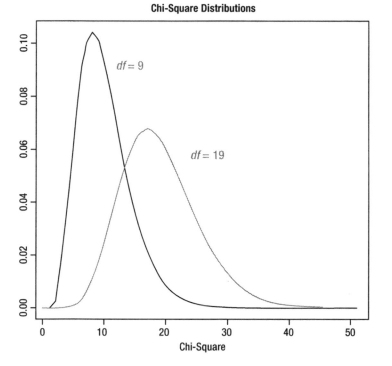

**Figure 8-2.** *Comparing two chi-square distributions*

# Confidence Intervals for Variances and Standard Deviations

Assume we have a normally distributed population with variance $\sigma^2$, and we have taken random samples of size $n$ from the population. A function of the sample variance $s^2$ follows the chi-square distribution:

$$\chi^2 = \frac{(n-1)s^2}{\sigma^2}$$

Because the chi-square distribution is not symmetrical, we must find a left-tailed and a right-tailed critical value by using the qchisq function. Assume we are interested in calculating a 95% confidence interval. The degrees of freedom are $n - 1$. We will find the values that separate the left .025 of the chi-square distribution and the right .025 from the middle .95. Let us return to our example of the weights of adult males who exercise regularly. We have 40 weights, so the degrees of freedom are 40 – 1 = 39. Here are our two critical values, as reported by the qchisq function in R:

```
> qchisq(.025, 39)
[1] 23.65432
> qchisq(.975, 39)
[1] 58.12006
```

Let us call these the left and right values of chi-square, respectively. To calculate the confidence interval, we use this formula:

$$\frac{(n-1)s^2}{\chi_R^2} < \sigma^2 < \frac{(n-1)s^2}{\chi_L^2}$$

For a confidence interval for the standard deviation, simply extract the square roots:

$$\sqrt{\frac{(n-1)s^2}{\chi_R^2}} < \sigma < \sqrt{\frac{(n-1)s^2}{\chi_L^2}}$$

Both the variance and chi-square are based on squared deviations, as we discussed earlier. Thus, it makes sense that the distribution of the sample variance would follow a chi-square distribution. Let us calculate our confidence interval and then write a function to accomplish the same purpose. The variance of the weights is 693.1195. We will calculate the confidence interval for the variance and the standard deviation. Note that the variance is in units of "squared pounds," which makes little sense, while the standard deviation is in a more meaningful unit of pounds, matching the original data.

$$\frac{(40-1)693.1195}{58.12006} < \sigma^2 < \frac{(40-1)693.1195}{23.65432}$$

$$\frac{(39)693.1195}{58.12006} < \sigma^2 < \frac{(39)693.1195}{23.65432}$$

$$\frac{27031.661}{58.12006} < \sigma^2 < \frac{27031.661}{23.65432}$$

$$465.1 < \sigma^2 < 1142.779$$

Now, we simply find the confidence limits for the standard deviation by taking the square roots, as described above.

$$\sqrt{465.1} < \sigma^2 < \sqrt{1142.779}$$

$$21.566 < \sigma < 33.805$$

Here is an R function to calculate the confidence interval for the variance and standard deviation. As before, we will default the alpha level to .05 for a 95% confidence interval.

```
confi.var <- function(x, n, alpha = .05) {
        chisqL <- qchisq(alpha/2, n-1)
        chisqR <- qchisq(1 - alpha/2, n-1)
        sampvar <- var(x)
        lower <- ((n - 1) * sampvar)/chisqR
```

```
upper <- ((n - 1) * sampvar)/chisqL
cat(1 - alpha,"% confidence interval for variance:","\n")
cat("sample variance:",sampvar,"\n")
cat("lower limit",lower,"\n")
cat("upper limit",upper,"\n")
cat("confidence interval for standard deviation:","\n")
cat("sample standard deviation",sd(x),"\n")
cat("lower limit",sqrt(lower),"\n")
cat("upper limit",sqrt(upper),"\n")
}
```

Once again, our function produces the same results as our hand calculations. We will use a little trick to tell R to find the length of the vector of weights, which means all we are really passing to the function are the raw data, as shown in this example:

```
> confi.var(weights, length(weights))
0.95 % confidence interval for variance:
sample variance: 693.1195
lower limit 465.1003
upper limit 1142.779
confidence interval for standard deviation:
sample standard deviation 26.32716
lower limit 21.56619
upper limit 33.80501
```

# Confidence Intervals for Differences between Means

If the original data come from two populations that are normally distributed, then two independent sample means (one from each population) are normally distributed. Thus, the differences between the sample means are normally distributed, so we can develop a confidence interval for the difference between the population means using either the normal distribution or the *t* distribution, depending on whether or not we know the population standard deviation (see Figure 8-1). As we have discussed, most statistical software provides *t*-based confidence intervals both for means and for differences between means, as the *t* distribution is more appropriate for small samples and becomes more similar to the standard normal distribution as the sample sizes increase.

Just as the one-sample *t* test produces a confidence interval, so does the two-sample *t* test. Let us return to the example data set from Chapter 1 in which we have the test scores for 20 students. We will do a two-sample *t* test comparing the ages of males and females.

To refresh your memory, the data are as follows.

|    | Gender | Age | Quiz1 | Quiz2 | Quiz3 | Quiz4 | Quiz5 |
|----|--------|-----|-------|-------|-------|-------|-------|
| 1  | 0      | 18  | 83    | 87    | 81    | 80    | 69    |
| 2  | 0      | 19  | 76    | 89    | 61    | 85    | 75    |
| 3  | 0      | 17  | 85    | 86    | 65    | 64    | 81    |
| 4  | 0      | 20  | 92    | 73    | 76    | 88    | 64    |
| 5  | 1      | 23  | 82    | 75    | 96    | 87    | 78    |
| 6  | 1      | 18  | 88    | 73    | 76    | 91    | 81    |
| 7  | 0      | 21  | 89    | 71    | 61    | 70    | 75    |
| 8  | 1      | 20  | 89    | 70    | 87    | 76    | 88    |
| 9  | 1      | 23  | 92    | 85    | 95    | 89    | 62    |
| 10 | 1      | 21  | 86    | 83    | 77    | 64    | 63    |
| 11 | 1      | 23  | 90    | 71    | 91    | 86    | 87    |

| 12 | 0 | 18 | 84 | 71 | 67 | 62 | 70 |
| 13 | 0 | 21 | 83 | 80 | 89 | 60 | 60 |
| 14 | 0 | 17 | 79 | 77 | 82 | 63 | 74 |
| 15 | 0 | 19 | 89 | 80 | 64 | 94 | 78 |
| 16 | 1 | 20 | 76 | 85 | 65 | 92 | 82 |
| 17 | 1 | 19 | 92 | 76 | 76 | 74 | 91 |
| 18 | 1 | 22 | 75 | 90 | 78 | 70 | 76 |
| 19 | 1 | 22 | 87 | 87 | 63 | 73 | 64 |
| 20 | 0 | 20 | 75 | 74 | 63 | 91 | 87 |

In the R code below, note the use of the tilde character (~) to show that we have used gender as the factor. Note also that R defaults to the conservative Welch *t* test that does not assume equal variances. We will discuss *t* tests in more detail in Chapter 9, but for now, focus on the confidence interval for the mean difference. The rather terse output from the t.test() function requires a bit of knowledge of statistics to interpret. See that the use of the confidence interval allows us to determine that zero or no difference is outside the confidence interval, which is an indication that we would conclude the mean difference is significantly different from zero.

```
> attach(dataset)
> t.test(Age ~ Gender)

        Welch Two Sample t-test

data:  Age by Gender
t = -2.849, df = 17.423, p-value = 0.0109
alternative hypothesis: true difference in means is not equal to 0
95 percent confidence interval:
 -3.652299 -0.547701
sample estimates:
mean in group 0 mean in group 1
          19.0            21.1
```

## Confidence Intervals Using the stats Package

The stats package provides many helpful functions, one of which is confint(). We can use this function after downloading and installing the stats package. We will use the lm() function to create a linear model of Age by Gender, with gender as a "factor." We then call the confint() function to develop the confidence interval as follows. Note that the confint() function requires a "model" in order to develop a confidence interval:

```
> require(stats)
> attach(dataset)
> factor(Gender)
 [1] 0 0 0 0 1 1 0 1 1 1 1 0 0 0 0 1 1 1 1 0
Levels: 0 1
> model <- lm(Age ~ Gender)
> confint(model)
                 2.5 %     97.5 %
(Intercept) 17.9049647 20.095035
Gender       0.5513862  3.648614
```

# Conclusion

Confidence intervals are very useful, as you have seen, and, in many cases, can be used to avoid some of the logical pitfalls of hypothesis testing. We will talk more about this in Chapter 19, after running down the list of the most commonly taught (and most widely used) statistical procedures.

In Chapter 8, you learned how to create confidence intervals for the sample mean, for proportions, and for the variance and standard deviation, as well as for the difference between means. In Chapter 9, we turn our attention to the use of the *t* distribution for tests of hypotheses concerning means and the differences between means.

# CHAPTER 9

■ ■ ■

# Performing *t* Tests

We use *t* tests to compare means. You have already seen that the t.test function can be used to display confidence intervals for means and differences between means. The t.test function in R is used for all three kinds of *t* tests: one-sample, paired-samples, and two-sample *t* tests.

In general, we calculate a mean difference and divide that by the standard error of the mean difference. Although we can conceivably perform one-sample, paired-samples, and two-sample *z* tests, and these are taught in some statistics classes and texts, for the reasons we have discussed repeatedly, the *t* tests work better than the *z* tests for small samples and just as well for large samples.

In this chapter, you learn how to do all three kinds of *t* tests. You also learn the differences between the two-sample *t* tests assuming equal variances and assuming unequal variances. You learn how to interpret the results of the tests of hypothesis.

## A Brief Introduction to Hypothesis Testing

Although this is not a statistics book, per se, I need to introduce some basic statistical terminology to help you understand the logic of hypothesis testing and to help you interpret the R output for various tests of hypothesis.

Null hypothesis significance testing (NHST) was the creation of R. A. Fisher, who also developed the analysis of variance (see the discussion below regarding the *t* distribution). In NHST, there are two competing hypotheses: the null hypothesis and the alternative hypothesis. The null hypothesis is presumptively true. A hypothesis is a statement about population parameters. The null hypothesis is always a statement of no difference, no effect, no change, or no relationship.

In the case of a *t* test, the null hypothesis is that there is no difference between two means. For example, a company changed its customer service practices and wants to compare customer satisfaction after the change to the customer satisfaction before the change. The null hypothesis is that there is no difference in customer satisfaction before and after the change. The alternative hypothesis is always a statement that there is a difference, effect, change, or relationship.

In our current example, the alternative hypothesis is either one-tailed (the customer satisfaction ratings are higher after the change) or two-tailed (the customer satisfaction is different after the change—it could have gone down). The null and alternative hypotheses are mutually exclusive (only one can be true) and exhaustive (one of them must be true).

The problem is that we rarely know the population, so we make inferences from samples. Our only decision is to reject or not to reject the null hypothesis. Based on our sample evidence, we conclude the null hypothesis should be rejected or should not be rejected. Of course, our decision could be incorrect, so we hedge our bets a little. We could make a Type I error (rejecting a true null hypothesis) or a Type II error (failing to reject a false null hypothesis). We call the probability of Type I error alpha and the probability of Type II error beta. Examine the following figure to understand the relationships among these errors, confidence, and statistical power (Figure 9-1).

| | Population State of Affairs | |
|---|---|---|
| | $H_0$ is True | $H_0$ is False |
| Reject $H_0$ | Incorrect Decision<br>Type I Error<br>$\alpha$ | Correct<br>Decision<br>Power$(1 - \beta)$ |
| Do Not<br>Reject $H_0$ | Correct<br>Decision<br>Confidence $(1 - \alpha)$ | Incorrect Decision<br>Type II Error<br>$\beta$ |

**Figure 9-1.** *Relationship of Type I and Type II errors to power and confidence*

See that we can only make a Type I error when the null hypothesis is true and we can only make a Type II error when the null hypothesis is false. We control the probability of a Type I error by selecting our alpha level (traditionally .05) in advance of the hypothesis test. A commonly accepted level of statistical power is .80. This means we are willing to make a Type II error up to 20% of the time. We cannot control a Type II error as directly as we can a Type I error, but all things being equal, the greater the sample size and the larger the effect size in the population, the more powerful our test will be.

The *p* value reported for our hypothesis is really a conditional probability. It is the probability of getting sample results as extreme as (or more extreme than) the ones we got, if the null hypothesis were true. As the discussion above implies, we could be making a mistake because we have an aberrant sample, or we could be making the right decision. Over-reliance on statistical significance is one of the shortcomings of the NHST approach, as an effect of any size will ultimately be shown to be statistically significant with a large enough sample size. For that reason, statisticians recommend we report not just the probability value, but also some measure of effect size. For the *t* tests we discuss in this chapter, the most commonly reported measure of effect size is Cohen's *d*.

# Understanding the *t* Distribution

The *t* distribution is interesting from a historical perspective. It was developed from the work of William S. Gosset, a chemist and mathematician who worked for Guinness Brewery. Gosset studied statistics with Karl Pearson at Pearson's London laboratory, and returned to Guinness to develop quality improvements for the brewery. Gosset's work with examining the sampling distribution of the means for small samples led to his development of the *t* distribution. Ironically, it was the other eminent statistician of the day, R. A. Fisher, who recognized the value of Gosset's work. Fisher saw the connection to his own work on degrees of freedom, and introduced the *t* form. Fisher, of course, ultimately extended the *t* distribution to the *F* distribution for simultaneous comparison of three or more means, which we discuss in Chapter 10. Guinness would not allow Gosset to publish under his real name for fear of giving away the trade secret that he had a statistician working for him to improve brewing output and efficiency. So Gosset published under the pseudonym "Student," and thus today we have the "Student's *t* test" and the "Studentized range statistic" among many other contributions of this mild-mannered man.

The R functions for the *t* distribution are dt, pt, qt, and rt, representing the density function, the cumulative probability, quantiles, and random samples. These, of course, correspond to the functions for other continuous statistical distributions.

The *t* distribution is flatter at the center and "fatter" in the tails than the standard normal distribution. As stated earlier, however, the *t* distribution converges to the normal distribution as the sample size increases.

Consider an example (Figure 9-2) of *t* distributions with 4, 9, and 19 degrees of freedom with the standard normal distribution as a point of reference. The R code to produce the graphic is shown below. I used color to show the different distributions. The normal curve is black, the *t* distribution with 19 *df* is purple, the *t* distribution with 9 *df* is blue, and the *t* distribution with 4 *df* is red. As before, we use the points() function to place multiple lines on the same graph.

```
> xaxis <- seq(-3.5, 3.5, .1)
> y1 <- dnorm(xaxis)
> y2 <- dt(xaxis, 4)
> y3 <- dt(xaxis, 9)
> y4 <- dt(xaxis, 19)
> plot(xaxis, y1, type = "l", main = "Comparing z and t Distributions")
> points(xaxis, y2, type = "l", col = "red")
> points(xaxis, y3, type = "l", col = "blue")
> points(xaxis, y4, type = "l", col = "purple")
```

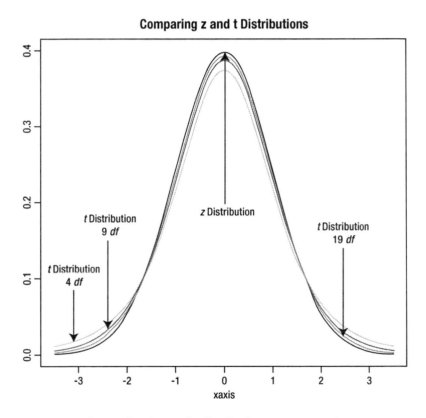

*Figure 9-2. Comparing the t and z distributions*

The graph makes it obvious that the *t* distribution quickly becomes more "normal" as the sample size increases.

# The One-sample *t* Test

In the one-sample *t* test, we are comparing a sample mean to a known or hypothesized population mean. We discussed this test briefly along with the topic of confidence intervals for the mean. As you will soon learn, the paired-samples *t* test can also be seen as a special case of the one-sample *t* test.

The formula for *t*, as you will remember from our previous discussion, is

$$t = \frac{\bar{x} - \mu}{\frac{s}{\sqrt{n}}}$$

The null hypothesis is that the expected mean difference between the sample mean and the population mean is zero, or in other words, that the expected value of the sample mean is equal to the population mean. We compare this value to the *t* distribution with $n - 1$ degrees of freedom to determine a right-tailed, left-tailed, or two-tailed probability. As you will recall, the t.test function also reports a confidence interval for the mean difference.

As an example, let us generate a simple random sample of 50 observations from a normal distribution with a mean of 500 and a standard deviation of 100. The R code to produce the same is shown below.

```
> rnorm1 <- rnorm(50, 500, 100)
> rnorm1
 [1] 513.5179 665.8870 611.5570 482.0871 461.4059 531.1799 398.8917 439.1047
 [9] 340.9291 502.2371 381.2369 551.1444 688.7814 661.5333 480.9378 706.3552
[17] 569.0833 487.7343 358.2330 615.8942 541.8217 741.3809 502.5116 554.4742
[25] 581.7286 453.0035 484.0431 462.2997 541.9050 549.1194 560.5631 541.6482
[33] 562.5287 568.8292 438.3408 307.5047 715.6810 649.1896 317.3438 389.4510
[41] 496.0802 595.7409 580.9330 496.8563 499.5228 574.5999 479.6650 323.9812
[49] 518.2375 389.7700
```

Now, let us examine the sample via the summary() function.

```
> summary(rnorm1)
   Min. 1st Qu.  Median    Mean 3rd Qu.    Max.
  307.5   461.6   515.9   517.3   573.2   741.4
```

The mean of 517.3 is higher than 500, but is it significantly higher? That's what we would use a one-sample *t* test to examine. Here is how to test the hypothesis that the sample came from a population in which $\mu = 500$. Of course, our contrived example is unrealistic, as the situations in which we actually know the population are either trivial ones or artificial ones. As we discussed above, in most applied situations, we do not know the population, so we make inferences about population parameters from sample estimates.

```
t.test(rnorm1, mu = 500)

        One Sample t-test

data:  rnorm1
t = 1.1682, df = 49, p-value = 0.2484
alternative hypothesis: true mean is not equal to 500
95 percent confidence interval:
 487.5180 547.1414
sample estimates:
mean of x
 517.3297
```

See that 500, our test value, is "in" the confidence interval. We fail to reject the null hypothesis and conclude that it is reasonable (with 95 % confidence) to state that the true population mean is between 478.52 and 547.14.

# The Paired-samples *t* Test

The `t.test` function in R will perform a paired-samples *t* test in addition to one-sample and two-sample tests. The test is variously known as a correlated *t* test, a repeated-measures *t* test, or a dependent *t* test, as there is a dependency between the two measures for each subject. As a matter of some statistical interest, the paired-samples *t* test can be easily recast as a one-sample *t* test, as I will demonstrate. For the paired-samples *t* test, the two data points for a single subject must be paired or matched in such a way that they represent two observations on the same individual or a matched pair such as mothers and daughters or twins. The real variable of statistical interest is not the two measures, but the difference between the two measures.

To calculate the value of *t*, we may use the "direct differences" method, as follows:

$$t = \frac{\bar{d} - \mu_d}{\sqrt{\frac{s_d}{n}}}$$

where $\bar{d}$ is the average difference between the pairs of data values, $\mu_d$ is the hypothesized mean difference (typically zero), $s_d$ is the standard deviation of the differences, and *n* in this case is the number of *pairs* of observations, not the total number of observations.

Let us illustrate the paired-samples *t* test with some data that represent before and after measures. The data (collected by me) represent student scores on a statistics test at the beginning of an introductory statistics class and the same students' scores on a parallel statistics test at the end of the semester-long course. Here are the data (Table 9-1):

***Table 9-1.*** *Pre-Course and Post-Course and Posttest Test Scores for a Statistics Class*

| Pretest | Posttest |
|---------|----------|
| 25.0 | 41.7 |
| 41.7 | 66.7 |
| 41.7 | 91.7 |
| 54.2 | 70.8 |
| 29.2 | 70.8 |
| 50.0 | 54.2 |
| 54.2 | 87.5 |
| 45.8 | 54.2 |
| 54.2 | 70.8 |
| 33.3 | 50.0 |
| 33.3 | 58.3 |
| 54.2 | 79.2 |
| 37.5 | 87.5 |
| 12.5 | 45.8 |
| 29.2 | 66.7 |
| 41.7 | 45.8 |

Let us import the data from a tab-delimited text file. (You could also use the R Data Editor to build the data frame.) To make it easier to access the separate variables, we attach the data frame.

```
> prepost <- read.table("prepost.txt", header = TRUE)
> attach(prepost)
```

To perform the paired-samples *t* test, use the following commands in R.

```
> t.test(Pretest, Posttest, paired = TRUE)

        Paired t-test

data:  Pretest and Posttest
t = -6.8695, df = 15, p-value = 5.328e-06
alternative hypothesis: true difference in means is not equal to 0
95 percent confidence interval:
 -33.08447 -17.41553
sample estimates:
mean of the differences
                -25.25
```

See that the average posttest score is 25.25 points higher than the average pretest score. To show the connection between the paired-samples *t* test and the one-sample *t* test, let us redo the test as a one-sample *t* test with a column of difference scores as our dependent variable and a test value of zero. First, let us calculate the vector of difference scores, and then run the one-sample *t* test. To make the differences positive, we subtract the pretest score from the posttest score.

```
> Differences <- Posttest - Pretest
> Differences
 [1] 16.7 25.0 50.0 16.6 41.6  4.2 33.3  8.4 16.6 16.7 25.0 25.0 50.0 33.3 37.5
[16]  4.1
> t.test(Differences)

        One Sample t-test

data:  Differences
t = 6.8695, df = 15, p-value = 5.328e-06
alternative hypothesis: true mean is not equal to 0
95 percent confidence interval:
 17.41553 33.08447
sample estimates:
mean of x
    25.25
```

We calculate the value of *t* as a positive one now, but other than reversing the sign, we get the same value as with the paired-samples *t* test, the degrees of freedom, and the confidence interval for the one-sample *t* test are identical to those values for the paired-samples *t* test.

---

■ **Tip**  We can also use the t.test function to get a positive value of *t* simply by reversing the order of the paired entries as follows: t.test(Posttest, Pretest, paired=TRUE). See the result below.

---

```
> t.test(Posttest, Pretest, paired=TRUE)

        Paired t-test

data:  Posttest and Pretest
t = 6.8695, df = 15, p-value = 5.328e-06
alternative hypothesis: true difference in means is not equal to 0
95 percent confidence interval:
 17.41553 33.08447
sample estimates:
mean of the differences
                  25.25
```

# Two-sample *t* Tests

R defaults to the "Welch" *t* test, which assumes the variances in the population are not equal. Many statisticians prefer this test to the "classic" version of the *t* test, which does assume equality of variance (homoscedasticity). When the two samples have the same number of observations, both tests produce equivalent results. When the two samples have different sample sizes and the sample variances are widely different (by a factor of two or more), the two tests produce different results. The Welch test makes use of the Welch-Satterthwaite correction to estimate the degrees of freedom, and the degrees of freedom can be fractional. The estimated degrees of freedom for the Welch *t* test will always be no larger than those for the "classic" test using a pooled variance estimate.

In addition to running both tests, we will discuss an expedient alternative, which is to test the equality of variance before performing the *t* test, and choosing the appropriate test based on whether we reject or fail to reject the null hypothesis that the variances are equal. This is the approach taken by the statistical software package SPSS, as illustrated below.

## The Welch *t* Test

This test is more conservative than the classic test, and I personally prefer it and use the default Welch test in my own research. Interestingly, though the Welch test is illustrated in many of the business and general statistics textbooks in my library, it is rarely discussed in behavioral statistics texts, and many behavioral researchers are apparently unaware of its existence or the justification for its use.

The Welch test does not pool the sample variances. The value of *t* is calculated as follows:

$$t = \frac{(x_1 - x_2) - (\mu_1 - \mu_2)}{\sqrt{\dfrac{s_1^2}{n_1} + \dfrac{s_2^2}{n_2}}}$$

Note that the difference ($\mu_1 - \mu_2$) is customarily assumed to be zero – that is, we are assuming the two means are equal in the population. The degrees of freedom for this test are calculated this way:

$$df = \frac{(s_1^2 / n_1 + s_2^2 / n_1)^2}{\dfrac{(s_1^2 / n_1)^2}{n_1 - 1} + \dfrac{(s_2^2 / n_2)^2}{n_2 - 1}}$$

Continuing with our example of statistics pretest and posttest scores, see the following data, which represent the pretest and posttest scores for two consecutive semesters of the same class (Table 9-2). We used the spring semester data to illustrate the paired-samples *t* test. For this illustration, we will compare the pretest scores and the posttest scores for the two semesters using an independent-samples *t* test.

***Table 9-2.*** *Pretest and Posttest Scores for Two Semesters*

| Fall | | Spring | |
|---|---|---|---|
| **Pretest** | **Posttest** | **Pretest** | **Posttest** |
| 54.2 | 62.5 | 25.0 | 41.7 |
| 50.0 | 54.2 | 41.7 | 66.7 |
| 41.7 | 41.7 | 41.7 | 91.7 |
| 37.5 | 50.0 | 54.2 | 70.8 |
| 37.5 | 41.7 | 29.2 | 70.8 |
| 37.5 | 50.0 | 50.0 | 54.2 |
| 37.5 | 41.7 | 54.2 | 87.5 |
| 33.3 | 33.3 | 45.8 | 54.2 |
| 33.3 | 33.3 | 54.2 | 70.8 |
| 33.3 | 29.2 | 33.3 | 50.0 |
| 33.3 | 37.5 | 33.3 | 58.3 |
| 33.3 | 41.7 | 54.2 | 79.2 |
| 33.3 | 37.5 | 37.5 | 87.5 |
| 29.2 | 41.7 | 12.5 | 45.8 |
| 29.2 | 33.3 | 29.2 | 66.7 |
| 29.2 | 25.0 | 41.7 | 45.8 |
| 25.0 | 33.3 | | |
| 25.0 | 37.5 | | |
| 20.8 | 41.7 | | |
| 20.8 | 33.3 | | |
| 12.5 | 33.3 | | |

I used lists to create a data structure and used the sapply() function to examine the means for these tests because the two classes have unequal numbers of students. This technique was illustrated in Chapter 2 when we compared test scores for three classes of different sizes. Note that the two pretest scores are fairly close, but the two posttest scores are widely different.

```
> PrePost <- list(Pretest1,Pretest2,Posttest1,Posttest2)
> PrePost
[[1]]
 [1] 54.16667 50.00000 41.66667 37.50000 37.50000 37.50000 37.50000 33.33333
 [9] 33.33333 33.33333 33.33333 33.33333 33.33333 29.16667 29.16667 29.16667
[17] 25.00000 25.00000 20.83333 20.83333 12.50000

[[2]]
 [1] 25.00000 41.66667 41.66667 54.16667 29.16667 50.00000 54.16667 45.83333
```

```
 [9] 54.16667 33.33333 33.33333 54.16667 37.50000 12.50000 29.16667 41.66667

[[3]]
 [1] 62.50000 54.16667 41.66667 50.00000 41.66667 50.00000 41.66667 33.33333
 [9] 33.33333 29.16667 37.50000 41.66667 37.50000 41.66667 33.33333 25.00000
[17] 33.33333 37.50000 41.66667 33.33333 33.33333

[[4]]
 [1] 41.66667 66.66667 91.66667 70.83333 70.83333 54.16667 87.50000 54.16667
 [9] 70.83333 50.00000 58.33333 79.16667 87.50000 45.83333 66.66667 45.83333

> sapply(PrePost, mean)
[1] 32.73810 39.84375 39.68254 65.10417
```

Now, we will perform the two-sample *t* test with the two classes' pretest scores. See the R commands below. Note that we can use both "stacked" data with indicator coding or side-by-side data as in the current example. I will illustrate both.

## Welch *t* Test for "Side-by-side" Data

If the data reside in separate vectors or as columns in a data frame, you can run the Welch two-sample *t* test as follows.

```
> t.test(Pretest1, Pretest2)

        Welch Two Sample t-test

data:  Pretest1 and Pretest2
t = -1.924, df = 27.403, p-value = 0.0648
alternative hypothesis: true difference in means is not equal to 0
95 percent confidence interval:
 -14.6781507   0.4668411
sample estimates:
mean of x mean of y
 32.73810   39.84375
```

See that the two sets of pretest scores are not significantly different, and a confirmation of this is the fact that zero or no difference is contained within the confidence interval. Also, note carefully the fractional degrees of freedom, as we discussed above.

Let us now compare the two classes' posttest scores.

```
> t.test(Posttest1, Posttest2)

        Welch Two Sample t-test

data:  Posttest1 and Posttest2
t = -5.7444, df = 21.885, p-value = 9.052e-06
alternative hypothesis: true difference in means is not equal to 0
95 percent confidence interval:
 -34.60233 -16.24092
sample estimates:
mean of x mean of y
 39.68254   65.10417
```

In this case, the posttest scores for the spring semester are significantly higher than those for the previous fall semester. Before you conclude anything of import about this significant difference, you should know that the posttest for the fall semester was not included in the course grade, but that it was included in the course grade for the spring semester. Thus, the two classes had very different motivations for doing well on the posttest.

## Doing the Welch *t* test with "Stacked" Data and Indicator Coding

It is quite common to stack the data in a single column and to use indicator coding to show group membership. In R, indicator coding is called a "factor." Factors can be verbal labels or numbers. Let us reconfigure the posttest scores for the two classes as stacked data. Some statistics programs like SPSS require independent-samples *t* tests to be set up this way, while others like Minitab and R are more flexible and allow either stacked or side-by-side data. Here are the reconfigured data. I used Excel to do the "surgery" on the data and then read the data frame into R via the read.table function.

```
> StackedData <- read.table("StackedData.txt", header = TRUE)
> StackedData
   PostTest Class
1  62.50000     1
2  54.16667     1
3  41.66667     1
4  50.00000     1
5  41.66667     1
6  50.00000     1
7  41.66667     1
8  33.33333     1
9  33.33333     1
10 29.16667     1
11 37.50000     1
12 41.66667     1
13 37.50000     1
14 41.66667     1
15 33.33333     1
16 25.00000     1
17 33.33333     1
18 37.50000     1
19 41.66667     1
20 33.33333     1
21 33.33333     1
22 41.66667     2
23 66.66667     2
24 91.66667     2
25 70.83333     2
26 70.83333     2
27 54.16667     2
28 87.50000     2
29 54.16667     2
30 70.83333     2
31 50.00000     2
32 58.33333     2
33 79.16667     2
34 87.50000     2
35 45.83333     2
```

```
36 66.66667    2
37 45.83333    2
```

Examine the use of the tilde character (~) to indicate that the *Class* vector contains the factor for the stacked data. See that the stacked data produce *t* test results identical to those of the side-by-side data.

```
> attach(StackedData)
> t.test(PostTest~Class)

        Welch Two Sample t-test

data:  PostTest by Class
t = -5.7444, df = 21.885, p-value = 9.052e-06
alternative hypothesis: true difference in means is not equal to 0
95 percent confidence interval:
 -34.60233 -16.24092
sample estimates:
mean in group 1 mean in group 2
       39.68254        65.10417
```

## The *t* Test Assuming Equality of Variance

As we discussed above, the "classic" version of the *t* test assumes equality of variance and pools the variances of the two samples to make the test more powerful. Many statistics texts in the behavioral and social sciences include only this test and do not make mention of the Welch test.

For this test, we calculate a pooled variance estimate as follows:

$$s_p^2 = \frac{(n_1 - 1)s_1^2 + (n_2 - 1)s_2^2}{n_1 + n_2 - 2}$$

We then calculate the value of *t*:

$$t = \frac{(\bar{x}_1 - \bar{x}_2) - (\mu_1 - \mu_2)}{\sqrt{\dfrac{s_p^2}{n_1} + \dfrac{s_p^2}{n_2}}}$$

The degrees of freedom for the *t* test are $n_1 + n_2 - 2$. Here is how to tell R to conduct the *t* test assuming equality of variance. We will use the same stacked data we just used for the Welch *t* test.

```
> t.test(PostTest~Class, var.equal = TRUE)

        Two Sample t-test

data:  PostTest by Class
t = -6.1879, df = 35, p-value = 4.37e-07
alternative hypothesis: true difference in means is not equal to 0
95 percent confidence interval:
 -33.76182 -17.08144
sample estimates:
mean in group 1 mean in group 2
       39.68254        65.10417
```

As we discussed, this test is more powerful than the Welch test, and thus produces a lower *p* value. To improve the statistical accuracy of our hypothesis tests, we could first conduct a test of equality of variance and then choose the appropriate *t* test, as mentioned above. To do that, we will use the `tapply` function to examine the two variances and then compare them using the `var.test` function.

```
> tapply(PostTest, Class, var)
       1        2
77.46362 254.34028
```

We note the wide discrepancy in the two variances, and thus suspect the two variances are unequal in the population. The `var.test` function confirms our suspicion. See that the significant *F* test indicates we should reject the null hypothesis that the two variances are equal. Thus, we are not justified in performing the equal variances "classical" *t* test. Because of the indicator coding used, R divided the smaller variance by the larger one to produce a strange left-tailed *F* ratio less than 1. To avoid this, you can simply divide the larger variance by the smaller one to get a more traditional *F* ratio, though the statistical results will be the same in either case.

```
> var.test(PostTest ~ Class)

        F test to compare two variances

data:  PostTest by Class
F = 0.3046, num df = 20, denom df = 15, p-value = 0.01435
alternative hypothesis: true ratio of variances is not equal to 1
95 percent confidence interval:
 0.1105144 0.7836799
sample estimates:
ratio of variances
          0.3045669
```

The SPSS package simply performs an equality of variance test and reports both the classic and the Welch tests, though its output is complicated and difficult to decipher. Here is the SPSS output for our current example (Figure 9-3). See that the significant results of the test of equality of variance indicate the user should report the *t* test that does not assume equality of variance. Note further that R and SPSS produce identical results for the two *t* tests and confidence intervals.

**Group Statistics**

|          | Class | N  | Mean       | Std. Deviation | Std. Error Mean |
|----------|-------|----|------------|----------------|-----------------|
| PostTest | 1     | 21 | 39.6825397 | 8.80134219     | 1.92061032      |
|          | 2     | 16 | 65.1041667 | 15.94804934    | 3.98701234      |

**Independent Samples Test**

|          |                              | Levene's Test for Equality of Variances | | t-test for Equality of Means | | | | | 95% Confidence Interval of the Difference | |
|----------|------------------------------|------|------|--------|--------|-------------------|-----------------|-----------------|--------------|--------------|
|          |                              | F    | Sig. | t      | df     | Sig. (2-tailed)   | Mean Difference | Std. Error Difference | Lower    | Upper        |
| PostTest | Equal variances assumed      | 8.35 | .007 | -6.188 | 35     | .000              | -25.42162698    | 4.10824971      | -33.76181729 | -17.08143668 |
|          | Equal variances not assumed  |      |      | -5.744 | 21.885 | .000              | -25.42162698    | 4.42549561      | -34.60233071 | -16.24092326 |

***Figure 9-3.*** *SPSS output for the independent-samples t test*

# A Note on Effect Size for the *t* Test

As mentioned at the beginning of this chapter, the most commonly reported measure of effect size for the *t* test is Cohen's *d*. This index shows how far apart the two means are in standard deviation units. For each form of the *t* test, we can identify a formula for Cohen's *d* based on the following general definition:

$$d = \frac{|\mu_1 - \mu_2|}{\sigma}$$

Note that the mean difference is divided by the standard deviation and not the standard error of the mean. Because we are using sample data, we will use sample statistics to estimate the population parameters. For the independent-samples *t* test, Cohen's *d* is calculated as

$$d = \frac{|\bar{x}_1 - \bar{x}_2|}{s_p}$$

where $s_p$ is the pooled standard deviation, which is the square root of the pooled variance estimate discussed above.
For the one-sample *t* test, Cohen's *d* can be calculated as

$$d = \frac{|\bar{x}_1 - \mu|}{s_x}$$

For the paired-sample *t* test, we can calculate Cohen's *d* as

$$d = \frac{|\bar{d}|}{s_d}$$

Note that we are using $\bar{d}$ to signify the mean difference, and Cohen's statistic is also called *d*. The term $s_d$ is the standard deviation (not the standard error) of the mean differences. It would clearly be simple to write an R function to perform a *t* test and calculate Cohen's *d*. That exercise is left to the reader.

Cohen suggested that a value of *d* of 0.2 represents a *small* effect, a value of 0.5 represents a *medium* effect, and a value of .8 or higher represents a *large* effect. These interpretations are irrespective of statistical significance or sample size.

The reporting of effect size indices is not built into the base version of R, but is implemented in the contributed R package pwr (for power) written by Stéphane Champely. We will discuss this package in more detail later, but for now, let it suffice to say the package implements power analysis as developed by Cohen. Each function in the pwr package requires you to enter three of four quantities (effect size, sample size, significance level, or power), and then calculates the value of the fourth quantity. As we have done throughout this text, the pwr package defaults to an alpha level of .05. All power analysis requires some level of assumption. Just as we assume a default alpha level of .05, we assume a default beta level of .80. We also assume the effect size in the population is "medium sized."

# Conclusion

In this chapter, you learned the basics of hypothesis testing, the R functions for the *t* distribution, and how to use R for three kinds of *t* tests. You also learned the differences between stacked and side-by-side data and the differences between the Welch *t* test and the classic *t* test assuming equal variances.

In the next chapter, you will learn how to use R for the analysis of variance, which is a direct extension of the *t* test to the simultaneous comparison of three or more means.

# CHAPTER 10

# One-Way Analysis of Variance

The analysis of variance (ANOVA) compares three or more means simultaneously. We determine whether the means are significantly different in the population by analyzing the variation in the dependent variable into separate sources. ANOVA takes advantage of the additivity property of variance, and we partition the variation into treatment effect (real differences) and error (differences due to sampling error or individual differences). The ratio of two variances follows the $F$ (named after R. A. Fisher) distribution. Some readers may have difficulty understanding why the analysis of variance components can be used to test hypotheses about means, but on reflection, one should realize that the variances themselves are based on squared deviations from means.

In this chapter, you learn how to conduct a one-way ANOVA and to conduct post hoc comparisons when appropriate using the Tukey honestly significant difference (HSD) criterion and Bonferroni corrections. In Chapter 11, you will learn how to conduct and interpret two-way and mixed model ANOVA, as well as the repeated-measures ANOVA.

Before we discuss the ANOVA, let us examine the properties of the $F$ distribution and the R functions for dealing with it. As you will see, the $F$ distribution cannot assume negative values because it is based on variances, which themselves are derived from squared deviations.

## Understanding the $F$ Distribution

The R functions for the F distribution are df, pf, qf, and rf, for the density, cumulative probability, quantiles, and random generator functions, respectively. Like the $t$ distribution, the $F$ distribution is based on degrees of freedom, and is thus a *family* of distributions. Unlike the $t$ distribution, the $F$ distribution has degrees of freedom for the numerator term and for the denominator term. Also unlike the $t$ distribution, the $F$ distribution is not symmetrical. Instead, the $F$ distribution is positively skewed, and peaks around a value of 1 (which would indicate the two variance estimates in ratio are equal). We will plot several representative $F$ distributions as we did with the $t$ distribution to see what happens as the degrees of freedom change.

Let us generate $F$ distributions for the following combination of degrees of freedom: (3, 10), (4, 15), and (10, 29). See that as the degrees of freedom increase, the $F$ distribution becomes more symmetrical. Here is our code for generating the $F$ distributions and the plot shown in Figure 10-1. We set the $x$ axis to range from 0 to 6 in increments of .1.

```
> xaxis <- seq(0,6,.1)> xaxis
 [1] 0.0 0.1 0.2 0.3 0.4 0.5 0.6 0.7 0.8 0.9 1.0 1.1 1.2 1.3 1.4 1.5 1.6 1.7 1.8
[20] 1.9 2.0 2.1 2.2 2.3 2.4 2.5 2.6 2.7 2.8 2.9 3.0 3.1 3.2 3.3 3.4 3.5 3.6 3.7
[39] 3.8 3.9 4.0 4.1 4.2 4.3 4.4 4.5 4.6 4.7 4.8 4.9 5.0 5.1 5.2 5.3 5.4 5.5 5.6
[58] 5.7 5.8 5.9 6.0
> y1 <- df(xaxis, 3, 10)
> y2 <- df(xaxis, 4, 15)
> y3 <- df(xaxis, 10, 29)
```

```
> plot(xaxis, y3, type = "l", main = "Comparing F Distributions")
> points(xaxis, y2, type = "l", col = "red")
> points(xaxis, y1, type = "l", col = "blue")
```

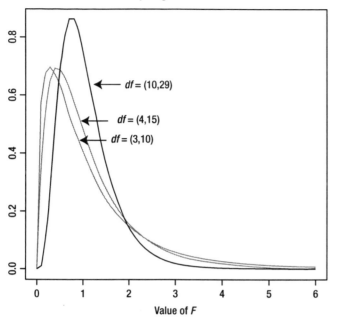

*Figure 10-1. Comparing F distributions with different degrees of freedom*

# Using the *F* Distribution to Test Variances

Because it is formed from the ratio of two variances, the *F* distribution can be used to test hypotheses about variances. In theoretical statistics books, students learn that the *F* and chi-square distributions have a mathematical connection, so it makes some sense that we develop confidence intervals for variances using the chi-square distribution and hypothesis tests about variances using the *F* distribution. In Chapter 9, you saw the use of the var.test function to compare two variances. Recall that the output of the var.test function is an *F* ratio.

Here is the result of the var.test function used to assess equality of variance from Chapter 9.

```
> var.test(PostTest~Class)

        F test to compare two variances

data:  PostTest by Class
F = 0.3046, num df = 20, denom df = 15, p-value = 0.01435
alternative hypothesis: true ratio of variances is not equal to 1
95 percent confidence interval:
 0.1105144 0.7836799
sample estimates:
ratio of variances
        0.3045669
```

Note the F ratio is less than 1 because the smaller variance was divided by the larger one. Such an *F* ratio is perfectly legitimate, but many students and researchers are thrown off by a "left-tailed" probability value in the *F* distribution. An easy way to avoid this is simply to divide the larger variance by the smaller one to make *F* at least 1 and the *p* value a "right-tailed" one. Recall that the variances for the two classes were 77.46 and 254.34, respectively:

```
> tapply(PostTest, Groups, var)
        1         2
 77.46362 254.34028
```

Let us divide the larger variance by the smaller one to get an *F* ratio greater than one: 254.34028 / 77.46362 = 3.283351. We can also simply find the reciprocal of the *F* ratio reported by the var.test function:

```
> 1/.3045669
[1] 3.283351
```

The *p* value will be the same whether we divide the larger or the smaller variance by the other. Note that this is a two-tailed probability because the alternative hypothesis is that the variances are unequal. Thus, we would double the one-tailed *p* value reported by R when we use the pf() function to determine the *p* value. See the following R code:

```
> TwoTailedP <- 2*(1 - pf(3.283351, 15, 20))
> TwoTailedP
[1] 0.01435193
```

Note that we had to reverse the numerator and denominator degrees of freedom, as we are now dividing the larger variance by the smaller one. The two-tailed *p* value is indeed the same as that reported by R's var.test function.

For the analysis of variance, we place $1 - \alpha$ to the left of a critical value of *F* and $\alpha$ to the right of the critical value. This leads some teachers erroneously to conclude that the *F* test is one-tailed. The test of hypothesis is based on a ratio of two variances, and variances are based on squared deviations, as we discussed above. For that reason, a negative difference between two means and a positive difference between two means will both produce a positive squared deviation. Therefore the *F* ratio increases as the differences (both positive and negative) between means increase relative to the within group variability, and the resulting increase in the *F* ratio reflects both positive and negative mean differences, making it a two-tailed test. SPSS and other statistics software packages report the *p* value (which SPSS inscrutably calls "Sig.") as two-tailed, and now you know why!

# Compounding Alpha and Post Hoc Comparisons

When we perform repeated hypothesis tests, the probability of a Type I error increases. This is especially true when we are comparing pairs of means. If we conduct *c* different comparisons between pairs of means, each at a nominal alpha level of .05, the overall Type I error rate will not be .05, but instead would be $1 - (1-.05)^c$, if the comparisons were independent, which they are not. To illustrate, assume we have six groups and are taking all possible pairs. Use the following formula to compute the number of pairwise comparisons:

$$_6C_2 = \frac{6!}{4!2!} = 15$$

Therefore the Type I error, if we assume independence, and if we perform each test at alpha = .05, will be

$$1-(1-.05)^{15} = 1-.95^{15} = 1-.4633 = .5367$$

This is clearly too high an error rate for hypothesis testing. ANOVA permits a simultaneous comparison of all 15 means at once, and controls the error rate to the nominal .05. If and only if the overall $F$ ratio is significant should we continue with post hoc comparisons to determine which pairs of means are significantly different. As with the overall $F$ test, we must make sure not to compound the error rate by performing each comparison at the nominal alpha level. There are several approaches to controlling the error rate of post hoc comparisons after a significant overall $F$ test, but in this chapter, we illustrate only the Tukey HSD criterion and Bonferroni corrections.

# One-Way ANOVA

In one-way ANOVA, we compare the means for three or more groups. Each group is defined by a different level of the factor (independent variable). If the overall $F$ test is significant, we are justified in conducting post hoc tests to determine which pairs of means are significantly different. One part of the total variation is the "treatment" variation, which is based on the differences among the three means. We compare each group mean to the overall average treating all the observations as a single group. The other partition is the "error" variation, which is based on differences among scores within each group. It is customary to call the treatment variation the "between" variation because it occurs between (or among) the groups. We customarily call the error variation the "within" variation because it occurs within the individual groups and is not affected by the differences between the means of the groups.

## The Variance Partition in the One-Way ANOVA

The total variation in the overall set of scores is known in ANOVA parlance as the total sum of squares. Technically, it should be called the sum of the squared deviations. We treat the entire set of data as one sample, calculate the grand mean, which we will call $\bar{\bar{x}}$, subtract the grand mean from each observation, square the deviations, and add them. Here is the conceptual formula for the total sum of squares. We would not actually calculate it this way because an algebraically equivalent computational formula produces the same result without the device of calculating and squaring deviations.

$$SS_{tot} = \sum (x - \bar{\bar{x}})^2$$

We partition the total variation into the between and within sums of squares.

$$SS_{tot} = SS_b + SS_w$$

We define the between groups sum of squares as

$$SS_b = \sum_{j=1}^{k} n_j (\bar{x}_j - \bar{\bar{x}})^2$$

The between variation (technically the between groups sum of squares) is divided by the between groups degrees of freedom to calculate the between groups mean square. The between groups degrees of freedom are $k - 1$ where $k$ is the number of groups. The between groups mean square is the variance due to treatment effects or "real" differences between the group means.

We define the within groups sum of squares as follows. The double summation simply means to add the squared deviations of each observation in each group from the group mean, and sum these across the groups.

$$SS_w = \sum_{j=1}^{k} \sum_{i=1}^{n_j} \left( x_{ij} - \bar{x}_j \right)^2$$

The within variation (technically the within groups sum of squares) is divided by the within groups degrees of freedom to calculate the within groups mean square. The within groups degrees of freedom is calculated as $N - k$ where $N$ is the overall sample size treating all the groups as a single sample. The within groups mean square is the variance due to "errors" within the groups.

The null hypothesis in one-way ANOVA is that all the means are equal in the population. The alternative hypothesis is that at least one of the means is different from the others.

## An Example of the One-Way ANOVA

The $F$ ratio is the between groups mean square divided by the within groups mean square. We compare this value to the theoretical $F$ distribution with $k$ and $N - k$ degrees of freedom. We will obtain a $p$ value, which is the two-tailed probability of finding an $F$ ratio as large as or larger than the one we did if the null hypothesis that the population means are equal is true.

Let us illustrate the one-way ANOVA with the following data, which represent the automobile mileage of 15 identical subcompact vehicles randomly assigned to three different brands of regular unleaded gasoline. Here is the R code for entering the data and creating a data frame:

```
> mpg=c(34,35,34.3,35.5,35.8,35.3,36.5,36.4,37,37.6,33.3,34,34.7,33,34.9)
> brand=c("A","A","A","A","A","B","B","B","B","B","C","C","C","C","C")
> mileage=data.frame(mpg=mpg,brand=brand)
> attach(mileage)
> factor(brand)
> mileage
    mpg brand
1   34.0    A
2   35.0    A
3   34.3    A
4   35.5    A
5   35.8    A
6   35.3    B
7   36.5    B
8   36.4    B
9   37.0    B
10  37.6    B
11  33.3    C
12  34.0    C
13  34.7    C
14  33.0    C
15  34.9    C
```

See that I formatted the data in "stacked" format with brand as a character value representing the factor (independent variable). Let us first examine side-by-side boxplots. Here is the R command to produce the boxplots shown in Figure 10-2. Remember to attach the data frame in order to access the individual variables.

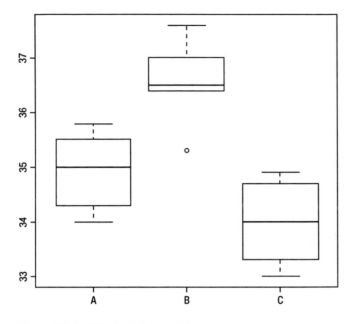

*Figure 10-2.* *Side-by-side boxplots*

```
> boxplot(mpg~brand)
```

It would appear brand B produces better gasoline mileage than A and C, but we must perform the analysis of variance to determine if the differences are significant. Let us create a factor from the brand column and call it group. We will then use the aov( ) function to perform the ANOVA, but save the results and then use the summary() function to display the customary ANOVA summary table. Note that the results are sufficient to determine the mean squares and the $F$ ratio. The summary function does this for you and formats the results nicely.

```
group <- factor(brand)
> group
 [1] A A A A A B B B B B C C C C C
Levels: A B C
```

Now, we can save the results of the ANOVA for additional use.

```
> results <- aov(mpg~group)
> results
Call:
   aov(formula = mpg~group)

Terms:
                  group Residuals
Sum of Squares  17.04933   8.02800
Deg. of Freedom        2        12
```

144

```
Residual standard error: 0.8179242
Estimated effects may be unbalanced
> summary(results)
            Df Sum Sq Mean Sq F value  Pr(>F)
group        2 17.049   8.525   12.74 0.00108 **
Residuals   12  8.028   0.669
---
Signif. codes:  0 '***' 0.001 '**' 0.01 '*' 0.05 '.' 0.1 ' ' 1
```

Remember you can call a function from another function, so you could get the ANOVA summary table with one statement if you prefer:

```
> summary(aov(mpg ~ group))
            Df Sum Sq Mean Sq F value  Pr(>F)
group        2 17.049   8.525   12.74 0.00108 **
Residuals   12  8.028   0.669
---
Signif. codes:  0 '***' 0.001 '**' 0.01 '*' 0.05 '.' 0.1 ' ' 1
```

The overall $F$ ratio is significant, so we can do post hoc comparisons to determine which pairs of means are significantly different. First, let us examine the means for each level of the grouping factor (gasoline brand). To accomplish this purpose, we will use the model.tables function. We will set the type to "means" and use the analysis of variance results as the argument:

```
> model.tables(results, type = "means")
Tables of means
Grand mean

35.15333

 group
group
    A     B     C
34.92 36.56 33.98
```

# Tukey HSD Test

The only post hoc procedure provided in the base version of R is the Tukey HSD criterion, but this is one of the most popular post hoc comparison approaches, and generally has desirable properties. It is more conservative than the original Fisher LSD (least significant difference) criterion, which many statisticians feel is too liberal. The Tukey HSD criterion is less conservative than the Scheffé procedure, which many statisticians consider too conservative. A good statistics or experimental design text will help those readers who want to explore alternatives to the HSD. To perform the HSD test, we use the TukeyHSD function. As with most statistical functions, the R implementation of the Tukey HSD test defaults to an *experiment-wise* (overall) alpha level of .05. Consider this code:

```
> TukeyHSD(results)
  Tukey multiple comparisons of means
    95 % family-wise confidence level

Fit: aov(formula = mpg ~ group)
```

```
$group
      diff       lwr        upr       p adj
B-A   1.64  0.2599123  3.0200877 0.0204273
C-A  -0.94 -2.3200877  0.4400877 0.2056606
C-B  -2.58 -3.9600877 -1.1999123 0.0008518
```

See that the difference between brands A and B is significant, as is that between brands B and C. Brands C and A are not significantly different. Brand B produces significantly higher gasoline mileage than the other two brands.

---

■ **Note**   The Tukey HSD criterion makes use of a quantity known as the "Studentized Range Statistic," which is frequently abbreviated as $q$. R has the continuous distribution of the Studentized range statistic built into it, along with the various continuous distribution functions we have discussed previously. Although Tukey's HSD is the only post hoc comparison procedure built into base R, the stats package has a number of other procedures for post hoc comparisons. For comparison purposes, we will use the pairwise.t.test function from the stats package as discussed below.

---

## Bonferroni-Corrected Post Hoc Comparisons

We can compare the means after a significant *F* test in several different ways, and in addition to the Tukey HSD test, another good way to do that is to use the `pairwise.t.test` function built into the `stats` package. Recall that you must download and install the `stats` package. (See Chapter 1 for a refresher if you need it.) You must then load the package into your workspace. If you need help, the R documentation explains these procedures. As a quick reminder, see the following:

```
> require(stats)
```

The `pairwise.t.test` function gives the user several choices for adjusting the *p* value to control for the overall Type I error rate. We will compare the means from our one-way ANOVA using Bonferroni-corrections and then see how that result compares with that of the Tukey HSD test. Here is the R code to produce the pairwise comparisons. The Bonferroni correction is simply the division of the overall alpha level by the number of comparisons, so the nominal alpha level for significance in this case is .05 / 3 = .0167 for each pairwise *t* test. The Bonferroni procedure is conservative, but not too conservative, and along with the Tukey HSD test, is a very commonly reported post hoc procedure. Here is the R output.

```
> require(stats)
> pairwise.t.test(mpg, group, p.adjust.method = "bonferroni")

        Pairwise comparisons using t tests with pooled SD

data:  mpg and group

  A       B
B 0.02420 -
C 0.28272 0.00095

P value adjustment method: bonferroni
```

Although the stated *p* values are slightly different, the Bonferroni-corrected comparisons lead us to the same conclusion as the Tukey HSD test, which is that brands A and B are different, brands B and C are different, and brands A and C are not different.

## Using the anova Function

As a last point about one-way ANOVA, see below that you can also use the anova function to conduct a one-way ANOVA by passing the lm (for linear model) argument to the anova function. Other than reporting one more decimal than the aov function, the anova function produces equivalent results and generates the summary table immediately. Here is the R code:

```
> anova(lm(mpg ~ group))
Analysis of Variance Table

Response: mpg
          Df Sum Sq Mean Sq F value   Pr(>F)
group      2 17.049  8.5247  12.742 0.001076 **
Residuals 12  8.028  0.6690
---
Signif. codes:  0 '***' 0.001 '**' 0.01 '*' 0.05 '.' 0.1 ' ' 1
```

## Conclusion

In this chapter, you learned about the theoretical F distribution, the R functions for working with the *F* distribution, and how to conduct a one-way ANOVA with post hoc comparisons using both the Tukey HSD test and Bonferroni-corrected comparisons. In the next chapter, you will learn more complex ANOVA designs and how to conduct and interpret them.

# CHAPTER 11

■ ■ ■

# Advanced Analysis of Variance

In Chapter 11 we dig deeper into ANOVA procedures, including two-way ANOVA, repeated-measures ANOVA, and mixed-factorial ANOVA. In general, these forms of ANOVA allow us to evaluate the combined effect of two or more factors or to examine multiple measurements on the dependent variable. In Chapter 13, where we discuss multiple regression, we will illustrate how the same linear model underlies both regression and ANOVA models and how we can use regression models, if preferred, to conduct ANOVAs as well.

Heed the following caution! ANOVA designs quickly become very complex, and their interpretation becomes equally complex.

---

■ **Caution**   The more complicated the ANOVA design becomes, the more difficult it is to ferret out the various effects and interactions, and the more likely it is that there will be difficulty in interpreting the results. As part of a rather quiet and gentle revolution in statistics over the past 20 years or so, statistics educators have concluded that simple designs, which are easy to interpret, are preferred over complicated designs, which can be difficult or impossible to interpret. This, of course, comes as welcome news to students who are learning statistics in order to complete their own research projects, theses, and dissertations.

---

## Two-Way ANOVA

In two-way ANOVA, there are two factors. We will illustrate only the most basic version of two-way fixed effects ANOVA, which is a *balanced factorial design*. Let us call the factors $A$ and $B$. If there are $c$ levels of $B$ and $r$ levels of $A$, there will be $r \times c$ total groups, each of which will have the same number of data values.

The variance partition in two-way ANOVA is as shown in Figure 11-1.

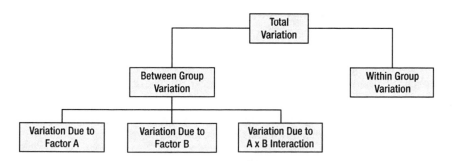

*Figure 11-1.* The variance partition in two-way ANOVA

It helps to visualize two-way ANOVA by considering a table such as the one shown in Figure 11-2. In the balanced factorial design, each cell will have the same number of observations.

|  | $B_1$ | $B_2$ |
|---|---|---|
| $A_1$ | $A_1B_1$ | $A_1B_2$ |
| $A_2$ | $A_2B_1$ | $A_2B_2$ |

**Figure 11-2.** *Visualizing two-way ANOVA*

In Figure 11-2, there are 2 rows and 2 columns for $r \times c = 4$ groups. Thus, for the simplest balanced factorial design, there will be four cell means to compare.

## Sums of Squares in Two-Way ANOVA

In two-way ANOVA, we have six sums of squares to compute, though one of them (the *SS* for cells) does not appear in our ANOVA summary table.

We can compute the sums of squares in two-way ANOVA as follows.

1.  We calculate the total sum of squares. This quantity will always be the same, regardless of the ANOVA model. It is the sum of the squared deviations from the grand mean considering each data point as an observation in a single sample.

$$SS_{tot} = \sum \left( x - \overline{\overline{x}} \right)^2$$

    The degrees of freedom are $N - 1$, where $N$ is the overall sample size. See that if we divide the sum of squares by the degrees of freedom, we get the completely obvious sample variance. In ANOVA, the actual variances being "analyzed" are called *mean squares*.

2.  The sum of squares for cells is derived from the cell means. We will subdivide the sum of squares for cells into sums of squares for A, B, and the $A \times B$ interaction.

$$SS_{cells} = SS_A + SS_B + SS_{AB}$$

    We calculate the sum of squares for cells the same way as any other sum of squares, and you may think of it as being the sum of squares for a one-way ANOVA considering all the groups as independent. The sum of squares for cells is useful for finding the interaction sum of squares, which we can find by subtraction.

3.  The sum of squares for A is found by calculating what would have been the between-groups sum of squares considering A as the only factor (see Chapter 10). The degrees of freedom for the sum of squares for A is the number of levels of A minus 1.

4.  The sum of squares for B is similarly found by calculating the between-groups sum of squares considering only the B factor. The degrees of freedom for the sum of squares for B is the number of levels of B minus 1.

5. The interaction sum of squares can be found most conveniently by subtraction:

$$SS_{AB} = SS_{cells} - SS_A - SS_B$$

The degrees of freedom for the interaction term are the product of the degrees of freedom for A and the degrees of freedom for B.

6. Finally, we calculate the error sum of squares by subtraction, too:

$$SS_{err} = SS_{tot} - SS_{cells}$$

The degrees of freedom for error are the total degrees of freedom minus the A, B, and AB degrees of freedom.

# An Example of a Two-Way ANOVA

The two-way ANOVA is an efficient design because it allows us to conduct three hypothesis tests. The three null hypotheses are:

- There is no main effect of A considered separately.

- There is no main effect of B considered separately.

- There is no interaction of A and B considered together.

The following hypothetical data represent college students' satisfaction measured on a 10-point scale (with 0 being *not at all satisfied* and 10 being *completely satisfied*). The students are randomly assigned to three course delivery formats and each student takes one of three class subjects. Here is the data set, which I read in from a CSV file:

```
> twowayexample <- read.csv("twowayexampledata.csv", header = TRUE)
> twowayexample
      Format      Subject Satisfaction
1      Online Statistics           10
2      Online Statistics            9
3      Online Statistics            8
4      Online      English          7
5      Online      English          6
6      Online      English          5
7      Online      Science          4
8      Online      Science          3
9      Online      Science          2
10     Hybrid Statistics            9
11     Hybrid Statistics            8
12     Hybrid Statistics            7
13     Hybrid      English          6
14     Hybrid      English          5
15     Hybrid      English          4
16     Hybrid      Science          3
17     Hybrid      Science          2
18     Hybrid      Science          1
19  Classroom Statistics            8
20  Classroom Statistics            7
21  Classroom Statistics            6
22  Classroom      English          5
```

```
23 Classroom    English         4
24 Classroom    English         3
25 Classroom    Science         2
26 Classroom    Science         1
27 Classroom    Science         0
```

As before, we will create factors from our course delivery format and class subject variables, as shown in the following R code.

```
> attach(twowayexample)
> Format <- factor(Format)
> Subject <- factor(Subject)
> Format
 [1] Online    Online    Online    Online    Online    Online    Online
 [8] Online    Online    Hybrid    Hybrid    Hybrid    Hybrid    Hybrid
[15] Hybrid    Hybrid    Hybrid    Hybrid    Classroom Classroom Classroom
[22] Classroom Classroom Classroom Classroom Classroom Classroom
Levels: Classroom Hybrid Online
> Subject
 [1] Statistics Statistics Statistics English    English    English
 [7] Science    Science    Science    Statistics Statistics Statistics
[13] English    English    English    Science    Science    Science
[19] Statistics Statistics Statistics English    English    English
[25] Science    Science    Science
Levels: English Science Statistics
```

We can use the aov() function to perform the two-way ANOVA. We must specify both factors when we provide the formula for the model. As before, we will save our results and then use the summary() function to produce a summary table. First, let us find the marginal means for the delivery method and the subject. Obviously, a statistics professor who teaches online classes fabricated these data. We will use the tapply() function to get the means.

```
> tapply(Satisfaction, Format, mean)
Classroom    Hybrid    Online
        4         5         6
> tapply(Satisfaction, Subject, mean)
  English    Science Statistics
        5         2          8
```

Now, we do the two-way ANOVA as follows:

```
> summary(results)
               Df Sum Sq Mean Sq F value  Pr(>F)
Format          2     18       9       9 0.00195 **
Subject         2    162      81      81   1e-09 ***
Format:Subject  4      0       0       0 1.00000
Residuals      18     18       1
---
Signif. codes:  0 '***' 0.001 '**' 0.01 '*' 0.05 '.' 0.1 ' ' 1
```

See that the Format and Subject main effects are both significant, but that the Format × Subject interaction is not significant. Let us use the Tukey HSD criterion for our post hoc comparisons to determine which pairs of means for Format and Subject are significantly different. Note that we use the ANOVA summary results, and we must tell the TukeyHSD() function each variable for which we are interested in having the comparisons performed.

```
> TukeyHSD(results, "Format")
  Tukey multiple comparisons of means
    95 % family-wise confidence level
Fit: aov(formula = Satisfaction~Format * Subject)

$Format

                   diff       lwr      upr       p adj
Hybrid-Classroom   1-0.2031012 2.203101 0.1135025
Online-Classroom   2  0.7968988 3.203101 0.0013531
Online-Hybrid      1-0.2031012 2.203101 0.1135025


> TukeyHSD(results, "Subject")
  Tukey multiple comparisons of means
    95% family-wise confidence level
Fit: aov(formula = Satisfaction~Format * Subject)

$Subject

                   diff       lwr      upr       p adj
Science-English    -3 -4.203101 -1.796899 1.54e-05
Statistics-English  3  1.796899  4.203101 1.54e-05
Statistics-Science  6  4.796899  7.203101 0.00e+00
```

The post hoc comparisons show that the online and the classroom formats are significantly different, and that all pairs of means are different when we compare the class subjects.

# Examining Interactions

Although the interaction in our current example was not significant, when there is a significant interaction, it "trumps" the main effects. We must examine the interaction to determine its nature before we make any conclusions about the main effects. One way to do this is to look at the means, as we did above, but a more effective way is to examine an interaction plot. Here is how to build such a plot in R. We enter the x-axis factor, the "trace factor" for which the lines will be drawn, and the response variable. The default function is the mean, so we need not specify it.

```
> interaction.plot(Format, Subject, Satisfaction)
```

Figure 11-3 shows the interaction plot displayed in the R Graphics Device. The plot shows that the online courses produce higher satisfaction levels for all subjects, and that statistics is the most popular subject (this is obviously a contrived example).

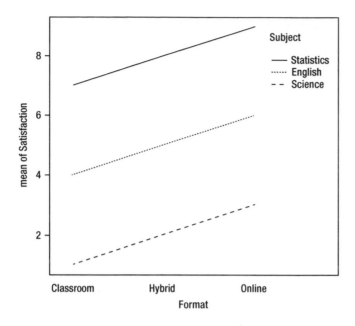

***Figure 11-3.*** *Plot showing parallel lines indicating a lack of interaction*

It is sometimes helpful to reverse the interaction plot by having the trace variable from the first plot become the *x* axis in the new plot. Here is an interaction plot with the course format as the trace variable and the class subject as the *x* axis (Figure 11-4).

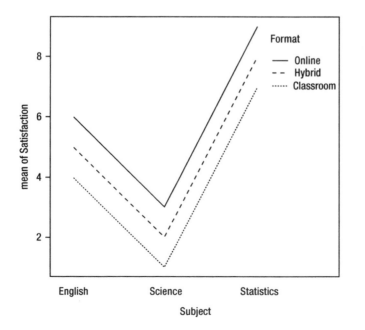

***Figure 11-4.*** *New interaction plot with Subject as the x axis*

# Plotting a Significant Interaction

Consider the following example, in which both factors and the interaction are significant. Assume we have a $3 \times 2$ factorial ANOVA. We have two medications and three different treatment conditions (*no treatment, conventional treatment,* and *experimental treatment*). We will compare the medications and the treatments, and test their possible interaction. The actual data are not presented as we merely wish to illustrate the type of graph that will appear if an interaction is present.

```
> results <- aov(Response ~ treat * drug)
> summary(results)
            Df Sum Sq Mean Sq F value   Pr(>F)
treat        2  72.47   36.23   6.858  0.00441 **
drug         1 149.63  149.63  28.322 1.84e-05 ***
treat:drug   2  38.07   19.03   3.603  0.04284 *
Residuals   24 126.80    5.28
---
Signif. codes:  0 '***' 0.001 '**' 0.01 '*' 0.05 '.' 0.1 ' ' 1
> interaction.plot(treat, drug, Response)
```

Figure 11-5 shows the interaction plot. It appears that drug 1 is more effective than drug 2, especially with treatment 3.

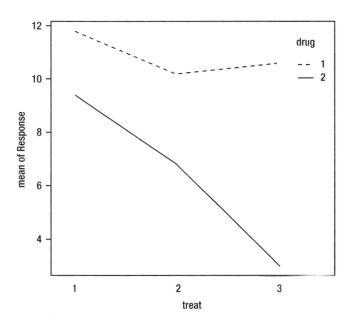

**Figure 11-5.** *Plot showing the significant interaction*

# Effect Size in the Two-Way ANOVA

In the two-way ANOVA, we can use "partial eta squared," symbolized by $\eta_p^2$, as an effect-size index. Although R does not routinely produce it, it is not difficult to calculate. We simply divide the sum of squares for each factor and the interaction by the total sum of squares. Here is the simple formula:

155

$$\eta_p^2 = \frac{SS_{effect}}{SS_{tot}}$$

To illustrate, the total sum of squares in the preceding example is
$72.467 + 149.663 + 38.067 + 126.800 = 386.967$. Dividing the treatment sum of squares by $386.967 = 72.467 / 386.967 = .19$, so we can conclude 19% of the total variation is due to treatment differences. We can calculate and interpret the partial eta squared coefficients for the drug and interaction effects in a similar fashion.

# Repeated-Measures ANOVA

The repeated-measures ANOVA is a direct extension of the paired-samples $t$ test to the examination of three or more measures for the same subjects. This is a within-subjects design in which each subject (or participant) serves as its (or his or her) own control. The advantage of the repeated-measures design is that individual differences are now considered as part of the "good" variation, and we can test their significance. The error term is thus considerably reduced, making repeated-measures ANOVA generally more powerful than between-groups (one and two-way) ANOVA. The increased power comes at a price, however, as repeated measures can lead to fatigue, learning, or order effects. We can sometimes control these effects through counterbalancing, and sometimes such effects as learning or fatigue are what we want to study.

We can consider the repeated-measures ANOVA as a special case of two-way ANOVA, in which each cell represents a single measurement for one research subject or participant. The columns are the repeated measurements, and the rows are the individual participants or subjects. The visualization of the repeated-measures ANOVA appears in Figure 11-6.

|  | Repeated Measures | | | |
|---|---|---|---|---|
|  | Column 1 | Column 2 | ... | Column $k$ |
| Row 1 |  |  | ... |  |
| Row 2 |  |  | ... |  |
| Row 3 |  |  | ... |  |
| ... | ... | ... | ... | ... |
| Row $n$ |  |  | ... |  |

*Figure 11-6.* *Visualizing the repeated-measures ANOVA*

## The Variance Partition in Repeated-Measures ANOVA

Examine Figure 11-7, which shows the variance partition for the repeated-measures ANOVA. In this analysis, individual differences are not part of the error term as they are in between-groups analyses, as we discussed above. Instead, individual differences are now part of the systematic (true) variation. Although it is possible to test the significance of individual differences with a separate $F$ ratio, this is rarely of concern to us, as we are usually convinced there will be individual differences. It is more important that we have removed this source of variation from the error term than that we can test them. The R output from the aov( ) function does not even provide the $F$ ratio for the within-subjects effect, though other programs such as Microsoft Excel do so. To perform the repeated-measures ANOVA in Excel, the user must specify the data analysis as a two-way ANOVA without replication (meaning each cell has one observation, as shown in Figure 11-8 in the next section).

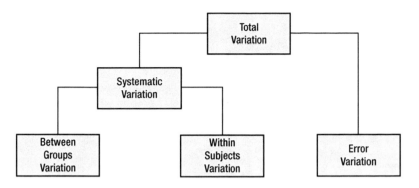

**Figure 11-7.** *The variance partition in the repeated-measures ANOVA*

## Example of a Repeated-Measures ANOVA

To conduct the repeated-measures ANOVA in R, we have to stack the data in such a way that we can use the subject identification number as a factor. We will use the same device with the mixed-factorial ANOVA, which combines between-group and within-subjects factors.

Let us use the following hypothetical data, in which the physical fitness rating on a scale of 0 (*completely unfit*) to 10 (*completely fit*) is measured in six research subjects who are engaged in a supervised residential fitness and weight loss program (think "Biggest Loser"). The fitness rating is provided by a team of exercise physiologists who combine various measurements including pulse rate, blood pressure, body mass index, body fat percentage, and vital capacity. Ratings are taken at the same time and under the same conditions every week. The first four weeks of data are as shown below:

```
> repeated <- read.csv("repeated.csv", header = TRUE)
> attach(repeated)
> repeated

   id time fitness
1   1    1       0
2   2    1       1
3   3    1       2
4   4    1       3
5   5    1       2
6   6    1       2
7   1    2       1
8   2    2       2
9   3    2       3
10  4    2       4
11  5    2       3
12  6    2       3
13  1    3       3
14  2    3       4
15  3    3       3
16  4    3       4
17  5    3       3
18  6    3       3
19  1    4       4
20  2    4       5
```

| 21 | 3 | 4 | 5 |
|----|---|---|---|
| 22 | 4 | 4 | 5 |
| 23 | 5 | 4 | 4 |
| 24 | 6 | 4 | 5 |

To understand this analysis more fully, examine the output from Microsoft Excel's Analysis ToolPak, treating the same data set as a special case of two-way ANOVA with one observation per cell (Figure 11-8). See that both the row and the column mean squares have the same error term with the within-subject (row) variation removed from the error term and treated as a separate source of systematic variation.

| ANOVA | | | | | | |
|---|---|---|---|---|---|---|
| Source of Variation | SS | df | MS | F | P-value | F crit |
| Rows | 8.333333333 | 5 | 1.666666667 | 5 | 0.006807263 | 2.901294536 |
| Columns | 28.5 | 3 | 9.5 | 28.5 | 1.92548E-06 | 3.287382105 |
| Error | 5 | 15 | 0.333333333 | | | |
| | | | | | | |
| Total | 41.83333333 | 23 | | | | |

**Figure 11-8.** *Microsoft Excel performs repeated-measures ANOVA as a special case of two-way ANOVA. Columns are the between-groups factor, and rows are individual subjects or participants*

SPSS also conducts the *F* test of the significance of the individual differences in the repeated-measures ANOVA (see Figure 11-9).

**Tests of Within-Subjects Effects**

Measure: MEASURE_1

| Source | | Type III Sum of Squares | df | Mean Square | F | Sig. |
|---|---|---|---|---|---|---|
| factor1 | Sphericity Assumed | 28.500 | 3 | 9.500 | 28.500 | .000 |
| | Greenhouse-Geisser | 28.500 | 1.271 | 22.420 | 28.500 | .001 |
| | Huynh-Feldt | 28.500 | 1.509 | 18.886 | 28.500 | .000 |
| | Lower-bound | 28.500 | 1.000 | 28.500 | 28.500 | .003 |
| Error(factor1) | Sphericity Assumed | 5.000 | 15 | .333 | | |
| | Greenhouse-Geisser | 5.000 | 6.356 | .787 | | |
| | Huynh-Feldt | 5.000 | 7.545 | .663 | | |
| | Lower-bound | 5.000 | 5.000 | 1.000 | | |

**Figure 11-9.** *SPSS output for repeated-measures ANOVA*

■ **Note**   Performing the repeated-measures ANOVA in SPSS requires the Repeated Measures SPSS add-on module. With the base version of SPSS, it is still possible to perform the repeated-measures ANOVA by treating this as a two-way ANOVA with the subject id as a random factor and time as the fixed (columns) factor. Apart from labeling, the results of the two-way ANOVA in SPSS base version will be identical to those produced by both Excel and the SPSS add-on module (see the output in Figure 11-10).

**Tests of Between-Subjects Effects**

Dependent Variable: fitness

| Source | | Type III Sum of Squares | df | Mean Square | F | Sig. |
|---|---|---|---|---|---|---|
| Intercept | Hypothesis | 228.167 | 1 | 228.167 | 136.900 | .000 |
| | Error | 8.333 | 5 | 1.667[a] | | |
| time | Hypothesis | 28.500 | 3 | 9.500 | 28.500 | .000 |
| | Error | 5.000 | 15 | .333[b] | | |
| id | Hypothesis | 8.333 | 5 | 1.667 | 5.000 | .000 |
| | Error | 5.000 | 15 | .333[b] | | |
| time * id | Hypothesis | 5.000 | 15 | .333 | . | . |
| | Error | .000 | 0 | .[c] | | |

a. MS(id)

b. MS(time * id)

c. MS(Error)

*Figure 11-10. Performing the repeated-measures ANOVA in the base version of SPSS by treating the subject id as a random factor*

To perform the same analysis in R, we identify the subject id as the within-subjects variable and treat it as a random factor. Remember to make both id and time into factors in order to perform the repeated-measures ANOVA. Unsurprisingly, we will get the same results with R that we got with SPSS and Excel.

```
> id <- factor(id)
> time <- factor(time)
> results <- aov(fitness ~ time + Error(id/time))
> summary(results)

Error: id
          Df Sum Sq Mean Sq F value Pr(>F)
Residuals  5  8.333   1.667

Error: id:time
          Df    Sum Sq  Mean Sq    F value     Pr(>F)
time       3    28.5    9.500      28.5        1.93e-06 ***
Residuals 15     5.0     .333
---
Signif. codes:  0 '***' 0.001 '**' 0.01 '*' 0.05 '.' 0.1 ' ' 1
```

Let us examine a line graph with the average fitness level plotted over time to see if the trend is a positive one (Figure 11-11). Here is the R code to summarize the means for each level and to plot the graph. We use the `tapply()` function to get the means, and use the `plot()` function, as shown in Chapter 5, to produce the line graph:

```
> result <- tapply(response, time, mean)
> plot(result, type = "o", xlab = "Time", ylab = "Fitness Level")
```

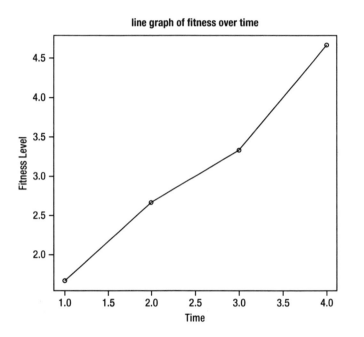

**Figure 11-11.** *Average fitness level over time*

## Effect Size for Repeated-Measures ANOVA

We also can use a partial eta squared as an effect-size index for repeated-measures ANOVA. The only minor adjustment from the formula for eta squared in two-way ANOVA is that the sum of squares for the effect in question (usually the column or treatment effect, but sometimes the within-subjects individual differences) is divided by the sum of the residual (error) sum of squares plus the particular effect sum of squares. Here is the formula:

$$\eta_p^2 = \frac{SS_{effect}}{SS_{effect} + SS_{error}}$$

# Mixed-Factorial ANOVA

It is possible to have an ANOVA in which there is at least one between-groups factor and at least one within-subjects factor. We will illustrate with a simple example in which we have two levels of a between-groups factor and three levels of a within-subjects (repeated-measures) factor. Such designs are generally known as mixed-factorial ANOVA designs, and they give us the benefits of both between-groups and within-subjects designs.

# Example of a Mixed-Factorial ANOVA

Let us consider the following data adapted from a classroom example of Dr. Gil Einstein of Furman University, a cognitive psychologist. We have a mixed-factorial design in which younger and older adults memorize words under three different distraction conditions (closed eyes, simple distraction, and complex distraction). Age is the between-groups factor, and the distraction conditions are the within-subjects factor. Note that in order to control for order effects, you could counterbalance or randomize the distraction conditions so that each subject receives them in a different order. There are 8 subjects, 4 of whom are young adults (age = 1), and the other 4 of whom are older adults (age = 2). Each person learns a different 10-item word list, matched for frequency of word use, under the three distraction conditions (1 = learning while listening to the words with one's eyes closed, 2 = learning while listening to the words while looking at an attractive photograph of a landscape, and 3 = learning while listening to the words while looking at an optical illusion showing apparent motion due to a phenomenon known as *peripheral drift*. The image was retrieved from http://www.ritsumei.ac.jp/~akitaoka/rotate-e.html.

Here is the data set, formatted for the mixed factorial ANOVA in R:

```
> mixed <- read.table("mixed.txt", header = TRUE)
> mixed
     id   age distr score
1    A  young     l     8
2    A  young     m     5
3    A  young     h     3
4    B  young     l     7
5    B  young     m     6
6    B  young     h     6
7    C  young     l     8
8    C  young     m     7
9    C  young     h     6
10   D  young     l     7
11   D  young     m     5
12   D  young     h     4
13   E    old     l     6
14   E    old     m     5
15   E    old     h     2
16   F    old     l     5
17   F    old     m     5
18   F    old     h     4
19   G    old     l     5
20   G    old     m     4
21   G    old     h     3
22   H    old     l     6
23   H    old     m     3
24   H    old     h     2
```

Now, remember to create factors from id, age, and distr. This is the code shown in the R Editor window:

```
within(mixed, {
       id <- factor(id)
       age <- factor(age)
       distr <- factor(distr)
       }
)
```

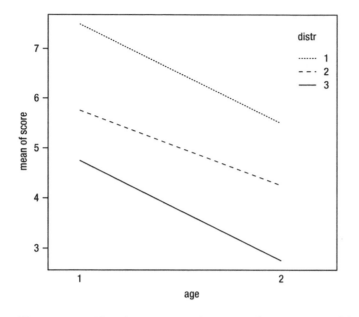

***Figure 11-12.*** *There is no apparent interaction between age and distraction*

First, let us examine a plot of the group means (see Figure 11-12).

```
> attach(mixed)
> interaction.plot(age, distr, score)
```

The ez package makes it easier to do analysis of variance. As you know by now, you must locate, download, and install the package. Figure 11-13 shows part of the R documentation for the ez package. We will make use of the ezANOVA function for our mixed-factorial design.

---

ez-package {ez}                                                      R Documentation

## Easy analysis and visualization of factorial experiments

## Description

This package facilitates easy analysis of factorial experiments, including purely within-Ss designs (a.k.a. "repeated measures"), purely between-Ss designs, and mixed within-and-between-Ss designs. The functions in this package aim to provide simple, intuitive and consistent specification of data analysis and visualization. Visualization functions also include design visualization for pre-analysis data auditing, and correlation matrix visualization. Finally, this package includes functions for non-parametric analysis, including permutation tests and bootstrap resampling. The bootstrap function obtains predictions either by cell means or by more advanced/powerful mixed effects models, yielding predictions and confidence intervals that may be easily visualized at any level of the experiment's design.

## Details

Package:    ez
Type:       Package
Version:    4.0-1
Date:       2012-08-06
License:    GPL-3
LazyLoad: yes

This package contains several useful functions:

- ezANOVA Provides simple interface to ANOVA, including assumption checks.

- ezBoot Computes bootstrap resampled cell means or lmer predictions

- ezCor Function to plot a correlation matrix with scatterplots, linear fits, and univariate density plots

---

**Figure 11-13.** *Part of the R documentation for the ez package*

Note that the ezANOVA function produces an ANOVA summary table and that age and distraction are both significant, but that as we predicted from our interaction plot, the interaction is not significant. Note that the ezANOVA function also runs a sphericity test, just as SPSS does with repeated measures (within-subjects) designs. The sphericity assumption is that the covariance matrices of the repeated measures are equal. Violation of this assumption will make it necessary to perform a corrected test.

We must tell the ezANOVA function where our data are stored, what the dependent variable is, what the subject id is, what the within-subjects (repeated measures) factor is, and what the between-groups factor is. If you have more than one within factor, or more than one between-groups factor, you must produce a list of the variable names.

```
> ezANOVA(mixed, score, id, distr, between = age)
$ANOVA
      Effect DFn DFd         F           p p<.05        ges
2        age   1   6 15.7826087 0.007343975     * 0.54260090
3      distr   2  12 19.5000000 0.000169694     * 0.64084507
4 age:distr   2  12  0.2142857 0.810140233       0.01923077
```

```
$'Mauchly's Test for Sphericity'
     Effect         W          p p<.05
3      distr 0.5395408 0.2138261
4 age:distr 0.5395408 0.2138261

$'Sphericity Corrections'
     Effect      GGe       p[GG] p[GG]<.05        HFe        p[HF] p[HF]<.05
3      distr 0.6847162 0.001321516         * 0.8191249 0.0005484227         *
4 age:distr 0.6847162 0.729793578           0.8191249 0.7686615724
Effect Size for the Mixed-Factorial ANOVA
```

Just as does SPSS, ezANOVA runs the Mauchly test for sphericity, and proposes a correction. In our case, the sphericity assumption can be assumed to have been met because the $p$ values are greater than .05.

For the mixed-factorial ANOVA, we can use a partial eta squared as our effect-size index, as we discussed above for two-way and repeated-measures ANOVAs. The sum of squares for the effect under consideration is divided by the sum of that effect plus the relevant error term.

To find out more about mixed-factorial ANOVA and more complex factorial designs, with and without within-subjects factors, you can consult the R and ANOVA tutorial posted at the R personality project. Code snippets and data files are available there as well. Here is the URL:

```
http://personality-project.org/r/r.anova.html
```

# Conclusion

We covered a lot of ground in this chapter. You learned how to conduct and interpret two-way, repeated-measures, and mixed-factorial ANOVAs. In Chapter 12, you will learn simple (bivariate) correlation and regression. In Chapter 13, you will learn multiple regression and correlation, and as a bonus, I will show you the underlying general model that makes ANOVA and $t$ tests a special case of regression, and how you can use multiple regression instead of ANOVA to accomplish the same result with more information than you get from ANOVA.

# CHAPTER 12

■ ■ ■

# Correlation and Regression

In Chapter 12 you learn simple (bivariate) correlation and regression. You discover how to use the R functions for correlation and regression and how to calculate and interpret correlation coefficients and regression equations. You also learn about fitting a curvilinear model and about confidence and prediction intervals for regression models. In Chapter 13, we will build on what you learn here, with multiple correlation and regression. In Chapter 13, you will also learn that ANOVAs and $t$ tests are special cases of regression. All these techniques are based on the same underlying general linear model.

Correlation and regression are versatile techniques used in a wide variety of practical applications from production forecasting to graduate admissions to selecting human resources. It is important to note that we are dealing (at least initially) with the determination of the degree (if any) of linear relationship between two variables measured at the interval or ratio level. If the linear relationship is not a good fit, you can try other kinds of fit, as you will learn.

## Covariance and Correlation

To help us understand *correlation*, let us first understand the term *covariance*. We have pairs of $(x, y)$ observations, where $x$ is the *predictor* (or independent) variable and $y$ is the *criterion* (or dependent) variable. We define the covariance of $x$ and $y$ as follows:

$$\sigma_{xy} = \frac{\sum (x - \mu_x)(y - \mu_y)}{N}$$

As the above formula shows, the covariance in the population is the sum of the cross products of the deviation scores for x and y divided by the number of pairs of observations. So, the covariance is by definition the average of the deviation cross products. In the absence of population data, we use sample estimators of the population parameters, along with the familiar $n - 1$ correction for degrees of freedom. The sample covariance is therefore defined as

$$s_{xy} = \frac{\sum (x - \bar{x})(y - \bar{y})}{n - 1}$$

We will find that $x$ and $y$ may have a positive covariance, negative covariance, or zero covariance. When the two variables have a positive covariance, increases in $x$ are associated with increases in $y$. When the two variables have a negative covariance, increases in $x$ are associated with decreases in $y$. We might expect two variables to covary because they have an obvious relationship, or because they are both affected by a third variable. For example, the number of births in the Stockholm area covaries positively with the number of storks. This is not because storks bring babies, but because both the number of storks and the number of humans born (because of denser population) are positively related to the proximity of water. Similarly, the crime rate covaries positively with the consumption of ice cream because both are affected by the weather. Both ice cream eating citizens and crime-committing criminals come out when the weather is nice. Some variables covary negatively, such as the demand for gasoline and the price of gasoline. We will discuss gas prices in more detail later in this chapter.

The covariance is obviously affected by the units of measurement of $x$ and $y$. Dividing the covariance by the product of the standard deviations of $x$ and $y$ produces a "scaleless" quantity known as the Pearson product-moment correlation coefficient. This coefficient ranges from −1 (representing a perfect *negative* or inverse relationship) through 0 (representing no relationship) to +1 (representing a perfect *positive* or direct relationship). We define the population correlation as

$$\rho_{xy} = \frac{\sigma_{xy}}{\sigma_x \sigma_y}$$

and the sample correlation coefficient as

$$r_{xy} = \frac{s_{xy}}{s_x s_y}$$

The R functions for covariance and correlation are cov() and cor(), respectively. You can supply two or more vectors of data to these functions. With two variables, you will get the covariance or the correlation. With more than two variables, you will get a *variance-covariance* matrix or an *intercorrelation* matrix.

To illustrate, assume we are able to find the heights in inches of the 40 adult men who exercise regularly. In actuality, I used the rnorm() function to generate a vector of heights with a mean of 70 (roughly the population mean), and a standard deviation of 6 inches. We will use the heights to predict the weights, so height is our $x$ variable and weight is our $y$ variable. Here is the R code to produce both vectors and show them in a side-by-side display by using the cbind function to produce a matrix.

```
> y <- sort(weights)
> y
 [1] 119.5 135.0 137.1 137.4 139.0 144.1 144.2 151.0 151.3 151.8 152.6 156.3
[13] 161.9 162.4 164.2 164.7 166.1 166.8 169.1 169.8 170.1 172.9 173.3 174.8
[25] 175.2 175.8 176.7 179.3 186.6 189.1 191.1 193.8 198.0 201.5 204.6 209.4
[37] 213.3 214.5 220.6 237.1

> x <- sort(rnorm(40, 70, 6))
> x
 [1] 58.03935 58.58117 60.12779 60.56782 61.83636 63.16131 63.22292 63.90711
 [9] 64.00655 65.25664 66.03604 66.39076 66.94539 68.10087 68.49093 68.50907
[17] 68.54162 68.62249 68.87835 68.88471 69.04019 69.14772 69.55085 69.61059
[25] 69.68665 69.80350 70.33496 71.26252 71.66794 71.92322 72.62133 72.98732
[33] 73.07877 73.49751 73.83431 78.55792 79.05835 79.93153 81.51535 81.74791

> matrix <- cbind(x, y)
```

Here are the first few rows of the matrix:

```
> head(matrix)
            x      y
[1,] 58.03935  119.5
[2,] 58.58117  135.0
```

```
[3,] 60.12779    137.1
[4,] 60.56782    137.4
[5,] 61.83636    139.0
[6,] 63.16131    144.1
```

We expect the covariance to be positive, and the correlation to be high because of the way we created the data vectors by sorting them in ascending order. Indeed, that is the case.

```
> cov(x,y)
[1] 151.0893
> cor(x,y)
[1] 0.9837487
```

We examine the scatterplot of *x* and *y* and see that there is very nearly a straight-line relationship (see Figure 12-1). The fit line was added, which you learned how to do in Chapter 5.

```
> plot(x, y, xlab = "height", ylab = "weight", main = "weights and heights")
```

Recall the use of the lm() function (for *linear model*) to fit the regression line.

```
> abline(lm(y ~ x))
```

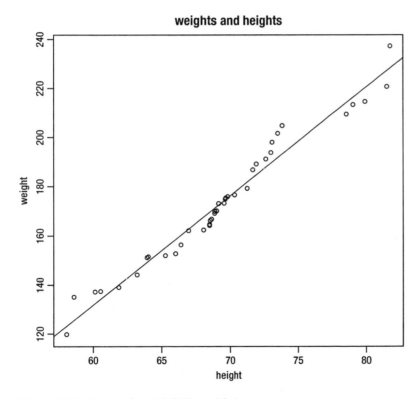

**Figure 12-1.** *Scatterplot with fit line added*

When there are three or more variables, we get a variance-covariance matrix or an intercorrelation matrix. Assume we add a *z* vector, which represents the resting pulse rates of the same 40 men who exercise regularly. Once again, I used the rnorm() function to generate the hypothetical data.

```
> z <- rnorm(40, 80, 10)
> z <- sort(z)
> z
 [1] 61.98885 62.84723 64.09291 65.85234 69.88917 72.11705 72.30176 72.45145
 [9] 73.09158 73.90444 73.91047 74.27552 74.53339 76.14059 76.14097 78.06199
[17] 78.20871 80.22371 81.35179 81.88351 83.04181 83.11799 83.33354 85.16001
[25] 85.70716 86.20246 86.55275 87.85077 88.43049 89.81758 91.15570 91.21423
[33] 91.54873 91.68754 91.77207 91.82445 92.58965 94.67990 95.34544 96.58870
```

The cov and cor functions are vectorized for both matrices and data frames. When you supply a matrix, you get a variance-covariance or an intercorrelation matrix, as we discussed above. We will examine a few of the cells to show the structure of the output matrices.

```
> matrix <- cbind(x,y,z)
> cov(matrix)
          x          y          z
x  34.03226  151.0893   53.20128
y 151.08927  693.1195  242.81819
z  53.20128  242.8182   92.24384

> cor(matrix)
          x          y          z
x 1.0000000 0.9837487 0.9495286
y 0.9837487 1.0000000 0.9603034
z 0.9495286 0.9603034 1.0000000
```

The variances are on the diagonal of the variance-covariance matrix, and the matrix is symmetric. Similarly, the correlation of each variable with itself is 1, and these 1 s make up the diagonal of the correlation matrix. Examine the code below to verify this.

```
> var(x)
[1] 34.03226
> cov(x,y)
[1] 151.0893
> cov(x,z)
[1] 53.20128
> cor(x,z)
[1] 0.9495286
```

# Regression

Francis Galton (1822 – 1911), who was a cousin of Charles Darwin, developed the idea of regression. He documented that the sons of tall men tended to be shorter than their fathers, and that the sons of short men tended to be taller than their fathers. Galton called this phenomenon "regression toward mediocrity," but today we call it "regression to the mean." Galton's student and intellectual protégé, Karl Pearson, worked out the mathematical formulas for correlation and regression, and thus we get the name Pearson product-moment correlation. The *r* used to symbolize the correlation coefficient is from the word *regression*.

It is helpful to see the direct connection between correlation and regression. We have a linear equation of the following form:

$$\hat{y} = a + bx$$

where $\hat{y}$ is the predicted value of $y$, $a$ is the y intercept term, and $b$ is the regression (slope) coefficient. First let us calculate the regression coefficient as follows:

$$b = r_{xy}\left(\frac{s_y}{s_x}\right)$$

This is the familiar slope term. In the simple bivariate case, testing the significance of the slope is equivalent to testing the significance of the correlation coefficient, and the standardized regression coefficient is equal to the correlation coefficient. To see why, note that when the variables are standardized, the standard deviations are both 1.

The intercept term, $a$, is found as follows:

$$a = \bar{y} - b\bar{x}$$

R gives us both these terms when we use the lm() function and specify the formula lm(y ~ x). Let us turn to a more realistic example, in which we obtain the grade point averages (GPAs) of 20 college students along with the number of hours each student studies per week (see below). We find the two variables are highly correlated, and we then use the lm() function to find the slope and intercept terms.

```
> hours
```

|    | Hours | GPA  |
|----|-------|------|
| 1  | 10    | 3.33 |
| 2  | 12    | 2.92 |
| 3  | 10    | 2.56 |
| 4  | 15    | 3.08 |
| 5  | 14    | 3.57 |
| 6  | 12    | 3.31 |
| 7  | 13    | 3.45 |
| 8  | 15    | 3.93 |
| 9  | 16    | 3.82 |
| 10 | 14    | 3.70 |
| 11 | 13    | 3.26 |
| 12 | 12    | 3.00 |
| 13 | 11    | 2.74 |
| 14 | 10    | 2.85 |
| 15 | 13    | 3.33 |
| 16 | 13    | 3.29 |
| 17 | 14    | 3.58 |
| 18 | 18    | 3.85 |
| 19 | 17    | 4.00 |
| 20 | 14    | 3.50 |

The correlation is .82:

```
> cor(Hours, GPA)
```

[1] 0.8174763

The linear model shows us that $a = 1.3728$ and $b = 0.1489$.

```
> lm(GPA ~ Hours)

Call:
lm(formula = GPA ~ Hours)

Coefficients:
(Intercept)          Hours
     1.3728         0.1489
```

As mentioned above, we can test the significance of the regression coefficient and of the correlation coefficient. We use a *t* test (or an equivalent analysis of variance) to determine whether these coefficients are statistically significantly different from zero. Let us apply the summary() function to our linear model and see what we find:

```
> results <- lm(GPA ~ Hours)
> summary(results)

Call:
lm(formula = GPA ~ Hours)

Residuals:
     Min       1Q   Median       3Q      Max
-0.52668 -0.17079  0.03171  0.12698  0.46796

Coefficients:
            Estimate Std. Error t value Pr(>|t|)
(Intercept)  1.37276    0.33329   4.119 0.000645 ***
Hours        0.14893    0.02473   6.022 1.08e-05 ***
---
Signif. codes:  0 '***' 0.001 '**' 0.01 '*' 0.05 '.' 0.1 ' ' 1

Residual standard error: 0.24 on 18 degrees of freedom
Multiple R-squared: 0.6683,     Adjusted R-squared: 0.6498
F-statistic: 36.26 on 1 and 18 DF,  p-value: 1.078e-05
```

As a matter of more than a little statistical interest, note that the *F* statistic testing the significance of the overall regression is the square of the *t* statistic testing the significance of the regression coefficient, and that the two *p* values are identical. The correct interpretation of the regression equation is that a student who did not study would have an estimated GPA of 1.3728, and that for every 1-hour increase in study time, the estimated GPA would increase by 0.1489 points. There is obviously a point at which this equation breaks down, as a 4.0 GPA is the maximum possible.

For instructive purposes, let us calculate a vector of predicted scores using the regression equation and also a vector of "residuals," which are the differences between the observed values of *y* (in this case, GPA) and the predicted values. To facilitate regression analysis, it is helpful to load the car (for *Companion to Applied Regression*) and stats packages. We can then achieve various goals without writing our own R functions. For example, to get the vector of predicted values, use the predict() function in the stats package. To get the vector of residuals, use the residuals() function in the same package. See the use of these functions in the following R output. We use cbind() to put the results in a column:

```
> predicted <- predict(results)
> predicted
> cbind(predicted)
   predicted
1    2.862038
2    3.159894
3    2.862038
4    3.606677
5    3.457749
6    3.159894
7    3.308822
8    3.606677
9    3.755605
10   3.457749
11   3.308822
12   3.159894
13   3.010966
14   2.862038
15   3.308822
16   3.308822
17   3.457749
18   4.053461
19   3.904533
20   3.457749
```

Now, let us compare the observed GPAs, the predicted GPAs, and the residuals:

```
> resid <- residuals(results)
> cbind(GPA, predicted, resid)
    GPA predicted        resid
1  3.33  2.862038  0.46796178
2  2.92  3.159894 -0.23989384
3  2.56  2.862038 -0.30203822
4  3.08  3.606677 -0.52667728
5  3.57  3.457749  0.11225053
6  3.31  3.159894  0.15010616
7  3.45  3.308822  0.14117834
8  3.93  3.606677  0.32332272
9  3.82  3.755605  0.06439490
10 3.70  3.457749  0.24225053
11 3.26  3.308822 -0.04882166
12 3.00  3.159894 -0.15989384
13 2.74  3.010966 -0.27096603
14 2.85  2.862038 -0.01203822
15 3.33  3.308822  0.02117834
16 3.29  3.308822 -0.01882166
17 3.58  3.457749  0.12225053
18 3.85  4.053461 -0.20346072
19 4.00  3.904533  0.09546709
20 3.50  3.457749  0.04225053
```

As you will learn in depth in Chapter 13, ANOVA and regression are closely related. We can perform an ANOVA on the results of our regression analysis with some interesting and useful results. But first, let us explore the relationships among the observed, predicted, and residual values we just calculated. We will calculate the sums of the squares of each by use of simple R formulas. We will call these the total sum of squares, the regression sum of squares, and the residual sum of squares—which we calculate as the sum of the squared residuals (see below).

```
> SStot <- sum((GPA - mean(GPA))^2)
> SStot
[1] 3.126455

> SSreg <- sum((predicted - mean(predicted))^2)
> SSreg
[1] 2.089308

> SSres <- sum(residual ^ 2)
> SSres
[1] 1.037147
```

The total degrees of freedom are the number of pairs of observations minus 1, for 20 – 1 = 19. The degrees of freedom for regression (Hours) are the number of variables minus 1, for 2 – 1 = 1. The residual degrees of freedom are the number of pairs minus 2, for 20 – 2 = 18. The total mean square is our familiar overall variance. We can calculate each mean square by dividing each sum of squares by its relevant degrees of freedom. We then can calculate an $F$ ratio to test the significance of the overall regression by dividing the regression mean square by the residual mean square:

```
> MSreg <- SSreg / 1
> MSreg
[1] 2.089308
> MSres <- SSres / 18
> MSres
[1] 0.05761926
> Fratio <- MSreg / MSres
> Fratio
[1] 36.26059
>
```

You should understand the relationship of the value of $r^2$ to the eta squared we calculated in Chapter 11. Recall that the treatment sum of squares divided by the total sum of squares in an ANOVA produces the ratio known as eta squared. In regression, dividing the regression sum of squares by the total sum of squares produces a value we know as $r^2$, the "coefficient of determination." This value is equivalent to eta squared calculated in an ANOVA. As with eta squared, $r^2$ can be directly interpreted as a percentage of variation. In this case, $r^2$ represents the percentage of the total variation that can be accounted for (explained or predicted) by the regression model. Examine the following output:

```
> rsquare <- SSreg / SStot
> rsquare
[1] 0.6682675
```

Keeping all this in mind, let us use the anova() function from the stats package. Note that the values we calculated above are duplicated in the ANOVA output.

```
> anova(results)
Analysis of Variance Table

Response: GPA
          Df Sum Sq Mean Sq F value    Pr(>F)
Hours      1 2.0893 2.08931  36.261 1.078e-05 ***
Residuals 18 1.0372 0.05762
---
Signif. codes:  0 '***' 0.001 '**' 0.01 '*' 0.05 '.' 0.1 ' ' 1
```

The anova() function labels the regression sum of squares as "Hours," and reports the same values of the sums of squares that we calculated with formulas. The Anova() (with a capital A) function in the car package also produces the same ANOVA summary table (see below). Remember you must download and install the car package in order to use its functions. If you have not loaded car into your workspace after installing it, you can do so by using the require() function.

```
> require(car)
Loading required package: car
Loading required package: MASS
Loading required package: nnet
> Anova(results)
Anova Table (Type II tests)

Response: GPA
          Sum Sq Df F value    Pr(>F)
Hours     2.0893  1  36.261 1.078e-05 ***
Residuals 1.0372 18
---
Signif. codes:  0 '***' 0.001 '**' 0.01 '*' 0.05 '.' 0.1 ' ' 1
```

Recall from the previous example of the lm() function that we can get both the regression equation and $r^2$ from the summary() function.

```
> summary(results)

Call:
lm(formula = GPA ~ Hours)

Residuals:
    Min      1Q  Median      3Q     Max
-0.52668 -0.17079 0.03171 0.12698 0.46796

Coefficients:
            Estimate Std. Error t value Pr(>|t|)
(Intercept)  1.37276    0.33329   4.119 0.000645 ***
Hours        0.14893    0.02473   6.022 1.08e-05 ***
---
Signif. codes:  0 '***' 0.001 '**' 0.01 '*' 0.05 '.' 0.1 ' ' 1

Residual standard error: 0.24 on 18 degrees of freedom
Multiple R-squared: 0.6683,    Adjusted R-squared: 0.6498
F-statistic: 36.26 on 1 and 18 DF,  p-value: 1.078e-05
```

The summary() function provides all the necessary information for interpreting the regression.

# An Example: Predicting the Price of Gasoline

The U.S. city average price of regular unleaded gasoline from 1982 to 2011, based on the Consumer Price Index Average Price data, can be obtained from the Bureau of Labor web site:

```
http://data.bls.gov/cgi-bin/surveymost?ap
```

In this extended example, we'll first examine the linear relationship between the annual city average price of gasoline and the year (really, an index number based on the year number, starting with 1 to make the calculations more sensible). We will then fit a curvilinear model to the same data to determine if the curvilinear model is better than a linear one. Here is the data:

```
> gas_prices <- read.csv("gas_prices.csv", header = TRUE)
> gas_prices
   Year   Jan   Feb   Mar   Apr   May   Jun   Jul   Aug   Sep   Oct   Nov   Dec average index
1  1982 1.358 1.334 1.284 1.225 1.237 1.309 1.331 1.323 1.307 1.295 1.283 1.260   1.296     1
2  1983 1.230 1.187 1.152 1.215 1.259 1.277 1.288 1.285 1.274 1.255 1.241 1.231   1.241     2
3  1984 1.216 1.209 1.210 1.227 1.236 1.229 1.212 1.196 1.203 1.209 1.207 1.193   1.212     3
4  1985 1.148 1.131 1.159 1.205 1.231 1.241 1.242 1.229 1.216 1.204 1.207 1.208   1.202     4
5  1986 1.194 1.120 0.981 0.888 0.923 0.955 0.890 0.843 0.860 0.831 0.821 0.823   0.927     5
6  1987 0.862 0.905 0.912 0.934 0.941 0.958 0.971 0.995 0.990 0.976 0.976 0.961   0.948     6
7  1988 0.933 0.913 0.904 0.930 0.955 0.955 0.967 0.987 0.974 0.957 0.949 0.930   0.946     7
8  1989 0.918 0.926 0.940 1.065 1.119 1.114 1.092 1.057 1.029 1.027 0.999 0.980   1.022     8
9  1990 1.042 1.037 1.023 1.044 1.061 1.088 1.084 1.190 1.294 1.378 1.377 1.354   1.164     9
10 1991 1.247 1.143 1.082 1.104 1.156 1.160 1.127 1.140 1.143 1.122 1.134 1.123   1.140    10
11 1992 1.073 1.054 1.058 1.079 1.136 1.179 1.174 1.158 1.158 1.154 1.159 1.136   1.127    11
12 1993 1.117 1.108 1.098 1.112 1.129 1.130 1.109 1.097 1.085 1.127 1.113 1.070   1.108    12
13 1994 1.043 1.051 1.045 1.064 1.080 1.106 1.136 1.182 1.177 1.152 1.163 1.143   1.112    13
14 1995 1.129 1.120 1.115 1.140 1.200 1.226 1.195 1.164 1.148 1.127 1.101 1.101   1.147    14
15 1996 1.129 1.124 1.162 1.251 1.323 1.299 1.272 1.240 1.234 1.227 1.250 1.260   1.231    15
16 1997 1.261 1.255 1.235 1.231 1.226 1.229 1.205 1.253 1.277 1.242 1.213 1.177   1.234    16
17 1998 1.131 1.082 1.041 1.052 1.092 1.094 1.079 1.052 1.033 1.042 1.028 0.986   1.059    17
18 1999 0.972 0.955 0.991 1.177 1.178 1.148 1.189 1.255 1.280 1.274 1.264 1.298   1.165    18
19 2000 1.301 1.369 1.541 1.506 1.498 1.617 1.593 1.510 1.582 1.559 1.555 1.489   1.510    19
20 2001 1.472 1.484 1.447 1.564 1.729 1.640 1.482 1.427 1.531 1.362 1.263 1.131   1.461    20
21 2002 1.139 1.130 1.241 1.407 1.421 1.404 1.412 1.423 1.422 1.449 1.448 1.394   1.358    21
22 2003 1.473 1.641 1.748 1.659 1.542 1.514 1.524 1.628 1.728 1.603 1.535 1.494   1.591    22
23 2004 1.592 1.672 1.766 1.833 2.009 2.041 1.939 1.898 1.891 2.029 2.010 1.882   1.880    23
24 2005 1.823 1.918 2.065 2.283 2.216 2.176 2.316 2.506 2.927 2.785 2.343 2.186   2.295    24
25 2006 2.315 2.310 2.401 2.757 2.947 2.917 2.999 2.985 2.589 2.272 2.241 2.334   2.589    25
26 2007 2.274 2.285 2.592 2.860 3.130 3.052 2.961 2.782 2.789 2.793 3.069 3.020   2.801    26
27 2008 3.047 3.033 3.258 3.441 3.764 4.065 4.090 3.786 3.698 3.173 2.151 1.689   3.266    27
28 2009 1.787 1.928 1.949 2.056 2.265 2.631 2.543 2.627 2.574 2.561 2.660 2.621   2.350    28
29 2010 2.731 2.659 2.780 2.858 2.869 2.736 2.736 2.745 2.704 2.795 2.852 2.985   2.788    29
30 2011 3.091 3.167 3.546 3.816 3.933 3.702 3.654 3.630 3.612 3.468 3.423 3.278   3.527    30
```

Let us create a plot of the gas prices by year and a linear model fit to the plot:

```
>attach(gas_prices)
> plot(index, average)
> abline(lm(average ~ index))
```

Examine the plot in Figure 12-2. It appears that a linear fit is not the best model for describing the increases in gas prices over the years.

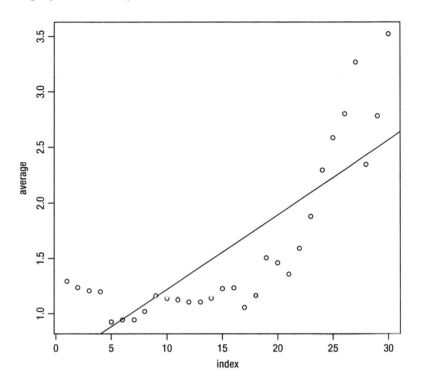

**Figure 12-2.** *The trend of rising gasoline prices over time does not appear to be linear in nature*

## Examining the Linear Relationship

Even with the visible departure from linearity, the linear relationship is statistically significant, as shown in the following regression analysis of the linear relationship between year and annual gas price.

```
> results <- lm(average ~ index)
> summary(results)

Call:
lm(formula = average ~ index)

Residuals:
    Min      1Q   Median      3Q      Max
-0.63185 -0.32280 -0.07582  0.34223  0.96130

Coefficients:
            Estimate Std. Error t value Pr(>|t|)
(Intercept) 0.546800   0.167200   3.270  0.00285 **
index       0.067297   0.009418   7.145 8.93e-08 ***
---
Signif. codes:  0 '***' 0.001 '**' 0.01 '*' 0.05 '.' 0.1 ' ' 1
```

```
Residual standard error: 0.4465 on 28 degrees of freedom
Multiple R-squared: 0.6458,     Adjusted R-squared: 0.6332
F-statistic: 51.06 on 1 and 28 DF,  p-value: 8.93e-08
```

## Fitting a Quadratic Model

We can account for roughly 65 % of the variability in gas prices by knowing the year. But what happens when we fit a *quadratic* model to the same data? We will calculate a new vector, the square of the index, and then fit a quadratic model as follows:

$$y = a + b_1 x + b_2 x^2$$

We are now broaching the subject of multiple regression, but in this case, the dual predictors are simply the raw score for the year index, and the same value squared. This will make our equation a second-order one. This is a common practice in curve-fitting analyses. We will discuss multiple regression in Chapter 13. Let us create the vector of squared values and use the cbind() function to add the values to our gas_prices data frame.

```
> indexsq <- index ^ 2
> indexsq
 [1]   1   4   9  16  25  36  49  64  81 100 121 144 169 196 225 256 289 324 361 400 441 484 529
576
[25] 625 676 729 784 841 900
> gas_prices <- cbind(gas_prices, indexsq)
```

We ultimately are still calculating a linear model by adding the squared term to make our model quadratic, because we are calculating the linear relationship between the observed prices and our linear combination of the index and squared index values. Here is the new model. We will then do a regression analysis to see if the fit is better than that of the original linear model.

```
> results <- lm(average ~ index + indexsq)
> summary(results)

Call:
lm(formula = average ~ index + indexsq)

Residuals:
     Min       1Q   Median       3Q      Max
-0.53327 -0.12358  0.02925  0.13339  0.58345

Coefficients:
             Estimate Std. Error t value Pr(>|t|)
(Intercept)  1.4659552  0.1350768  10.853 2.38e-11 ***
index       -0.1050448  0.0200863  -5.230 1.64e-05 ***
indexsq      0.0055594  0.0006287   8.843 1.85e-09 ***
---
Signif. codes:  0 '***' 0.001 '**' 0.01 '*' 0.05 '.' 0.1 ' ' 1

Residual standard error: 0.2304 on 27 degrees of freedom
Multiple R-squared: 0.9091,     Adjusted R-squared: 0.9024
F-statistic:   135 on 2 and 27 DF,  p-value: 8.73e-15
```

The quadratic model clearly does a better job of fitting the data than does the linear model. We can now account for 91% of the variation in in gas prices by using our quadratic model. R's plot function can be applied to the results of our linear fit model with beneficial results. In reality, you are using the plot.lm function, but the plot function recognizes our model as an object of the class "lm," so you can leave that out. See the following code to verify this.

```
> class(results)
[1] "lm"
```

In particular, we will receive four useful diagnostic plots based on the "residuals," which are the differences between the observed and predicted values of y. You will have to press <Enter> to advance from one plot to the next.

```
> results <- lm(average ~ index + indexsq)
> plot(results)
Waiting to confirm page change...
Waiting to confirm page change...
Waiting to confirm page change...
Waiting to confirm page change...
```

See the four plots on the following pages. Each provides helpful information about the regression model. First, we see in Figure 12-3 the plot of the residuals against the fitted values.

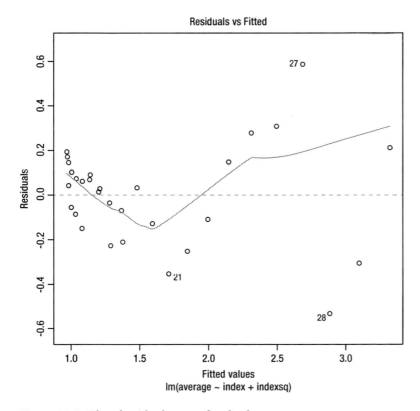

*Figure 12-3.* *Plot of residuals versus fitted values*

Next, we examine the scale-location plot in Figure 12-4.

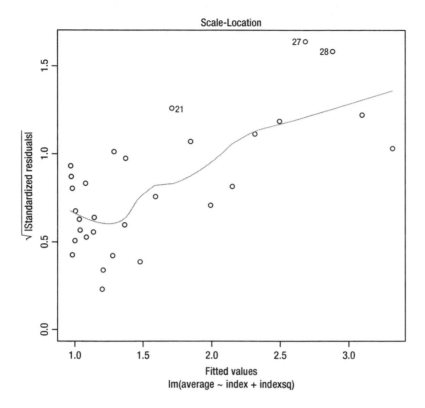

***Figure 12-4.*** *Scale location plot*

In particular, examine Figure 12-5 to see the normal Q-Q (quantile-quantile) plot derived from using the plot function with our results. With the exception of a couple of outliers, the virtual straight-line nature of this plot shows the quadratic model is an excellent fit. The rapid drop in oil prices that occurred in the year 2009 caused the strange residuals for years 27 and 28. If you remember the news from that year, many analysts attributed the drop, which was followed by a fairly quick correction, to speculation in the oil markets.

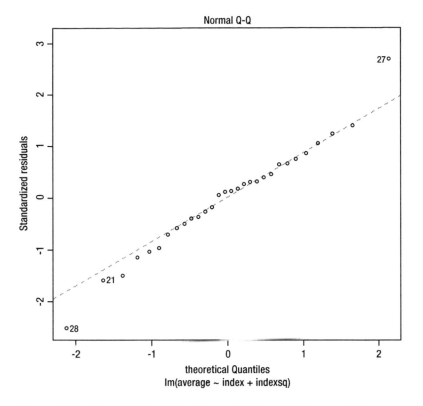

***Figure 12-5.*** *Normal Q-Q plot for the quadratic model shows good fit*

The residuals versus leverage plot appears in Figure 12-6.

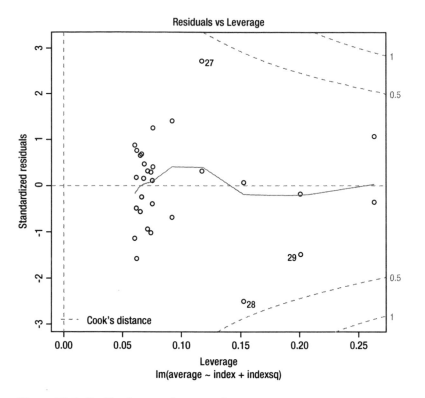

**Figure 12-6.** *Residuals versus leverage plot*

Let us use the predict() function to produce the predicted gasoline prices from the quadratic model. We will call the predicted value predquad.

```
> predquad <- predict(results)
> gas_prices <- cbind(gas_prices, predquad)
```

Note the considerably better fit of the quadratic model to the observed data (see Figure 12-7). I used the lines() function to add the predicted values from the new regression equation with the quadratic term added. Here is the R code to produce the plot and add the line.

```
> plot(index, average, main = "quadratic model")
> lines(predquad)
```

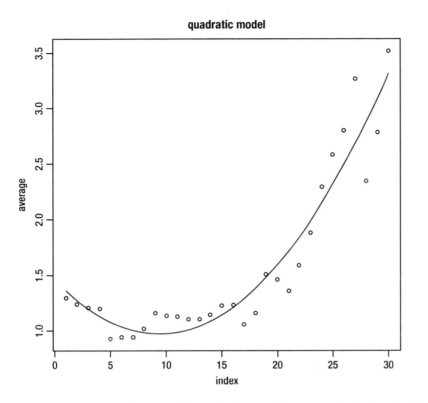

**Figure 12-7.** *The quadratic model fits the observed data more closely than the linear model does*

---

■ **Note** The quadratic model obviously works well, and certainly better than the linear one. You can also try fitting other curvilinear models to the data, with perhaps even better results than those we obtained with the quadratic model. Possible candidates are a *power* curve, a *logarithmic* curve, or an *exponential* curve. Consult a good statistics or multiple regression text to understand these additional models.

---

# Determining Confidence and Prediction Intervals

For our final topic in this chapter, let us turn our attention to the calculation and interpretation of confidence and prediction intervals for a regression model. In the process, you will learn about the *standard error of estimate*. We will use the *t* distribution for our confidence and prediction intervals. Let us continue to work with the gasoline-price data set.

First, let us define the standard error of estimate:

$$s_{y \cdot x} = \sqrt{\frac{\sum (y - \hat{y})^2}{n - 2}}$$

The standard error of estimate is the square root of the residual mean square, and is an estimate of the population standard deviation for *y* at a given value of *x*. If the standard error is small, the data points will lie close to the line of best fit, and if it is large, there is more dispersion in the data points, and many of them will lie farther away from the line of best fit.

We assume the error terms (residuals) are normally distributed and have equal variances at all levels of $y$. However, as we go farther into the extremes of the x distribution, we will see that the errors tend to increase on both ends of the scale, which means that we will do less well with our predictions at smaller and larger values of $x$ than we will in the middle of the scale. We can show this graphically by creating confidence and prediction intervals. The confidence interval is an interval describing the ranges of the means of $y$ for each value of $x$. The prediction interval, on the other hand, describes the ranges of the predicted individual values of $y$ for each value of $x$. For this reason, the prediction interval will always be wider than the confidence interval.

We define the confidence interval this way:

$$y \pm t(s_{y \cdot x}) \sqrt{\frac{1}{n} + \frac{(x - x)^2}{\sum (x - \overline{x})^2}}$$

The prediction interval is defined as:

$$y \pm t(s_{y \cdot x}) \sqrt{1 + \frac{1}{n} + \frac{(x - x)^2}{\sum (x - \overline{x})^2}}$$

Let us determine the confidence and prediction intervals for the predicted $y$ values for our linear model and compare those to the confidence and prediction intervals for the predicted $y$ values using the quadratic model. The predict() function in the stats package allows us to produce both confidence and prediction intervals. See the following R code:

```
> results <- lm(average ~ index)
> predlin <- predict(results)
> conf <- predict(results, interval = "confidence")
> pred <- predict(results, interval = "prediction")
Warning message:
In predict.lm(results, interval = "prediction") :
  Predictions on current data refer to _future_ responses
```

Now, we will plot the averages against the index number along with the fit line, the confidence interval, and the prediction interval, as discussed above. Let us display both of these on a plot for the linear model to predict gasoline prices. See Figure 12-8, in which the line of best fit is surrounded by first the confidence interval and then the prediction interval. The more generous limits of the prediction interval are obvious, and all the individual observed data values are within (or on) the prediction interval. Here is the R code to produce the plot. We use the points() function to add the confidence and prediction intervals so we can use different colors.

```
> plot(index, average)
> lines(fit)
> points(conflwr, col = "blue", type = "l")
> points(confupr, col = "blue", type = "l")
> points(predlwr, col = "red", type = "l")
> points(predupr, col = "red", type = "l")
```

Observe in Figure 12-8 that the confidence interval indeed widens at both ends of the $x$ scale and narrows in the center, as mentioned above.

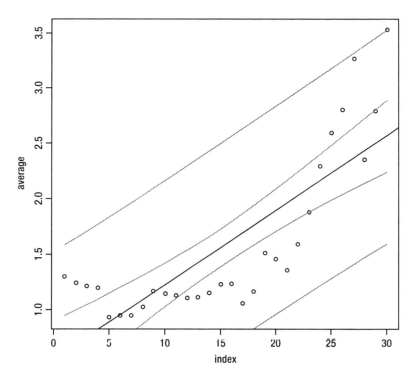

**Figure 12-8.** *Fit line surrounded by confidence and prediction intervals*

## Conclusion

In this chapter, you learned how to use R to calculate correlation and covariance, and how to perform linear regression. You also learned how to apply a quadratic model to fit a curvilinear data set, as well as how to calculate and interpret confidence and prediction intervals for a regression model. You examined a number of diagnostic plots provided by R that help you to understand the nature of the regression model. We have laid the foundation for our discussion of multiple regression in Chapter 13.

# CHAPTER 13

■ ■ ■

# Multiple Regression

In Chapter 13, you learn about multiple regression, which is the linear combination of two or more predictor variables to optimize the relationship between the observed and predicted variables. You also learn, as promised earlier, that the general linear model underlying multiple regression also underlies ANOVA and $t$ tests, and you can use regression instead of those procedures to obtain the same (or more informative) results. You discover R's functions for dealing with both continuous and dichotomous predictor variables, and how to dummy code your data to achieve the most useful information. As a bonus, I show you how to use matrix algebra to solve a regression model. This will enhance both your R skills and your statistical understanding, and will help you with more advanced topics such as multivariate analyses (which are beyond the scope of this beginning text).

Many analysis of variance designs are based on the assumption of independence between the factors (as in the completely crossed balanced factorial design we considered in Chapter 11). However, in data we observe in the real world, there is often a lack of independence between predictors. We need a general model to allow us to work with such situations, and with predictors that are continuous in nature, and multiple regression is a good solution in these cases.

It is important to note that in multiple regression the predicted value of $y$ is a *linear combination* of the values of the predictors. We calculate and interpret residuals in multiple regression in exactly the same fashion we do in bivariate regression. Just as we can add quadratic terms in simple regression, we can do so in multiple regression.

A variety of modern statistical techniques are based on multiple regression. We will limit ourselves in this beginning book to a single dependent (criterion) variable and multiple predictors (either continuous or dichotomous), but you should be aware of the existence of a technique called *canonical correlation*, which is a generalization of regression models. In canonical correlation, we seek a simultaneous linear combination of multiple $y$ variables and multiple $x$ variables. The general linear model shows that all linear correlational and ANOVA designs are subsets of canonical correlation.

## The Multiple Regression Equation

The multiple regression equation is an extension of the simple (bivariate) regression equation to accommodate two or more predictors. Let us make a slight adjustment and label our intercept coefficient $b_0$ rather than $a$. You will learn later why this is an improvement. Here is the general form of our regression equation with multiple predictors:

$$\hat{y} = b_0 + b_1 x_1 + b_2 x_2 + \cdots + b_k x_k$$

The regression coefficients (often called "beta weights" when we use the standardized versions) are derived in such a way as to minimize the sum of the squares of the deviations of the observed and predicted values of $y$. This is called "least squares" or "ordinary least squares" (OLS) regression. We calculate the coefficient of multiple correlation, which is symbolized as $R$, which we call "multiple $R$," by correlating the predicted and observed values of *y*. The direction of the relationship (positive or negative) between the individual predictors and each other and between the predictors and the criterion is taken into account in the calculation of the regression coefficients. For that reason, *R* will always range between 0 and 1 and cannot achieve negative values (though I have seen "statistics" books that claim there is such a thing as negative *R*). The square of *R*, $R^2$, is the coefficient of determination and the equivalent of eta squared in ANOVA terminology. Multiple $R^2$ tells us the proportion of the total variation that can be accounted for by the regression equation, and as such is an effect-size index.

## Multiple Regression Example: Predicting Job Satisfaction

Let us use multiple regression to see if we can predict the job satisfaction of respondents to the National Opinion Research Center's General Social Survey (GSS). The data were retrieved from the following web site:

http://www3.norc.org/gss+website/

After cleaning the data I was able to retain the 2010 GSS survey responses for 964 people. The data fields we will use are the respondent's income (on a scale of 1 to 12), age, job satisfaction (with 1 being the highest), years at the current job, and belief that his or her job is secure (with 1 being the highest). Here are the first few lines of the relevant data:

```
> gssdata <- read.csv("gssdata.csv", header = TRUE)
> head(gssdata)
  rincome age satjob1 yearsjob jobsecok
1       7  23       3     0.75        4
2      12  46       2    10.00        2
3      11  31       3     0.75        2
4      12  58       2     7.00        2
5      12  35       2    13.00        1
6      12  49       2    28.00        2
```

We will use job satisfaction as the dependent (criterion) variable, and the other variables as predictors.

```
> attach(gssdata)
> mulreg <- lm(satjob1 ~ rincome + age + yearsjob + jobsecok)
> summary(mulreg)

Call:
lm(formula = satjob1 ~ rincome + age + yearsjob + jobsecok)

Residuals:
     Min      1Q   Median      3Q      Max
-1.67405 -0.50569 -0.04992 0.40383  2.56341

Coefficients:
             Estimate Std. Error t value Pr(>|t|)
(Intercept)  1.548183   0.111874  13.839  < 2e-16 ***
rincome     -0.001547   0.007717  -0.200  0.84113
age         -0.008073   0.001746  -4.624 4.28e-06 ***
yearsjob    -0.008431   0.002868  -2.940  0.00336 **
jobsecok     0.331870   0.024512  13.539  < 2e-16 ***
---
Signif. codes:  0 '***' 0.001 '**' 0.01 '*' 0.05 '.' 0.1 ' ' 1
```

```
Residual standard error: 0.6603 on 959 degrees of freedom
Multiple R-squared: 0.2059,     Adjusted R-squared: 0.2026
F-statistic: 62.17 on 4 and 959 DF,  p-value: < 2.2e-16
```

We see that the respondent's income is not a significant predictor, so we drop it from the analysis and run the regression again. Now, the value of $R$ squared remains the same, but the significance of the regression is greater.

```
> mulreg <- lm(satjob1 ~ age + yearsjob + jobsecok)
> summary(mulreg)

Call:
lm(formula = satjob1 ~ age + yearsjob + jobsecok)

Residuals:
    Min      1Q    Median      3Q      Max
-1.66128 -0.50756 -0.04729  0.40303  2.56970

Coefficients:
             Estimate Std. Error t value Pr(>|t|)
(Intercept)  1.533169   0.083075  18.455  < 2e-16 ***
age         -0.008087   0.001744  -4.638    4e-06 ***
yearsjob    -0.008540   0.002814  -3.034  0.00248 **
jobsecok     0.332151   0.024459  13.580  < 2e-16 ***
---
Signif. codes:  0 '***' 0.001 '**' 0.01 '*' 0.05 '.' 0.1 ' ' 1

Residual standard error: 0.6599 on 960 degrees of freedom
Multiple R-squared: 0.2059,     Adjusted R-squared: 0.2034
F-statistic: 82.96 on 3 and 960 DF,  p-value: < 2.2e-16
```

As with bivariate regression, we test the significance of the overall regression with an ANOVA, by partitioning the variance into regression and residual sums of squares. We also test the significance of the intercept (when this is of interest) and of the regression coefficients with $t$ tests. In the case of multiple regression, the tests of the regression coefficients do not coincide with the overall test of the regression, in contrast to the simple regression case we discussed in Chapter 12. We see that in this particular case, the overall regression is statistically significant—we can account for roughly 20% of the variation in job satisfaction by knowing an individuals' age, the number of years on the job, and his or her sense of job security.

```
>plot(mulreg)
```

First, examine the plot of the residuals against the fitted values (Figure 13-1):

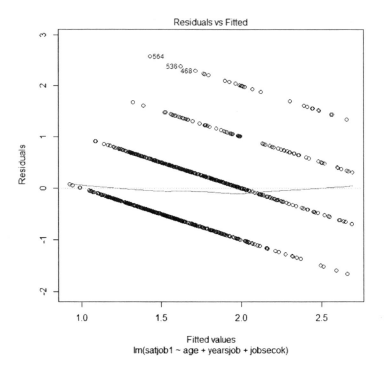

**Figure 13-1.** *Residuals versus fitted values*

Figure 13-2 shows the normal Q-Q plot:

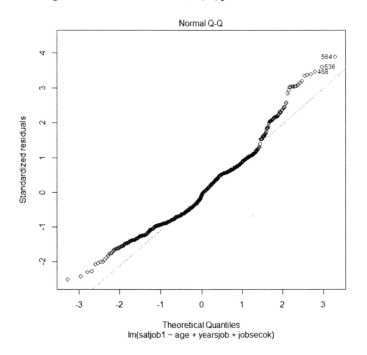

**Figure 13-2.** *Normal Q-Q plot*

The normal Q –Q plot shows that the relationship is fairly well described by a straight line. The scale location plot appears in Figure 13-3, and the residuals versus leverage plot is in Figure 13-4.

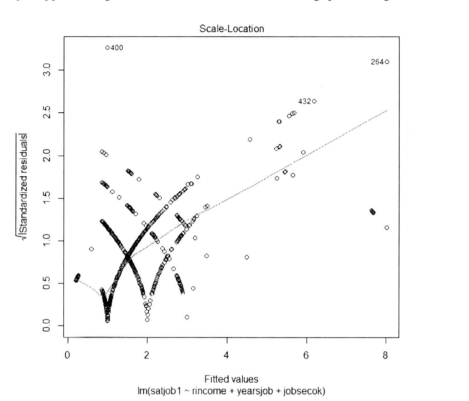

***Figure 13-3.*** *Scale location plot*

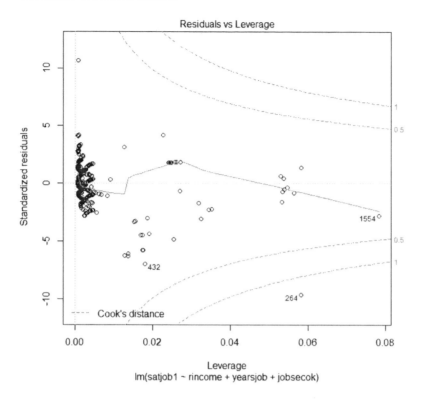

***Figure 13-4.*** *Residuals versus leverage plot*

We will also plot the predicted and observed values, along with a confidence interval and a prediction interval, as you learned to do in Chapter 12. To make this easier to comprehend, the values were first sorted in ascending order. Because of the discrete nature of the job satisfaction ratings, 95% confidence limits do not plot a smooth line (see Figure 13-5).

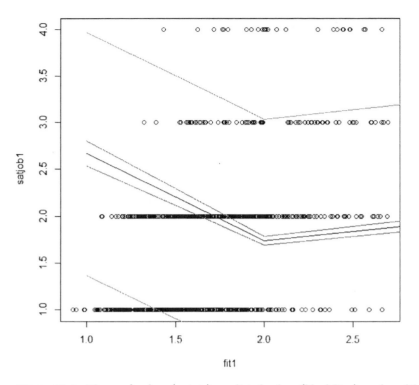

**Figure 13-5.** *Observed values (points), predicted values (black line), and confidence limits (red and blue lines)*

As a reminder, we can use the predict() function to get the fitted values and the confidence intervals:

```
> confint <- predict(mulreg, interval = "confidence")
> predint <- predict(mulreg, interval = "prediction")
Warning message:
In predict.lm(mulreg, interval = "prediction") :
  Predictions on current data refer to _future_ responses
```

A little data manipulation helps us get the data we need for the intervals.

```
> intervals <- cbind(confint, predint)
> intervals <- edit(intervals) ## Here we simply change the column headings to remove  +
  duplication

> head(intervals)
      fit1 lwrconf uprconf    fit2 lwrpred uprpred
1 2.669363 2.536859 2.801868 2.669363 1.3675079 3.971219
2 1.740063 1.695023 1.785102 1.740063 0.4441851 3.035940
3 1.940365 1.878468 2.002262 1.940365 0.6437920 3.236938
4 1.668638 1.601060 1.736215 1.668638 0.3717812 2.965494
5 1.471250 1.400903 1.541596 1.471250 0.1742459 2.768254
6 1.562080 1.449084 1.675075 1.562080 0.2620651 2.862095
```

Here is how we build the plot with our fitted values and our intervals.

```
plot(fit1,satjob1)
> lines(fit1)
> points(lwrpred, col = "red", type = "l")
> points(uprpred, col = "red", type = "l")
> points(lwrconf, col = "blue", type = "l")
> points(uprconf, col = "blue", type = "l")
```

# Using Matrix Algebra to Solve a Regression Equation

As you learned in Chapter 1, it is possible to do matrix algebra in R. We can use the matrix algebra operations of R to solve a regression equation. We can convert our data frame from the previous section to a matrix by using the as.matrix() function, or we can attach the data frame and use the cbind() function to combine the relevant variables into a matrix. We add a column of 1's, for reasons you will understand more fully in a short time.

Let us make an **X** matrix using the column of 1's and the three predictors.

```
> xcol <- rep(1, 964)
> Xij <- cbind(xcol, age, yearsjob, jobsecok)
> head(Xij)
     xcol age yearsjob jobsecok
[1,]    1  23     0.75        4
[2,]    1  46    10.00        2
[3,]    1  31     0.75        2
[4,]    1  58     7.00        2
[5,]    1  35    13.00        1
[6,]    1  49    28.00        2
> Xij
```

Now, we make a one-column matrix of our job satisfaction scores, and call it **Y**.

```
> Y <- as.matrix(satjob1)
> head(Y)
     [,1]
[1,]    3
[2,]    2
[3,]    3
[4,]    2
[5,]    2
[6,]    2
```

Here is the matrix algebraic solution to the linear regression equation. The column of 1's in our **X** matrix will allow us to calculate the intercept coefficient. We use matrix multiplication to produce a square matrix of our predictors by multiplying the transpose of the **X** matrix by the **X** matrix. We then invert (solve) that matrix and multiply the inverse by **X'Y**:

$$\mathbf{B} = \left(\mathbf{X'X}\right)^{-1}\mathbf{X'Y}$$

The resulting vector will consist of the intercept ($b_0$), $b_1$, and $b_2$. Let us illustrate the calculations using matrix operations. First, we calculate our square matrix and invert it.

```
> transpose <- t(Xij)
> solved <- solve(transpose %*% Xij)
> solved
                   xcol           age      yearsjob       jobsecok
xcol       1.584651e-02 -2.559229e-04  4.067362e-05 -2.302653e-03
age       -2.559229e-04  6.980049e-06 -4.988232e-06 -4.646113e-06
yearsjob   4.067362e-05 -4.988232e-06  1.818813e-05  1.664574e-05
jobsecok  -2.302653e-03 -4.646113e-06  1.664574e-05  1.373650e-03
```

Just to check, we will multiply the inverse by the original matrix to make sure the inverse is proper.

```
> square <- transpose %*% Xij
> identity <- solved %*% square
> identity
                   xcol           age      yearsjob       jobsecok
xcol       1.000000e+00  2.436662e-13  3.141064e-14  9.207045e-15
age       -1.064339e-16  1.000000e+00 -1.190003e-15 -2.217973e-16
yearsjob   3.349846e-17  1.202597e-15  1.000000e+00  7.238744e-17
jobsecok  -7.572068e-16 -4.467954e-14 -1.042569e-14  1.000000e+00
```

The matrix is quite close to an identity matrix (1s on the diagonal and 0 s on the off-diagonals), as the following rounding makes clear.

```
> round(identity, digits = 3)
          xcol age yearsjob jobsecok
xcol         1   0        0        0
age          0   1        0        0
yearsjob     0   0        1        0
jobsecok     0   0        0        1
```

Next, we'll solve for our regression coefficients. First, however, recall the terms we found using the lm() function:

```
Coefficients:
              Estimate Std. Error t value Pr(>|t|)
(Intercept)   1.533169   0.083075  18.455  < 2e-16 ***
age          -0.008087   0.001744  -4.638    4e-06 ***
yearsjob     -0.008540   0.002814  -3.034  0.00248 **
jobsecok      0.332151   0.024459  13.580  < 2e-16 ***
```

Now, observe the results of our matrix manipulations. Unsurprisingly, the matrix operations produce exactly the same coefficients as the lm() function does.

```
> B <- solved %*% (transpose %*% Y)
> B
                 [,1]
xcol       1.533168528
age       -0.008087098
yearsjob  -0.008540087
jobsecok   0.332150789
```

**Caution**   Many people (including myself) use Microsoft Excel for basic statistics. It is true that you can do the same matrix manipulations illustrated above in Microsoft Excel, but you should be aware that the matrix inversion algorithms in Excel do not produce precise answers, and the resulting vector of regression coefficients may be close, or sometimes not close at all, to the regression coefficients produced by Excel's built-in regression functions or the regression tool in the Analysis ToolPak. It is also quite easy to come up with data that cause Excel's algorithms to produce inaccurate answers or even to stop working altogether. The moral of the story (from a confirmed Excel addict), is that Excel is a general-purpose spreadsheet program, but not a very good statistics package.

# Brief Introduction to the General Linear Model

Although we could use a variety of examples to illustrate the general linear model, let us restrict ourselves to a few simple ones. I present the examples here not as mathematical proof of the underlying statistical theory, but rather as illustrations of the equivalence of several procedures. Of these, multiple regression is by far the most general. In the following discussion, you will see the equivalence of the *t* test and ANOVA. Some modern statistics texts do not even cover *t* tests, because an ANOVA with two groups is equivalent mathematically and statistically to a *t* test. You may have wondered earlier why we use *t* tests to examine the significance of regression coefficients. Indeed, many statistics students are surprised to learn that we can use bivariate correlation and regression to gain exactly the same (or more) information as we could with a two-sample *t* test.

## The *t* Test as a Special Case of Correlation

Let us begin with the connection between the *t* test and correlation and regression. We will return to our example of a two-sample *t* test from Chapter 9. We make only a small adjustment to our stacked data used previously. We will let Class 1 now be represented by a 0 and Class 2 be symbolized by a 1. You will understand why this is important momentarily. Here is how the stacked data are now reconfigured, with the first few and last few rows shown below. Recall that these are the comparisons of the posttest scores of two different classes.

```
> head(ttestdata)
  PostTest Class
1 62.50000     0
2 54.16667     0
3 41.66667     0
4 50.00000     0
5 41.66667     0
6 50.00000     0

> tail(ttestdata)
   PostTest Class
32 58.33333     1
33 79.16667     1
34 87.50000     1
35 45.83333     1
36 66.66667     1
37 45.83333     1
```

CHAPTER 13 ■ MULTIPLE REGRESSION

Here, for the sake of reference, is the *t*-test output for the test that assumes the variances are equal in the population. This assumption of equality of variance is common to ANOVA and regression, so we will run the equivalent *t* test. We will make Class a factor, as before. The steps in attaching the file and making the factor are not shown, but if you need a refresher, you can revisit Chapter 9.

```
> t.test(PostTest~Class, var.equal = TRUE)

        Two Sample t-test

data:  PostTest by Class
t = -6.1879, df = 35, p-value = 4.37e-07
alternative hypothesis: true difference in means is not equal to 0
95 percent confidence interval:
 -33.76182 -17.08144
sample estimates:
mean in group 0 mean in group 1
       39.68254        65.10417
```

Now, let us run a regression analysis on the same data using the lm( ) function. Statistically, we are *regressing* the vector of test scores onto the dummy-coded *factor* that represents class membership. You will note some interesting equivalencies when we compare the *t*-test output above to the summary of the regression model below.

```
> results <- lm(PostTest~Class)
> summary(results)

Call:
lm(formula = Posttest~Class)

Residuals:
    Min      1Q  Median      3Q     Max
-23.406  -6.386   1.594   5.694  26.594

Coefficients:
            Estimate Std. Error t value Pr(>|t|)
(Intercept)   39.686      2.703  14.682  < 2e-16 ***
Class         25.421      4.110   6.185 4.41e-07 ***
---
Signif. codes:  0 '***' 0.001 '**' 0.01 '*' 0.05 '.' 0.1 ' ' 1

Residual standard error: 12.39 on 35 degrees of freedom
Multiple R-squared: 0.5222,     Adjusted R-squared: 0.5085
F-statistic: 38.25 on 1 and 35 DF,  p-value: 4.415e-07
```

First, note that the intercept term is equivalent to the mean of Class 1, and the slope term is equivalent to the mean difference. Second, see that the *t* test on the regression coefficient (slope) is identical to the *t* test on the mean difference in the *t*-test results above. Third, observe that the *F* statistic testing the overall "regression" of the posttest onto the grouping vector of 0's and 1's is the square of the value of *t* for both the *t* test and the slope coefficient. None of these equivalences are accidental or coincidental. In fact, they are statistical and mathematical realities based on the equivalence of the two procedures.

## The *t* Test as a Special Case of ANOVA

Now, let us recast the same test as an ANOVA. We will do a one-way ANOVA with only two groups. This will still give us an *F* ratio, but in this case, the numerator degrees of freedom will be 1 because there are 2 groups. See the ANOVA and the results below. The *t* test for two groups is identical to the ANOVA for 2 groups, and the value of *t* squared is equal to the value of *F* (which is the same whether we have done an ANOVA or a regression), the only difference being the labeling of the output.

```
> results <- aov(PostTest ~ Class)
> summary(results)
            Df Sum Sq Mean Sq F value   Pr(>F)
Class        1   5868    5868   38.25 4.41e-07 ***
Residuals   35   5370     153
---
Signif. codes:  0 '***' 0.001 '**' 0.01 '*' 0.05 '.' 0.1 ' ' 1
```

As in the comparison of the ANOVA and multiple regression, the $r^2$ (or "Multiple R-squared" in the R output) is equivalently an eta-squared when we look at the analysis as a comparison of groups. Some statistics teachers try to make the distinction that *t* tests and ANOVAs are used to *compare groups*, and correlation and regression are means of *examining relationships*, and indeed that is the traditional and historical distinction between the two families of statistical procedures. However, the statistical truth of the matter is that this is a difference without a distinction, as the discussion and illustrations above indicate.

## ANOVA as a Special Case of Multiple Regression

For our last demonstration of the general linear model, we will recast our one-way ANOVA as a multiple regression problem. As with the *t* test, we will use vectors of 0 s and 1 s to represent group membership. Note because there are $k - 1$ degrees of freedom, where $k$ represents the number of groups, we will use $k - 1$ columns of 0 s and 1 s, as the final group will be identified by the absence of a code. (This will make more sense after the example.)

Let us return to the one-way ANOVA example from Chapter 10. For your convenience, the ANOVA summary table is repeated below. As you recall, we were using gas mileage as the dependent variable and the gasoline brand as the grouping variable.

```
> results <- aov(mpg~brand)
> results
Call:
   aov(formula = mpg~brand)

Terms:
                  group Residuals
Sum of Squares  17.04933   8.02800
Deg. of Freedom        2        12

Residual standard error: 0.8179242
Estimated effects may be unbalanced
> summary(results)
            Df Sum Sq Mean Sq F value  Pr(>F)
brand        2 17.049   8.525   12.74 0.00108 **
Residuals   12  8.028   0.669
---
Signif. codes:  0 '***' 0.001 '**' 0.01 '*' 0.05 '.' 0.1 ' ' 1
```

Now, let us perform the same analysis, but this time we must come up with columns to code the gasoline brand as 0 or 1. As mentioned, we will need only 2 columns, though there are 3 gasoline brands. Here are the reconfigured data for the multiple regression analysis.

```
> mileage <- read.table("mileage.txt", header = TRUE)
> mileage
    mpg x1 x2
1  34.0  1  0
2  35.0  1  0
3  34.3  1  0
4  35.5  1  0
5  35.8  1  0
6  35.3  0  1
7  36.5  0  1
8  36.4  0  1
9  37.0  0  1
10 37.6  0  1
11 33.3  0  0
12 34.0  0  0
13 34.7  0  0
14 33.0  0  0
15 34.9  0  0
```

We now use the lm( ) function to do the multiple regression analysis:

```
> attach(mileage)
> x1 <- factor(x1)
> x2 <- factor(x2)
> results <- lm(mpg~x1 + x2)
> summary(results)

Call:
lm(formula = mpg~x1 + x2)

Residuals:
   Min    1Q Median    3Q    Max
 -1.26 -0.65   0.02  0.65   1.04

Coefficients:
            Estimate Std. Error t value Pr(>|t|)
(Intercept)  33.9800     0.3658  92.896  < 2e-16 ***
x11           0.9400     0.5173   1.817 0.094239 .
x21           2.5800     0.5173   4.987 0.000316 ***
---
Signif. codes:  0 '***' 0.001 '**' 0.01 '*' 0.05 '.' 0.1 ' ' 1

Residual standard error: 0.8179 on 12 degrees of freedom
Multiple R-squared: 0.6799,    Adjusted R-squared: 0.6265
F-statistic: 12.74 on 2 and 12 DF,  p-value: 0.001076
```

Once again, note the equivalence of the $F$ ratio in the multiple regression to the $F$ ratio in the one-way ANOVA. As before, this equivalence is based on the statistical fact that the underlying general linear model for ANOVA and multiple regression is identical, and we are using a special case of multiple regression when we do ANOVA, whether that fact has been made known to us or not.

It is not difficult to show that the paired-samples (repeated-measures) $t$ test and the repeated-measures ANOVA are also both special cases of multiple regression, and that the repeated-measures $t$ test is also a special case of the repeated-measures ANOVA.

# More on Multiple Regression

Entire textbooks have been written on multiple regression, and deservedly so. In this chapter, we have concentrated on rather simple examples. There are many other techniques that make use of multiple regression, some of them quite sophisticated, but we have stuck to the basics here.

Even with fairly simple multiple regression problems, there is still the problem of which variables to enter into the regression equation, and which method to use for deciding the order of variable entry. There are also problems in many regression models with multicollinearity and variance inflation. Some data sets, especially time series data, violate the assumption of independence. We have previously discussed the problem of heteroscedasticity (inequality of variance). Techniques, diagnostic tools, and statistics have been developed to deal with these problems, but beyond mentioning them briefly, their actual illustration and application are beyond our current scope.

## Entering Variables into the Regression Equation

One of the key considerations in multiple regression is which predictor variables to enter into the regression equation, and in which order to enter these variables. There are numerous approaches. One approach I like to use when there is no particular theoretical basis for the analysis is to enter all the predictors (the full model), and then to use "backward elimination," in which each predictor that does not have a significant regression coefficient is dropped from the equation and the analysis is run again. When all the remaining variables in the equation each have a significant regression coefficient, and the overall regression is significant, we have identified a reasonable model. Another approach is "stepwise regression," in which the variable with the highest zero-order correlation with the criterion is entered first, the variable with the second-highest zero-order correlation is entered next, and so on, until the addition of any new variable will not improve the regression model. Many statisticians (myself one of them) object to the stepwise approach, as it is opportunistic in nature and tends to "overfit" the predictors. Other, more sensible, approaches to deciding which variables to enter and what order to enter them have been developed, as discussed below.

A more recent approach to the question of the order of entry of predictors is "hierarchical regression." In this approach, variables are entered in blocks. The blocks, in turn, are based on some theory or hypothesis that specifies the importance of the variables to the regression model. We can test (via ANOVA) the increase in multiple R (what is called "R-squared change") to determine if the additional block of variables adds significantly to the predictive power of the regression equation. If you're interested in learning more, refer to the R documentation and to a good statistics or multiple regression text. My personal favorite is the text by Elazar Pedhazer entitled *Multiple Regression in Behavioral Research: Explanation and Prediction*, 3rd edition (1997). I studied the earlier 1973 book by Kerlinger and Pedhazer in my own graduate training in multiple regression. Although dated, both books are well worth consulting, even in today's technological world. Quaintly, the 1973 book talks about FORTRAN-IV routines to run multiple regression analysis!

## Dealing with Collinearity

One must also understand that the relationships between predictors affect their contributions to the overall prediction of $y$ from a linear combination of $x$s. The correlations among the predictors can be high enough to cause a problem known as multicollinearity. To see why this is a problem, consider the Venn diagrams shown in Figure 13-6. In case A, we have three uncorrelated predictors, each of which predicts some amount of the variation in the criterion. In case B, we have three predictors, but they are correlated with each other. The effect of this collinearity is that the amount of y being predicted in the second case is less than the amount in the first case. Because of the possibility of multicollinearity in the data, it is necessary to examine the correlation matrix of the predictors carefully to determine if any of the variables have too high a correlation.

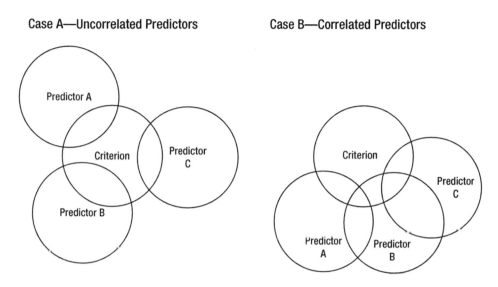

**Figure 13-6.** *Comparing uncorrelated and correlated predictors*

As a rule of thumb, an ideal multiple regression model will be more like case A than case B. To the extent that we have relatively independent predictors, each of which predicts some significant proportion of the dependent (criterion) variable, their combination can lead to increases in predictive accuracy.

# Conclusion

In this chapter, you learned about multiple correlation and regression, and also about the general linear model underlying regression, *t* tests, and ANOVA. We addressed some simple cases of multiple regression and hinted at some more complex approaches. Additionally, you learned some of the issues that concern those who do multiple regression in their research or in their professions. These issues include the selection of predictors and the intercorrelation of predictors. Multiple regression is a very general technique, as you learned, and both ANOVA and *t* tests can easily be recast as regression problems. As a bonus, you also learned how to use matrix algebra to solve for the vector of regression coefficients. Matrix algebraic formulas are a very compact way to represent regression and many other multivariate techniques based on the general linear model.

In Chapter 14, we will address the topic of logistic regression, which has become a very popular method in a variety of disciplines.

# CHAPTER 14

■ ■ ■

# Logistic Regression

In bivariate and multiple regression (Chapters 12 and 13), we used a continuous dependent variable. There are occasions in which the outcome is an either-or (0, 1) binary outcome. Fisher developed a technique known as discriminant analysis for predicting group membership (by maximizing the combination of predictor scores to separate the two groups). This is a fine technique, and one that has been around for a long time. There is, however, one major problem with discriminant analysis, namely that it can take advantage only of continuous predictors. A more modern technique to the prediction (and classification as desired) of group membership in two groups represented by 0s and 1s is known as logistic regression. Logistic regression allows the use of both continuous and binary predictors.

In this chapter, you learn what logistic regression is and how to use R for both simple binary logistic regression with one dependent variable and one predictor and for multiple binary logistic regression with a single outcome variable and two or more predictors. Logistic regression has proven to be quite versatile and useful. I have used it as a way to predict student retention at a university as well as a way to predict the success of a telephonic wellness-coaching program sponsored by an insurance company. In still another application, I used logistic regression to predict the success rate of hormone treatment in producing pregnancy in artificially inseminated cows. A quick search of the scientific literature in a variety of disciplines will show just how frequently logistic regression is being used.

## What Is Logistic Regression?

Logistic regression enables us to predict a dichotomous (0, 1) outcome while overcoming the problems with linear regression and discriminant analysis. Examples of binary outcomes include the presence and absence of defects, attendance and absenteeism, and student retention versus dropout. Fisher used discriminant function analysis as his approach to predicting a binary outcome (which you can think of as group membership). This approach essentially involves finding the linear combination of predictors that maximizes the difference between groups, and thus serves as a way to predict group membership. Discriminant analysis has been a very useful tool but suffers from being technically applicable only with continuous predictors (though many of my textbooks show the use of dichotomous predictors anyway). Logistic regression provides a superior alternative.

When we have a binary outcome measure, we can treat this as a binomial process, with $p$ being the proportion of 1s, and $q = 1 - p$ being the proportion of 0s. We call a 1 a "success" and a 0 a "failure," as we discussed in Chapter 6. As you may recall, the difference between success and failure is often a matter of choice, but sometimes the 1s really do represent "success," such as with student retention in the examples discussed below.

As I mentioned above, there is a problem with using correlation and regression to predict a (0, 1) outcome. Typically, we will have predicted values less than 0 and greater than 1, and of course these are theoretically impossible. The logistic curve, on the other hand, has a very nice property of being asymptotic to 0 and 1 and always lying between 0 and 1. Thus, logistic regression avoids the problems of both linear regression and discriminant function analysis for predicting binary outcomes.

We can convert a probability to *odds*, and we use odds in logistic regression. If *p* is the probability of success, the odds in favor of success, *o*, are:

$$odds = \frac{p}{q} = \frac{p}{1-p}$$

Odds can also be converted to probabilities quite easily. If the odds in favor of an event are 5:1, then the probability of the event is 5/6. Note that odds, unlike probabilities, can exceed 1. For example, if the probability of rain is .25, the odds in favor of rain are .25 / .75 = .33, but the odds against rain are .75 / .25 = 3.00.

In logistic regression we work with a term called the *logit*, which is the natural logarithm of the odds. We develop a linear combination of predictors and an intercept term to predict the logit:

$$ln(odds) = b_0 + b_1 x_1 + b_2 x_2 + \ldots + b_k x_k$$

Examining this model carefully, we see that we have simply described a linear regression on the logit transform of *y*, where *y* is the proportion of success at each value of *x*. Remember that a 1 is considered a success and a 0 is considered a failure. Logistic regression allows us to model the probability of "success" as a function of the logistic curve, which is never less than 0 and never greater than 1. Because we are not accustomed to thinking in terms of logarithms, we typically convert the logit to odds, which make more intuitive sense to us.

We can convert the logit to odds as follows:

$$odds = e^{b_0 + b_1 x_1 + \ldots + b_k x_k}$$

Remember *e* is the base of the natural logarithms.

This brief introduction gives us the background needed to illustrate logistic regression. We will begin with the simplest of cases, that of a single dichotomous predictor. This will allow us the luxury of working out the logistic regression manually before learning how to do it in R.

# Logistic Regression with One Dichotomous Predictor

Let us start with a simple example, one in which we have a dichotomous criterion and a dichotomous predictor. We have already used tests of proportions and chi-square tests to deal with such data, but we can also envision the use of logistic regression for the same kind of data. Say we have 50 pairs of observations, which represent the dangerous phenomenon of binge drinking and a sample of 25 male and 25 female college students. We will use binge drinking as the dichotomous criterion and the students' gender as the dichotomous predictor. These data are fabricated, but were generated to match national percentages of binge drinking reported among college students. Here are the first and last few rows of data from the data frame called `bingedata`. We use 0 to represent the absence of binging and 1 to represent binge drinking (defined as having five or more drinks in a row for males and four or more for females) in the last two-week period. We represent males by 1 and females by 0.

```
> head(bingedata)
  binges gender
1      0      1
2      1      1
3      1      1
4      1      1
5      0      1
6      0      1
```

```
> tail(bingedata)
   binges gender
45      1      0
46      0      0
47      0      0
48      0      0
49      0      0
50      0      0
```

Let us look at the cross-tabulation of the data. We will also do a chi-square test of independence, as you learned previously.

```
> table(bingedata)
       gender
binges  0   1
     0 20  13
     1  5  12

    > chisq.test(table(bingedata))

            Pearson's Chi-squared test with Yates' continuity correction

    data:   table(bingedata)
    X-squared = 3.2086, df - 1, p-value = 0.07325
```

We see that the chi-square test is "approaching" significance, and might be significant with a larger sample. We will keep working with a small data set for now to make the calculations simpler and easier to communicate. In this first simple case, we will find the logistic regression model easier to understand, and that understanding will form the basis of interpreting more complex cases.

Now, let us model this problem as one of odds and ultimately perform the binary logistic regression for the data. First, let us calculate the proportion of men and women who are binge drinkers using our sample data. Let us call these values $\hat{p}_1$ and $\hat{p}_0$ respectively:

$$\hat{p}_1 = \frac{12}{25} = .48$$

$$\hat{p}_0 = \frac{5}{25} = .20$$

So the odds in favor of a man being a binge drinker are:

$$odds_m = \frac{\hat{p}_1}{\hat{q}_1} = \frac{.48}{.52} = 0.9231$$

And the odds in favor of a woman being a binge drinker are:

$$odds_f = \frac{\hat{p}_0}{\hat{q}_0} = \frac{.20}{.80} = .25$$

In our current simplified case, the logistic regression model simplifies to:

$$\ln\left(\frac{\hat{p}_1}{q_1}\right) = b_0 + b_1 x$$

Because we coded gender with a zero for females, the estimate of the intercept term will be the log(odds) for the females.

$$b_0 = \ln(.25) = -1.386294$$

The estimated slope will be the difference between the log(odds) for the men and the log(odds) for the women. We will calculate the log(odds) for males and then find the difference.

$$\ln(0.9231) = -0.08001771$$
$$b_1 = -0.08001771 - (-1.386294) = 1.30627629$$

Here is how to do the logistic regression in R. We use the glm procedure, and identify the model as a binary logistic one.

```
> results <- glm(binges~gender, family = "binomial")
> summary(results)

Call:
glm(formula = binges~gender, family = "binomial")

Deviance Residuals:
    Min      1Q   Median      3Q     Max
 -1.1436  -1.0247  -0.6681   1.2116   1.7941

Coefficients:
            Estimate Std. Error z value Pr(>|z|)
(Intercept)  -1.3863     0.5000  -2.773  0.00556 **
gender        1.3063     0.6405   2.039  0.04141 *
---
Signif. codes:  0 '***' 0.001 '**' 0.01 '*' 0.05 '.' 0.1 ' ' 1

(Dispersion parameter for binomial family taken to be 1)

    Null deviance: 64.104  on 49  degrees of freedom
Residual deviance: 59.637  on 48  degrees of freedom
AIC: 63.637

Number of Fisher Scoring iterations: 4
```

Examine the R output, and see that apart from the number of decimals reported, our earlier hand calculations and the R output are consistent. We interpret the results of the R output just as we would those of any regression. Interestingly, though the chi-square test of independence was nonsignificant, the logistic regression led to the conclusion that gender is a significant predictor of binge drinking.

Now that you understand both the concepts and the R commands for logistic regression, let us move toward the case of a continuous predictor.

# Logistic Regression with One Continuous Predictor

Let us now consider the case where we are predicting a dichotomous outcome with a continuous predictor. Say we want to predict retention of college students from their freshman to their sophomore years. Students who started as freshmen and returned as sophomores will get a 1, and those who did not register as sophomores will get a 0. We will use high school GPA (HSGPA) as our predictor variable and college retention as our criterion.[1]

The data for this study required me to take information from Access, Excel, SPSS, and CSV files. R made it easy to build a unified data set. The criterion variable was whether the student returned as a sophomore (1) or did not return (0). Of all the variables we considered in this study, the one best predictor of retention was a dichotomous variable (as discussed in the previous section), which was whether or not the student really wanted to attend that university (as witnessed by putting the university first on the list of schools to receive the SAT scores). In this case, we also found that a student's previous academic performance is a good predictor of future academic performance. This is yet one more application of the age-old adage that the best predictor of future behavior is past behavior.

The data included a binary outcome (retained as a sophomore versus not retained), and eight potential predictors (preference for the university – based on whether the university was listed first on the FAFSA form, number of hours taken in the first semester as a freshman, gender, high school GPA, ethnic group, race, total SAT score, and status as a scholarship athlete). Here are the first few lines of the data set.

```
> head(retention)
  Retained Pref FRTerm FRHours Gender HSGPA Ethnic Race SATtot Athlete
1        1    1  20051    16.0      1  3.40      3    0    950       0
2        1    0  20061    16.0      1  3.27      1    1    900       0
3        0    0  20051    10.0      1  2.87      1    1    980       0
4        1    1  20071    15.0      0  3.88      1    1   1030       0
5        1    1  20061    15.5      1  4.04      1    1   1010       0
6        0    1  20051    16.0      1  3.47      2    0    930       0
```

The records of 958 freshmen were analyzed in this archival study, dating back to the fall term of 2005. Note the $p$ value for the HSGPA variable is highly significant, showing that it is a good predictor of retention. This certainly makes intuitive sense, as the best predictor of future grades is previous grades, and many of the students who did not return as sophomores either dropped out or were dismissed for poor grades in college. A two-sample $t$ test (see Chapter 9) reveals that indeed those students who returned as sophomores had initially higher HSGPA scores than those who did not return:

```
> t.test(HSGPA~Retained)

        Welch Two Sample t-test

data:  HSGPA by Retained
t = -7.843, df = 738.317, p-value = 1.542e-14
alternative hypothesis: true difference in means is not equal to 0
95 percent confidence interval:
 -0.3546878 -0.2126715
sample estimates:
mean in group 0 mean in group 1
      3.375714        3.659394
```

---

[1]This example is adapted from a study I did for a private liberal arts university.

Now, let us do the logistic regression and study the results.

```
> results <- glm(Retained~HSGPA, family = "binomial")
> summary(results)

Call:
glm(formula = Retained~HSGPA, family = "binomial")

Deviance Residuals:
    Min        1Q    Median        3Q       Max
 -1.7975   -1.2313    0.7555    0.9673    1.5944

Coefficients:
             Estimate Std. Error z value Pr(>|z|)
(Intercept)   -2.8675     0.4504  -6.367 1.93e-10 ***
HSGPA          0.9533     0.1273   7.490 6.87e-14 ***
---
Signif. codes:  0 '***' 0.001 '**' 0.01 '*' 0.05 '.' 0.1 ' ' 1

(Dispersion parameter for binomial family taken to be 1)

    Null deviance: 1272.3  on 957  degrees of freedom
Residual deviance: 1212.4  on 956  degrees of freedom
AIC: 1216.4

Number of Fisher Scoring iterations: 4
```

To conclude this example, let us find the predicted (fitted values) for retention and plot them against the HSGPA. See the following code to generate the predicted value for each student, and to produce the plot shown in Figure 14-1.

```
> results <- glm(Retained~HSGPA, family = "binomial")
> predicted <- results$fitted.values
> plot(HSGPA, predicted)
```

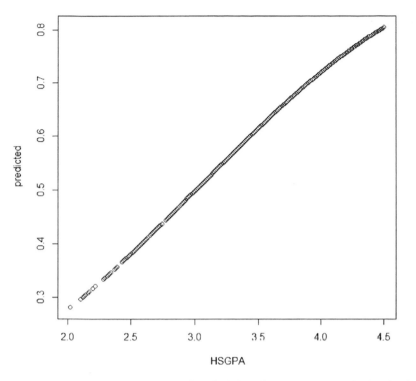

**Figure 14-1.** *A plot of the predicted probability of retention against high school grade point average*

Note that the graph is monotonic increasing, so that the predicted probability of retention increases as a function of the student's grade point average. Students with a high school grade point average lower than 3.0 have less than a .50 probability of returning after their freshman year. Also, notice that students with a HSGPA of 4 or above have about a .70 probability of returning for their sophomore year.

# Logistic Regression with Multiple Predictors

Having seen how you can use either a single dichotomous predictor or a single continuous predictor in logistic regression, we can look at how logistic regression works with multiple predictors, both dichotomous and continuous. We will continue to work with the retention data. You will learn how to assess several of the objects returned by the call to glm. We save the results of the general linear model with a logistic regression option and then provide the summary.

```
> results <- glm(Retained ~ Pref + Athlete + FRHours + HSGPA + SATtot + Gender, family =
+ "binomial")

> summary(results)

Call:
glm(formula = Retained ~ Pref + Athlete + FRHours + HSGPA + SATtot +
    Gender, family = "binomial")
```

```
Deviance Residuals:
    Min       1Q    Median       3Q       Max
-2.6351   -0.9610    0.3044    0.8861    2.1750

Coefficients:
              Estimate Std. Error z value Pr(>|z|)
(Intercept) -5.9111678  0.9113405  -6.486 8.80e-11 ***
Pref         1.4817399  0.2057348   7.202 5.93e-13 ***
Athlete      2.9579003  0.3624216   8.161 3.31e-16 ***
FRHours      0.0666602  0.0506562   1.316   0.1882
HSGPA        0.7797138  0.1592518   4.896 9.78e-07 ***
SATtot       0.0011058  0.0006552   1.688   0.0915 .
Gender      -0.0199795  0.1671598  -0.120   0.9049
---
Signif. codes:  0 '***' 0.001 '**' 0.01 '*' 0.05 '.' 0.1 ' ' 1

(Dispersion parameter for binomial family taken to be 1)

    Null deviance: 1272.3  on 957  degrees of freedom
Residual deviance: 1011.2  on 951  degrees of freedom
AIC: 1025.2

Number of Fisher Scoring iterations: 5
```

We see that gender, freshman hours, and total SAT scores are not significant predictors, so we omit them and run the logistic regression again:

```
> summary(results)

Call:
glm(formula = Retained ~ Pref + Athlete + HSGPA, family = "binomial")

Deviance Residuals:
    Min       1Q    Median       3Q       Max
-2.6377   -0.9712    0.2972    0.8918    2.2626

Coefficients:
            Estimate Std. Error z value Pr(>|z|)
(Intercept)  -4.3629     0.5280  -8.263  < 2e-16 ***
Pref          1.5078     0.2049   7.358 1.87e-13 ***
Athlete       2.9732     0.3608   8.240  < 2e-16 ***
HSGPA         0.9326     0.1412   6.603 4.04e-11 ***
---
Signif. codes:  0 '***' 0.001 '**' 0.01 '*' 0.05 '.' 0.1 ' ' 1

(Dispersion parameter for binomial family taken to be 1)

    Null deviance: 1272.3  on 957  degrees of freedom
Residual deviance: 1016.4  on 954  degrees of freedom
AIC: 1024.4

Number of Fisher Scoring iterations: 5
```

Now, all the predictors are significant. The "Wald *z* statistic" should be interpreted like any other test statistic. The overall model fit is measured by the Akaike information criterion (AIC), which is a relative measure of the information lost when the model is used to describe the outcome variable. The AIC can be used in model selection. All other things equal, the model with the lowest AIC should be chosen. See below how we can perform an overall test of model fit with a chi-square test of the difference between the null deviance (the null model) and our fitted model. The chi-square value of 261.11 with 6 degrees of freedom is highly significant, indicating our model fit is good.

```
> with(results, null.deviance - deviance)
[1] 261.1064
> with(results, df.null - df.residual)
[1] 6
> with(results, pchisq(null.deviance - deviance, df.null - df.residual,
+     lower.tail = FALSE))
[1] 1.732426e-53
```

One of the objects returned by the glm function is fitted.values, as we illustrated in the example of predicting retention by use of the student's HSGPA alone. In the case of logistic regression, we have a predicted probability of retention. Here are the first several predicted values.

```
> head(results$fitted.values)
        1         2         3         4         5         6
0.5782717 0.2119206 0.1562471 0.6820747 0.7135189 0.5941055
> cbind(head(results$fitted.values))
        [,1]
1 0.5782717
2 0.2119206
3 0.1562471
4 0.6820747
5 0.7135189
6 0.5941055
```

You can think of the fitted values as the risk assessment for each student. We can turn these into 0s and 1s by rounding .5 and up to 1, and less than .5 to 0. Then we can determine how good our model fit is by comparing the original retention data with the predicted retention. Assuming we can beat the baseline value, our model will be useful for predicting retention and therefore risk for the next incoming freshman class. Of the freshman in the sample of 958, 594 or 62% returned as sophomores. Here are the first few lines of the data with the fitted values and the risk added. Now, we can determine the association between our predicted retention (risk) and the actual retention (and whether it is significant) by performing another chi-square test.

```
> head(retention)
  Retained Pref FRTerm FRHours Gender HSGPA Ethnic Race SATtot Athlete
1        1    1  20051    16.0      1  3.40      3    0    950       0
2        1    0  20061    16.0      1  3.27      1    1    900       0
3        0    0  20051    10.0      1  2.87      1    1    980       0
4        1    1  20071    15.0      0  3.88      1    1   1030       0
5        1    1  20061    15.5      1  4.04      1    1   1010       0
6        0    1  20051    16.0      1  3.47      2    0    930       0
  results$fitted.value risk
1            0.5782717    1
2            0.2119206    0
3            0.1562471    0
```

```
4           0.6820747    1
5           0.7135189    1
6           0.5941055    1

> table(Retained, risk)
        risk
Retained   0    1
       0 187  177
       1  81  513
```

Examine the table above to see that the "hits" (correct classifications) are on the diagonals. There were 700 correct classifications, or a 73% hit rate. This is an 11% improvement over the baseline prediction of 62%. A chi-square test reveals the strong association between the actual retention and the predicted retention. For example:

```
> chisq.test(table(Retained,risk))

        Pearson's Chi-squared test with Yates' continuity correction

data:  table(Retained, risk)
X-squared = 157.6508, df = 1, p-value < 2.2e-16
```

As with linear regression, you can use the plot() function to produce diagnostic graphs for logistic regression. Simply use plot(results) to produce these. The plots are as shown in Figures 14-2 through 14-5.

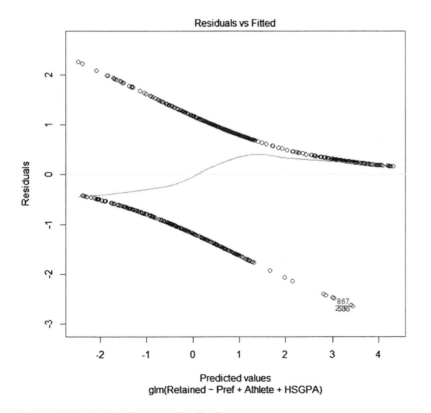

*Figure 14-2.* *Residuals versus fitted values*

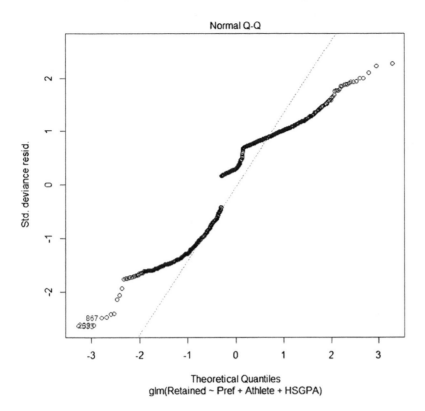

*Figure 14-3.* *Normal Q-Q plot*

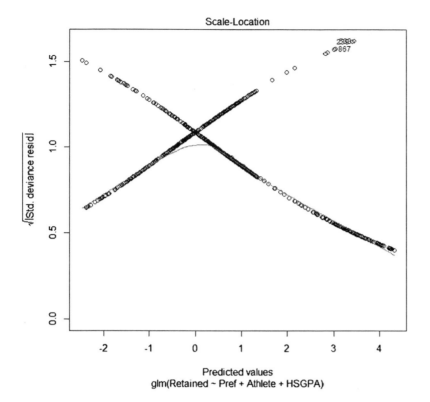

***Figure 14-4.*** *Scale-location plot*

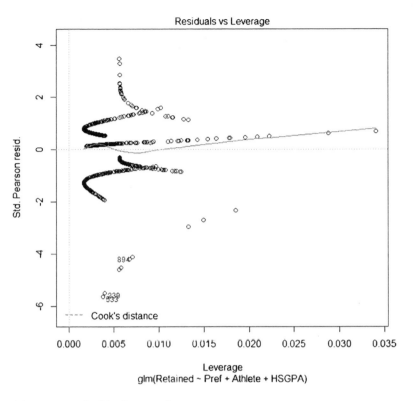

**Figure 14-5.** *Residuals versus leverage*

We can also plot our fitted values against the logits of the predicted risk. Remember to turn the probability into odds, we take the natural logarithm of the probability divided by 1 - the probability. Here is how to do this in R, as well as how to plot the curve (see Figure 14-6). The plot has the characteristic "S" shape of the logistic curve. I renamed the fitted values from `results$fitted.value` to `fitted` and then transformed the fitted values to logits as we discussed earlier:

```
> for (i in 1:958) logits[i] = log((fitted[i])/(1-fitted[i]))
> plot(logits, fitted)
```

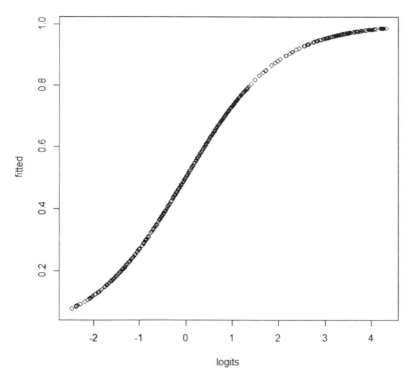

**Figure 14-6.** *Fitted values plotted against logits*

You may be interested to know that the logistic regression analysis discussed above resulted in not just the prediction of retention but the identification of at-risk students. Under the leadership of a forward-thinking dean, the university implemented interventions for these high-risk students, including personal contacts by faculty members, peer mentoring, and a revamped first year experience class (FYE). The logistic regression formula was used to predict the risk for all new incoming freshman students. Those assessed as having less than a .50 probability of being retained were identified as at-risk, and the interventions were used as dropout prevention strategies. In the face of a declining market base, the university was able to raise its retention from 62% to nearly 80%.

# Comparing Logistic and Multiple Regression

For comparison purposes, I ran the standard linear model with Retained as the criterion and the same three predictors we used for the logistic regression model. The multiple linear regression was significant, as the following output shows:

```
> summary(mulreg)
Call:
lm(formula = Retained ~ Pref + Athlete + HSGPA)

Residuals:
    Min      1Q  Median      3Q     Max
-0.99909 -0.41175  0.06959  0.34937  0.97567
```

```
Coefficients:
            Estimate Std. Error t value Pr(>|t|)
(Intercept) -0.34563    0.09109  -3.794 0.000157 ***
Pref         0.29618    0.03584   8.263 4.70e-16 ***
Athlete      0.39471    0.03528  11.187  < 2e-16 ***
HSGPA        0.18315    0.02531   7.235 9.55e-13 ***
---
Signif. codes:  0 '***' 0.001 '**' 0.01 '*' 0.05 '.' 0.1 ' ' 1

Residual standard error: 0.428 on 954 degrees of freedom
Multiple R-squared: 0.2257,    Adjusted R-squared: 0.2233
F-statistic: 92.69 on 3 and 954 DF,  p-value: < 2.2e-16
```

However, note the histogram of the fitted values from the multiple regression model. As indicated at the beginning of this chapter, the predicted values can be lower than 0 and greater than 1, which is not possible for probabilities. See Figure 14-7.

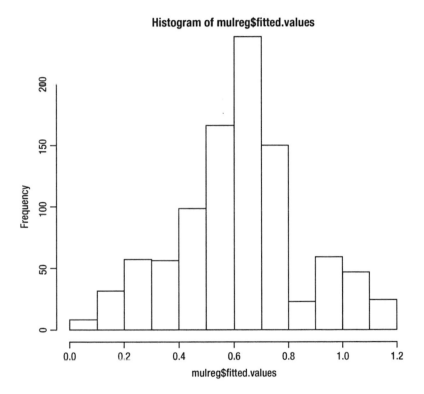

***Figure 14-7.*** *Histogram of fitted values from the multiple regression model*

# Alternatives to Logistic Regression

When we have a dichotomous criterion, there are several different approaches to data analysis. In situations where the sample sizes are small, a form of logistic regression called *exact logistic regression* is available. We have already discussed discriminant function analysis, and you have seen that multiple regression is a possible choice, but not a very good one. There are other alternatives, however:

- **Hotelling's $T^2$.** This approach is essentially a way to turn the dichotomous outcome into a grouping variable and to use the multiple predictors as outcomes. This produces an overall test, but does not give individual coefficients. It is also unclear how the "predictors turned outcomes" are adjusted for the impact of the other variables. When there are more than two groups, this analysis becomes the MANOVA (multivariate analysis of variance).

- **Probit regression.** This approach will produce results similar to those of logistic regression. Like logistic regression, probit regression is intended for binary outcome variables. The probit model is based on the cumulative normal distribution, and probit regression typically uses maximum likelihood methods to estimate the coefficients.

You may not need these approaches, but they at least worth knowing about. You can research them if you're interested in using them.

# Conclusion

Logistic regression is an excellent way to predict a dichotomous outcome using one or more dichotomous or continuous predictor variables. In this chapter, you learned how to conduct and interpret a logistic regression analysis, how to assess the model fit, and how to assess the effectiveness of the classifications based on the model.

This concludes our discussion of regression. In Chapter 15, we will examine chi-square tests of goodness of fit and independence.

# CHAPTER 15

■ ■ ■

# Chi-Square Tests

You learned about the chi-square distribution when we discussed confidence intervals for the variance and standard deviation in Chapter 8. Another contribution of Karl Pearson, the chi-square distribution has proven to be quite versatile. We use chi-square tests for determining goodness of fit and for determining the association or lack thereof for cross-tabulated categorical variables.

Earlier in the book, in Chapter 2, I used the example of Benford's Law to detect fraudulent activity by a refund officer. Although we did not discuss it in much depth at that time, we did a chi-square test of goodness of fit to determine that the observed frequencies of the leading digits in the check amounts were not distributed in accordance with Benford's Law.

The chi-square distribution is continuous, as we discussed in Chapter 8, but in this chapter, we use chi-square tests with nominal data, specifically frequencies. You will learn that there is a statistical relationship between the standard normal distribution and chi-square, and that a test of two proportions could be cast as either a chi-square test or a z test with equivalent results. We will consider chi-square tests of goodness of fit both with equal and unequal expected frequencies. We will also cover chi-square tests of independence.

## Chi-Square Tests of Goodness of Fit

With chi-square tests of goodness of fit, we compare the observed frequencies in the different levels of a categorical variable to the frequencies we would expect if some null hypothesis were true. The null hypothesis might be that there are no differences among the categories, and thus that the frequencies should be distributed equally. In that case, if the null hypothesis happened to be true, any deviations from expectation could be explained by chance. In other cases, the expected frequencies could be based on some other theoretical distribution. For example, we might divide the nominal variable into categories and then determine the expected frequencies if the data were distributed, say, normally. In more sophisticated applications, we use chi-square as a measure of "model fit," just as we use F ratios to test the significance of linear models or the change from one linear model to another. Chi-square, which is based on squared deviations, has the same additivity property that variance does, and we can thus examine the change in chi-square as a chi-square variate itself. In this book, we will stick with the basic uses of chi-square.

Recall from Chapter 2 that we calculated the value of chi-square as:

$$\chi^2 = \sum \left( \frac{(O-E)^2}{E} \right)$$

# Goodness-of-Fit Tests with Equal Expected Frequencies

You will recall our previous example of the use of Benford's Law. As you learned, humans are not very good at making up numbers that follow Benford's Law, but it is still a legitimate question as to whether people make up numbers in a random fashion. A few years ago, I asked one of my classes to poll fellow students and ask them to come up with a number between 1 and 10 inclusive. The class members collected 196 such numbers from people they encountered on campus. Here is the distribution of the digits provided by the participants. Let us use a chi-square test of goodness of fit to determine whether the numbers are provided with equal frequencies – that is, whether people are good "random number generators." I will add the calculations for chi-square at the same time, so you can see how chi-square is calculated in the case of equal expected frequencies (see Table 15-1).

**Table 15-1.** *Calculating Chi-Square with Equal Expected Frequencies*

| X | Observed | Expected | $(O-E)^2/E$ |
|---|---|---|---|
| 1 | 9 | 19.6 | 5.73 |
| 2 | 13 | 19.6 | 2.22 |
| 3 | 20 | 19.6 | 0.01 |
| 4 | 10 | 19.6 | 4.70 |
| 5 | 22 | 19.6 | 0.29 |
| 6 | 23 | 19.6 | 0.59 |
| 7 | 72 | 19.6 | 140.09 |
| 8 | 10 | 19.6 | 4.70 |
| 9 | 10 | 19.6 | 4.70 |
| 10 | 7 | 19.6 | 8.10 |
| Sum | 196 | 196 | 171.14 |

The expected frequencies do not need to be integers, though the observed ones obviously will be. The degrees of freedom for the chi-square test of goodness of fit (also known as a one-sample chi-square test) are the number of categories minus 1, so in this case the degrees of freedom are nine. We can use the pchisq() function to determine the *p* value of our calculated value of chi-square with 9 degrees of freedom. The probability of achieving such a value of chi-square if the null hypothesis is true is virtually 0. Observe also that the number 7 is clearly the most popular (due to superstitions about numbers being lucky and unlucky). Obviously, people are no better at generating random numbers than they are at following Benford's Law. See the R code to check the *p* value below:

```
> 1-pchisq(171.14, 9)
[1] 0
```

Now, here is how to perform the chi-square test in R. If we do not specify the probabilities of the expected frequencies, R will assume we have equal expected frequencies, which is true in this particular case. We need only to supply the observed frequencies, and the chisq.test() function does the rest of the work for us.

```
> o
[1]  9 13 20 10 22 23 72 10 10  7
> chisq.test(o)
```

```
        Chi-squared test for given probabilities
data:  o
X-squared = 171.1429, df = 9, p-value < 2.2e-16
```

Indeed, the *p* value is very close to 0.

## Goodness-of-Fit Tests with Unequal Expected Frequencies

As indicated above, and as we demonstrated with the Benford's Law example, it is possible to have unequal expected frequencies. The null hypothesis is typically that the data do not depart significantly from some theoretical distribution. This is one case where researchers are often interested in finding that the null hypothesis should not be rejected, as the rejection would indicate a significant departure from the theoretical distribution. This is particularly true when we are using chi-square to test distributional assumptions, such as normality.

Other than the unequal expected frequencies, there is no difference in this form of the goodness-of-fit test and the one with equal expected frequencies. The degrees of freedom are calculated in the same manner as before, by subtracting 1 from the number of categories.

As an example of the goodness-of-fit test with unequal frequencies, imagine taking a random sample of 500 people from our city and determining their blood types (using the ABO blood groups). We would expect the following percentages (for the U.S. population), as shown in Table 15-2.

*Table 15-2.* *Expected Percentages of Various (ABO) Blood Types*

| type | pct | Obs | Exp |
|------|-----|-----|-----|
| O+ | 37.4 | 195 | 187 |
| A+ | 35.7 | 165 | 178.5 |
| B+ | 8.5 | 47 | 42.5 |
| AB+ | 3.4 | 15 | 17 |
| O- | 6.6 | 30 | 33 |
| A- | 6.3 | 35 | 31.5 |
| B- | 1.5 | 8 | 7.5 |
| AB- | 0.6 | 5 | 3 |

When there are unequal expected frequencies, one supplies a vector of probabilities to the chisq.test() function. We will use the vector x we created above and specify that it is the vector of exepected probabilities under the null hypothesis. Here is how to do the chi-square test with unequal expected frequencies.

```
> exp <- c(.374, .357, .085, .034, .066, .063, .015, .006)
> obs <- c(195, 165, 47, 15, 30, 35, 8, 5)
> chisq.test(obs, p = exp)

        Chi-squared test for given probabilities

data:  obs
X-squared = 4.1033, df = 7, p-value=0.7678
```

```
Warning message:
In chisq.test(obs, p = exp) : Chi-squared approximation may be incorrect
```

The value of chi-square is 4.10, and the *p* value with 7 degrees of freedom is .768. We are not able to reject the null hypothesis, and we conclude that the blood types are distributed in accordance with our expectation (and that any deviations from expectation are due to chance).

# Chi-Square Tests of Independence

Chi-square tests of independence are used to determine whether there is an association between the categories of two nominal variables, each of which has at least two levels. The data are conveniently cross-tabulated in a two-way contingency table, which as you learned earlier in Chapter 5, can be accomplished in R using the table() function. Let *r* be the number of rows in the table, and let *c* be the number of columns. The degrees of freedom for the chi-square test of independence are $(r - 1) \times (c - 1)$. Although it is a matter of statistical and mathematical indifference as to which variable defines the rows and which defines the columns, it is a practical expedient to use the variable with fewer categories as the column variable. This makes the resulting tables narrower and easier to manage in R and in other applications.

The formula for the chi-square test of independence is as follows. The double summation simply means that you subtract the expected value for each cell from the observed value, square that difference, divide the squared difference by the expected value, and then sum across all cells to get the value of chi-square:

$$\chi^2 = \sum_{j=1}^{c} \sum_{i=1}^{r} \left( \frac{(O_{ij} - E_{ij})^2}{E_{ij}} \right)$$

Let us illustrate the chi-square test of independence with the following data. When we already have a summary table, we can submit it to the chisq.test() function. When we have raw data, we can cross-tabulate the data with the table() function and then do the chi-square test. Assume a newspaper editor collects a sample of subscribers and is interested in the relationship between the type of community the subscriber lives in and the section of the paper he or she reads first. Here are some sample data, in which the location is 1 = *city*, 2 = *suburb*, and 3 = *rural*. The sample consists of 1024 subscribers.

```
  location news sports comics
1        1  170    124     90
2        2  120    112    100
3        3  130     90     88
```

Here is one way to make this table in R:

```
> location <- c(1, 2, 3)
> news <- c(170, 120, 130)
> sports <- c(124, 112, 90)
> comics <- c(90, 100, 88)
> paper <- cbind(location, news, sports, comics)

> paper
```

```
     location news sports comics
[1,]        1  170    124     90
[2,]        2  120    112    100
[3,]        3  130     90     88
```

The expected frequencies in the chi-square test of independence are calculated by multiplying the marginal totals for each cell and dividing that product by the sample size. We can conveniently calculate the expected frequencies with a little matrix algebra in R. We define vectors with the column and row marginal totals, and then transpose the column margins into a column-wise matrix. Next we use matrix multiplication to get all the products at once. Finally, we divide each product by the sample size to get the expected frequencies. As before, note that the expected frequencies are assuming no association between the row and column variables (also known as complete independence), and the expected frequencies are not required to be integers. Examine the data with the totals and then the R code to calculate the expected frequencies:

```
> paper
                 coltot
row1    170 124  90    384
row2    120 112 100    332
row3    130  90  88    308
rowtot  420 326 278   1024

> colmargin <- c(384,332,308)
> rowmargin <- c(420,326,278)
> sampsize <- 1024
> colmargin <- t(colmargin)
> colmargin
       [,1]
[1,]   384
[2,]   332
[3,]   308
> expected <- (colmargin %*% rowmargin)/sampsize
> expected
            [,1]      [,2]      [,3]
[1,]  157.5000 122.25000 104.25000
[2,]  136.1719 105.69531  90.13281
[3,]  126.3281  98.05469  83.61719
>
```

We perform the chi-square test of independence in R as follows. Notice that we omit the column of locations to keep from calculating an incorrect value of chi-square. Our hypothesis test is not significant, and we conclude there is no association between location and the section of the paper read first.

```
> chisq.test(paper[2:4])

        Pearson's Chi-squared test

data:  newspaper[2:4]
X-squared = 7.3399, df = 4, p-value = 0.119
```

# A Special Case: Two-by-Two Contingency Tables

When we have two-by-two tables, there will obviously be 1 degree of freedom. The value of chi-square for a two-by-two contingency table can be improved by a correction for continuity called the Yates correction.

As I mentioned at the beginning of this chapter, we can recast a test of two proportions as a chi-square test. You learned in Chapter 8 that the standard normal distribution is used for confidence intervals for proportions. We can also use the standard normal distribution for a confidence interval or a hypothesis test about the difference between two proportions. As you will now discover, the z test for two proportions is statistically and mathematically equivalent to a chi-square test with one degree of freedom based on a two-by-two contingency table.

Let us use the following data for our chi-square test of independence, and then recast the problem as a test of the difference between two proportions. We will imagine we have a sample of 240 adults, 120 males, and 120 females. According to the Migraine Research Foundation, about 18% of adult women and about 6% of adult men suffer from migraine headaches. (For more information, see:
http://www.migraineresearchfoundation.org/about-migraine.html.)

Assume we have the following contingency table (see Table 15-3).

**Table 15-3.** *Hypothetical Migraine Data*

|             | Female | Male | Total |
|-------------|--------|------|-------|
| Migraine    | 18     | 10   | 28    |
| No Migraine | 102    | 110  | 212   |
| **Total**   | 120    | 120  | 240   |

Let's do the chi-square test first. R uses the Yates correction for continuity by default.

```
> female<-c(18,102)
> male<-c(10,110)
> migraine<-cbind(female,male)
> migraine
     female male
[1,]     18   10
[2,]    102  110
> chisq.test(migraine)

        Pearson's Chi-squared test with Yates' continuity correction

data:  migraine
X-squared = 1.9811, df = 1, p-value = 0.1593
```

We determine that the chi-square test fails to reject the null hypothesis that gender and migraine susceptibility are independent. If the ratio of female to male migraine sufferers is indeed 18:6, then our result is not what we had hoped for. We may have an unusual sample or we may simply need a larger sample to obtain statistical significance.

# Relating the Standard Normal Distribution to Chi-Square

As mentioned at the beginning of this chapter, we can recast a test of two proportions as a chi-square test. You learned in Chapter 8 that the standard normal distribution is used for confidence intervals for proportions.

We can also use the standard normal distribution for a confidence interval or a hypothesis test about the difference between two proportions. As you will now learn, the *z* test for two proportions is statistically and mathematically equivalent to a chi-square test with one degree of freedom based on a two-by-two contingency table.

We continue with our example of the migraine data. Let us redo the chi-square test without the Yates continuity correction:

```
> chisq.test(migraine, correct = FALSE)

        Pearson's Chi-squared test

data:  migraine
X-squared = 2.5876, df = 1, p-value=0.1077
```

Now, extract the square root of chi-square. You will learn why we did this shortly. The square root of 2.5876 is 1.6086. The prop.test() function available in the stats package also provides the facility to compare two proportions and results in output identical to that of the chisq.test() function. We configure our data slightly differently to get the test to work correctly. We can simply use the numbers of males and females who suffer from migraines and the totals to get the test to run. Here is how.

```
> count <- c(18,10)
> total <- c(120, 120)
> prop.test(count, total, correct = FALSE)

        2-sample test for equality of proportions without continuity
        correction

data:  count out of total
X-squared = 2.5876, df = 1, p-value = 0.1077
alternative hypothesis: two.sided
95 percent confidence interval:
 -0.01412271  0.14745604
sample estimates:
    prop 1      prop 2
0.15000000 0.08333333
```

We will now recast our test as a *z* test for two proportions. Note from the above output that we have proportions of .15 and .08333 for females and males, respectively. The traditional two-sample *z* test for proportions is not built into R, but it is easy enough to calculate the value of *z*. We will implement the following formula for *z*.

$$z = \frac{(p_1 - p_2)}{\sqrt{\dfrac{p_1 q_1}{n_1} + \dfrac{p_2 q_2}{n_2}}}$$

Here is the code to compute the above value. The denominator term is the standard error of the difference between proportions. This could obviously be accomplished with fewer computations, but the code illustrates the formula above.

```
> p1 <- .15
> p2 <- .08333
> q1 <- 1 - p1
> q2 <- 1 - p2
> var1 <- p1 * q1
> var2 <- p2 * q2
> n1 <- 120
> n2 <- 120
> se <- sqrt(var1/n1 + var2/n2)
> z = p1 - p2) / se
> z
[1] 1.617437
> z^2
[1] 2.616101
```

Observe that the value of $z$ is very close to the square root of the chi-square value we calculated above, an indication that the square of the z distribution is distributed as chi-square with 1 degree of freedom. If you like, you can build a function for a test of the difference between proportions. Also, observe that the test statistic $z = 1.617$ is less than 1.96 in absolute value. Because 95% of standard normal random values fall between -1.96 and +1.96, we would fail to reject the null hypothesis that the proportions of male and female migraine sufferers are different. Since studies have shown that the proportions of migraine sufferers are in fact different for males and females, our result that failed to detect this difference is due to an unrepresentative sample or due to an insufficiently large sample.

# Effect Size for Chi-Square Tests

For the chi-square goodness of fit test, Cohen suggests an effect size index called omega hat, which is represented by the symbol $\hat{\omega}$. We can calculate the value of omega as follows:

$$\hat{\omega} = \sqrt{\sum \left( \frac{(p_o - p_e)^2}{p_e} \right)}$$

where $p_o$ is the observed proportion and $p_e$ is the expected proportion. Cohen suggests that a value of .1 is a *small* effect size, .3 is a *medium* effect, and .5 is a *large* effect.

For the chi-square test of association, the phi coefficient ($\phi$) is an effect-size index for two-by-two tables such as those we discussed above. For contingency tables with three or more columns or rows, the appropriate effect-size index is called Cramér's $V$, which is an extension of the phi coefficient. We calculate these two quantities as follows:

$$\phi = \sqrt{\frac{\chi^2}{n}}$$

where we divide the calculated value of chi-square by the sample size and take the square root. Cramér's $V$ is sometimes known as Cramér's phi, confusing the issue somewhat.

$$V = \sqrt{\frac{\chi^2}{n(df_{smaller})}}$$

where $df_{smaller}$ is the degrees of freedom for the variable with the smaller number of levels. Recall that the degrees of freedom for the chi-square test of independence are $(r - 1) \times (c - 1)$. Note that phi is a special case of $V$ for a two-way table, as $df = 1$.

We can interpret both indices as we did omega above. However, a more complete interpretation is shown in the following (Table 15-4).

**Table 15-4.** *Guide to Interpreting Effect Size for φ or V*

| Value of $\varphi$ or V | Strength of Association |
| --- | --- |
| .00 and under .10 | Negligible |
| .10 and under .20 | Weak |
| .20 and under .40 | Moderate |
| .40 and under .60 | Relatively Strong |
| .60 and under .80 | Strong |
| .80 to 1.00 | Very Strong |

As examination of Table 14-3 reveals, both $\phi$ and $V$ are "correlation"-like statistics that can range from 0 to 1. See the note below for some interesting statistical background.

---

■ **Note** The phi coefficient is a special case of the correlation coefficient. If you measure two categorical variables as 0 and 1, and then correlate the two vectors of 0s and 1s, you will obtain the same value as you would with the correlation coefficient. Following is a demonstration.

---

# Demonstrating the Relationship of Phi to the Correlation Coefficient

Examine the percentages in Table 15-5. We are interested in the association between college major and gender. The data table shows the first semester choice of major for graduate students attending Texas A&M University. You can retrieve the entire study from the following web site:

http://theop.princeton.edu/reports/wp/ANNALS_Dickson_Manuscript%20(Feb%2009).pdf

**Table 15-5.** *First Semester Choice of Major for Texas A&M Graduate Students*

| First Semester Major | Female | Male | Total |
| --- | --- | --- | --- |
| Science | 47% | 35% | 42% |
| Business | 1% | 1% | 1% |
| Social sciences | 14% | 7% | 11% |
| Engineering and computer science | 10% | 35% | 22% |
| Humanities and other majors | 27% | 22% | 25% |

Assume we are interested in determining if there is an association between gender and the choice of engineering and computer science or social sciences. The following hypothetical data are based on a proposed sample of 44 students. We will perform the chi-square analysis and calculate the phi coefficient as described above. Then we will perform the analysis as a correlation with vectors 0s and 1s. The data is as follows (Table 15-6).

**Table 15-6.** *Hypothetical College Major Choice by Gender Data*

| Major | Female | Male |
|---|---|---|
| Engineering and computer science | 5 | 18 |
| Social sciences | 7 | 14 |

Let us enter the data in a matrix and perform the chi-square test of independence. We will use the version without the continuity correction. We see that there is no association between gender and choice of these majors, though at least in this sample, both are male-dominated.

```
> sexmajor <- c(5,18)
> eng <- c(5,18)
> soc <- c(7,14)
> sexmajor <- rbind(eng,soc)
> sexmajor
    [,1] [,2]
eng    5   18
soc    7   14
> chisq.test(sexmajor, correct = FALSE)

        Pearson's Chi-squared test

data:  sexmajor
X-squared = 0.744, df = 1, p-value = 0.3884
```

Now, calculate the value of phi using the formula shown in the previous section.

$$\phi = \sqrt{\frac{\chi^2}{n}} = \sqrt{\frac{0.744}{44}} = .13$$

We can calculate phi directly from the contingency table, as well. See Table 15-7, in which the basic layout of a two-by-two contingency table is shown with the letters A -D representing the cells.

**Table 15-7.** *Basic Two-by-Two Table Layout*

| Y\X | 0 | 1 | Totals |
|---|---|---|---|
| 1 | A | B | A + B |
| 0 | C | D | C + D |
| Totals: | A + C | B + D | N |

Here is the summary of the majors and genders from the above example.

```
       Females Male Total
eng          5   18    23
soc          7   14    21
coltot      12   32    44
```

We can calculate the phi coefficient as follows: phi = (BC – AD)/sqrt((A+B)(C+D)(A+C)(B+D)). Let's do it in R.

```
> A <- 5
> B <- 18
> C <- 7
> D <- 14
> phi <- (B*C - A*D)/sqrt((A+B)*(C+D)*(A+C)*(B+D))
> phi
[1] 0.1300316
```

The psych package has the phi coefficient built into it. The sign of the phi coefficient is immaterial, because we could change the sign by reversing the 0s and 1s. We interpret only the absolute value.

```
> install.packages("psych")
> require(psych)
Loading required package: psych
> t <- sexmajor
> t
    [,1] [,2]
eng    5   18
soc    7   14
> phi(t, digits = 2)
[1] -0.13
```

To complete our demonstration, let us create columns of 1s and 0s to represent the cell membership in the contingency table, and then correlate the two vectors. Here is how to arrange the data. Observe that each cell is coded 0 or 1, and the combinations are (0,0), (0,1), (1,0), and (1,1). We enter the combination for each individual in the sample to represent the cells, starting with (0,0) for the first cell, which we enter 5 times. We then repeat this process for the remaining cells so that we ultimately have all 44 individuals represented by cell membership with 0s and 1s.

```
> V1 = c(rep(0,23), rep(1,21))
> V2 = c(rep(0,5),rep(1,18),rep(0,7),rep(1,14))
> phicorrelation<-cbind(V1,V2)
> phicorrelation
   V1 V2
1   0  0
2   0  0
3   0  0
4   0  0
5   0  0
6   0  1
7   0  1
8   0  1
```

```
9    0   1
10   0   1
11   0   1
12   0   1
13   0   1
14   0   1
15   0   1
16   0   1
17   0   1
18   0   1
19   0   1
20   0   1
21   0   1
22   0   1
23   0   1
24   1   0
25   1   0
26   1   0
27   1   0
28   1   0
29   1   0
30   1   0
31   1   1
32   1   1
33   1   1
34   1   1
35   1   1
36   1   1
37   1   1
38   1   1
39   1   1
40   1   1
41   1   1
42   1   1
43   1   1
44   1   1
```

Now, note the correlation between the vectors, which is the same value as that of phi reported by the psych package. To reiterate, the phi coefficient is actually a special case of the correlation coefficient.

```
> cor(V1, V2)
[1] -0.1300316
```

# Conclusion

In this chapter, you learned how to use R to conduct chi-square tests of goodness of fit and of independence. The chi-square tests discussed here are nonparametric: You are not estimating population parameters and you are working with frequency data. Another class of nonparametric statistics exists, as well. We will consider order-based statistics and the associated hypothesis tests in Chapter 16.

■ ■ ■

# Nonparametric Tests

As you learned in Chapter 15, when we use chi-square tests for frequency data and we are not estimating population parameters, we are conducting *nonparametric* tests. A whole class of nonparametric procedures is available for data that are ordinal (ranks) in nature. Some data are ordinal by their very definition, such as employee rankings, while in other cases we convert interval or ratio data to ranks because the data violate distributional assumptions such as linearity, normality, or equality of variance. As a rule of thumb, nonparametric tests are generally less powerful than parametric tests, but that is not always the case.

In this chapter, you learn how to conduct nonparametric alternatives to *t* tests, correlation, and ANOVA. We will be looking at methods based primarily on the order relationships among the values in a data set. Although these tests are generally easy to perform, and the logic behind each is based on simple probability theory, it is common to introduce nonparametric tests after the foundation has been laid with parametric procedures. This is because, although the tests are simple to calculate, their use should be restricted to situations in which they are justified and appropriate.

There is a wide variety of nonparametric procedures and tests, but we will limit our discussion to the tests that are most commonly used and taught. The reason for the popularity of these particular tests is that they compare favorably to parametric tests in terms of statistical power when the appropriate assumptions are met, and in some cases, they outperform parametric tests.

## Nonparametric Alternatives to *t* Tests

There are several nonparametric tests that serve as alternatives to independent-samples and paired-samples *t* tests. I will illustrate the Mann-Whitney *U* test for independent samples, and the Wilcoxon signed ranks test for dependent (paired) samples. Both tests are frequently presented as tests of the differences between medians, but statistically, it is more precise to interpret them as tests of the overall distribution of the two variables. The logic behind this is that we assume the null hypothesis to be true that all possible orderings of the data are equally likely, and then test the likelihood of the ordering of our actual data if the null hypothesis is true. Unlike *t* tests that test a single parameter or the difference between parameters, order-based tests most commonly are testing the equality of the entire distribution when the rankings are compared. One way to conceptualize this is that these tests compare the *locations* of the two distributions, with a null hypothesis that the two distributions have the same location, and the alternative hypothesis that there is a significant shift in the location of one distribution as compared to the other.

### The Mann-Whitney *U* Test

The Mann-Whitney *U* Test is used to compare two ranked data sets. We either convert the data to ranks or we start with ordinal (ranked) data. The test statistic, *U*, is based on the comparison of ranks for the two distributions. Although we are using ranks, we make the assumption that the underlying dimension on which the groups are being compared is continuous in nature. To calculate *U*, we rank the combined data from both groups, from smallest to largest, and then find the value $T_1$, which is the sum of the ranks of the smaller group if the sample sizes are unequal. We then find $U$ as follows:

$$U = N_1 N_2 + \frac{N_1(N_1 + 1)}{2} - T_1$$

If $U$ is larger than $N_1 N_2/2$, then we take $U' = N_1 N_2 - U$. The test statistic is the smaller of $U$ or $U'$. Historically, we would consult tables of critical values of the $U$ statistic, but modern technology makes the tables less important.

In R, the same function is used for both the Mann-Whitney test and the Wilcoxon signed-ranks test for paired data. The function is called `Wilcox.test`, and it is located in the `stats` package. For the two-sample test, we provide a formula much like that for the linear models we have considered before, where the first value is the numeric ranking (using a correction for tied ranks), and the second value is a factor with two levels giving the corresponding groups. Thus, the layout of the data would be similar to the "stacked" data we used when examining $t$ tests.

## The Mann-Whitney Test with Small Samples

Here is an example of the Mann-Whitney test, given a small sample. Assume we have the following raw data:

```
> mannwhitney
  score group
1     8     A
2     3     A
3     4     A
4     6     A
5     1     B
6     7     B
7     9     B
8    10     B
9    12     B
```

When there are ties in the ranks, the customary correction is to assign the average rank to each instance of the same original raw score. R provides the `rank()` function for this purpose. In our example there are no ties, but we will use a data set with ties in our next example. Here is the R code to get the rankings and to combine them with the data using the `cbind()` function:

```
> order <- rank(score)
> order
[1] 6 2 3 4 1 5 7 8 9
> mannwhitney <- cbind(mannwhitney, order)
> mannwhitney
  score group order
1     8     A     6
2     3     A     2
3     4     A     3
4     6     A     4
5     1     B     1
6     7     B     5
7     9     B     7
8    10     B     8
9    12     B     9
```

Recall from our previous discussions that you can use the `tapply()` function to get the sums of ranks for the two groups.

```
> tapply(order, group, sum)
 A  B
15 30
```

In keeping with our discussion above, let us calculate the value of $U$:

$$U = N_1 N_2 + \frac{N_1(N_1+1)}{2} - T_1$$

$$= (4)(5) + \frac{4(5)}{2} - 15$$

$$= 20 + 10 - 15 = 15$$

As this value is larger than $N_1 N_2 / 2$, or 10, we take $U'$ as instructed above.

$$U' = N_1 N_2 - U = (4)(5) - 15 = 5$$

The customary approach with the Mann-Whitney test is to use a table of critical values of $U$. R provides the `qwilcox()` function, which we can use to make a table of critical values. Assume we want to have a table of critical values for $N_1$ and $N_2$ with values from 1 to 20 for each. We will create a matrix with 20 rows and 20 columns in R, and then we will write a nested loop to look up the critical values for a .05 significance level. We could repeat this process for the .01 level simply by changing that value. Here is the R code to produce the matrix, which we will call qtable. We will fill the 400-cell matrix with the numbers 1 to 400 to begin with and then look up the critical values using our loops.

```
> n1 <- 20
> n2 <- 20
> N <- n1 * n2
> Utable <- matrix(c(1:N), ncol <- n1, byrow = TRUE)
```

This produced our 400-cell matrix with 20 rows and 20 columns. Now, we write a short script with our nested loop, which does the work for us, looking up the 400 critical values and then writing them into our table one row at a time:

```
for(m in n1) {
        for(n in n2) {
                Utable[m,n] <- qwilcox(.05, m, n)
        }
}
```

Here are the first few rows of our table of critical values (Figure 16-1):

```
> head(Utable)
     [,1] [,2] [,3] [,4] [,5] [,6] [,7] [,8] [,9] [,10] [,11] [,12] [,13] [,14] [,15] [,16] [,17] [,18] [,19] [,20]
[1,]    0    0    0    0    0    0    0    0    0     0     0     0     0     0     0     0     0     0     0     1
[2,]    0    0    0    0    1    1    1    2    2     2     2     3     3     3     4     4     4     5     5     5
[3,]    0    0    0    1    2    3    3    4    4     5     6     6     7     8     8     9    10    10    11    12
[4,]    0    0    1    2    3    4    5    6    7     8     9    10    11    12    13    15    16    17    18    19
[5,]    0    1    2    3    5    6    7    9   10    12    13    14    16    17    19    20    21    23    24    26
[6,]    0    1    3    4    6    8    9   11   13    15    17    18    20    22    24    26    27    29    31    33
```

***Figure 16-1.*** *Table of critical values of U for a .05 significance level*

We could if, we liked, dress up the table by adding names for the columns, rather than the R indexes, but we really do not need to have a table of critical values. In the case of R, the exact *p* value is reported automatically, making critical value tables unnecessary. To perform the test in R, do the following:

```
> wilcox.test(order ~ group)

        Wilcoxon rank sum test

data:  order by group
W = 5, p-value = 0.2857
alternative hypothesis: true location shift is not equal to 0
```

Observe that R calls the test statistic *W* instead of *U*, because the statistic is also known by that label (for Wilcox, of course). The *p* value is higher than the customary alpha level of .05, and we conclude the distributions are approximately equal. Although I calculated the ranks and included them for the purpose of demonstration, you should be aware that you really can use the original raw data and get the same result, as shown here:

```
> wilcox.test(score ~ group)

        Wilcoxon rank sum test

data:  score by group
W = 5, p-value = 0.2857
alternative hypothesis: true location shift is not equal to 0
```

## The Mann-Whitney Test with Larger Samples

When the number of observations in one group is 20 or higher and the group sizes are roughly equal, we can take advantage of the fact that the expected value of $U$ becomes normally distributed. If we assume that all possible random arrangements of the ranks are equally likely, the expected value of $U$ will be:

$$E(U) = \frac{N_1 N_2}{2}$$

and the variance of the sampling distribution is:

$$\sigma_U^2 = \frac{N_1 N_2 (N_1 + N_2 + 1)}{12}$$

Therefore, when we have relatively large samples, we can test the hypothesis of no difference in the population distributions by using the standard normal distribution:

$$z = \frac{U - E(U)}{\sigma_U}$$

We can use either $U$ or $U'$ for a two-tailed test, as the absolute value of $z$ will be the same for either. If, on the other hand, the test is one tailed, the sign of the $z$ score should be considered. Let us conduct this test with a larger sample size and use the $z$ score approach explained above. Imagine we have the following data, which represent the psychological need for competence of student leaders and a nonequivalent control group consisting of a randomly selected class at the same university.[1] There are 19 leaders and 23 nonleaders in the sample. Let us analyze this data the same way we did the smaller sample, finding the sums of ranks for each group. Note that when we obtain the ranks from these real data (collected by me as part of a research project), there are tied ranks, which we correct by giving the average rank to each tied data value. Here are the data, along with the ranks.

```
> mwlarge
   competence      group       order
1        78.6     leader        26.0
2        76.2     leader        22.5
3        85.7     leader        32.5
4        81.0     leader        28.5
5        97.6     leader        40.5
6        61.9     leader         9.0
7        88.1     leader        35.5
8        59.5     leader         7.0
9        73.8     leader        19.0
10       57.1     leader         5.0
11       81.0     leader        28.5
12       92.9     leader        38.0
13       83.3     leader        30.0
14       78.6     leader        26.0
15      100.0     leader        42.0
16       88.1     leader        35.5
17       76.2     leader        22.5
18       76.2     leader        22.5
19       78.6     leader        26.0
20       66.7   nonleader       13.5
21       71.4   nonleader       17.0
22       57.1   nonleader        5.0
23       52.4   nonleader        2.0
24       57.1   nonleader        5.0
25       85.7   nonleader       32.5
26       76.2   nonleader       22.5
27       64.3   nonleader       11.5
28       54.8   nonleader        3.0
29       92.9   nonleader       38.0
30       73.8   nonleader       19.0
31       97.6   nonleader       40.5
32       64.3   nonleader       11.5
33       69.1   nonleader       15.5
34       85.7   nonleader       32.5
35       50.0   nonleader        1.0
36       69.1   nonleader       15.5
37       92.9   nonleader       38.0
38       61.9   nonleader        9.0
39       61.9   nonleader        9.0
```

[1]This example is taken from Pace, L. A. (2008). *The Excel 2007 data and statistics cookbook* (2nd ed.). Anderson, SC: TwoPaces.com.

```
40      66.7    nonleader    13.5
41      73.8    nonleader    19.0
42      85.7    nonleader    32.5
```

We find that the variances are different, and though we could use the *t* test assuming the variances are not equal (which you learned how to do in Chapter 9), let us use the Mann-Whitney test here for illustrative purposes.

```
> tapply(competence, group, var)
   leader nonleader
 133.9461  186.0542
```

Again, we use the `tapply()` function for finding the sums of ranks for the two groups.

```
> tapply(order, group, sum)
   leader nonleader
    496.5     406.5
```

Now, we calculate $U$:

$$U = N_1 N_2 + \frac{N_1(N_1+1)}{2} - T_1$$
$$= (23)(19) + \frac{23(24)}{2} - 406.5$$
$$= 437 + 276 - 406.5 = 306.5$$

As before, this value is greater than $N_1 N_2/2 = 218.5$, so we find U'.

$$U' = N_1 N_2 - U = (23)(10) - 306.5 = 130.5$$

Now, let us compare the $z$ score approach and the Mann-Whitney U test. Note that the `wilcox.test()` function computes the same value of $U$ we did but does not compute $U'$. The function also warns us that the $p$ values are not exact when there are tied ranks.

```
> wilcox.test(competence ~ group)

        Wilcoxon rank sum test with continuity correction

data:  competence by group
W = 306.5, p-value = 0.02674
alternative hypothesis: true location shift is not equal to 0

Warning message:
In wilcox.test.default(x = c(78.6, 76.2, 85.7, 81, 97.6, 61.9, 88.1,  :
  cannot compute exact p-value with ties
```

Now, let us calculate the required $z$ score for the normal approximation:

$$E(U) = \frac{N_1 N_2}{2} = \frac{(23)(19)}{2} = \frac{437}{2} = 218.5$$

$$\sigma_U^2 = \frac{(23)(19)(23+19+1)}{12} = \frac{18791}{12} = 1565.9167$$

$$z = \frac{306.5-218.5}{\sqrt{1565.9167}} = \frac{88}{39.5717} = 2.2238$$

Next, we find the $p$ value for this $z$ score, using a two-tailed probability. Remember, we use the `pnorm()` function for this purpose. We double the probability to get the two-tailed $p$ value.

```
> 2*(1-pnorm(2.2238))
[1] 0.0261619
```

Note how closely our $p$ value of .0262 agrees with the $p$ value from the Mann-Whitney test above, which was .0267. The difference of only .0005 indicates the normal approximation was very effective in this case. Let us also do the $t$ test for unequal variances, just for the sake of comparison. We see that all three approaches lead us to the same conclusion. Student leaders have a significantly higher need for competence than does the average member of a randomly selected class.

```
> t.test(competence ~ group)

        Welch Two Sample t-test

data:  competence by group
t = 2.2586, df = 39.96, p-value = 0.02944
alternative hypothesis: true difference in means is not equal to 0
95 percent confidence interval:
  0.9238253 16.6519184
sample estimates:
   mean in group leader mean in group nonleader
              79.70526                70.91739
```

## The Wilcoxon Signed-Ranks Test

The Wilcoxon signed-ranks test is the nonparametric equivalent to the paired-samples $t$ test. As with the Mann-Whitney test, we will find that the normal distribution can be used with larger samples.

### The Wilcoxon Signed-Ranks Test for Small Samples

In R, much as we did with the one-sample and paired-samples $t$ tests, we can supply either the vector of differences as $x$ or the paired scores as $x$ and $y$. For the matched-pairs test, we must specify `paired = TRUE`. Assume we have the following (hypothetical) data, which represent the length of time a participant can keep his or her hand in ice water before (control) and after (treatment) taking an experimental painkiller:

```
> signedRanks
  id treatment control
1  A        15      10
2  B        17      15
3  C        10      11
```

```
4   D        14      13
5   E        13       7
6   F        10       5
7   G         8       5
```

We perform the Wilcoxon signed-ranks test as follows:

```
> wilcox.test(treatment, control, paired = TRUE)

        Wilcoxon signed rank test with continuity correction

data:  treatment and control
V = 26.5, p-value = 0.04179
alternative hypothesis: true location shift is not equal to 0

Warning message:
In wilcox.test.default(treatment, control, paired = TRUE) :
  cannot compute exact p-value with ties
```

The test is significant at $p = .042$, which indicates the painkiller is working. R gives us a warning about tied ranks. Let us understand the test statistic that R calls $V$. Most statistics books call this value $T$ (not to be confused with the $t$ distribution). Using the sign of the difference as a factor, calculate the sum of the absolute value of the ranks for both plus and minus signs. In other words, we rank the differences ignoring sign and then apply the sign of the difference to the ranks (thus the name signed-ranks test).

Here is how we can work this out:

```
> diffs <- treatment - control
> diffs
[1]  5  2 -1  1  6  5  3
> order <- rank(diffs)
> order
[1] 5.5 3.0 1.0 2.0 7.0 5.5 4.0
> signs <- c(1,1,-1,1,1,1,1)
> signed <- order * signs
> signed
[1]  5.5  3.0 -1.0  2.0  7.0  5.5  4.0
```

Now that we have our signed ranks, let us put everything in the same place, namely our data frame:

```
> signedRanks <- cbind(signedRanks, diffs, order, signs, signed)
> signedRanks
  id treatment control diffs order signs signed
1  A        15      10     5   5.5     1    5.5
2  B        17      15     2   3.0     1    3.0
3  C        10      11     1   1.5    -1   -1.5
4  D        14      13     1   1.5     1    1.5
5  E        13       7     6   7.0     1    7.0
6  F        10       5     5   5.5     1    5.5
7  G         8       5     3   4.0     1    4.0
> tapply(signed, signs, sum)
  -1    1
-1.5 26.5
```

Note that the statistic R is calling $V$ is the larger of the two sums of the signed ranks. It is immaterial whether to use the larger or the smaller sum when you are conducting a two-tailed test. To conduct this test, remember, we needed to calculate the differences between the pairs, rank their absolute values from lowest to highest, and then assign the sign of the original difference to the ranks (thus the name signed ranks). Now, we take the absolute value of the sum of the ranks for the sign (in our current case the minus sign) with the lower frequency. We call this value $T$ (or $V$), which we just calculated.

## The Wilcoxon Signed-Ranks Test for Larger Samples

For larger samples, the expected value of $T$ is

$$E(T) = \frac{N(N+1)}{4}$$

and the variance is

$$\sigma_T^2 = \frac{N(N+1)(2N+1)}{24}$$

We can then use the following z score for our test statistic:

$$z = \frac{T - E(T)}{\sigma_T}$$

Let us calculate the $z$ score in R, and compare the $p$ value to that of the wilcox.test() function. To show the choice to use $T' = 40$ or $T = 15$ is immaterial, we will calculate both z scores and find they differ only in sign:

```
> ET <- (10 * 11) / 4
> VT <- (10 * 11) * ((2 * 10) + 1) / 24
> T
[1] 15
> Tprime <- 40
> z <- (Tprime - ET) / sqrt(VT)
> z
[1] 1.274118
> z2 <- (T - ET) / sqrt(VT)
> z2
[1] -1.274118
```

Now, we look up the two-tailed probability for a z score of 1.274118. The $p$ value is similar to that found by the wilcox.test() function.

```
> 2*(1 - pnorm(z))
[1] 0.2026216
```

# Nonparametric Alternatives to ANOVA

The two most commonly used nonparametric alternatives to ANOVA are the Kruskal-Wallis "analysis of variance" of ranks for independent groups and the Friedman test for repeated measures. Both tests are illustrated below.

# The Kruskal-Wallis Test

In R, this test is called the kruskal.test and is located in the stats package. It is useful to think of the Kruskal-Wallis test as a direct extension of the Mann-Whitney $U$ test to three or more groups, and in fact if you use the Kruskal-Wallis test with only two groups, your results will be equivalent to those from the Mann-Whitney test.

To perform this test, we rank all observations, treating the data set as a single group. We analyze the ranks in a fashion similar to the one-way ANOVA. Note that if the ranking has been done correctly, the sum of the ranks will always be the quantity:

$$T = \frac{N(N+1)}{2}$$

We sum the ranks for each group, and then calculate the test statistic $H$. Assume we have $k$ groups.

$$H = \frac{12}{N(N+1)} \sum_{j=1}^{k} \frac{T_j^2}{n_j} - 3(N+1)$$

When we have large enough sample sizes, $H$ is distributed as chi-square with $k - 1$ degrees of freedom. Technically, when there are tied ranks, we can improve the estimate by a correction factor, but the adjustment makes little difference unless the number of ties is large and $N$ is small. Further, when the tied ranks are within the same group, the correction has no effect at all. The interested reader should consult a text on nonparametric statistics for more detail.

To illustrate the Kruskal-Wallis test, let us return to the data we used in Chapter 10 for the one-way ANOVA. Here are the data again. We have 15 identical vehicles, each driven the same number of miles (by use of a dynamometer, which simulates highway driving conditions). The vehicles were randomly assigned to three groups, and each group used a specific brand of regular unleaded gasoline.

Let us calculate $H$ using the formulas above. We need to calculate the total of the ranks for each brand. As you have probably already guessed, we will use tapply() for this purpose. First, however, we must rank the MPG figures for the entire sample.

```
> order <- rank(mpg)
> order
 [1]  3.5  8.0  5.0 10.0 11.0  9.0 13.0 12.0 14.0 15.0  2.0  3.5  6.0  1.0  7.0
> kruskal <- cbind(kruskal, order)
> kruskal
    mpg brand order
1  34.0    A   3.5
2  35.0    A   8.0
3  34.3    A   5.0
4  35.5    A  10.0
5  35.8    A  11.0
6  35.3    B   9.0
7  36.5    B  13.0
8  36.4    B  12.0
9  37.0    B  14.0
10 37.6    B  15.0
11 33.3    C   2.0
12 34.0    C   3.5
13 34.7    C   6.0
14 33.0    C   1.0
15 34.9    C   7.0
```

```
> tapply(order, brand, sum)
   A    B    C
37.5 63.0 19.5
```

The sum of these MPG ranks is also the overall sum of the ranks, as stated above. See the following:

```
> sum(order)
[1] 120
> length(order)
[1] 15
> (15 * 16) / 2
[1] 120
```

Now, we can calculate $H$.

$$H = \frac{12}{N(N+1)} \sum_{j=1}^{k} \frac{T_j^2}{n_j} - 3(N+1)$$

$$= \frac{12}{15(16)} \sum_{j=1}^{k} \frac{T_j^2}{n_j} - 3(16)$$

$$= \frac{12}{240} \left[ \frac{37.5^2}{5} + \frac{63^2}{5} + \frac{19.5^2}{5} \right] - 3(16)$$

$$= 0.05[281.25 + 793.8 + 76.05 - 48]$$

$$= 0.05(1151.1) - 48$$

$$= 9.555$$

This value will be distributed as chi-square with k – 1 = 3 – 1 = 2 degrees of freedom. Let us find the p value using the built-in chi-square distribution.

```
> 1 - pchisq(9.555, 2)
[1] 0.008417015
```

Now, let us perform the Kruskal-Wallis test using the kruskal.test() function in R. To do the test, we supply the dependent variable and the grouping factor. As I indicated in the discussion above, the correction for tied ranks applied by the R function changes the value of $H$ slightly. The nonparametric test finds a significant difference both with and without the correction for ties, and the p values differ only very slightly. The effect of the correction is to improve the test's power by a very small amount.

```
> kruskal.test(mpg, brand)

        Kruskal-Wallis rank sum test

data:  mpg and brand
Kruskal-Wallis chi-squared = 9.5721, df = 2, p-value = 0.008345
```

Recall the ANOVA results from Chapter 10, which are repeated below. Comparisons of the p values reveal the nonparametric test is less powerful than the parametric procedure.

```
> results <- aov(mpg ~ brand)
> summary(results)
```

```
          Df Sum Sq Mean Sq F value  Pr(>F)
brand      2 17.049   8.525   12.74 0.00108 **
Residuals 12  8.028   0.669
---
Signif. codes:  0 '***' 0.001 '**' 0.01 '*' 0.05 '.' 0.1 ' ' 1
```

## The Friedman Test for Repeated Measures or Randomized Blocks

The Friedman test can be used as a nonparametric alternative to the repeated-measures ANOVA, or for data that would equate to a randomized block design in ANOVA terminology. These designs have unreplicated observations – that is, a single observation per cell. The R function is in the stats package and is called friedman.test().

To perform this test, we set up the data as though we have a repeated-measures analysis, with each column representing a separate measure, and each row representing a single unit or participant. We will use $K$ to represent the number of individuals and $J$ to represent the number of measures. We will rank the observations within each row, using the customary correction for ties, and then sum the resulting ranks by columns. Each column, then, has a total of ranks, which we will symbolize as $T_j$. The test statistic for large samples is:

$$\chi^2 = \frac{12}{KJ(J+1)}\left[\sum_{j=1}^{J} T_j^2\right] - 3K(J+1)$$

To illustrate the Friedman test, let us return to the data from Chapter 11 used to demonstrate the repeated-measures ANOVA. Here are the data, reconfigured as is customary for the Friedman test:

```
> friedman
  time1 time2 time3 time4
1     0     1     3     4
2     1     2     4     5
3     2     3     3     5
4     3     4     4     5
5     2     3     3     4
6     2     3     3     5
```

Remember, we must convert each row into ranks, so each row will consist of ranks rather than raw scores. Because there are four repeated measures, each row will have four rankings. We will deal with ties as usual. Here are the ranks by rows:

```
1    2     3     4
1    2     3     4
1    2.5   2.5   4
1    2.5   2.5   4
1    2.5   2.5   4
1    2.5   2.5   4
```

Here is our chi-square statistic:

$$\chi^2 = \frac{12}{KJ(J+1)}\left[\sum_{i=1}^{J} T_j^2\right] - 3K(J+1)$$

$$= \frac{12}{6\times4\times5}\left[6^2+14^2+16^2+24^2\right] - 3\times6\times5$$

$$= \frac{12}{120}\left[36+196+256+576\right] - 90$$

$$= 0.1\times1064 - 90$$

$$16.4$$

This value of chi-square is obviously significant with $J - 1 = 4 - 1 = 3$ degrees of freedom. To do the Friedman test in R, let us put the data back into "long" format:

```
   id time fitness
1   1   1      0
2   2   1      1
3   3   1      2
4   4   1      3
5   5   1      2
6   6   1      2
7   1   2      1
8   2   2      2
9   3   2      3
10  4   2      4
11  5   2      3
12  6   2      3
13  1   3      3
14  2   3      4
15  3   3      3
16  4   3      4
17  5   3      3
18  6   3      3
19  1   4      4
20  2   4      5
21  3   4      5
22  4   4      5
23  5   4      4
24  6   4      5
```

Now, we can do the Friedman test as follows:

```
> friedman.test(fitness, time, id)

        Friedman rank sum test

data:  fitness, time and id
Friedman chi-squared = 17.5714, df = 3, p-value = 0.0005391
```

And, indeed, the chi-square is highly significant. As with Kruskal-Wallis test, the Friedman test function in R uses a correction for tied ranks, which increases the power of the test. Observe by comparing the Friedman test results to those of the repeated-measures ANOVA that, in this case, the nonparametric test, which is testing the ranks rather than the raw scores, is fairly powerful, though less powerful than the parametric procedure.

```
> id <- factor(id)
> time <- factor(time)
> results <- aov(fitness ~ time + Error(id/time))
> summary(results)

Error: id
          Df Sum Sq Mean Sq F value Pr(>F)
Residuals  5  8.333   1.667

Error: id:time
          Df Sum Sq Mean Sq F value   Pr(>F)
time       3   28.5   9.500    28.5 1.93e-06 ***
Residuals 15    5.0   0.333
---
Signif. codes:  0 '***' 0.001 '**' 0.01 '*' 0.05 '.' 0.1 ' ' 1
```

# Nonparametric Alternatives to Correlation

We will examine two nonparametric alternatives to linear correlation. In each case, we convert the data to ranks (or collect the data as ranks initially). The two indices are the Spearman rank correlation and Kendall's tau statistic.

## Spearman Rank Correlation

When we have pairs of ordinal data, we can correlate the ranks. This index is known as Spearman's Rho, or the Spearman rank correlation coefficient. Because with ranks there are no equal intervals, this index will give us a measure of whether the relationship between two variables is *monotonically* increasing or decreasing, but will not give us an indication of a linear relationship. When there are tied ranks, the best way to calculate $r_s$ is to rank the observations and use the cor() function. However, when there are no tied ranks, the following simpler computational form can be used:

$$r_s = 1 - \left( \frac{6\left(\sum_{i=1}^{N} D_i^2\right)}{N(N^2 - 1)} \right)$$

where $D_i$ is the difference between ranks associated with the particular individual $i$, and $N$ is the total number of individuals.

We interpret the rank correlation in a fashion similar to that of the standard correlation coefficient. To illustrate, let us examine the number of locations and the revenues generated by the 15 largest fast food establishments in the U.S. (These data were obtained from Yahoo Finance.). The sales figures are 2011 annual sales in billions of dollars.

```
> spearman <- read.csv("spearman.csv", header = TRUE)
> spearman
          Brand Locations Sales
1     McDonald's     14098 34.20
2         Subway     24722 11.40
```

```
3        Starbucks    10787  9.75
4          Wendy's     5876  8.50
5      Burger King     7231  8.50
6        Taco Bell     5674  6.80
7   Dunkin' Donuts     7015  5.92
8        Pizza Hut     7595  5.40
9              KFC     4793  4.50
10     Chick-Fil_A     1600  4.05
11           Sonic     3531  3.68
12         Domino's    4907  3.40
13    Panera Bread     1480  3.30
14          Arby's     3484  3.03
15  Jack in the Box    2221  3.01
```

Let us rank the number of locations and the sales figures for these data.

```
> LocRank <- rank(Locations)
> SalesRank <- rank(Sales)
> spearman <- cbind(spearman, LocRank, SalesRank)
> spearman
              Brand Locations Sales LocRank SalesRank
1         McDonald's    14098 34.20      14      15.0
2            Subway    24722 11.40      15      14.0
3         Starbucks    10787  9.75      13      13.0
4           Wendy's     5876  8.50       9      11.5
5       Burger King     7231  8.50      11      11.5
6         Taco Bell     5674  6.80       8      10.0
7    Dunkin' Donuts     7015  5.92      10       9.0
8         Pizza Hut     7595  5.40      12       8.0
9               KFC     4793  4.50       6       7.0
10      Chick-Fil_A     1600  4.05       2       6.0
11            Sonic     3531  3.68       5       5.0
12         Domino's     4907  3.40       7       4.0
13     Panera Bread     1480  3.30       1       3.0
14           Arby's     3484  3.03       4       2.0
15  Jack in the Box     2221  3.01       3       1.0
```

There is a correlation of $r = .57$ between sales and the number of locations, but examination of the scatterplot (see Figure 16-2) shows the relationship is not particularly well described by a straight line.

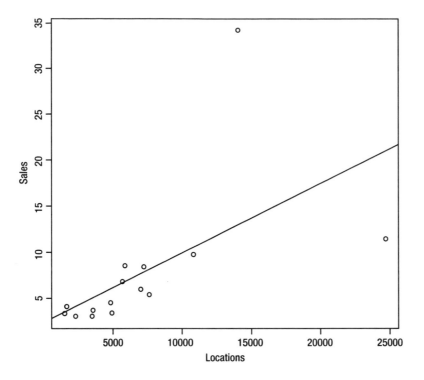

**Figure 16-2.** *Scatterplot of sales and locations of the most profitable fast food restaurants*

Let us calculate the rank correlation using the formula shown above. We need to add a column of difference scores, which is easy to do in R:

```
> diffs <- LocRank - SalesRank
> spearman <- cbind(spearman, diffs)
```

Now, we can use R to calculate the sum of the squared differences:

```
> diffssq <- sum(diffs ^ 2)
> diffssq
[1] 67.5
```

First, we will correlate the ranks and see what we get when we use the simple formula shown above and repeated below for your convenience. Interestingly, the rank correlation is substantially higher than the product-moment correlation, showing the lack of linearity in the data.

```
> cor(salesrank, locationrank)
[1] 0.8793569
```

We see that this formula produces the same value as the cor() function applied to the ranks:

$$r_s = 1 - \left( \frac{6\left( \sum_{i=1}^{N} D_i^2 \right)}{N(N^2 - 1)} \right)$$

$$= 1 - \left( \frac{6(67.5)}{15(15^2 - 1)} \right)$$

$$= 1 - \left( \frac{405}{15(225 - 1)} \right)$$

$$= 1 - \frac{405}{3360} = .8794$$

# The Kendall Tau Coefficient

The Kendall tau coefficient is very different from the correlation of ranks. Instead, the coefficient is based on the number of *inversions* in order for pairs of observations a and b when a > b is one ranking and b > a is the other ranking. When the two rankings are identical, there is no inversion. The τ statistic is defined as follows:

$$\tau = 1 - \left[ \frac{2(\text{number of inversions})}{\text{number of pairs}} \right]$$

This is essentially a difference in proportions: the proportion of "agreements" between the two rankings and the proportion of "disagreements." As the method of calculating τ in most statistics texts is a graphic rather than a solely numeric one, I will not show it here.

R provides the cor.test() function, which is located in the stats package to calculate τ. The same function can be used to calculate and test the significance of the Spearman rank correlation and the Pearson product-moment correlation coefficient. Although the R documentation refers to τ as a "rank correlation," we will limit our use of rank correlation to describe only the Spearman coefficient. We will calculate the Kendall coefficient for the same data we just used for the Spearman rank correlation. Technically, it is better to call the τ coefficient an index of agreement or concordance. Here is the R code to calculate τ, which we will see is between the values of the correlation coefficient (.57) and Spearman's rank correlation (.88):

```
> cor.test(salesrank, locationrank, method = "kendall")

        Kendall's rank correlation tau

data:  salesrank and locationrank
z = 3.6665, p-value = 0.0002459
alternative hypothesis: true tau is not equal to 0
sample estimates:
      tau
0.7081421

Warning message:
In cor.test.default(salesrank, locationrank, method = "kendall") :
  Cannot compute exact p-value with ties
```

# Conclusion

An entire branch of statistics has been devoted to nonparametric procedures. Some of the "new" statistical approaches, which are based on resampling the same data from a sample and not on estimating parameters, are also nonparametric in that sense. The statistics invented by Pearson and Fisher about 100 years ago, and then developed for the next 50, have stood us in good stead, but are being replaced by techniques that allow us to make inferences without having to estimate population parameters or having to know the sampling distribution of a certain statistic. We will refer to these techniques later in Chapter 18, after discussing using R for simulation in Chapter 17.

# CHAPTER 17

■ ■ ■

# Using R for Simulation

R shines as a tool for simulations of all kinds. Simulations have been around for a very long time. I remember doing Monte Carlo simulations as a graduate student with FORTRAN-IV programs I wrote. That was fun, but R is far more versatile, and as a result, more fun.

In this chapter, we quickly revisit mathematical operations and also cover additional ones. We will also revisit input and output in R, adding to our current knowledge and skills new ways to get data into and out of R. But the most important topic of Chapter 17 is simulation. I will introduce the topic in a conceptual way and then illustrate it with examples. We will not get too sophisticated here, but you will learn some useful techniques and will build a foundation for performing simulations of your own.

## Defining Statistical Simulation

The term *simulation* has a variety of meanings, but we will limit ourselves to *statistical simulation*. I define this term to mean the generation of random variables followed by the statistical analysis of those variables. The purposes of simulation are to solve inference and decision problems, for example, to understand the distribution of quantities that are not well described by mathematical functions or formulas, and to understand the real world by the creation and analysis of artificial (but still very meaningful) data. Simulation is also often called *modeling*, but to avoid confusion we will not use that term. Throughout this book, when we refer to simulation, we mean statistical simulation.

The general steps in simulation are the following:

1. Describe possible outcomes.

2. Explain how each outcome is linked to one or more random numbers.

3. Generate a list of random numbers.

4. Choose one of the random numbers.

5. Simulate the outcome for that random number.

6. Repeat steps 4 and 5 many times.

7. Examine the outcomes to determine if there is a stable pattern.

8. Analyze and report the simulated outcomes and their meaning.

Although this book does not assume any mathematical background beyond college algebra or any programming experience, you will understand this chapter more fully if you have had advanced mathematical and statistical training and if you have programmed in another language besides R. I will cover only a few basic techniques in this chapter, but enough to help you understand the rich complexity of R.

# Random Numbers

At the heart of simulation is the generation of random (really *pseudorandom*) numbers. For practical purposes, pseudorandom numbers behave enough like truly random numbers. All computer-based random number generators work in the same way:

1. A seed number is needed by the process or function that generates the random number. The seed can be supplied by the user, but is often supplied (generated) by the computer as needed.

2. The seed number is then supplied to the mathematical function used to generate a random number. The process or function returns the random number and a new seed for generating the next random number.

Specifically, the way R implements this approach is that we can use the set.seed() function to declare the seed for the random number generator. If we do that, we can then get the same random numbers when we use the random number generator whenever we supply the same seed. For example, see what happens when we use rnorm() to generate two vectors of $z$ scores from the standard normal distribution. The seed will automatically be reset by R, so we must set it a second time. Note the vectors are identical.

```
> set.seed(7)
> z1<- rnorm(10)
> z1
 [1]  2.2872472 -1.1967717 -0.6942925 -0.4122930 -0.9706733 -0.9472799
 [7]  0.7481393 -0.1169552  0.1526576  2.1899781
> set.seed(7)
> z2<- rnorm(10)
> z2
 [1]  2.2872472 -1.1967717 -0.6942925 -0.4122930 -0.9706733 -0.9472799
 [7]  0.7481393 -0.1169552  0.1526576  2.1899781
> z1 - z2
 [1] 0 0 0 0 0 0 0 0 0 0
```

Now, observe what happens when we do not set the seed, but simply allow R to select it for us. We will generate two additional vectors or random normal deviates. As we would expect to be the case, our two new vectors are not identical because the seed was changed.

```
> z4<- rnorm(10)
> z5<- rnorm(10)
> cbind(z4, z5)
                z4          z5
 [1,] -2.113736990  0.27647884
 [2,] -0.370527471 -2.05087766
 [3,]  0.522867793  0.01419021
 [4,]  0.517805536  0.58226648
 [5,] -1.402510873 -0.03472639
 [6,] -0.485636726 -0.11666415
 [7,]  0.008498139 -0.64498209
 [8,] -1.282113287  1.74441160
 [9,] -1.111578841  0.36609447
[10,]  0.300665411 -0.06680993
> z4 == z5
 [1] FALSE FALSE FALSE FALSE FALSE FALSE FALSE FALSE FALSE FALSE
```

When deciding whether or not to use the set.seed() function, the key question is whether you want the results to be reproducible. If so, then use set.seed(). If you want the results to be more "random," then you may choose not to set the seed.

You will recall that we can generate random variables for many probability distributions in R. These include the normal distribution, the *t* distribution, the *F* distribution, and the chi-square distribution. We have already used some of these functions in various demonstrations, and thus we have already been doing simulations without bringing attention to that fact. Very often the use of simulated data is preferable to the study of "real" data because we have more control over the characteristics of the simulated data.

## Sampling and Resampling

Another hallmark of simulation is sampling. R gives us the ability to sample from a larger set of observations, one we often treat as a population. The sampling can be accomplished either with or without replacement. Sampling without replacement is associated with a technique known as *jackknifing*, while sampling with replacement is used in a technique known as *bootstrapping*. We will discuss and illustrate these techniques in Chapter 18.

Along with sampling, we often do *resampling*, taking samples with replacement from the original data set. This allows us to extrapolate from the sample data without making any assumptions about a population, and to estimate the confidence intervals for statistics derived from these multiple samples. What is interesting about this is that we do not need any prior knowledge of the sampling distribution of the statistic, and we can even derive new statistics and study their distributional properties without having access to a population or making any assumptions about population parameters. We will talk more about this in Chapter 18.

## Revisiting Mathematical Operations in R

Before we proceed with our discussion on simulation, let us quickly revisit doing math in R. In Chapters 1 to 3, you learned how to use R as a command-line calculator, and then how to program and write functions in R. These skills are important if you want to become more than a casual R user. We spoke in Chapter 1 about the various mathematical operators built into R. R also has some other useful mathematical capabilities.

As you know by now, we can do various mathematical operations in R either from the command line or through scripts and functions. You already learned the R operators for addition, subtraction, division, multiplication, and exponentiation. R functions are useful for various other mathematical calculations, including roots, logarithms, and trigonometric functions. In our simulations, we will often use a for() loop to capture the statistic of interest in a vector. We will use some customary ways to analyze and report these statistics, including confidence intervals, summaries, counts, and probabilities.

# Some Simulations in R

In the following sections, I illustrate the use of R for various kinds of simulations. This set of simulations is not meant to be exhaustive but illustrative (and instructive) only. The possibilities are almost limitless. You will see how I often use explicit looping to capture the values of interest, as mentioned above. A combination of numerical and graphical analyses will help us understand the principles and concepts being illustrated.

## A Confidence Interval Simulation

To illustrate how simulations can be performed in R, let us perform 100 simulations of a sample of a population with a mean of 500 and a standard deviation of 100. We will calculate a 95% confidence interval for each simulation, and in the process, see whether the "true" population mean of 500 is "in" or "out" of the confidence interval. We will assume in this case the population variance is known. Here is some code to accomplish our purposes. We set up our simulation with the number of simulations, a vector for the lower confidence limits and a vector for the upper confidence limits. We define the sample size, the mean, and the standard deviation as well:

```
nreps <- 100
ll <- numeric(nreps)
ul <- numeric(nreps)
n <- 100
mu <- 500
sigma <- 100
for(i in 1:nreps) {
        print(i)
        set.seed(i)
        x <- rnorm(n, mu, sigma)
        ll[i] <- mean(x) - qnorm(0.975)*sqrt(sigma^2/n)
        ul[i] <- mean(x) + qnorm(0.975)*sqrt(sigma^2/n)
        }
```

See that we use a for() loop to set the seeds for the 100 successive simulations, and produce a vector, x, which is our simulated sample from the normal distribution with a mean of 500 and a standard deviation (sigma) of 100. We can print out the value of $i$ as confirmation that our loop in fact looped.

Now, we can explore our confidence intervals by looking at ranges, the mean of each, and the coverages to see how many of our 100 confidence intervals have "captured" the true population value of mu, which is 500. There are a number of ways we can do this. One of them is to use the which() function you learned about earlier to identify any intervals in which the value of 500 is either below the lower limit or above the upper limit. Following is some R code to illustrate how to determine whether the population value is inside the confidence limits. We sort the limits and then "eyeball" them to see which limits do not contain the value 500. We find that only one of the 100 intervals in this case does not contain 500. All the lower limits are below 500, and 500 is below only one of the upper limits. Thus, we have 1% of the confidence limits that do not contain the true population mean, and 99% that do (higher than the expected 5% and 95%, respectively). Note the use of the mean() function and the vectorized & to examine the coverage with a single expression.

```
> which(ul <= 500)
[1] 85

> mean((ll <= 500) & (500 <= ul))
[1] 0.99
```

We can also use the table() function to get a count of the number of confidence intervals in which 500 is outside the limits of the interval. The output from the table() function will make it clearer what the mean() function shown above is doing.

```
> table(ll >= 500)

FALSE
  100
> table(ul <= 500)

FALSE   TRUE
   99      1
```

In practice, many more than 100 replicates of the statistic in question are calculated and analyzed. For example, if we repeat our simulation not 100, but 10,000 times, we will learn more about the confidence intervals we construct. Let us change the number of simulations and construct the tables again. We would expect 250 of the 10,000 intervals to have lower limits higher than 500 and 250 of the intervals to have upper limits below 500. The simulated intervals are very close to our expectation. This is an illustration of the law of large numbers.

```
> nreps <- 10000
> ll <- numeric(nreps)
> ul <- numeric(nreps)
> n <- 100
> mu <- 500
> sigma <- 100
> for(i in 1:nreps) {
+ set.seed(i)
+ x <- rnorm(n, mu, sigma)
+ ll[i] <- mean(x) - qnorm(0.975)*sqrt(sigma^2/n)
+ ul[i] <- mean(x) + qnorm(0.975)*sqrt(sigma^2/n)
+ }
```

We use the table() function again to determine how many of the lower limits are less than and greater than 500, as well as how many of the upper limits are above and below 500.

```
> table(ll <= 500)

FALSE   TRUE
  239   9761
> table(ul >= 500)

FALSE   TRUE
  263   9737
```

A histogram of the limits shows that, like the random variates we generated, they tend to have a very "normal-looking" distribution. See Figure 17-1 for the histogram of the lower limits we just generated.

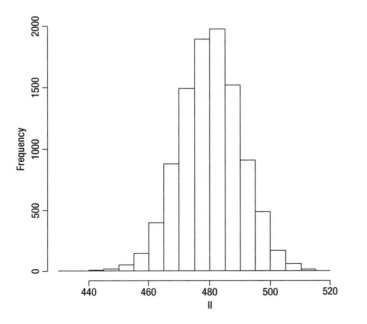

**Figure 17-1.** *With 10,000 replications, the histogram shows a very "normal looking" distribution of lower limits*

# A *t* Test Simulation

In the simulation we just completed, we made the assumption that we know the population standard deviation, a tenuous assumption at best. The more common situation is one in which we do not know the population standard deviation. As you have learned earlier, we use the *t* distribution in such cases to make inferences about means.

Let us illustrate with a one-sample *t* test for simulated data, again from a normally distributed population with a mean of 500 and a standard deviation of 100. This time, however, we will not assume we know the population standard deviation and will use the sample standard deviation as an estimate. We will also check to see whether 500 is contained in the confidence interval by using conditional logic. Here is our simulation. The script is shown as it appears in the R Editor:

```
mu <- 500
sigma <- 100
n <- 100
nreps <- 1000
pv <- rep(NA, nreps)
inout <- rep(NA, nreps)
for(i in 1:nreps){
        print(i)
        set.seed(i)
        x <- rnorm(n, mu, sigma)
        pv[i] <- t.test(x, mu = 500)$p.value
        lower <- t.test(x, mu = 500)$conf.int[1]
        upper <- t.test(x, mu = 500)$conf.int[2]
        inout[i] <- ifelse(500 >= lower & 500 <= upper,1,0)
        }
```

We can determine the probability of a Type I error by using the following expression:

```
> mean(1 - inout)
[1] 0.041
```

We can also examine histograms of our confidence limits (not shown, as these are similar to the one shown previously in Figure 17-1) and the *p* values (see Figure 17-2), which plot very nearly a uniform distribution.

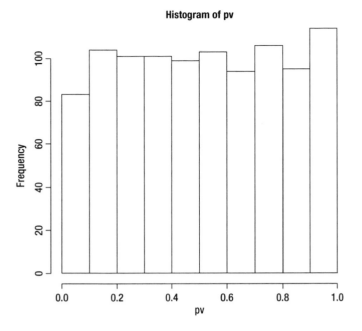

**Histogram of pv**

*Figure 17-2.* *The p values plot very nearly a uniform distribution*

## A Uniform Distribution Simulation

Looking at the *p* values above, we saw that they were distributed in a nearly uniform way. Let us use R to generate a distribution of values from 1 to 4. We will then do a chi-square test to determine if the simulated distribution matches our expectation.

For this simulation, we will use the runif() function, which unfortunately looks more like "*run if*" to a seasoned programmer than "*random uniform*," which is really what it is. We will create a vector of 1000 numbers between 1 and 4 inclusive, using the runif() function, and then we will perform a chi-square test to see if the observed values (those we simulated) are significantly different from our expectation, which is that each will have a frequency of 250. The R code is very compact. Note the use of the ceiling() function to round the generated value between 0 and 3 inclusive up to 1 to 4 inclusive. In this case, we need no explicit looping because we are using vectorized operations in R.

```
> chivector <- ceiling(runif(1000, min = 0, max = 4))
> table(chivector)
chivector
  1   2   3   4
262 221 254 263
> chisq.test(table(chivector))

        Chi-squared test for given probabilities

data:  table(chivector)
X-squared = 4.68, df = 3, p-value = 0.1968
```

Here is an even more compact way to produce the vector of numbers between 1 and 4, as well as to determine the results of the chi-square test. Instead of using the runif() function, we will sample with replacement from the sequence 1 to 4:

```
> chivector <- sample(1:4, 1000, replace = TRUE)
> result <- table(chivector)
> chisq.test(result)

        Chi-squared test for given probabilities

data:  result
X-squared = 0.5, df = 2, p-value = 0.7788
```

The nonsignificant values of chi-square indicate our generated distributions do not depart significantly from the uniform distribution. A bar plot (see Figure 17-3) makes conformance to uniform distribution even clearer. The R command for the bar plot is:

```
> barplot(table(chivector))
```

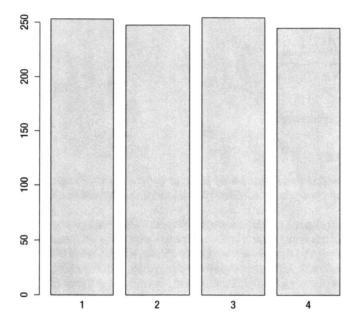

*Figure 17-3.* *The bar plot shows the snumbers are nearly uniformly distributed*

## A Binomial Distribution Simulation

For our last simulation in this chapter, let us simulate 1000 tosses of a fair coin. We will track the number of heads by assigning heads 1 and tails 0. We will then examine the performance of our process over time. If the law of large numbers is correct, the empirical probability of heads should converge on the theoretical probability, which of course is .50. When we use 0 s and 1 s, the mean of the vector is simply the proportion of 1s. We specify the number of trials, the number of outcomes, and the probability of success for each outcome and pass these values (or variables) to the rbinom( ) function:

```
> x<- rbinom(1000, 1, .5)

> table(x)
x
```

```
  0   1
491 509
> mean(x)
[1] 0.509
```

Note that the mean of the distribution, and therefore the proportion of heads, is .51, indeed close to the theoretically expected .50. We can expand on our simulation for an even more convincing demonstration of the law of large numbers. Let us simulate 1000 coin tosses, and keep a moving average of the proportion of heads. We will use a for() loop and the cumsum() function to calculate the average.

```
nsim <- 1000
p <- .50
n <- 1
o <- 1
y <- 0
heads <- rep(NA, nsim)
        for (i in 1:nsim){
                x <- rbinom(n, o, p)
                y <- y + x
                heads[i] <- cumsum(y)/length(1:i)
        }
```

Examine the graph of the proportion of heads as the number of trials increases (Figure 17-4). You see extreme fluctuations at the beginning, but over a large number of trials the binomial process begins to stabilize close to the true proportion. Here is how to make the graph in R:

```
> plot(heads, type = "l", xlab = "Number of Trials",
+ ylab = "Proportion of Heads", main = "Proportion of Heads")
```

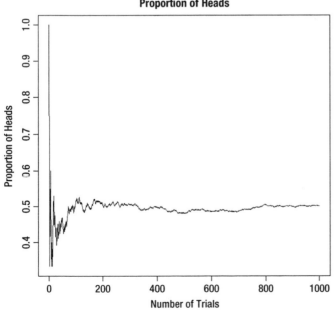

**Figure 17-4.** *Proportion of heads over 1000 trials of a fair coin toss*

# Conclusion

In this chapter, you learned how to do simulations in R. We covered the use of explicit looping to capture values of interest to the analysis, the generation of random variables, and the numerical and graphical analysis of simulated data. Together with the earlier concepts that we've revisited, what you've learned in this chapter provides the necessary base for your exploration of the "new" statistics in Chapter 18.

■ ■ ■

# The "New" Statistics: Resampling and Bootstrapping

In Chapter 17 you learned how you can do simulations of various statistical processes in R by generating random data. In Chapter 18, we turn the tables and work only with sample data. We will still be simulating, however, because we will use resampling and bootstrapping to generate multiple samples with replacement from our original data. In essence these are *nonparametric* techniques, because we are not making assumptions about populations when we analyze the sample data.

The techniques presented in this chapter have actually been around (at least conceptually) for a very long time. The problem was that the computations were intensive and time consuming, and a more advanced computer was necessary for them to be fully implemented, but did not exist at the time the ideas were developed. Today, the situation is entirely different. There is more computing power in the laptop computer I am using to write this chapter than there was in the mainframe computer at the University of Georgia when I was a graduate student in the 1970s. High-speed computers and programs like R allow us to bootstrap and resample in an instant.

Along with a star-studded cast of eminent statisticians, I have been so bold as to say that the techniques of bootstrapping, resampling, and permutation tests will eventually supplant null hypothesis significance testing (NHST), which was the invention of Ronald Fisher. There are both logical and practical problems with NHST, and many authorities, including a task force of the American Psychological Association, have concluded that the emphasis on hypothesis testing is misplaced and counterproductive. In this chapter we discuss these issues briefly before exploring how R makes it possible to do what was virtually impossible just a few years ago – that is, to use a sample to build a sampling distribution and find confidence intervals for virtually any statistic imaginable.

## The Pitfalls of Hypothesis Testing

When we test hypotheses, we must assume, de facto, that the null hypothesis is true. This is necessary because we would not know the sampling distribution of the test statistic otherwise. We then calculate a conditional probability, the probability of observing the sample result we have, or a result more extreme, if the null hypothesis is indeed true. The problem is that we never have the "unconditionals," or what we might call the prior probabilities in a Bayesian framework. Thus, we never prove anything with our hypothesis test, but simply make a decision to reject or not reject the null hypothesis.

We are advised by experts to avoid the statement that we have proven the alternative or that we "accept" the null hypothesis. If we do reject the null hypothesis, we claim statistical significance and behave as though we have found support for our research hypothesis. One problem with this reliance on hypothesis testing is that an effect of any size will eventually be found to be significant given a large enough sample size. People who fund research often require the researchers to conduct a priori power analyses for the very purpose of determining the required sample size to obtain significance, presumably to justify the funding.

If we do not reject the null hypothesis, we are in the unfortunate position of a *triple negative*—we have *not* found sufficient evidence to reject the *null* hypothesis of *no effect*. At this point, we have made a *non-decision*, and must decide whether to increase our sample size or look for a different research question. This has the effect of making hypothesis testing and achieving statistical significance more important than advancing knowledge. This bias is also practiced by journal editors, and research that fails to show significance is seen as insignificant and is therefore more likely to remain unpublished.

Because we never truly know the population state of affairs (as to whether the null hypothesis is true or false), we also never really know when we make Type I or Type II errors. When we do power analysis we are really not much better off. We must assume an effect of *some size* in the population in order for the power analysis to be possible, and as a result to allow us to "shift" our test distribution such as $t$ or $F$ to a different expected value (this is what is known as the *noncentrality* parameter).

Interestingly, many researchers are completely unaware of modern robust statistical methods. Most statistics texts and courses taught in departments other than math, statistics, or computer science tend to stress the classical statistics of hypothesis testing and parameter estimation. The field of statistics has advanced greatly since the 1960s, but most researchers are more concerned with staying up to date in their own field than they are in learning the newest statistical techniques.

Even though they typically use parametric tests such as $t$ tests and ANOVA, many researchers blithely ignore the results of the tests of the distributional assumptions of linearity, homoscedasticity, and normality. The whole house of cards collapses when we realize that without a prior distribution (the actual probabilities of Type I error or true knowledge of whether the effect exists or does not, or what I previously called the "unconditionals"), we simply have not made any advancement in knowledge whether we have rejected or failed to reject the null hypothesis. This is why many experts advocate the complete abandonment of NHST. I agree with them.

# The Bootstrap

The basic idea behind bootstrapping is quite simple. Instead of assuming anything about the population, we sample the data in our own sample repeatedly. We sample *with replacement*, which allows us to generate a variety of new samples, all of which will have only values that are in our original data set. We can then calculate any statistic of interest and study its distribution. Quite interestingly, this allows us to study the distribution of common statistics as well as new statistics we create. Because we do not need to make assumptions about populations, we can simply study the distribution of any statistic we can imagine and calculate, and develop confidence intervals from our multiple resamples. We usually take around 1,000 samples with replacement from our original data.

To some, bootstrapping seems mysterious and even a little suspect, as though we are creating data from thin air. However, the data we generate with our resampling are not really substitutes for gathering additional data, but rather a method of determining empirically whether certain properties of the data are well described by a certain distribution or function. In practice, the reuse of data is perfectly legitimate, as we use the same data to calculate the mean and the variance of a given data set and then turn around and use this same information and the sample size to calculate the standard error of the mean (or the standard error of the mean difference).

Bootstrapping has a very interesting "plug-in" aspect that we will exploit in our examples:

---

■ **Note**   The plug-in principle of bootstrapping tells us that to estimate a parameter, which is of course a measurable characteristic of a population, we use the statistic that is the corresponding quantity for the sample. Application of this principle allows us to model sampling distributions when we have little or no information about the population, and when the data do not meet the traditional distributional assumptions required for parametric tests.

---

# Bootstrapping the Mean

Let us illustrate bootstrapping using our familiar example of 40 adult males who exercise regularly. We will bootstrap the mean and then the median. We will put the weights in a vector called x, and then we will sample with replacement taking 999 resamples. Next we will calculate the mean for each sample and save these means in a new vector we call boot. Finally, we will study the distribution of the means and compare a confidence interval developed for our resampled data to one computed in the traditional way. Here is our R script. Note that we can write a compact for() loop in one line of code. As a reminder, here is the vector of weights.

```
> weights
 [1] 169.1 144.2 179.3 175.8 152.6 166.8 135.0 201.5 175.2 139.0 156.3 186.6
[13] 191.1 151.3 209.4 237.1 176.7 220.6 166.1 137.4 164.2 162.4 151.8 144.1
[25] 204.6 193.8 172.9 161.9 174.8 169.8 213.3 198.0 173.3 214.5 137.1 119.5
[37] 189.1 164.7 170.1 151.0
```

See how we can produce the vector of 999 sample means:

```
boot <- numeric(999)
x <- weights
for (i in 1:length(boot)) boot [i] <- mean(sample(x, replace = TRUE))
mean(boot)
LL <- quantile(boot, 0.025)
UL <- quantile(boot, 0.975)
hist(boot)
```

Here is the result of executing the code shown above:

```
> mean(boot)
[1] 172.4271

> cat("Empirical 95 % Confidence Interval:",LL,UL,"\n")
Empirical 95 % Confidence Interval: 164.5424 180.3569
```

Now, compare the bootstrapped confidence interval with the one produced by traditional means using the t.test() function. Our bootstrap confidence interval is slightly narrower than the one reported by the one-sample t test.

```
> t.test(x)

        One Sample t-test

data:  x
t = 41.4516, df = 39, p-value < 2.2e-16
alternative hypothesis: true mean is not equal to 0
95 percent confidence interval:
 164.1302 180.9698
sample estimates:
mean of x
   172.55
```

Studying the histogram of our bootstrapped means shows that the sample size of 40 here allows us to invoke the central limit theorem and claim that the distribution of means is very "normal" in appearance (see Figure 18-1).

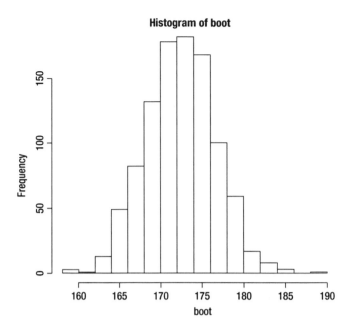

***Figure 18-1.*** *The histogram of the means from 999 resamples of the 40 weights appears "normal"*

It should be obvious from the discussion above that we can use resampling in place of hypothesis testing. For example, we conducted a one-sample *t* test to determine if the weights of men who exercise are significantly lower than the national average (they are). We could just as easily have concluded the same thing by looking at our confidence intervals (either the one based on parameter estimation or our resampling distribution).

## Bootstrapping the Median

One small change to our script allows us to bootstrap the median and study its distribution. We simply replace the mean() function with the median() function. Note that we are taking advantage of the plug-in principle explained above.

```
> boot <- numeric(999)
> x <- weights
> for (i in 1:length(boot)) boot [i] <- median(sample(x, replace = TRUE))
> mean(boot)
[1] 170.4499
> LL <- quantile(boot, 0.025)
> UL <- quantile(boot, 0.975)
> hist(boot)
> cat("Empirical 95% CI for the Median:",LL,UL,"\n")
Empirical 95% CI for the Median: 163.3 176.25
```

For comparison, here is the summary of the original data set:

```
> summary(weights)
   Min. 1st Qu.  Median    Mean 3rd Qu.    Max.
  119.5   152.4   170.0   172.6   189.6   237.1
```

The bootstrapped confidence interval for the median, unsurprisingly, "captures" the median of the original data. Here is the histogram (Figure 18-2) of the distribution of the resampled medians. Note that there is no parametric procedure for developing a confidence interval for the median, so bootstrapping is our only choice in this particular case.

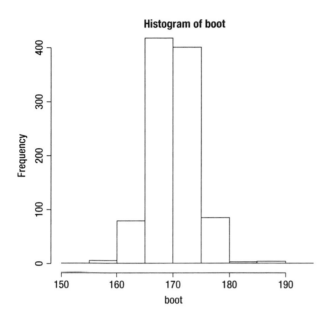

**Figure 18-2.** *Histogram of the medians from 999 resamples of the original data*

# Jackknifing

Jackknifing preceded bootstrapping historically. In this technique, a particular statistic such as the mean is calculated by omitting each individual value (or some number of values) in the data set until all the possible samples are taken. We then study the distribution of the statistic in question and can calculate bias and standard error terms. Unlike bootstrapping, jackknifing uses systematic partitions of the data and thus will always produce the same results for a given sample of data. We owe the credit for the jackknife technique to Quenouille, who suggested the technique to estimate the bias of a statistic , and credit for the term itself to John Tukey, who coined the term *jackknife* for this method and showed that it is also useful for estimating the variance of a statistic.

The primary use of jackknifing today is still the estimation of bias and variance of a statistic. We systematically recompute the statistic, leaving out one or more observations at a time from the sample data. We then calculate the estimate of bias from this set of replicates of the statistic in question. The traditional omit one value jackknifing is less general than bootstrapping, and should technically be used only with "smooth differentiable" statistics such as totals, means, proportions, ratios, and odds ratios. Jackknifing should not be used with medians or quantiles.

To illustrate the jackknife, let us return to an earlier example. We calculated the coefficient of variation (CV) in Chapter 2. Remember the CV is the ratio of the standard deviation to the mean. Technically, the CV should be calculated only for ratio measurements – that is, values with a true zero point. The advantage of using the CV rather than the standard deviation is that the CV is dimensionless like the correlation coefficient. The CV is independent of the unit in which the measure is taken. Thus, it is much easier to compare two sets of scores with different units of measurement or widely different means using the CV than the standard deviation. One disadvantage of the CV, however, is that it cannot be used directly to construct confidence intervals for the mean.

To jackknife a sample, we will compute the CV with each successive value of the data set removed. This will necessitate explicit looping, which we will handle in a fashion similar to what we did in Chapter 17 on simulation. Let us continue to work with the data from the 40 adult males who exercise regularly. We will create a jackknife sample vector with length $n - 1$. We then calculate a partial estimate of the test statistic using the sample, and turn the partial estimate into a "pseudovalue" as follows. We will call our jackknife estimator $\hat{\theta}$ ("theta hat"). We will generate a jackknife vector of samples with each value $x_i$ removed. We will use this sample to compute the $i^{th}$ partial estimate of the test statistic.

$$\hat{\theta}_i(x_i \cdots x_{i-1}, x_i \cdots x_n)$$

Next, we turn the partial estimate into a pseudovalue as follows.

$$\hat{\theta}_i^* = n\hat{\theta} - (n-1)\hat{\theta}_i$$

where $\hat{\theta}$ is the estimate using the full dataset. We will use nested for() loops to achieve our "omit one" calculations. Here is the Rw script to make all this happen:

```
cv <- function(x) sd(x)/mean(x)
x <- weights
jack <- numeric(length(x) - 1)
pseudo <- numeric(length(x))
for(i in 1:length(x)) {
for(j in 1:length(x)) {
if(j<i) jack[j] <- x[j] else if(j>i) jack[j-1] <- x[j]
}
pseudo[i] <- length(x)*cv(x) - (length(x)-1)*cv(jack)
}
```

The mean of the pseudo vector is our estimate of the CV, and the variance divided by the sample size is our variance estimate. We can then calculate a confidence interval by using the $t$ distribution. Here are the calculations:

```
> mean(pseudo)
[1] 0.1535138
> varest <- var(pseudo)/length(pseudo)
> varest
[1] 0.0002589396
> tcrit <- qt(0.975, length(pseudo)-1)
> tcrit
[1] 2.022691
> LL <- mean(pseudo) - tcrit * sqrt(varest)
> LL
[1] 0.1209654
> UL <- mean(pseudo)+tcrit * sqrt(varest)
> UL
[1] 0.1860621
```

For comparison purposes, let us bootstrap the CV for 999 samples and compare the empirical confidence interval from that approach to the one we just calculated with the jackknife. The intervals are similar (especially the lower limits).

```
boot <- numeric(999)
x <- weights
for (i in 1:length(boot)) boot [i] <- cv(sample(x, replace = TRUE))
mean(boot)
LL <- quantile(boot, 0.025)
UL <- quantile(boot, 0.975)
hist(boot)

> cat("Empirical 95% CI for the CV from Bootstrap:",LL,UL,"\n")
Empirical 95% CI for the CV from Bootstrap: 0.1202669 0.1772276
```

The histogram for the bootstrapped CVs is very "normal looking" (Figure 18-3).

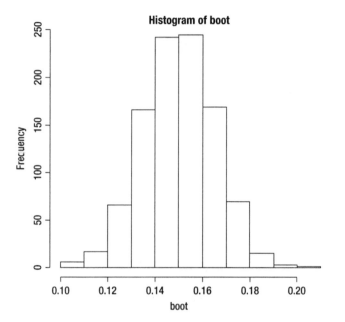

***Figure 18-3.*** *Histogram of the CVs from 999 resamples of the original data*

# Permutation Tests

Once we have derived a distribution of a statistic, we can study the distribution and also develop confidence intervals, as we just demonstrated. This is also the essence of a *permutation test*. By using permutations of the sample data (meaning we resample the data by sampling with replacement many times), we are able to study the distribution of statistics including common ones like the mean, variance, and median. We are also able to study distributions of less common statistics like the coefficient of variation. Beyond that we can study distributions of statistics we invent, such as the ratio of two means or the difference between two medians.

The confidence intervals we develop for population parameters such as the mean or functions of parameters such as the difference between two means are derived *only* from the data in the sample! Thus, we do not have the dilemma discussed earlier. We do not have to assume normality, linearity, or homoscedasticity. In fact, we do not have to assume anything. Computers allow us to step away from the assumption-driven approach to NHST and to move toward sample-based inferences that need few if any population and distribution assumptions. Permutation tests are also called *randomization* tests or *exact* tests. This approach evolved from the work of R. A. Fisher and E. J. G. Pitman in the 1930s. It is a little ironic that the man who gave us NHST also gave us a better alternative. Also, a little ironic is the fact that the first randomization test, the Fisher exact test, was Fisher's rejoinder to Pearson's chi-square test. (Remember the two were bitter enemies.) Chi-square tests are really approximations and only good ones when the number of categories is large, and the expected cell frequencies are at least 5 each. In a bit of statistical humor from nearly 100 years ago, Fisher pointed out rather triumphantly that Pearson incorrectly calculated the degrees of freedom for his own chi-square test, basing them on sample size rather than the number of categories. Spats between superstars of statistics notwithstanding, the logic of permutation tests is compelling, and the use of R and other technologies to conduct permutation tests moves this whole topic from a conceptual to an applied practical one.

Probably the most common statistical test in the research literature in a number of disciplines is the two-sample $t$ test. Let us redo the two-sample $t$ test from Chapter 9 as a permutation test. In the process, you will learn how permutations work more generally. Recall that we compared the statistics posttest scores for two sections of the same class taught in two different semesters. The class sizes were unequal, so we resorted to using a list to study the means , and we wound up using vectors of data to conduct the independent-samples $t$ test. For convenience, the $t$-test results are repeated below. The slight differences from the results reported in Chapter 9 are due to rounding in the recreated data to make them a little more tractable. We found that the fall semester's students had considerably (and significantly) lower posttest scores than the students from the following spring.

```
> t.test(posttest2, posttest1)

        Welch Two Sample t-test

data:  posttest2 and posttest1
t = 5.7418, df = 21.898, p-value = 9.089e-06
alternative hypothesis: true difference in means is not equal to 0
95 percent confidence interval:
 16.23637 34.60470
sample estimates:
mean of x mean of y
 65.10625  39.68571
```

To run this as a permutation test, we will calculate the difference between the means of the two samples. Then, we will pool the samples and record the differences in sample means for every possible way of dividing the combined data into two groups of size $n_1$ and $n_2$. The resulting set of calculated differences is the exact distribution of possible differences under the null hypothesis that there are no differences (the means are equal). We calculate a $p$ value by determining the proportion of the sampled permutations in which the absolute mean differences was equal to or greater than the mean difference for the original samples. We can also easily make this into a left-sided or right-sided test if the alternative hypothesis is one-tailed.

Permutation tests are computationally expensive. In another interesting downside, the permutation $t$ test, like the pooled variance test, assumes equality of variance, making the permutation test inappropriate when the variance ratio is high. Several R packages provide one- and two-sample permutation tests. We will illustrate with the use of the perm package, which is fairly new on the scene, having been contributed early in 2012 by Michael Fay. Recall how we install a package. First we must find the archive (I used the Carnegie Mellon mirror site), and then we must install the package from our downloaded packages folder (you can see the path to mine below).

```
> install.packages("perm")
Installing package(s) into 'C:/Users/Larry/Documents/R/win-library/2.15'
(as 'lib' is unspecified)
--- Please select a CRAN mirror for use in this session ---
trying URL 'http://lib.stat.cmu.edu/R/CRAN/bin/windows/contrib/2.15/perm_1.0-0.0.zip'
Content type 'application/zip' length 52171 bytes (50 Kb)
opened URL
downloaded 50 Kb
```

```
package 'perm' successfully unpacked and MD5 sums checked
```

```
The downloaded binary packages are in
        E:\Apress\R Workspace for Book\Rtmp4IpRhb\downloaded_packages
```

As an alternative to using install.packages, in the RGui, you can click on **Packages > Install package(s) from local zip files...**(see Figure 18-4).

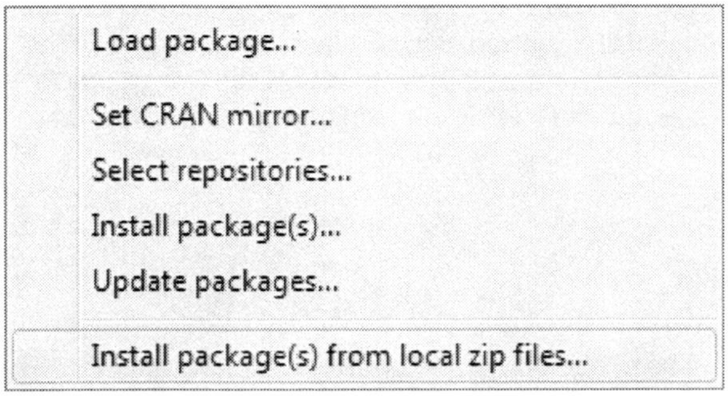

**Figure 18-4.** *Installing a package from a local zip file*

Before we run the permutation test, let us test the homoscedasticity assumption with a var.test(). Note the $F$ ratio is significant, indicating a violation of that assumption. After we do the permutation test, we will redo the test as a bootstrap test. Unlike the permutation test, the bootstrap test will not be exact, but with a large number of resamples, it will be quite effective nonetheless. Here is the variance equality test followed by the permutation test. Remember as a rule of thumb if the ratio of the variances is 2:1 or higher, our variances are considered "too unequal."

```
> var.test(posttest2, posttest1)

        F test to compare two variances

data:  posttest2 and posttest1
F = 3.2772, num df = 15, denom df = 20, p-value = 0.0145
alternative hypothesis: true ratio of variances is not equal to 1
95 percent confidence interval:
 1.273658 9.031764
sample estimates:
ratio of variances
        3.277244
```

The two-sample permutation test in the perm package uses a $z$ statistic to compare the two groups. The function is permTS(). We see the permutation test is significant, just as was our original $t$ test.

```
> permTS(posttest2, posttest1)

        Permutation Test using Asymptotic Approximation

data:  posttest2 and posttest1
Z = 4.3357, p-value = 1.453e-05
```

```
alternative hypothesis: true mean posttest2 - mean posttest1 is not equal to 0
sample estimates:
mean posttest2 - mean posttest1
                    25.42054
```

As a final demonstration of this comparison, let us calculate a number of resamples of each group using our customary approach, calculate the mean differences, and then study their distribution. We will make an adjustment to the posttest scores for each group to equate their means. Then we can examine a bootstrapped distribution of mean differences for a number of resamples. By inspecting the distribution of differences, we can see where our observed mean difference of 25.42054 falls on that distribution. We calculate the average of all the scores by combining the groups, and then we use that average as a way to adjust the means of the two groups to make them equal. (This is what is expected under the null hypothesis.) Here is our adjustment, and we now have two vectors with equal means from which to resample.

```
> n1 <- length(posttest1)
> n2 <- length(posttest2)
> adj <- sum(posttest1, posttest2)/(n1 + n2)
> adj
[1] 50.67838
> for(i in 1:n1) post1adj <- posttest1 - mean(posttest1) + adj
> for(i in 1:n2) post2adj <- posttest2 - mean(posttest2) + adj
> mean(posttest2) - mean(posttest1)
[1] 25.42054
> mean(post2adj) - mean(post1adj)
[1] 0
```

Now, we can resample each transformed test, calculate the mean difference, and then examine the distribution of mean differences. Here is the R code:

```
nreps <- 999
diffs <- numeric(nreps)
for(i in 1:nreps){
        diffs[i]<-mean(sample(post2adj,replace=TRUE))-mean(sample(post1adj,replace=TRUE))
        }
```

The histogram of the mean differences (see Figure 18-5) shows that our observed mean difference of 25.42054 is far in the right tail of the sampling distribution, making a test of the hypothesis virtually unnecessary. A 95% confidence interval for the differences is found as usual with the quantile() function.

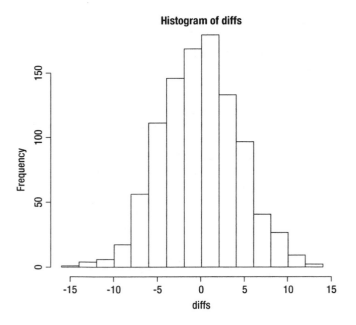

**Figure 18-5.** *Histogram of bootstrapped mean differences under the null hypothesis*

Here is our 95% confidence interval:

```
> quantile(diffs, 0.025)
     2.5%
-8.090238
> quantile(diffs, 0.975)
    97.5%
8.456339
```

In this extended example, we have shown that bootstrapping, a permutation test, and the traditional *t* test all lead to the same conclusion, namely that the scores on posttest2 are significantly higher than those on posttest1. You may rightly wonder, "If all these techniques lead to the same conclusion, which one is the best, or are they all the same?" The answer, quite simply, is that the permutation test is the best way statistically to conclude that the means are different. The *t* test requires an assumption of normality, as well as homoscedasticity. Although the permutation test also requires the assumption of homoscedasticity, it does not require normality. If the distributional assumptions are met, the *t* test will give a very good *p* value, but if they are not, the *p* value may be inexact. On the other hand, the permutation test will always give an exact *p* value. Bootstrapping is also a very good approach here, but it also produces an approximate (though quite accurate) *p* value because of the nature of resampling.

The bottom line is that permutation tests are the gold standard for assessing a variety of statistical procedures, including two-sample *t* tests. Bootstrapping is more effective for parameter estimation, and permutation tests are more effective for hypothesis testing. You might think of these procedures much in the way Tukey thought of the jackknife. They are useful tools that should be applied when they work best to solve the problem at hand.

# More on Modern Robust Statistical Methods

In this chapter, I hope to have whetted your appetite for modern statistical procedures and that you are thinking of ways you can use bootstrapping, resampling, jackknifing, and permutation tests in your own research. We have really only scratched the surface of the modern robust statistical methods available to us in R, SPSS, SAS, and other statistical packages.

Often, as we have done in this chapter, we will analyze our data set both with the traditional statistical methods and with modern ones. When the results of the analyses are consistent, the debate about which method is better is moot. When the two approaches lead to different conclusions, we will often find that the breakdown is in the data themselves. Real data sets are rarely normally distributed. Real data distributions frequently have huge variance ratios, and real data frequently have outliers that skew the mean and statistics based on the mean. Thus, when the methods produce different results, we will find on many occasions that the modern method may be more accurate than the traditional one. We can deal with outliers and other problems in the data by a variety of devices, some of which we have discussed previously in this text, such as a trimmed mean.

A particularly promising, robust approach to hypothesis testing proposed by Keselman and others uses a combination of trimmed means, Winsorized variances, and bootstrapping. Keselman and his colleagues call this solution the *adjusted degrees of freedom* (ADF) approach. Both a test statistic and a *p* value are calculated. At this writing, the implementation of the ADF approach was limited to the SAS/IML platform, but I am positive that an R package will soon be forthcoming!

# Conclusion

The topics we covered in Chapter 18 were a combination of "modern" methods of data analysis that make few or no assumptions about populations. Though the techniques have been around for longer than most people realize, their use has been limited. However, in my estimation (and I am in good company), the techniques we have discussed in this chapter will eventually supplant null hypothesis significance testing with its many traps and pitfalls. In Chapter 19, we turn our attention to the creation of an R package, discussing and illustrating the mechanics of that process by making a (very small) package of our own.

# CHAPTER 19

# Making an R Package

One of the strengths of R is the ability to share software as packages. Packages give users a reliable, convenient, and standardized way to access R functions, data, and documentation. Package authors have a means of communicating with users and a way to organize software for the purpose of sharing it with others and reusing it themselves.

In this chapter, you learn the mechanics of making an R package. Although you may not create your own package, you still need to understand how packages work if you need to modify an existing one or if you have problems installing one. There are four good reasons to take the time and effort to learn how to create an R package. The first, and most important, is that it gives you the ability to share your code, data, and documentation with others, including perhaps the R community at large. The second reason is that this will force you to document your code, which will help both you and others, as we have discussed previously. The third is that it will force you to test your code to make sure it works properly, and the fourth is that building a package makes it easier for you to use your own R functions and data.

As of this writing, R has been updated to version 2.15.1, and there are currently 3960 contributed packages at the CRAN repository. There are undoubtedly other packages elsewhere. All of the packages at CRAN, and many of those in other places, are free of charge. Though they are distributed in an "as is" condition, most of the packages contributed to CRAN are quite good. The R Core Team, of course, is vigilant about keeping the language itself and the base version of R as clean and efficient as possible.

## The Concept of a Package

The purpose of a package, in general, is to make it easier to share and distribute software. This idea has certainly taken off in the R community; thousands of contributed packages are available for a very wide variety of purposes. An R package is a collection of related source code and other files. When the package is correctly installed by R, you can access the functions and other items in the package by a call to the library() function. While the package is under development, it is wise to put all the related files into a single source directory. When you are ready to create the package, you store the source as a compressed file. R provides tools for installing and testing packages. Users of Linux and Mac operating systems will find the R tools sufficient. Windows users, on the other hand, will have to use some additional utilities. I will discuss these, as we have been using R in the Windows environment throughout this book.

We will illustrate the construction of a package with a simple example. Although we will not include code from other languages, you should know that an R package can contain other kinds of software code in addition to R code. If you include code written in other languages, of course, you will also need to have compiler tools for those languages. Remember R is a command-line interpreted language and does not have (or need) a compiler, though there are discussions of an R compiler being developed one day. We will include only R code, documentation, and data in our package. In the process of building our package, we will tie together many loose ends, and you will see how the various strands we have explored separately in this book come together to make a nice (and perhaps even pretty) tapestry.

Let us define several key terms (adapted from the tutorial on creating R packages by R Core Team member Friedrich Leish). The tutorial is available at the CRAN web site.

**Package**: An extension of the R base system with code, data, and documentation in a standardized format

**Library**: A directory containing installed packages

**Repository**: A web site providing packages for installation

**Source**: The original version of a package with text and code

**Binary**: A compiled version of a package

**Base packages**: Part of the R source tree, maintained by the R Core Team

**Recommended packages**: Part of every R installation, but not necessarily maintained by R Core Team

**Contributed packages**: All the rest

Following Leish's lead, let us create a couple of functions and build a package. In the process, you will learn how to do this on a larger scale when desired.

---

■ **Note**   The R documentation for creating packages is available at the following URL: http://cran.r-project.org/doc/manuals/R-exts.html. The R documentation on creating help files in the Rd format is here: http://cran.r-project.org/doc/manuals/R-exts.html#Writing-R-documentation-files.

---

# Some Windows Considerations

R, which has its roots in Unix, uses *paths* to search for files, so you need to let R know where to find the proper tools. You must edit the path in your Windows environment to include the path to the RTools, to the R binary file, and to the program RCmd (which is under the R directory). To get to the path in Windows 7, use the following procedure. Right-click on the Computer icon or open the Control Panel and locate the **System Properties** (see Figure 19-1). Click on **Environment Variables**.

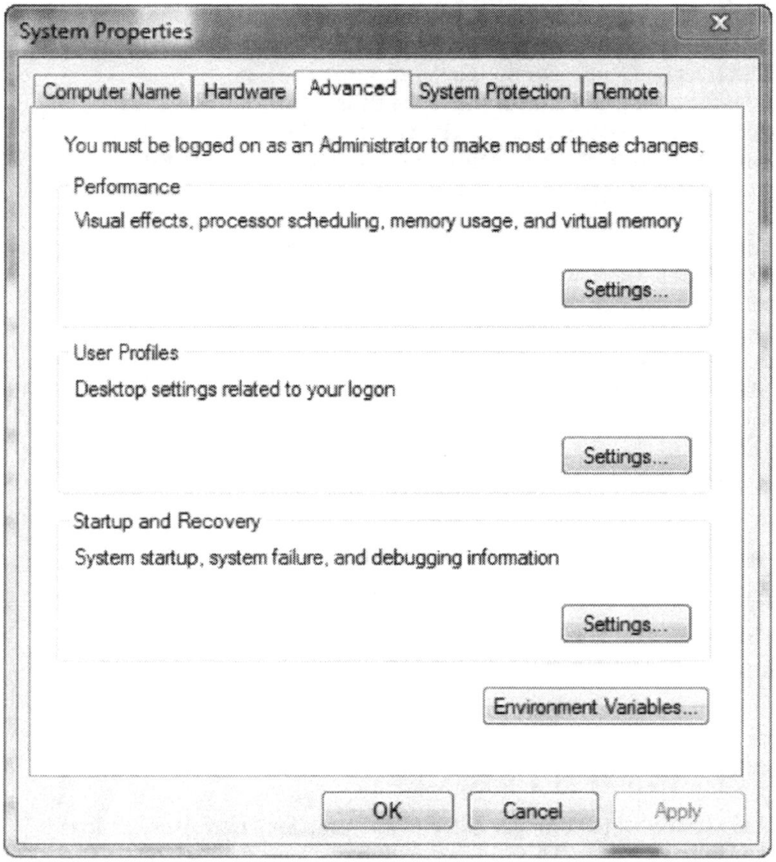

**Figure 19-1.** *Accessing the Environment Variables to edit the path*

In the **Environment Variables** dialog box, locate the **System variables** and scroll to **Path**. Click on **Edit**. It is a good idea to copy the path into a text editor and to make the changes there rather than trying to edit inside the small one-line box (see Figure 19-2). That way, you can save the current path and restore it if it is not correct.

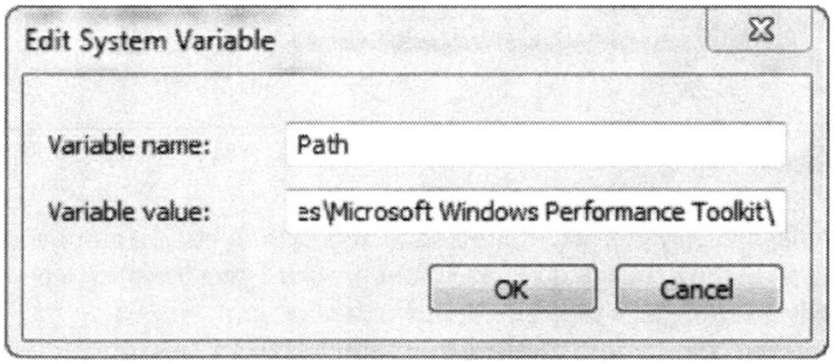

**Figure 19-2.** *Editing the system path*

If you are planning to use code from any language other than R, you must have the proper compilers, as mentioned previously. In addition, if you intend to contribute your package to CRAN, you will need to produce proper documentation. A tool like MiKTeX is a good choice for this purpose.

Below is my path, which now includes the path to the R tools and to the RCmd program. See that the path also includes Perl, the HTML Help Workshop, and MiKTeX, all of which may be needed if you will eventually contribute your packages to CRAN. The order of the entries is very important. The R Tools must be the first or second entry in the path.

```
C:\Rtools\bin;c:\Rtools\gcc-4.6.3\bin;C:\Program Files (x86)\MiKTeX 2.9\miktex\bin\;C:\Program
Files\R\R-2.15.1\bin\i386;C:\Program Files (x86)\HTML Help Workshop;C:\Program Files (x86)\
Common Files\Microsoft Shared\Windows Live;C:\Windows\system32;C:\Windows;C:\Windows\System32\
Wbem;C:\Windows\System32\WindowsPowerShell\v1.0\;C:\Program Files (x86)\Common Files\Roxio
Shared\DLLShared\;C:\Program Files (x86)\Common Files\HP\Digital Imaging\bin;C:\Program Files
(x86)\HP\Digital Imaging\bin\;C:\Program Files (x86)\HP\Digital Imaging\bin\Qt\Qt 4.3.3;C:\
Program Files (x86)\Common Files\Teleca Shared;C:\Program Files (x86)\Common Files\HP\Digital
Imaging\bin;C:\Program Files (x86)\HP\Digital Imaging\bin\;C:\Program Files (x86)\HP\Digital
Imaging\bin\Qt\Qt 4.3.3;C:\Program Files (x86)\QuickTime\QTSystem\;C:\Program Files\Microsoft
Windows Performance Toolkit\;
```

---

■ **Tip**  You can opt to edit the path when you install the R tools package, and if so, the path to the Rtools binary files will be added automatically to the beginning of your path. I manually added the path to the tools on one computer and let the installation do it on another computer, and both worked fine.

---

# Establishing the Skeleton of an R Package

It is a good idea to use the R package.skeleton utility to automate some of the setup for a new package. In the example for this function, you will find the following code. This will ensure that you have the path set up correctly and can create the package. We will use the example from the package.skeleton documentation to build our simple package, which you see in the following code. We will create an addition function and a subtraction function, as well as two data sets. One data set will be a very simple data frame, and the other will be a vector of 1000 random normal deviates.

```
require(stats)
## two functions and two "data sets" :
f <- function(x,y) x+y
g <- function(x,y) x-y
d <- data.frame(a=1, b=2)
e <- rnorm(1000)

package.skeleton(list=c("f","g","d","e"), name="mypkg")
```

The functions are uninspiring, as are our data sets, but they give us enough code and data to build a simple package. See that we pass a list of our package contents to the package.skeleton function and give the package a name. If the code executes correctly, a directory named mypkg will be created under the current working directory. It will have a directory called man (think *manual*) for documentation, one called data for (you guessed it) data, and one called R for our R code (see Figure 19-3). You will need to create another directory called src if you have source code from C/C++/or FORTRAN. If you have compiled code from other languages, it will also be necessary to compile that source code, as we have discussed already. You must also add a useDynLib() directive to the NAMESPACE file for any compiled code.

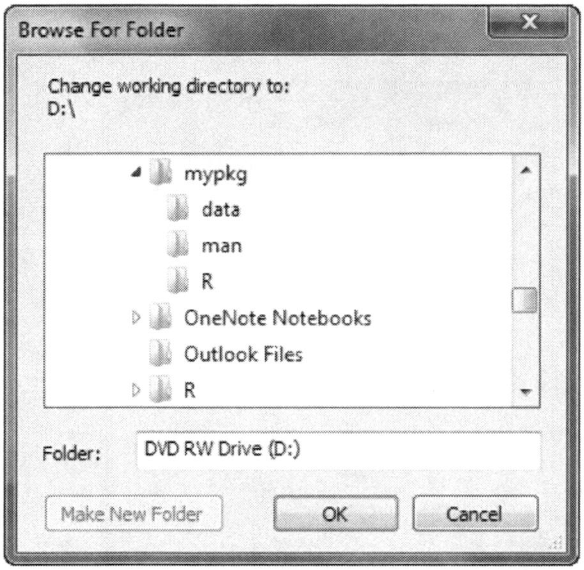

*Figure 19-3. The* package.skeleton *function creates a directory and subdirectories*

Now that we have created the package skeleton, let us change the working directory to it. See that we have a data folder, a man folder, and an R folder. Let's peek at the contents of these folders and see what we find. Use Windows Explorer to access the folders. Note that our data files were copied into the data directory (Figure 19-4).

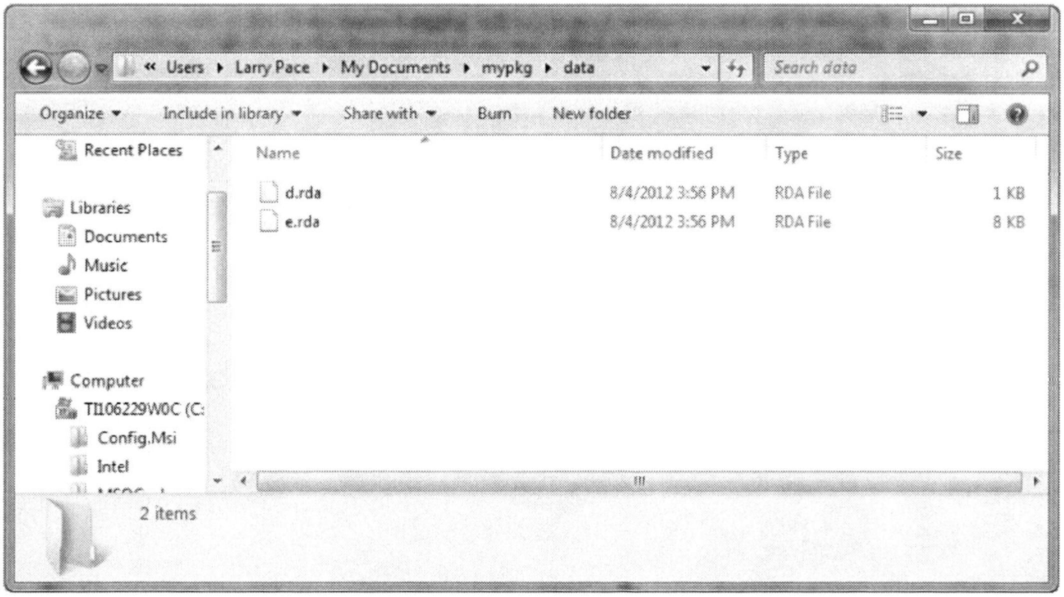

*Figure 19-4. The data files are in the* data *directory*

The R directory contains our R functions (Figure 19-5).

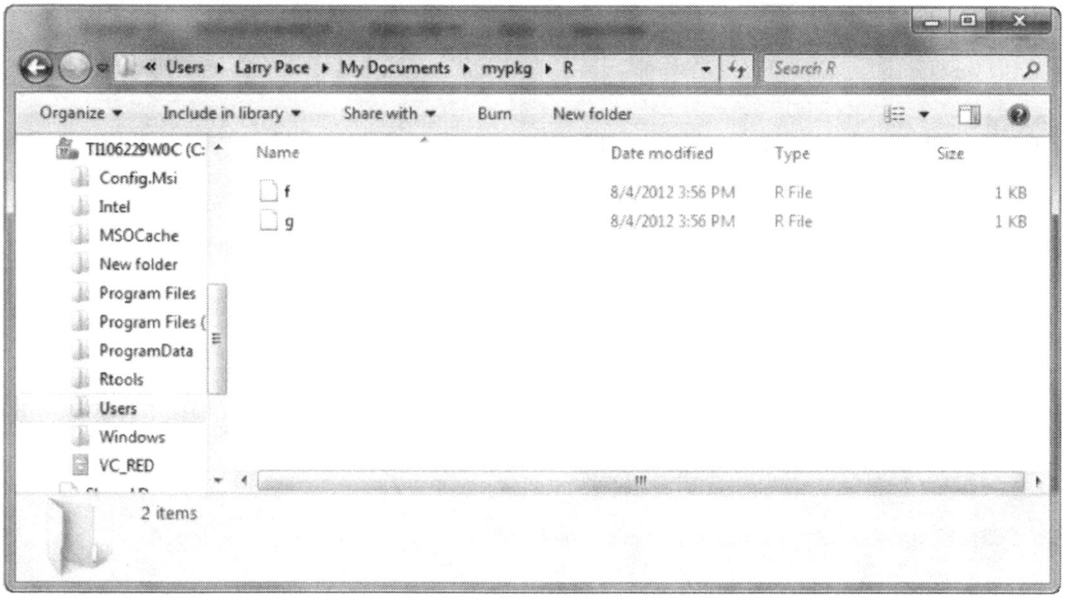

***Figure 19-5.*** *The* R *directory contains the R functions*

The mypkg directory also contains a NAMESPACE file, a DESCRIPTION file, and a "read and delete" file explaining the next steps:

```
* Edit the help file skeletons in 'man', possibly combining help files
  for multiple functions.
* Edit the exports in 'NAMESPACE', and add necessary imports.
* Put any C/C++/Fortran code in 'src'.
* If you have compiled code, add a useDynLib() directive to
  'NAMESPACE'.
* Run R CMD build to build the package tarball.

Read "Writing R Extensions" for more information.
```

The man directory gives us the skeleton for our package documentation:

```
\name{mypkg-package}
\alias{mypkg-package}
\alias{mypkg}
\docType{package}
\title{
What the package does (short line)
~~package title~~
}
```

```
\description{
More about what it does (maybe more than one line)
~~A concise (1-5 lines) description of the package~~
}
\details{
\tabular{ll}{
Package: \tab mypkg\cr
Type: \tab Package\cr
Version: \tab 1.0\cr
Date: \tab 2012-08-04\cr
License: \tab What license is it under?\cr
}
~~An overview of how to use the package, including the most important~~
~~functions~~
}
\author{
Who wrote it

Maintainer: Who to complain to< yourfault@somewhere.net>
~~The author and/or maintainer of the package~~
}
\references{
~~Literature or other references for background information~~
}
~~Optionally other standard keywords, one per line, from file KEYWORDS in~~
~~the R documentation directory~~
\keyword{ package }
\seealso{
~~Optional links to other man pages, e.g. ~~
~~\code{\link[<pkg>:<pkg > -package]{<pkg>}}~~
}
\examples{
~~simple examples of the most important functions~~
}
```

Note we also need to document our functions and data sets. The R documentation is in a "text-like" format called *.Rd. The DESCRIPTION file also has a standardized format:

```
package: mypkg
Type: Package
Title: What the package does (short line)
Version: 1.0
Date: 2012-08-04
Author: Who wrote it
Maintainer: Who to complain to< yourfault@somewhere.net>
Description: More about what it does (maybe more than one line)
License: What license is it under?
```

The NAMESPACE file is used to manage imports and exports. Here is the skeleton:

```
exportPattern("^[[:alpha:]]+")
```

The DESCRIPTION and documentation files must be edited in order for the R package to install properly. You can use virtually any text editor, including Notepad, but you may want to try an R GUI, such as RStudio, for the purpose of building packages more easily. Like R Commander (see Chapter 20), RStudio allows you to access the functions of the R Console, but adds features. The RStudio download site is here:

http://rstudio.org/download/desktop

RStudio comes in both server and desktop varieties, and is a free download. Here is the RStudio desktop interface (Figure 19-6):

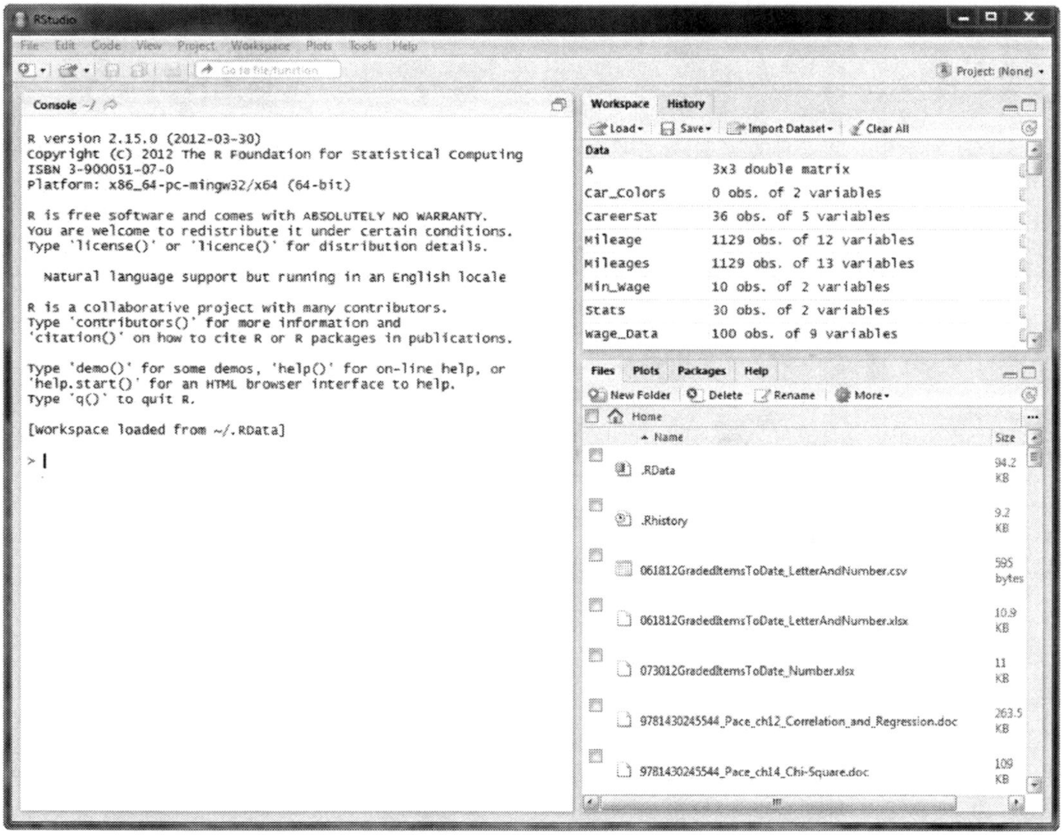

***Figure 19-6.*** *The RStudio interface*

Unlike R Commander, RStudio does not separate the script and output windows, but it does automatically show the data in the current workspace. It also allows you to import data using a drop-down menu. We will use RStudio to edit our documentation and DESCRIPTION files.

# Editing the R Documentation

When you open a text file in RStudio, a new window opens above the R Console. Let us open and edit the DESCRIPTION file for our package (Figure 19-7).

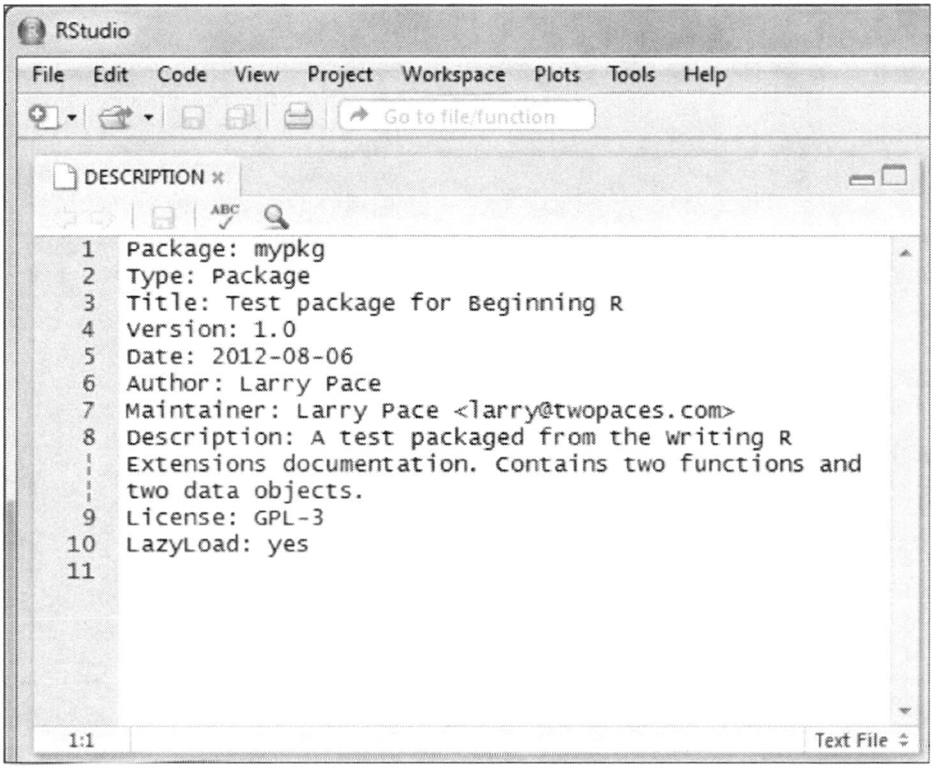

**Figure 19-7.** *Editing the* DESCRIPTION *file in RStudio*

See how I have edited the DESCRIPTION file. Although the LazyLoad feature is not really needed here, it is a good idea to include it in your packages, especially those with larger data sets. LazyLoad was introduced with R 2.0, and makes it easier to load code and data, especially large data sets. You can learn more about lazy loading from the CRAN documentation. The URL is:

```
http://cran.r-project.org/doc/manuals/R-ints.html#Lazy-loading
```

The LazyLoad: yes syntax in Figure 19-7 enables the feature for the package being edited.

Similarly, we will edit the documentation files in the man directory. Let's start with the most complicated one:

```
\name{mypkg-package}
\alias{mypkg-package}
\alias{mypkg}
\docType{package}
\title{Sample test package}
\description{Based on the R documentation for writing extensions.}
\details{
\tabular{ll}{
Package: \tab mypkg\cr
Type: \tab Package\cr
Version: \tab 1.0\cr
Date: \tab 2012-08-04\cr
License: \tab GPL-3\cr
}
}
```

```
\author{Larry Pace
Maintainer: Larry Pace< larry@twopaces.com>}
\references{Package source is in the help file for package.skeleton}
\keyword{package}
\examples{
test <- f(x <- 1, y <- 2)
}
```

Even with a good text editor or R Studio, this is a tedious process, and one to which you must pay very close attention. We will edit the help files for the data sets and the R functions. Following is the edited documentation for the d data set. The documentation for the e data set is similar and is not shown.

```
\name{d}
\alias{d}
\docType{data}
\title{sample data object}
\description{This is a simple data frame with two variables.}
\usage{data(d)}
\format{
  A data frame with 1 observations on the following 2 variables.
  \describe{
    \item{\code{a}}{a numeric vector}
    \item{\code{b}}{a numeric vector}
  }
}
\details{No additional details}
\source{The R documentation for writing R extensions}
\references{There are no references}
\examples{
data(d)
## maybe str(d) ; plot(d) ...
}
\keyword{datasets}
```

Here is the edited documentation for the f function:

```
\name{f}
\alias{f}
\title{Addition Function}
\description{A function to add two numbers}
\usage{
f(x, y)
}

\arguments{
  \item{x}{The first item to add}
  \item{y}{The second item to add}
}
\details{no additional details}
\value{Returns the sum of two numbers}
\references{The R documentation for writing R extensions}
\author{Larry Pace}
```

```
\note{no additional notes}

\examples{
x <- 1
y <- 2
test <- f(x,y)
print(test)
}

\keyword{ addition }
```

The documentation for the g function is similar and is not shown. As I mentioned above, all the edited documentation is required for the package to be built properly.

## Building and Checking the Package

Assuming we have correctly documented our code, and that our path is set correctly, we are now ready to build our R package. To do this, we must use the command prompt, which means we will be working in an MS-DOS window rather than in Windows. To get to the command prompt, you click on the Windows button at the bottom left of the Windows Vista or Windows 7 interface, and then type Command in the "Search programs and files" field (see Figure 19-8).

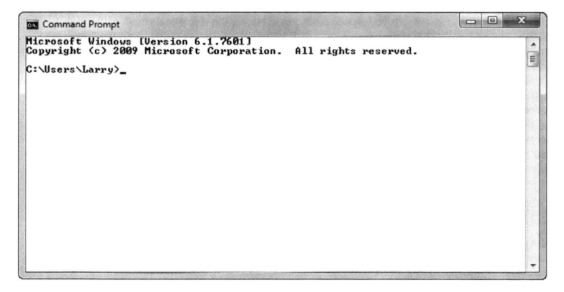

**Figure 19-8.** *The command prompt*

You need to change to the working directory under which you have the package files. In my case, it is on the flash drive I am using, which is drive E. Use the cd command to change to the working directory, and then use R CMD build mypkg to build the package (Figure 19-9). If successful, this will create a compressed archive essentially like that of all the R packages at CRAN. You can then use the command R CMD INSTALL mypkg to install the package.

```
C:\Users\Larry>cd E:\Apress\R Workspace for Book

C:\Users\Larry>cd E:
E:\Apress\R Workspace for Book

C:\Users\Larry>E:

E:\Apress\R Workspace for Book>R CMD build mypkg
* checking for file 'mypkg/DESCRIPTION' ... OK
* preparing 'mypkg':
* checking DESCRIPTION meta-information ... OK
* checking for LF line-endings in source and make files
* checking for empty or unneeded directories
* looking to see if a 'data/datalist' file should be added
* building 'mypkg_1.0.tar.gz'
cygwin warning:
  MS-DOS style path detected: E:/Apress/R Workspace for Book/mypkg_1.0.tar.gz
  Preferred POSIX equivalent is: /cygdrive/e/Apress/R Workspace for Book/mypkg_1
.0.tar.gz
  CYGWIN environment variable option "nodosfilewarning" turns off this warning.
  Consult the user's guide for more details about POSIX paths:
    http://cygwin.com/cygwin-ug-net/using.html#using-pathnames

E:\Apress\R Workspace for Book>_
```

***Figure 19-9.*** *Change to the working directory and build the package*

After building the package, and before installing it in your R library, you should check it using the command `R CMD check mypkg`. This will run a series of checks, including a check to see that the package can be installed. Assuming that the package is installable, you should do so, but checking it first is recommended. In my experience, the most difficult part of getting a package built is writing the documentation correctly. The second most difficult part is making sure you have the path specified correctly, and that the proper read/write permissions are set in Windows for the folders you are using. Windows 7 has an annoying habit of setting document folders to read only, and you must have a TMPDIR setting in the Windows environment that R can use to build temporary files during the package build. You will undoubtedly have to tinker with this a little to make sure the settings in Windows are correct. The R tools will create a number of directories as they build, check, and install the package.

The package builds with minor incident. (I got a warning about using an MS-DOS file path, when R preferred a POSIX equivalent, but the R tools went ahead and built my package anyway.) Note in Figure 19-9 that R created a file named `mypkg_1.0.tar.gz`. You are not ready to use the package quite yet. You still must install the package in your R library.

# Installing the Package

To install the package, use the command `R CMD INSTALL mypkg` (the use of all caps for `INSTALL` is necessary). When successful, this command will place the package in your R library. See Figure 19-10 to verify the package is now in the library.

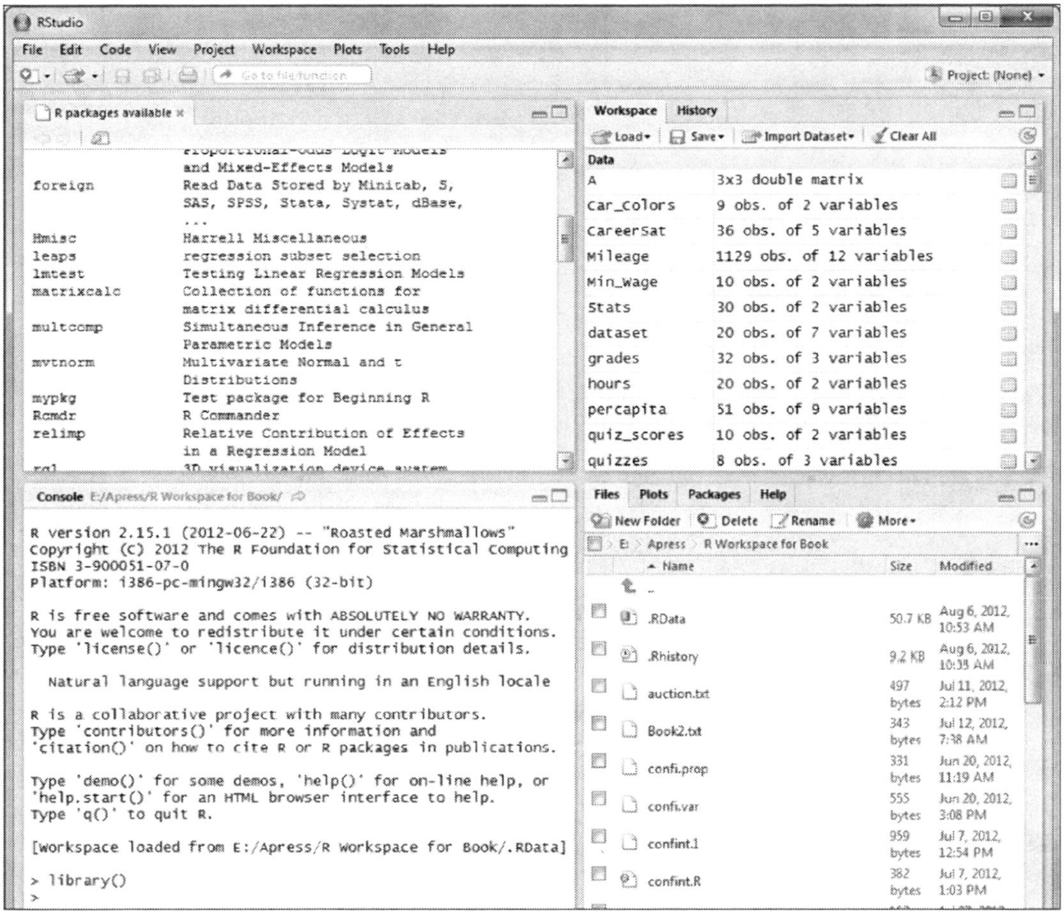

*Figure 19-10.* *The installed package now appears in the R library*

# Making Sure the Package Works Correctly

We load the package by using library(mypkg) or require(mypkg). The HTML help file is accessed by using ?mypkg (see Figure 19-11). Let us load the package, look at the documentation, and then run the example to make sure the package works.

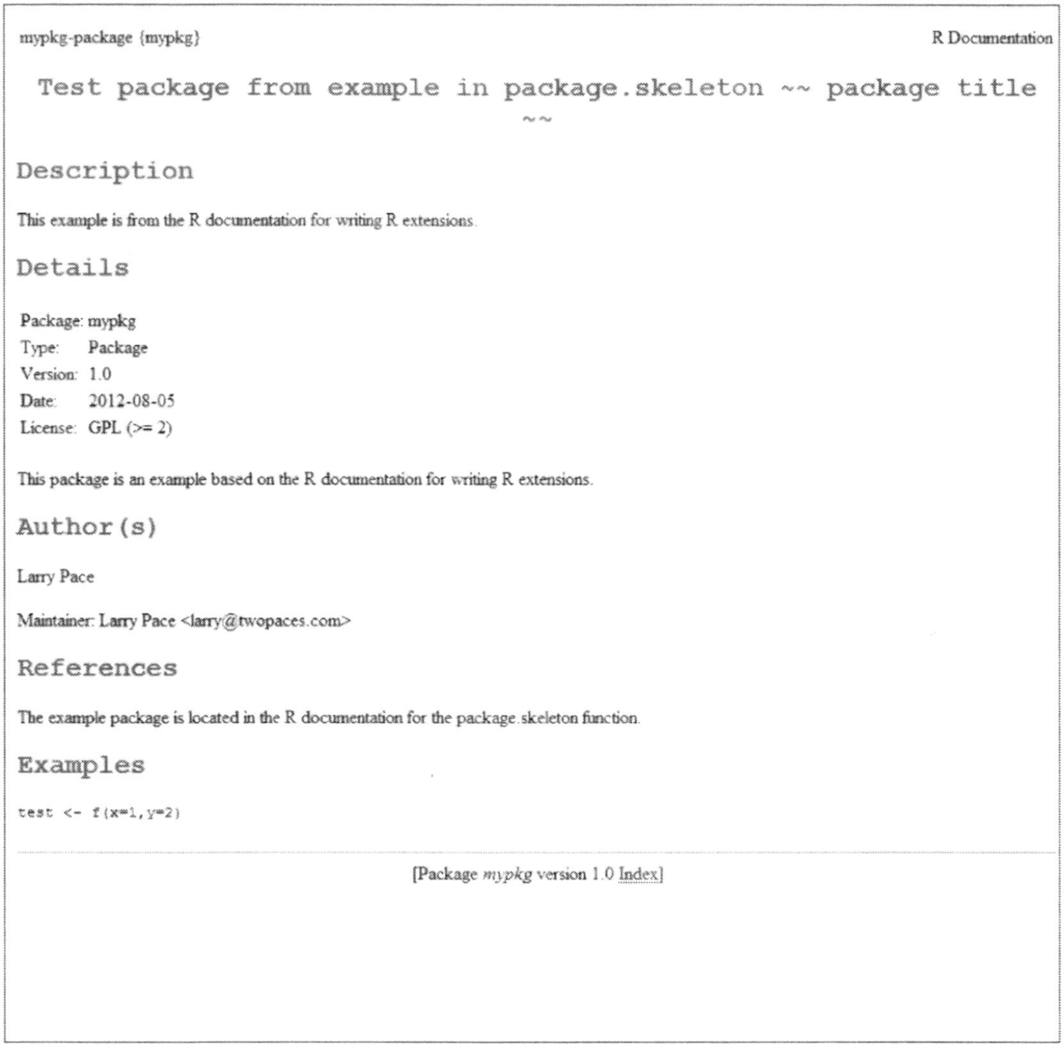

---

mypkg-package {mypkg}                                                                                    R Documentation

# Test package from example in package.skeleton ~~ package title
~ ~

## Description

This example is from the R documentation for writing R extensions.

## Details

Package: mypkg
Type:    Package
Version: 1.0
Date:    2012-08-05
License: GPL (>= 2)

This package is an example based on the R documentation for writing R extensions.

## Author(s)

Larry Pace

Maintainer: Larry Pace <larry@twopaces.com>

## References

The example package is located in the R documentation for the package.skeleton function.

## Examples

```
test <- f(x=1,y=2)
```

---

[Package *mypkg* version 1.0 Index]

***Figure 19-11.*** *The R documentation for the package*

Following is the code to launch the package, look at the help file, and run the example from the help file. Observe that the f function for addition works properly.

```
> library(mypkg)
> ?mypkg
starting httpd help server ... done
> test <- f(x=1,y=2)
>
> test
[1] 3
```

Let us access the help file for the f function by typing ?f at the command prompt. The resulting R documentation appears as follows (Figure 19-12).

```
f {mypkg}                                                    R Documentation
                        Addition function
```

## Description

This function adds two numbers

## Usage

```
f(x, y)
```

## Arguments

```
x  The first number
y  The second number
```

## Details

No additional details

## Value

This function returns the sum of two numbers. The result is of numeric() class.

## Note

No additional notes

## Author(s)

Larry Pace

## References

This function is found in the help file for package.skeleton.

## Examples

```
x <- 10
y <- 20
test <- f(x, y)
```

***Figure 19-12.*** *The R documentation for the* f *function*

The data objects also have documentation. See the documentation for the data frame called d (Figure 19-13). The other functions and objects have similar documentation, and you can see from the figures above that the R tools produce a consistent and standardized format for the documentation files. This makes R packages highly predictable in terms of the way they work, the way they look, and the way to access help and examples.

d {mypkg}                                                                            R Documentation

## Sample data

## Description

The data frame has two elements

## Usage

```
data(d)
```

## Format

A data frame with 1 observations on the following 2 variables.

a

   a numeric vector

b

   a numeric vector

## Details

No additional details

## Source

The help file for package.skeleton

## References

There are no references

## Examples

```
data(d)
## maybe str(d) ; plot(d) ...
```

---

[Package *mypkg* version 1.0 Index]

**Figure 19-13.** *The R documentation for a data object*

The data objects are available immediately. Just do what the documentation says and access the data frame by using the command data(d). For example, let us run both functions on the variables a and b in data frame d. See that our functions work correctly.

```
> data(d)
> attach(d)
> f(a, b)
[1] 3
> g(a, b)
[1] -1
```

We could go on with examples, but because our package is so simple, the examples are obvious. The main point is that we have created, checked, installed, loaded, and now tested an R package.

# Maintaining Your R Package

After you create a package, you may want to add functions or functionality to it, edit the documentation to improve it or correct errors, or add objects and classes to your code. All of this is done in exactly the same way we built our package initially, with the exception that we do not need to use package.skeleton() again unless we are creating a new package. You create the code and documentation, build the function, check it, and then install it. It is important to test the package to make sure it works correctly.

## Adding a New Function

Let us add a new function, one for multiplying two numbers. In keeping with our minimalist labeling strategy, we will call our new function h. We test the function with the example data in our data frame.

```
h <- function(x, y) {
        product <- x * y
        return(product)
        }
h(a, b)
[1] 2
```

We must build our package again after producing the proper documentation and adding the h function to the package, along with its associated help file. Using an R GUI such as RStudio makes this a little easier, and the fact that our function is so similar to the others makes it easier to edit one of the existing documentation files than to create a new one from scratch. Here is our new function's documentation.

```
\name{h}
\alias{h}

\title{
Multiplication Function
}
\description{
This function multiplies y and x
}

\usage{
h(x, y)
}

\arguments{
  \item{x}{
First number
}
  \item{y}{
Second number
}
}
\details{
No additional details
}
\value{
```

```
Returns the value of x * y. The class is numeric().
}
\references{
Created for the book Beginning R published by Apress.
}
\author{
Larry Pace
}
\note{
No additional notes
}

\examples{
x <- 10
y <- 5
print(g(x,y))
}
\keyword{ arithmetic }
\keyword{ multiplication }
```

## Building the Package Again

The steps for adding the new function are straightforward. Copy the R function into the R directory and the documentation into the man directory. Then use the build, check, and INSTALL commands to rebuild the function, as illustrated above. You can change the version number if you like, or make any other cosmetic or substantive changes necessary to improve the package.

I will not show all the steps again, as that would be repetitious, but I will show that the new function is in the updated package. Maintaining your R packages should become a regular practice.

```
> require(mypkg)
> h
function (x, y)
{
    product <- x * y
    return(product)
}

> h(2,3)
[1] 6
> g(2,3)
[1] -1
> f(2,3)
[1] 5
```

Note that RStudio allows you to keep the console open while you access the documentation. This is quite handy (Figure 19-14).

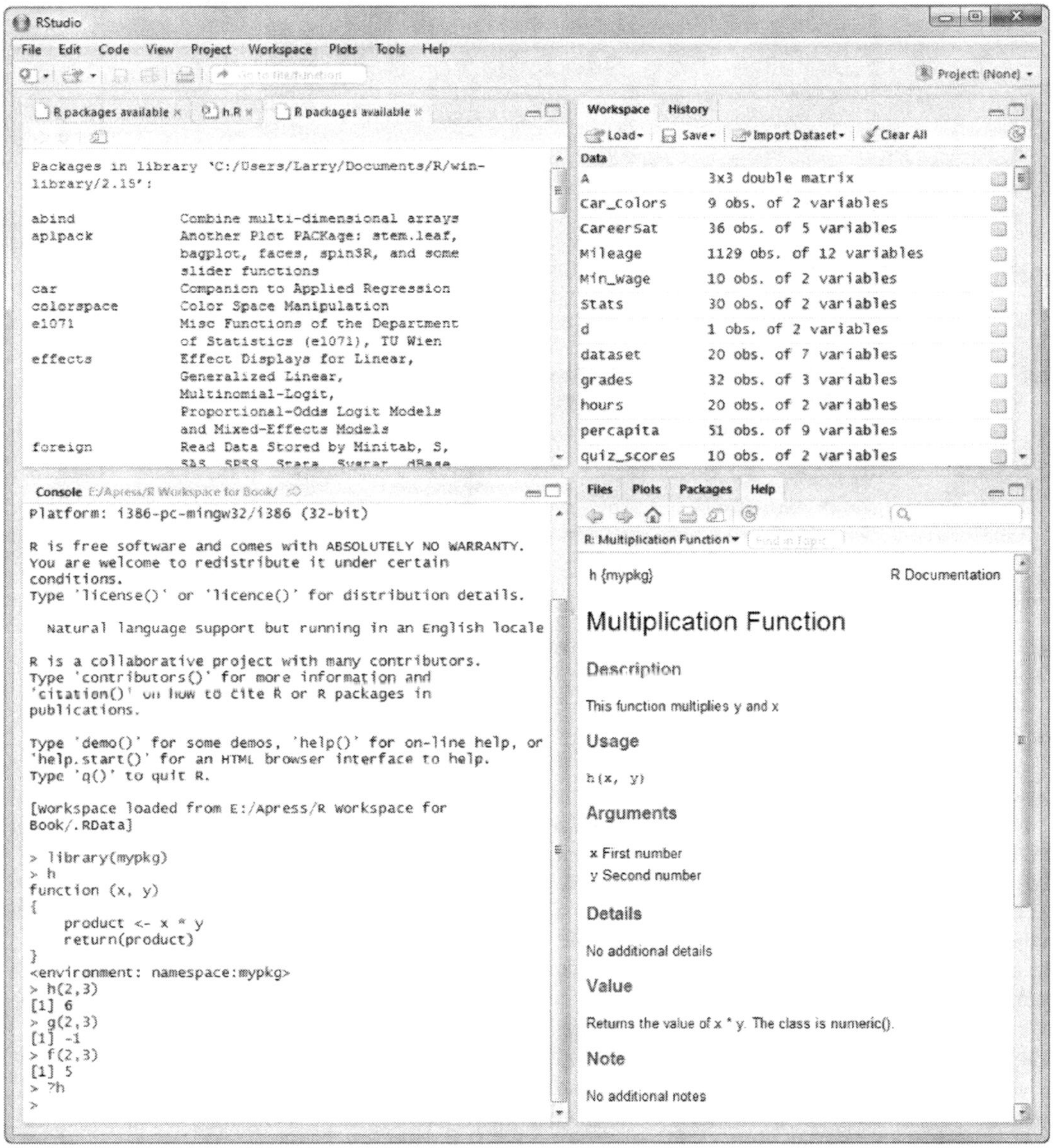

**Figure 19-14.** *RStudio allows you to see the console and the R documentation side-by-side*

Now that we have added an additional function and rebuilt our package, let's take a look at the index file created by the R tools. You will find a link to this file at the bottom of each R documentation file for the package. Here is the index HTML file, which is quite helpful (Figure 19-15). The index file has a very familiar "R look," and has navigation buttons, as well as hyperlinks to all the R documentation. Although it is possible to build your own index file and include it in the package build, my experience is that the R tools do a great job and save you time and effort.

```
Test package for Beginning R  ®R

                    ⌒  ⌒

       Documentation for package 'mypkg' version 1.0

  • DESCRIPTION file.

                        Help Pages

mypkg-package          Test package from example in package.skeleton ~~ package title ~~
d                      Sample data
e                      Generate 1000 random normal variables
f                      Addition function
g                      Subtraction Function
h                      Multiplication Function
mypkg                  Test package from example in package.skeleton ~~ package title ~~
```

***Figure 19-15.*** *The index file (generated by the R tools) for our updated package*

# Conclusion

By studying and following the examples in Chapter 19, you have learned all the steps required to make R packages. My advice is that you create a simple package like the one in this chapter before you try to produce more complex ones. Serious programmers will undoubtedly incorporate code from other languages and add elements beyond the simple ones we have illustrated here, but you have learned the rudiments.

John Chambers suggests that you learn to create R packages early in your R journey, and if you do, you will be well on the way to moving from a user to a programmer to finally a contributor. As I have said repeatedly, the R community is a vibrant and friendly one with plenty of advice, instruction, and shared code as well as shared experience.

As a reminder, R packages force you to document and test your code, which are always good things to do. Packages also allow you to share your code across platforms. If you are a developer, an instructor, or a student of statistics or computer science, you will learn quite a bit not just about R but about your operating system as well, as I found when trying to make the R tools work the first time!

In this chapter, you saw glimpses of an effective R GUI, namely the RStudio interface. I like it a lot and find it very useful for software development. It automates many of the steps we have done manually (for instructive purposes) in our current chapter and throughout this book, including simple but frustrating things like making sure your parentheses are balanced. If your focus is more on data analysis or teaching data analysis than it is on developing R functions and packages, you may find another R GUI, namely John Fox's R Commander package, to be superior for that purpose. Using a well-developed package like R Commander is the subject of Chapter 20, our final chapter.

# CHAPTER 20

■ ■ ■

# The R Commander Package

If you are interested in developing R software, you probably found Chapter 19 to be interesting and useful. However, if you plan to use R simply for statistical analyses or if you need to teach (or take) a statistics course, you may want to consider the R Commander package written by John Fox. R Commander is a graphical user interface you invoke from the R command line. It is an R package itself, and must be downloaded and installed like any other R package. Once you have initiated R Commander, however, you are no longer working with the traditional R GUI, but with a different one, as you will learn here.

R Commander is one of several available R GUIs, such as RStudio we previewed in Chapter 19, but in my opinion it is one of the easiest to learn and use, and the one that is most like dedicated statistics packages such as Minitab, SPSS, and SAS. Other R GUIs are more suited for software development than for data analysis, which is where R Commander shines. Students appreciate R Commander's ease of use and the familiar point and click interface. Teachers may prefer to use R Commander if their purpose is simply to teach data analysis rather than statistical programming.

## The R Commander Interface

To invoke R Commander, you must be running R. Download and install the R Commander packages as you would any other package. You can download and install R Commander from the CRAN web site or from a mirror site. You can also visit John Fox's Rcmdr web site for the download and installation instructions:

http://socserv.mcmaster.ca/jfox/Misc/Rcmdr/

Here is one way to get R Commander working on your system:

```
> install.packages("Rcmdr")
Installing package(s) into 'C:/Users/Larry Pace/Documents/R/win-library/2.15'
(as 'lib' is unspecified)
--- Please select a CRAN mirror for use in this session ---
trying URL 'http://lib.stat.cmu.edu/R/CRAN/bin/windows/contrib/2.15/Rcmdr_1.9-0.zip'
Content type 'application/zip' length 3069600 bytes (2.9 Mb)
opened URL
downloaded 2.9 Mb

package 'Rcmdr' successfully unpacked and MD5 sums checked
```

```
The downloaded binary packages are in
        C:\Users\Larry Pace\AppData\Local\Temp\RtmpmOhGfD\downloaded_packages
> library(Rcmdr)
Loading required package: tcltk
Loading Tcl/Tk interface ... done
Loading required package: car
Loading required package: MASS
Loading required package: nnet
also installing the dependencies 'XLConnectJars', 'rJava'

trying URL 'http://lib.stat.cmu.edu/R/CRAN/bin/windows/contrib/2.15/XLConnectJars_0.2-0.zip'
Content type 'application/zip' length 16486857 bytes (15.7 Mb)
opened URL
downloaded 15.7 Mb

trying URL 'http://lib.stat.cmu.edu/R/CRAN/bin/windows/contrib/2.15/rJava_0.9-3.zip'
Content type 'application/zip' length 746108 bytes (728 Kb)
opened URL
downloaded 728 Kb

trying URL 'http://lib.stat.cmu.edu/R/CRAN/bin/windows/contrib/2.15/XLConnect_0.2-1.zip'
Content type 'application/zip' length 1358587 bytes (1.3 Mb)
opened URL
downloaded 1.3 Mb

package 'XLConnectJars' successfully unpacked and MD5 sums checked
package 'rJava' successfully unpacked and MD5 sums checked
package 'XLConnect' successfully unpacked and MD5 sums checked

The downloaded binary packages are in
        C:\Users\Larry Pace\AppData\Local\Temp\RtmpmOhGfD\downloaded_packages

Rcmdr Version 1.9-0

Attaching package: 'Rcmdr'

The following object(s) are masked from 'package:tcltk':

    tclvalue

Warning messages:
1: package 'Rcmdr' was built under R version 2.15.1
2: package 'car' was built under R version 2.15.1
```

The package is quite large, so the installation will take time. You will need to install other objects in addition to the Rcmdr package. After you have properly installed R Commander, you simply type Rcmdr at the command prompt. R Commander launches, and you now have a point-and-click interface for doing various analyses (see Figure 20-1). R Commander has separate script and output windows, along with a menu system similar to that of SPSS or Mintab. You can access data sets directly from R Commander and read in a variety of file types including SPSS, Minitab, STATA, Access, Excel, and dBase.

**Figure 20-1.** *The R Commander interface*

When you exit R Commander, you will receive a prompt to save the script (or scripts) in the script window as well as the output. You can use R Commander to enter scripts, just as you can write scripts in the R Editor. You can then press the Submit button (see Figure 20-1) to execute the selected script. When you use R Commander's point-and-click interface, the scripts generated by your actions will also appear in the script window. Somewhat more flexibly than the RGui, R Commander allows you to select and delete the output directly in the R Commander windows.

In the following paragraphs, we will explore using R Commander for some of the same analyses we have done previously. First, however, let's run down the menus. We will start with the File menu (Figure 20-2). Then you will see in Figures 20-3 through 20-10 various additional menus in R Commander.

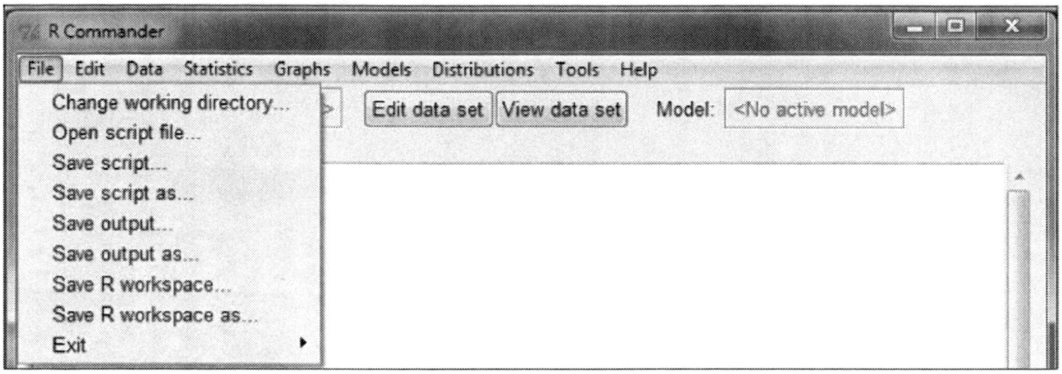

*Figure 20-2.* *The R Commander File menu*

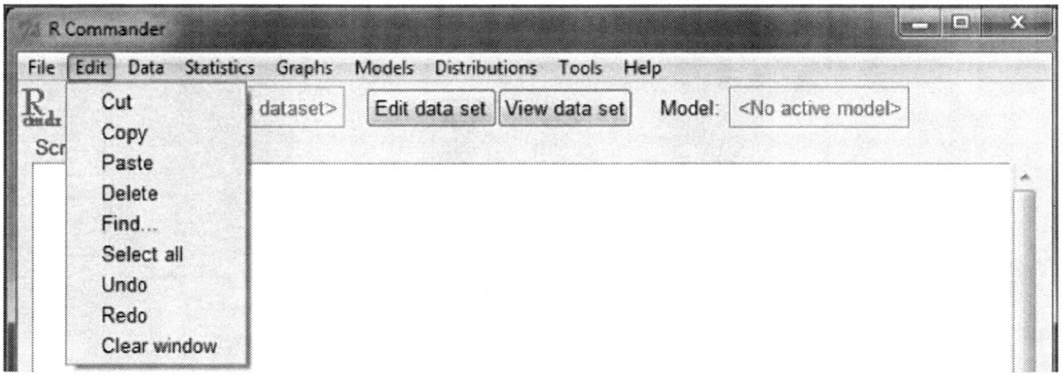

*Figure 20-3.* *The R Commander Edit menu*

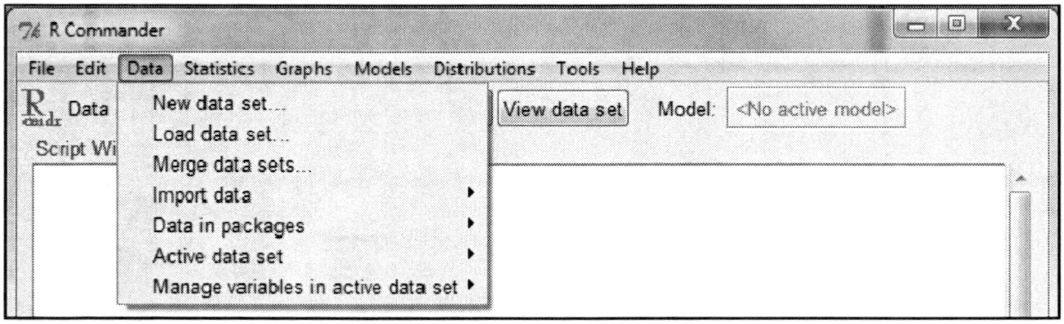

*Figure 20-4.* *The R Commander Data menu*

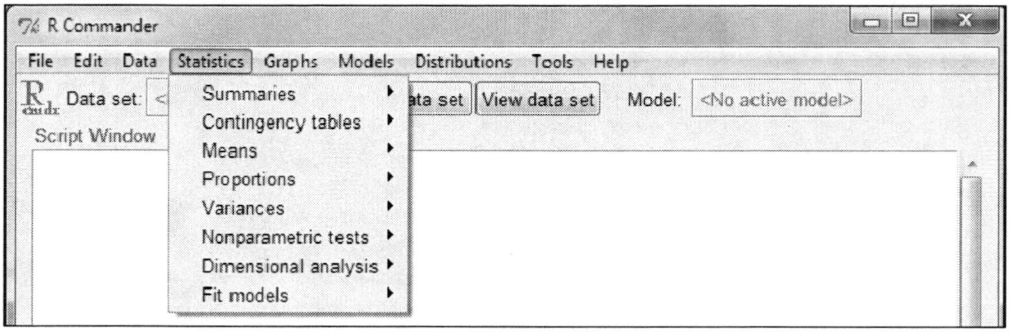

***Figure 20-5.*** *The R Commander Statistics Menu*

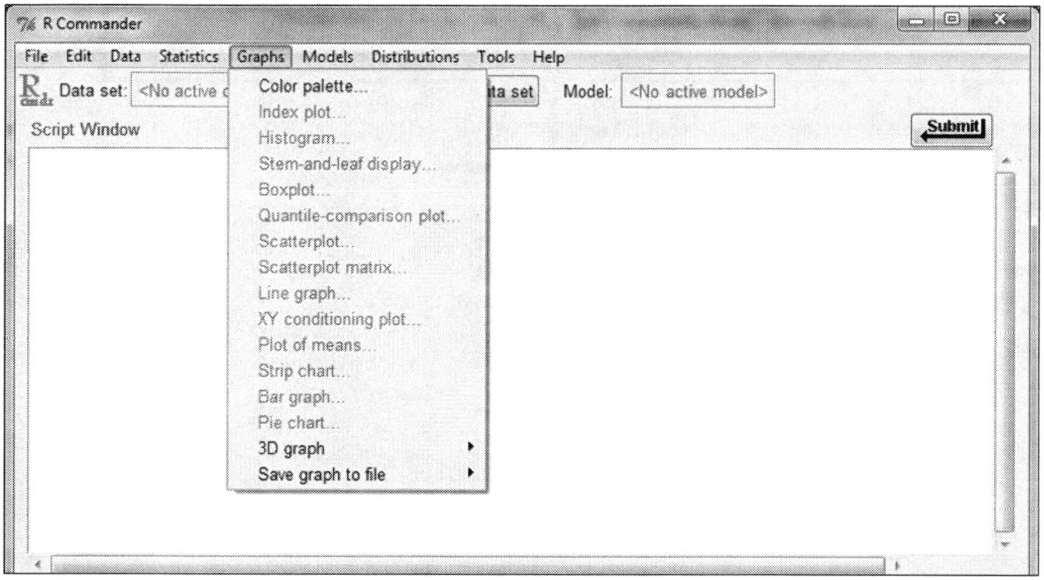

***Figure 20-6.*** *The R Commander Graphs menu*

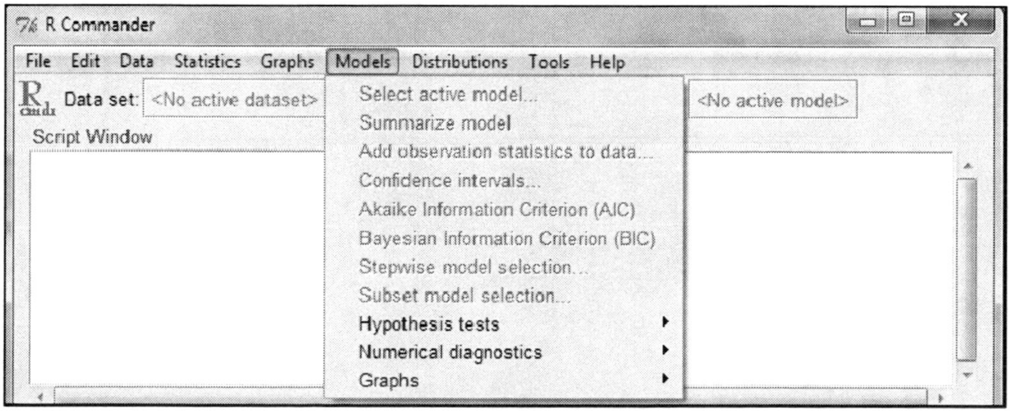

***Figure 20-7.*** *The R Commander Models menu*

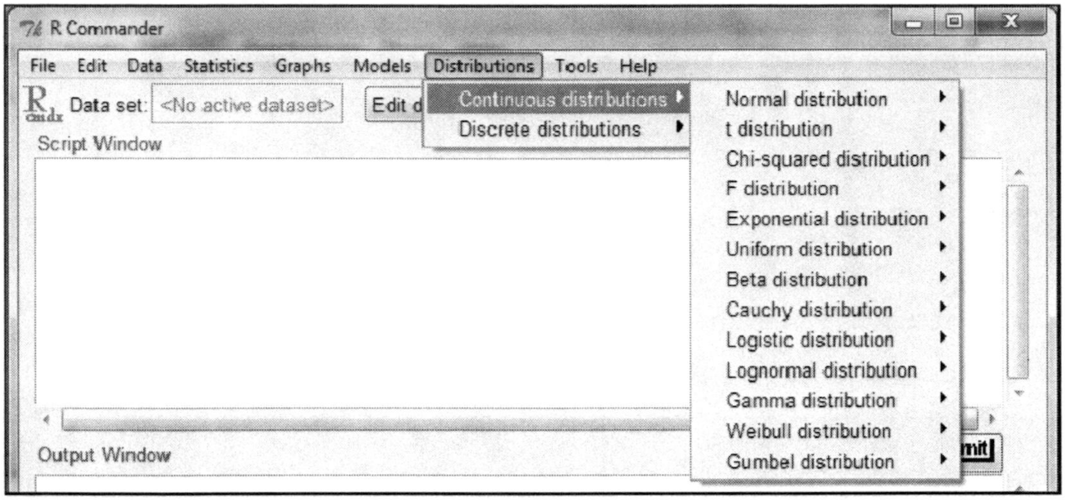

**Figure 20-8.** *Continuous distributions available in R Commander*

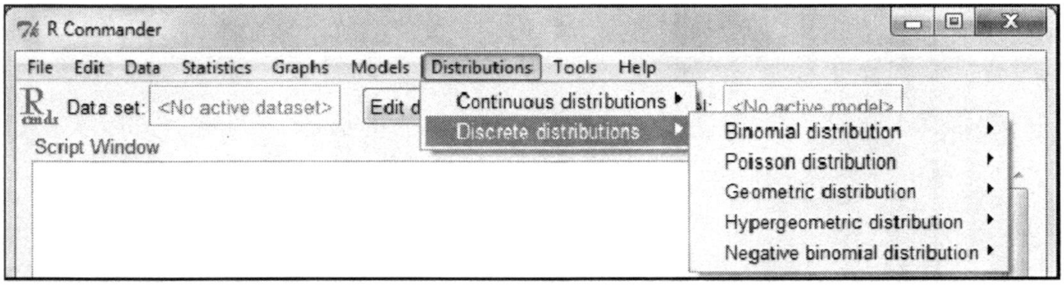

**Figure 20-9.** *Discrete distributions available in R Commander*

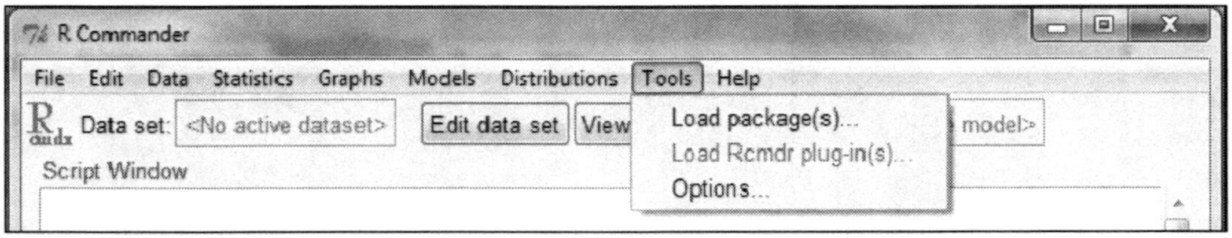

**Figure 12-10.** *The R Commander Tools menu*

Finally, the Help menu (not shown) provides help on R Commander and access to the R help system.

# Examples of Using R Commander for Data Analysis

For the sake of brevity, we will not repeat every analysis we have done throughout this text, but a couple of examples will show you how R Commander works and will either convince you that you don't want to waste your time using it, or that you want to use it exclusively and save your statistical programming for another day. If you have come this far in this book, you are fully capable of making either decision. Or you may want to do what I do, which is to use R Commander for "stock-in-trade" analyses, and R proper or RStudio for developing functions and packages and doing more specialized analyses.

## Confidence Intervals in R Commander

Let us import a data file into R Commander using the Data menu, and then develop confidence intervals. We will work with a familiar example: the weights of 40 men who exercise regularly. First, we make the vector into a data frame so R Commander will recognize it as a data set. Then we use the Data menu to make weights the active data set.

```
> weights
 [1] 169.1 144.2 179.3 175.8 152.6 166.8 135.0 201.5 175.2 139.0 156.3 186.6
[13] 191.1 151.3 209.4 237.1 176.7 220.6 166.1 137.4 164.2 162.4 151.8 144.1
[25] 204.6 193.8 172.9 161.9 174.8 169.8 213.3 198.0 173.3 214.5 137.1 119.5
[37] 189.1 164.7 170.1 151.0
> weights <- as.data.frame(weights)
```

Now, when we invoke R Commander, we can access this data frame. Click Data > Active data set > Select active data set. Select the desired data frame, and see that you can edit and view the data directly from R Commander (Figure 20-11).

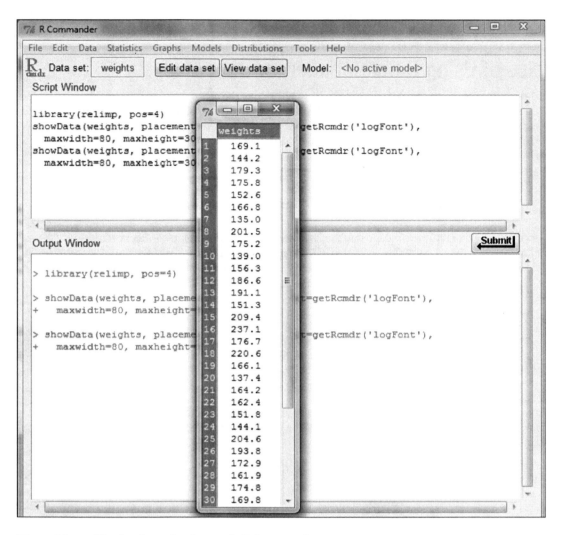

***Figure 20-11.*** *Viewing the active data set in R Commander*

Just as you can do with R proper, you invoke the one-sample *t* test to construct a 95% confidence interval for the weights (Figure 20-12). Select Statistics ➤ Means ➤ Single-sample t-test.

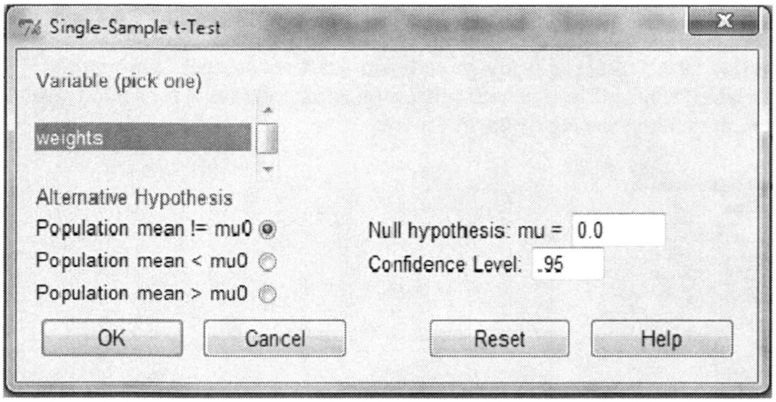

**Figure 20-12.** *Using the one-sample t test to find a confidence interval in R Commander*

See that R Commander is simply doing what you already know how to do in R. It is using the built-in
t.test() function and using R's own output. As with SPSS, you are recording the R syntax in a script window
when you use the point-and-click interface of R Commander (Figure 20-13).

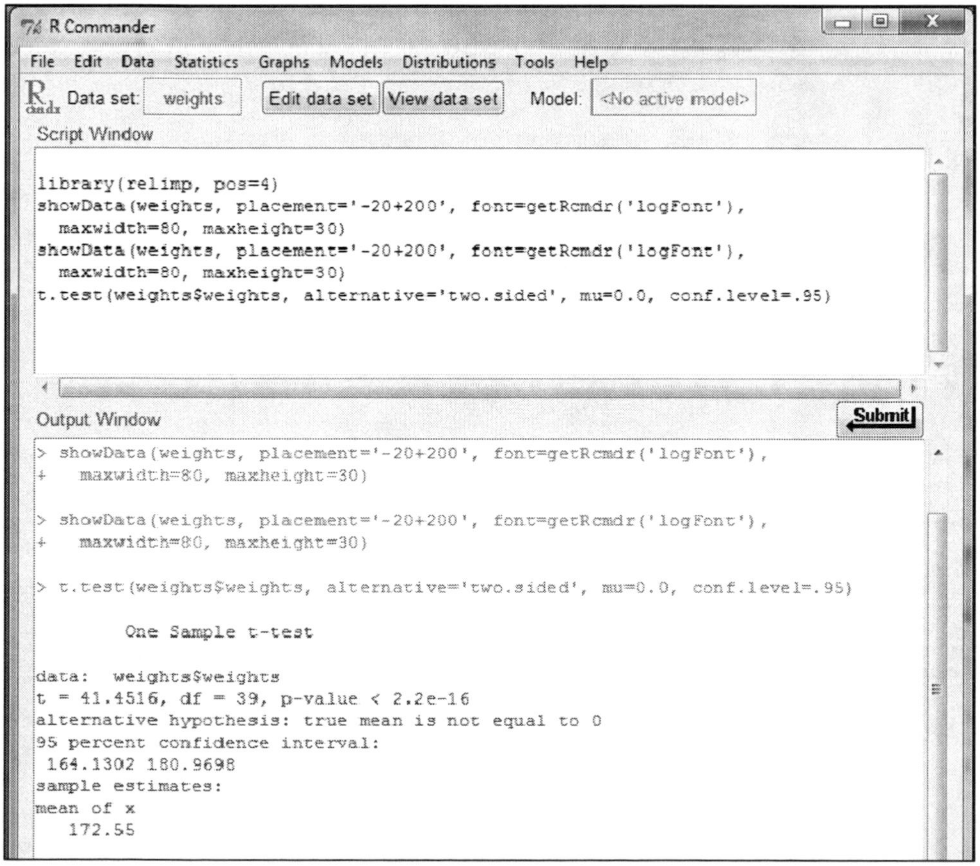

**Figure 20-13.** *R Commander uses the one-sample t test to produce a confidence interval for the mean*

## Using R Commander for Hypothesis Testing

Let us treat the following data as repeated measures and perform a paired-samples *t* test using R Commander (see Figure 20-14). Note the data have to be in "stacked" format with a factor (grouping variable) for a two-sample *t* test, and thus the option is grayed out in the dialog (see Figure 20-15).

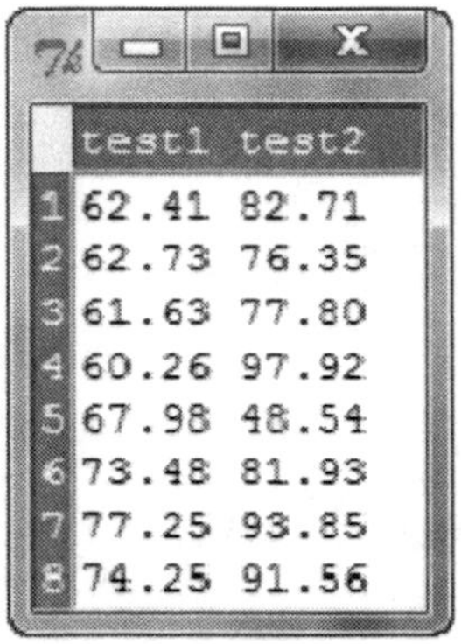

***Figure 20-14.*** *Data for a paired-samples t test*

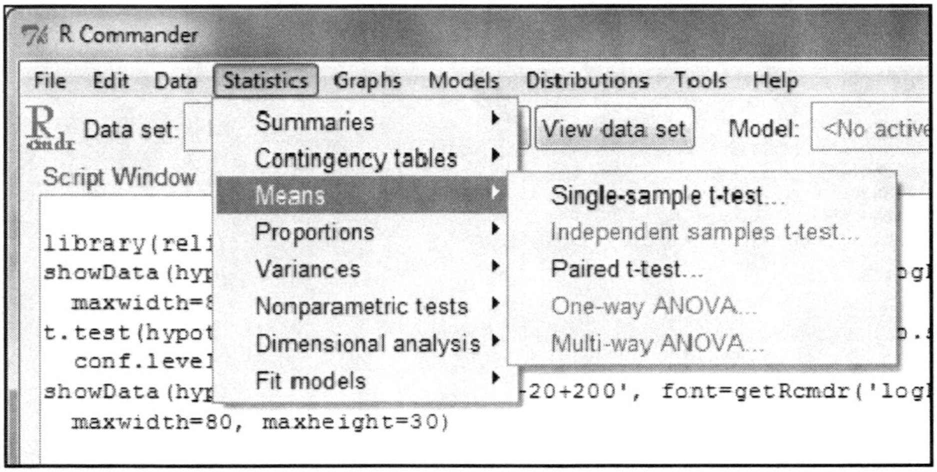

***Figure 20-15.*** *Performing a paired-samples t test in R Commander*

To do the paired-samples *t* test, select Statistics ➤ Means ➤ Paired t-test. In the Paired t-Test dialog box, select the two variables, the direction of the alternative hypothesis, and the confidence level (see Figure 20-16).

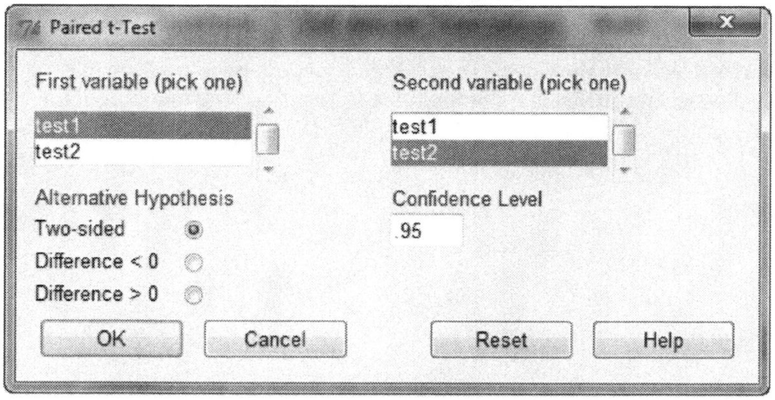

**Figure 20-16.**  *The Paired t-Test dialog box in R Commander*

When you click OK, the test results appear in the output window (Figure 20-17).

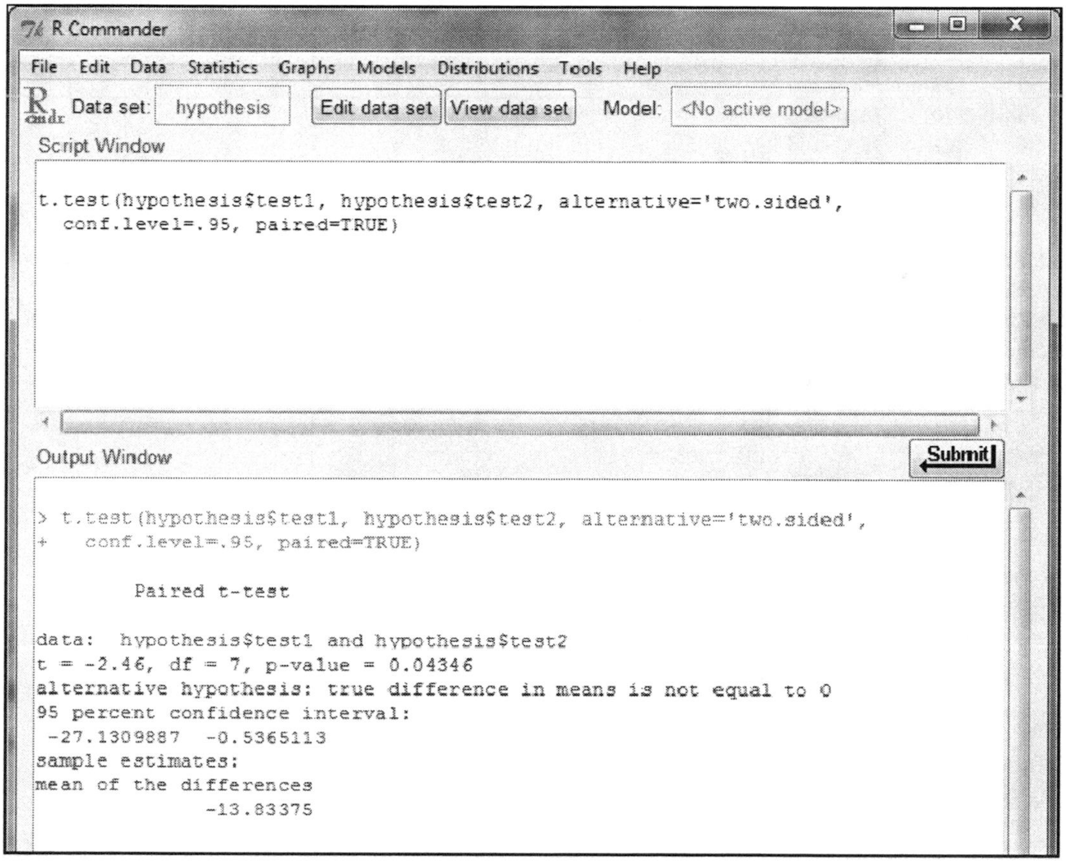

**Figure 20-17.**  *The paired-samples t test output in R Commander*

## Using R Commander for Regression

The following data is a subset of one provided by Fox in the `car` package, which is a companion package to R Commander, and which will also be installed when you install R Commander. Here are the first few rows of the complete data set:

```
> head(Davis)
  sex weight height repwt repht
1   M     77    182    77   180
2   F     58    161    51   159
3   F     53    161    54   158
4   M     68    177    70   175
5   F     59    157    59   155
6   M     76    170    76   165
```

We want to select only the males and create a new data frame in order to use weight (in kilograms) to predict height (in centimeters). To accomplish this, we will use the `subset()` function.

```
> males <- subset(Davis, sex == "M")
> head(males)
  sex weight height repwt repht
1   M     77    182    77   180
4   M     68    177    70   175
6   M     76    170    76   165
7   M     76    167    77   165
8   M     69    186    73   180
9   M     71    178    71   175
```

There are 88 males whose self-reported weights and heights are listed. See the row numbers show that these records were taken as a subset of the larger data set. Now let us use R Commander to regress height onto weight for males. We make `males` the active data set. Click Data ➤ `Active data set` ➤ `Select active data set`. Then we use Statistics ➤ Fit Models ➤ Linear Regression. In the resulting dialog box, enter height as the response variable and weight as the explanatory variable (see Figure 20-18).

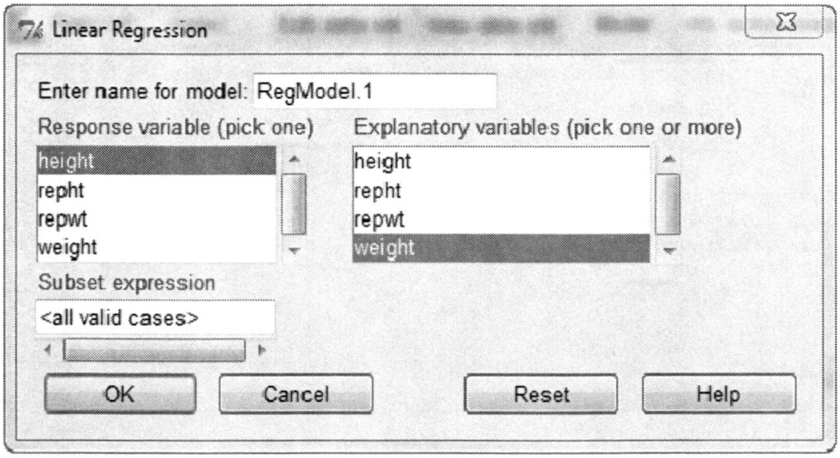

*Figure 20-18.* *The Linear Regression dialog box*

Unsurprisingly, R Commander uses the lm() function to perform the regression, which is significant (Figure 20-19).

*Figure 20-19. The R Commander output for the linear regression*

We can use the Models menu in R Commander to get a summary ANOVA table for the regression model. Select Models ➤ Hypothesis tests ➤ ANOVA table. The output is shown below (Figure 20-20).

```
Output Window                                                        Submit

(Intercept) 155.84010    3.77832  41.246  < 2e-16 ***
weight        0.29212    0.04919   5.939 5.92e-08 ***
---
Signif. codes:  0 '***' 0.001 '**' 0.01 '*' 0.05 '.' 0.1 ' ' 1

Residual standard error: 5.455 on 86 degrees of freedom
Multiple R-squared: 0.2908, Adjusted R-squared: 0.2826
F-statistic: 35.27 on 1 and 86 DF,  p-value: 5.922e-08


> Anova(RegModel.1, type="II")
Anova Table (Type II tests)

Response: height
          Sum Sq Df F value    Pr(>F)
weight    1049.6  1  35.269 5.922e-08 ***
Residuals 2559.4 86
---
Signif. codes:  0 '***' 0.001 '**' 0.01 '*' 0.05 '.' 0.1 ' ' 1
```

***Figure 20-20.*** *An ANOVA summary table for the regression model*

# Conclusion

In this chapter, you have learned how to use a comprehensive R package, R Commander. As the several examples have shown, R Commander makes R into a point-and-click statistics program similar to SPSS, SAS, or Minitab. R Commander is a very capable package because it is built as a wrapper for the R system itself. R Commander has been extended with plug-ins, which themselves are also R packages. You now know enough about how R Commander works to explore these additional features on your own.

This is our final chapter together, and I hope you have enjoyed learning how to use R, as well as how to write your own functions, how to use R for a variety of statistical analyses, how to make your own package, and how to use the many excellent contributed R packages.

# Index

## ■ U, V

## ■ W, X, Y, Z

CPSIA information can be obtained at www.ICGtesting.com
Printed in the USA
LVOW091755231012

304104LV00002B/1/P